The Ultimate Consignment
&
Thrift Store Guide

*An international guide to the world's best
consignment, thrift, vintage & secondhand stores*

by Carolyn Schneider

Published by Consignment & Thrift Store Publishing, Inc.
442 Route 202-206 North Suite 274
Bedminster, New Jersey 07921
USA

Phone: 908-781-2589
Fax: 908-781-8598
e-mail: carolyn@net-lynx.com
carolyn@consignmentguide.com
Web site: www.consignmentguide.com

The Ultimate Consignment & Thrift Store Guide copyright © 1998

by Consignment & Thrift Store Publishing, Inc. All rights
reserved. Previous edition copywritten in 1997.
No portion of this book in part or whole may be reproduced, adapted or copied
in any form or by any means, electronic or mechanical such as photo copying,
recording or by any information retrieval and storage items without written permission
from Consignment & Thrift Store Publishing.
ISBN 0-9656571-1-6

Front Cover Design by Ray Sternesky Advertising Phone: 212-226-2707
Book Design: Consignment & Thrift Store Publishing, Inc.
Cover photograph by Justin Baiter Photographer Phone: 908-221-9226
Senior Editor: Marcia Schneider
Database Manager: Marjorie Sanfratello
Contributor: Walter Schneider

Printed in The United States of America
Library of Congress Catalog Number: 98-92494
Published by Consignment & Thrift Store Publishing, Inc.
442 Route 202-206 North Suite 274
Bedminster, New Jersey 07921
Phone: 908-781-2589
1-800-361-5171
Fax: 908-781-8598
e-mail: carolyn@net-lynx.com
Web site: www.consignmentguide.com

*Dedicated to all the thrifty shoppers
around the globe*

*Thanks to Marcia & Walter, Aaron, Marge, Larry, Nicole, Mim,
Bob, Giorgio, Ruben & Lorraine for their support*

*A special note of thanks to Play It Again Sports, TVI Inc.,
Sean James Enterprises, The Clothes Tree Consignment Boutique,
Apparel Revisited & Nicole's Revival*

Thanks again to Ron, Cathy Cheo-Isaacs & Rick King for their assistance

G l o s s a r y

Consignment Store: A store that accepts merchandise from a consignor and agrees to try to sell the merchandise within a certain time frame. After the merchandise is sold the owner of the store splits the profit with the consignor. The split may vary 40% to 60%, depending upon the store.

Thrift Store: A nonprofit thrift store is a store that accepts donations. The proceeds usually benefit a worthy cause. A thrift store for profit usually purchases merchandise from charities in bulk & sells the merchandise for a profit.

Resale Store: A store that purchases merchandise outright for cash.

Handy Tips for Consignment & Thrift Shopping

1. Visit a wide variety of stores as often as you can. Merchandise is constantly changing therefore you never know what treasures you will find.
2. When you find a favorite store let the store owner know what type of items you may be seeking. Many stores offer a wish list for that "special" item.
3. Sizes can be misleading therefore try on clothing whenever possible.
4. Inspect all garments & items carefully before purchasing them.
5. If you like something, buy it. It may not be there next time.
6. Look for stores that offer bag sales, clearance racks, frequent shopper cards & other shopper incentives.
7. Some stores offer pick-up and closet audits for your convenience. Check with each store for details.
8. Be prepared to look around the entire store. You never know what you will discover.
9. Keep an open mind. When you set out on your shopping venture looking for one specific item, you may find some other item of interest.
10. Shop resale on-line. Many secondhand stores offer convenient, easy to order on-line catalogs such as www.theclothesetree.com & www.savers.com. Check with each site for their return & exchange policy.

Handy Tips For Consigning & Donating Merchandise

1. Make a list of all the items you would like to consign or donate.

2. Use The Ultimate Consignment & Thrift Store Guide to locate the stores in which you would like to consign or donate merchandise.

3. When consigning merchandise keep in mind items must be cleaned, in excellent condition & usually on hangers. Check with each store to see if they accept seasonal merchandise. Ask for a copy of the consignment contract which explains all the details. Make sure you fully understand the consignment policy & the amount you will receive when your item sells.

4. Once your item sells verify when & how you will receive payment.

5. When consigning merchandise keep track of your time limit. After your consignment period is over, verify if items need to be picked -up.

6. Be patient. If items have not sold after the consignment period has ended, try consigning items with another store. Certain items may be more suitable for specific stores.

7. Be realistic. Prices may vary depending upon the item and the demand for it.

8. When donating merchandise ask if you may be provided with a receipt for tax purposes. Check if pick-up is available for your convenience.

9. Please do not discard salvageable items. Keep in mind that there are thousands of nonprofit organizations worldwide who are more than happy to receive donations. Items donated to these organizations help provide programs for those in need.

Table of Contents

Alexander City

**A Second Act
Unique Re-Sale &
Consignment Shop
640 Cherokee Road
Alexander City, Alabama
35010**

Store Hours:
Monday-Saturday 9:30am-5:30pm
Thursday 9:30am-7pm
Sunday 1pm-4pm (Winter)

Phone: 205-329-3621

New & "nearly new" clothing for
the entire family, toys, children's
furniture, maternity wear, plus
sizes & uniforms

Store Specials: Clothing rentals
from the 50's, 60's & 70's,
costumes, prom & bridal dresses

```
┌─────────────────────────────┐
│   Present this coupon at     │
│        A Second Act          │
│      640 Cherokee Road       │
│    Alexander City, Alabama   │
│       & save 10% off         │
│     purchase over $5.00      │
│  (Limit one coupon per customer & │
│  coupon can not be used for formal, │
│     new items & special sales)   │
│     Expiration Date: 12/31/99    │
└─────────────────────────────┘
```

Birmingham

**Alabama Thrift Stores, Inc.
1248 Centerpoint Parkway
Birmingham, Alabama 35215**

Store Hours:
Monday-Saturday 7:30am-9:30pm

Contact: Buford Salmon
Phone: 205-856-1234

Clothing for the entire family &
electronics

Thrift Policy: Donations welcome

**Birmingham Antique Mall
2211 Magnolia Avenue
Birmingham, Alabama 35205**

Store Hours:
Monday-Friday 10am-5pm
Sunday 1pm-5pm

Contact: Connie Nolan
Phone: 205-328-7761

Furniture, china, crystal, art glass,
jewelry & much more!

**Collage Consignment
Boutique
2810 Crescent Avenue
Birmingham, Alabama 35209**

Store Hours:
Monday-Friday 10am-6pm
Saturday 10am-4pm

Contact: Tracy True Dismukes
Phone: 205-879-6163

Upscale apparel & accessories
for women
Accepts cash, checks, Visa,
Mastercard, Discover/Novus

Consignment Policy:
50/50 split
Items consigned for 90 days
Better labels & current style

Store Specials:
Weekly specials &
semiannual clearance sales

Alabama

Second Hand Rose
2015 Valleydale Road Suite 5
Birmingham, Alabama 35244

Store Hours:
Monday-Saturday 10am-5pm

Contact: Nancy Klasterka
Phone: 205-987-7027
Fax: 205-987-7027
e-mail: SHANDROSE@aol.com
Web site: www.htmp.net/ves/sh-rose

Upscale women's & children's clothing and lots of great accessories
Accepts cash, checks, all major credit cards

Consignment Policy:
50/50 split
No appointment necessary to consign items; items accepted Monday-Friday 10am-3pm
Friday 10am-3pm

Second Hand Rose features exceptional jewelry from world-wide designers, i.e. Judith Leiber, Lagos & Stephen Dweck, in addition to many unique pieces.

Hoover

Deja Vu, Inc.
2146 Tyler Road
Suite 200
Hoover, Alabama 35226

Store Hours:
Monday, Tuesday, Wednesday & Friday 10am-6pm
Thursday 10am-7pm
Saturday 10am-4pm

Contact: Jackie MacFarland
Phone: 205-822-8835

Upscale clothing for men, women & children including plus sizes, formal wear, wedding dresses, shoes, handbags, belts, lots of jewelry & some new items too!

Consignment Policy: 50/50 split
An appointment is necessary to consign merchandise

Deja Vu offers great clothing & great prices all the time!

Huntsville

Act II Consignment Shop
Act II After Five and Bridal
6125 University Drive
Suite D14-D20
Huntsville, Alabama 35806

Store Hours:
Monday-Saturday 10am-6pm
Sunday 1pm-5pm

Contact: Judy Chassay
Phone: 205-971-2282

Choose from three fantastic shops of merchandise. The first shop carries upscale gently used designer clothing & accessories for women. The second shop carries children's & maternity wear & some casual wear for men. The third shop carries After Five & Bridal wear. Some new items can be found here too!

Store Specials: Check with the shop for daily markdowns

Madison

Chic Street
181-4 Hughes Plaza
Madison, Alabama 35758

Store Hours:
Monday-Friday 10am-6pm
Saturday 10am-5pm
Contact: Anita Homsley
Phone: 205-461-9650

Clothing for the entire family, furniture & accessories

Store Specials: Half price & dollar racks

Mobile

Fine Things
220 Airport Blvd.
Mobile, Alabama 36606

Store Hours:
Monday-Saturday 10am-5pm

Contact: Crystal Daw
Phone: 334-478-6111

Gently used clothing for women & children

Consignment Policy: 50/50 split
Items consigned for 90 days

Thrift Town
261 Western Drive
Mobile, Alabama 36607

Store Hours:
Monday-Saturday 9am-9pm
Sunday 12pm-6pm

Phone: 334-476-9504

Clothing for the entire family & much more!

Store Specials: Tuesdays seniors receive a 20% discount

Thousands of new items added to stock daily!!

Montgomery

Kids Kloset
2055 Carter Hill Road
Montgomery, Alabama 36016

Store Hours:
Monday-Friday 10am-5pm
Saturday 10am-4pm

Alabama

Phone: 334-262-4946

Clothing for newborn to preteens,
shoes & toys
Accepts cash & checks

Store Policy: Items purchased
outright

Anchorage

**Alaska Society For The
Prevention of Cruelty
To Animals, Inc.
A.S.P.C.A.
549 W. International
Airport Road, Suite B-2
Anchorage, Alaska 99518**

Store Hours:
Monday-Saturday 10am-6pm
Sunday 1pm-5pm

Contact: Dee Hipom
Phone: (907)-562-1092

General thrift merchandise
including furniture, jewelry,
fine art, antiques & collectibles

Store Policy: Donations are
welcome & consignments
accepted on certain items, i.e.
furniture. The consignor
receives 50% of the selling price
for furniture & 60% of the selling
price on other items. A tax
receipt is provided for donated
items.

Palmer

**Bishop's Attic No. 2
840 South Bailey
Palmer, Alaska 99645**

Store Hours:
Monday, Tuesday, Wednesday &
Saturday 10am-5pm
Thursday & Friday 10am-6pm

Contact: Cloudy Rockwell
Phone: (907) 745-4215

Clothing & bric & brac

Store Policy: Donations welcome
& a receipt is provided for tax
purposes

Store Specials: Monthly select
color tag sales

All proceeds are donated to local
charities which include food
banks, parishes, women's shelters
& runaway houses, in addition to
helping those in dire need.

Arizona

Bisbee

On Consignment In Bisbee
100 Lowell Traffic Circle
Bisbee, Arizona 85603

Store Hours:
Tuesday-Saturday
10:30am-5:30pm & the first
Sunday of every month
12pm-5pm

Phone: 520-432-4002

Over 12,000 square feet of
antiques, jewelry, glass,
kitchenware, dolls, toys, furniture
& much more!
Accepts cash, Visa, Mastercard &
Discover

Consignment Policy: Items
accepted must be in good
condition. Clothing or crafts are
not accepted.

Chandler

Rose's Closet
6045 W. Chandler Blvd. #13
Chandler, Arizona 85226

Store Hours:
Monday-Friday 10:30am-6pm
Saturday 10am-5pm

Contact: Rose McCoy
Phone: 602-961-1837

Designer apparel for women,
bridal wear, mother-of-the-bride &
after-five gowns

Consignment Policy: 50/50 split

Store Specials: Birthday discount

Hardy

Hardy Thrift Shop
Highway 62-412
Hardy, Arizona 72542

Store Hours:
Monday-Saturday 9am-4pm

Phone: 501-856-3547

Clothing, books, furniture & bric-
a-brac

Proceeds from the shop benefit
St. Jude Children's Research
Hospital for cancer research.

Lake Havasu City

Sherry's Consignments
2169 Swanson Ave
Lake Havasu City, Arizona
86403

Store Hours:
Monday-Saturday 9am-5pm
Closed on Sunday

Phone: 520-680-9677

High quality gently used clothing
for women, accessories & small
household items

Consignment Policy: 50/50 split

Mesa

Cash For Clothes®
Clothing Outlet-Buy, Sell &
Trade
830 West Southern
NWC Southern & Extension
(next to Circle K

Mesa, Arizona 85201

Store Hours:
Monday-Friday 10am-7pm
Saturday 10:30am-6pm
Sunday 12pm-5pm

Phone: 602-464-1791

Second Location:
Cash For Clothes
2050 North Alama
School Road
NWC Alma School & Warner
Chandler, Arizona 85224

Store Hours:
Monday-Friday 10am-7pm
Saturday 10:30am-6pm &
Sunday 12pm-5pm

Phone: 602-963-0663

Clothing for guys, gals & kids.
Lots of denim jeans, dresses &
jackets for under ten dollars.
Featuring labels i.e. the Limited,
Gap, Levi's, Calvin Klein & more!

Store Policy: Items purchased
outright

Wear It Again Kids
730 E. Brown Road #17
Mesa, Arizona 85203

Store Hours:
Monday-Saturday 10am-5pm

Contact: Donna Winton
Phone: 602-644-0484

Clothing for children, toys &
equipment
Accepts cash, checks, Mastercard,
Visa & Discover

Store Policy: Buy or trade

Phoenix

My Sister's Closet
Recycled Design Apparel
2033 East Camelback
Phoenix, Arizona 85016

Store Hours:
Monday-Tuesday 10am-7pm
Wednesday-Friday 10am-8pm
Saturday-Sunday 10am-6pm

Contact: Ann Siner
Phone: 602-954-6080

Designer apparel sizes 2-22 &
accessories for women

Consignment Policy: No
appointment is necessary to
consign items
Consignor receives 55% of the
selling price for the item in store
credit or 45% in cash

Store Specials: January & August
annual sale

Named *"Best of Phoenix"* by *The
New Times* in 1994 & 1996!

People's Thrift Shop
2946 N. 7th Avenue
Phoenix, Arizona 85013

Store Hours:
Monday-Saturday 10am-5pm

Contact: Kaye Counts
Phone: 602-274-3451

Clothing for the entire family,
furniture, jewelry & dishes
Accepts cash, checks, Visa,
Mastercard, American Express &
Discover

Arizona

**Yesterdaze Wearables &
Costuming
2413 E. Osborn
Phoenix, Arizona 85016**

Store Hours:
Wednesday-Friday 11am-6pm
Saturday 12pm-4pm
Vintage & Bridals by appointment

Contact: Ann Grossman
Phone: 602-957-3944

Featuring sales & rental of period
& vintage wear
Accepts cash, checks & debit cards

Store Specials: Specially marked
items discounted 20% & 50%

This coupon entitles the
bearer to save 10% off an
undiscounted item or rental
at *Yesterdaze Wearables &
Costuming
2413 E. Osborn
Phoenix, Arizona 85016*
Expiration Date: 12/31/99

Scottsdale

**Back To The Rack Kids
7121 E 5th Avenue
Scottsdale, Arizona 85251**

Store Hours:
Monday-Saturday 10am-5:30pm

Contact: Mary Ellen O'Connor
Phone: 602-949-9609

Clothing for kids, maternity wear,
toys, baby equipment & more
Accepts cash, Mastercard & Visa

Consignment Policy: Items are
consigned for six months

Store Specials: Items reduced 10%
to 25%

**Consigning Women
7120 E. Indian School Road
Scottsdale, Arizona 85251**

Store Hours:
Tuesday-Saturday 10am-5pm
Sunday 12pm-5pm

Phone: 602-947-1717
e-mail: CONSIGN602@aol.com

Featuring American & European
designer resale fashions on
consignment

Consignment Policy: 50/50 split
Items are consigned for 90 days

Present this coupon at
*Consigning Women
7120 E. Indian School Road
Scottsdale, Arizona* & save
$5.00 off a minimum purchase
of $25.00 or more
(Excludes jewelry)
Expiration Date: 12/31/99

**Gigi's Second Time
Around Ltd.
7126 E. Becker Lane
Scottsdale, Arizona 85254**

Store Hours:
Monday-Friday 9am-6pm
Saturday 9am-4pm

Contact: Gigi McMillen
Phone: 602-998-5978

Upscale resale clothing for women featuring labels designed by Escada, Christian Dior, Chanel, Carol Little & more, lots of North Beach Leather, sizes casual to plus & accessories

Secrets/What The Butler Saw
4436 N. Miller Road #100-200
Scottsdale, Arizona 85251

Store Hours:
Monday-Saturday 10am-5:30pm

Phone: 602-941-0167

Upscale clothing for women, bridal wear & jewelry

Consignment Policy: Designer & couture labels only, less than three years old

Tempe

Gracie's Cottage
1520 E. Apache Blvd.
Tempe, Arizona 85283

Store Hours:
Monday, Tuesday, Wednesday, Friday & Saturday 9am-6pm
Thursday 9am-7pm

Contact: Linda Smith
Phone: 602-967-5231
Web site:
www.theclothestree.com/shops/
Graciescottage

Clothing for the entire family, furniture, household items and a great book department

Store Policy: Donations accepted
Store Specials: Seniors receive a 20% discount on Tuesdays

Proceeds from Gracie's Cottage benefit the Grace Community Church.

Tucson

Thrift Store For Children
3601 N. Flowing Wells Road
Tucson, Arizona 85705

Store Hours:
Tuesday, Wednesday & Thursday 10am-3pm
Friday & Saturday 10am-4pm

Contact: Dorothy Howard
Phone: 520-293-8873

Clothing for the entire family, housewares, small furniture, books, records, jewelry, artwork and much more!
Accepts cash only

Store Policy: Donations welcome at the back door

Store Specials: Adult clothing-three pieces for one dollar & special sales at the holidays
Proceeds benefit the Arizona

Booneville

The Store - A division of the Logan County Day Service Center
1234 East Main (Highway 10)
Booneville, Arkansas 72927

Store Hours:
Monday-Saturday 9:30am-4:30pm

Contact: Marcia Anderson
Phone: 501-675-3533
Fax: 501-675-5218

Gently used clothing for the entire family, shoes, handbags, linens, housewares, books & small miscellaneous items
Accepts cash

Store Policy: Donations welcome & a receipt is provided for tax purposes

The Store is a non profit thrift shop run by the Logan County Day Service Center. Proceeds benefit adults & children with developmental challenges.

Fayetteville

Experienced Denim
509 W. Spring St. Suite 6
Fayetteville, Arkansas 72701

Store Hours:
Monday-Friday 9am-5:30pm
Saturday 11am-5pm

Phone: 501-521-3767
Fax: 501-521-8331

Retro, contemporary & vintage clothing including jeans

Accepts cash, checks, Visa, Mastercard & Discover

Store Policy: Items purchased outright

Kathryn's Closet, Inc.
778 Happy Hollow Road
Fayetteville, Arkansas 72701

Store Hours:
Monday-Saturday 10am-5pm

Contact: Kathryn Keck
Phone: 501-521-9046
Web site:
www.theclothestree.com/shops/Kathryn'sCloset/

More than 2000 square feet of clothing for the entire family! Including a special enclosed play area for children.
Accepts cash, checks, Visa & Mastercard

Consignment Policy:
60/40 on casual wear & 40/60 on formal wear
An appointment is necessary to consign merchandise
Items are consigned for 60 days

Store Specials: Color coded discounts from 25% to 50% off

Rogers

Consigning Women
318 S. First Street
Rogers, Arkansas 75756

Store Hours:
Monday-Friday 9am-6pm
Saturday 9am-5pm

Phone: 501-636-0169

Gently used clothing for women,
bridal & prom gowns

Consignment Policy:
50/50 split

Consigning Women is a non profit
thrift shop. Proceeds benefit
the Office of Human Concern.

Member of The National
Association Resale &Thrift Shops

California

Atwater

Beverly Ann's Thrift Shop
1149 Broadway
Atwater, California 95301

Store Hours:
Monday-Friday 10am-5pm
Saturday & Sunday 10am-4pm

Contact: Beverly Marion
Phone: 209-357-0102

Clothing & bric-a-brac

Store Specials: Lay-a-ways
available

Auburn

Assistance League
Thrift Shop
1249 Grass Valley Highway
Auburn, California 95603

Store Hours:
Tuesday-Friday 10am-4pm
Saturday 11am-3pm

Phone: 916-885-1982

Clothing, furniture, small
appliances, jewelry & collectibles

Store Policy: Donations welcome
and a receipt is provided for tax
purposes

Assistance League Thrift Shop is a
non profit shop whose proceeds
benefit families in need within
the community.

Kids Stuff
1269 Grass Valley Highway
Auburn, California 95603

Store Hours:
Tuesday-Saturday 10am-5pm

Contact: Linda Bearden
Phone: 530-885-7873

Children's clothing, toys, books &
baby equipment

Consignment Policy:
50/50 split
Call before bringing items to
consign
Items must be in excellent
condition

With almost 3000 consignors on
the roster at Kids Stuff you are
sure to find a great selection of
merchandise

Brownsville

Country Consignments
16849 Willow Glenn Road
PO Box 353
Brownsville, California 95919

Store Hours:
Tuesday-Friday 12pm-4pm
Saturday 10am-4pm

Phone: 530-675-0825

Everything from clothing to
antiques

Store Specials:
25% to 50% off select items
$1.00 rack

Country Consignment is one the
best kept secrets in the foothills
of California.

Burbank

Junk For Joy
Halloween & Vintage
3314 W. Magnolia Blvd.
Burbank, California 91505

Store Hours:
Tuesday-Saturday 12pm-6pm

Phone: 818-569-4903
e-mail: j4j@junkforjoy.com
Web site: www.junkforjoy.com

Never worn clothing & accessories from the 60's & 70's for all tastes
Accepts cash, checks, Mastercard, Visa, American Express & ATM Debit cards

Store Specials: Movie, TV & promotion folks receive a 10% discount when purchasing large quantities of merchandise

Burlingame

Circles-Women's
Resale Boutique
1113 Burlingame Avenue
Burlingame, California
94010

Store Hours:
Monday-Saturday 10am-5:30pm

Contact: Sora Lei Newman & Michelle Newman-Light
Phone: 650-347-6162

New & "nearly new" designer clothing for women & children & accessories
Accepts cash, checks, Visa & Mastercard

Consigment Policy:
Consignments accepted by appointment
40/50 split
Items consigned for 60 to 90 days

Canyon Lake

The Elegant Lady
Consignment Boutique
31682 Railroad Canyon
Road #5
Canyon Lake, California
92587

Store Hours:
Monday-Friday 10am-5pm &
Saturday 12pm-6pm

Phone: 909-244-9203

Elegant clothing & accessories for women, jewelry, fine paintings & antiques

13

California

Carmichael

Rambling Rose -Boutique-
5907 Fair Oaks Blvd.
Carmichael, California 95608

Store Hours:
Monday-Saturday 10am-6pm
Sunday 12pm-4pm
Phone: 916-944-7742

New & "nearly new" clothing for women

Store Policy: Buy, sell or trade

Claremont

Silent Partners East
346 N. Yale Avenue
Claremont, California 91711

Store Hours:
Tuesday-Saturday 11am-5pm
Sunday 12pm-4pm

Contact: Kym Sorenson
Phone: 909-624-0696

Designer clothing for women

Consignment Policy:
Items must be current & seasonal

Store Specials: Always featuring 50% off items

> This coupon entitles the bearer
> to save 10%
> off one non-sale item
> at
> *Silent Partners East*
> *346 N. Yale Avenue*
> *Claremont, California*
> Expiration Date: 12/31/99

Compton

Alameda Thrift Store
124 South Alameda Street
Compton, California 90221

Store Hours:
Monday-Saturday 9am-6pm
Sunday 11am-5pm

Contact: Margaret Flores
Phone: 310-639-4900
Fax: 310-693-4905

Clothing for the entire family, toys, dishes, knickknacks, collectibles, antiques, small furniture, small appliances, linens, towels, curtains, rugs, bed frames & more
Accepts cash, checks, Visa, Mastercard, American Express & Explorer

Store Policy: Donations accepted

Store Specials: Select color tags 50% off
Seniors & disabled veterans receive a 10% discount

Established in 1958, Alameda Thrift has been offering great merchandise at affordable prices!

> Present this coupon at
> *Alameda Thrift Store*
> *124 South Alameda Street*
> *Compton, California*
> &
> save 10% off one single purchase
> (This coupon can not be combined with any other specials)

Concord

Cambridge Closet
1135 Lacey Lane
Concord, California 94520

Store Hours:
Tuesday, Wednesday & Thursday
10am-8pm
Friday & Saturday 10am-5pm
Sunday-open seasonally

Phone: 510-798-1078

Designer label clothing for women
& men featuring labels such as
Ralph Lauren, Anne Klein, JNY,
Escada & Armani

Consignment Policy: Consignments accepted by appointment
only

Store Specials: Half price sale in
January & July

Coronado

Reruns
The Children's Resale Shop
1015 C Avenue
Coronado, California 92118

Store Hours:
Monday-Saturday 10am-5pm
Sunday 12pm-3pm

Phone: 619-435-5444

Upscale children's clothing sizes
newborn-teens
Accepts cash, checks, Visa &
Mastercard

Consignment Policy:
Consignments accepted by
appointment only

Consignor receives 40% of the
selling price for the item

Danville

Something Old-
Something New
442 & 482 Hartz Avenue
Danville, California 94526

Store Hours:
Monday-Friday 10am-6pm
Saturday 10am-5pm

Phone: 510-838-4492

Upscale clothing & accessories for
women

Consignment Policy: 50/50 split
Consignments accepted by
appointment

Store Specials: Clearance room

Dublin

Kids Again/Fashion Court
6891 Village Parkway
Dublin, California 94568

Store Hours:
Monday-Saturday 10am-5pm
Thursday until 7pm
Sunday 12pm-4pm

Contact: Lynn Cole
Phone: 925-828-7334
Fax: 925-803-0691

Kids Again features apparel for
infants & children sizes 0-10,
toys, accessories, baby
furniture & equipment, maternity
wear. New infant & teen furniture
at factory-direct prices. Save up
to 60% below retail! Over 1000

California

different items each week.
Accepts cash, checks,
Visa & Mastercard

Furnish Again
6891 Village Parkway
Dublin, California 94568

Store Hours:
Monday-Saturday 10am-5pm
Thursday 10am-7pm
Sunday 12pm-4pm

Contact: Ken Pfeifer
Phone: 925-828-7207
Fax: 925-803-0691

Better quality home furnishings,
accessories, gift items, crystal,
fine dinnerware, decorative items
& fine art
Accepts cash, checks, Visa &
Mastercard

Kids Again/Fashion Court &
Furnish Again is one of the largest
consignment department stores in
Northern California. All shoppers
are welcome to stop in and
browse.

Fair Oaks

Moth Hole
Simply the Best in
Consignment
11787 Fair Oaks Blvd.
Fair Oaks, California 95628

Store Hours:
Monday-Friday 10am-8pm
Saturday 10am-6pm
Sunday 12pm-4pm

Phone: 916-965-5542
Fax: 916-965-4360

16

Web site: http://
www.theclothestree.com/shops/
TheMothHole

Women's current designer
clothing & accessories

Consignment Policy:
50/50 split
Items consigned for 120 to 150
days
Moth Hole also buys some items
outright for cash

Located in the most fashionable
shopping center in Sacramento,
California, the Moth Hole
offers over 3700 square feet of
fantastic items worn by celebrities
and consignors from all parts of
the United States.

Folsom

KidStuff
306 Natoma Street
Folsom, California 95630

Store Hours:
Monday-Friday 10am-5:30pm
Saturday 10am-5pm
Sunday 11am-4pm

Phone: 916-985-0606

Featuring gently used clothing for
children sizes birth to 14,

furniture & maternity clothing. Huge inventory includes gently used items, manufacturer's samples & discontinued items
Accept cash or checks

Store Policy: Call for buying schedule & requirements
Cash or credit given when you bring in your quality items

This coupon entitles the bearer to save 10% off all clothing & shoe purchases at
KidStuff
306 Natoma Street,
Folsom, California
Expiration Date: 12/31/99

Fort Bragg

Good Stuff!
310 North Franklin Street
Fort Bragg, California 95437

Store Hours:
Monday-Saturday 11am-5pm
Sunday 12pm-3pm

Phone: 707-964-3032

Vast selection of vintage clothing from vintage to retro, some contemporary clothing items too & featuring one of the largest selections of costume jewelry in northern California!
Accepts cash & all major credit cards

Store Specials:
Lay-a-way available
Dealer discount

25% off the entire shop during the weekend of the Fort Bragg Festival & the week after Christmas

The shop has been featured in *The Santa Rose Press Democrat, Coast Magazine & The Advocate.*

Present this coupon at
Good Stuff!
310 North Franklin Street
Fort Bragg, California &
save 10% off any item over $20.00
Expiration Date: 12/31/99

Paul Bunyan Thrift Shop
242 N. McPherson
Fort Bragg, California 95437

Store Hours:
Monday-Friday 9:30am-5pm
Saturday 12pm-5pm

Contact: Laura Welter
Phone: 707-964-4471

Clothing for the entire family, household items, books, small appliances including computers, knick-knacks & much more!
Accepts cash & checks

Store Policy: Donations of merchandise in good condition are accepted

Proceeds from the shop benefit developmentally disabled people in the Fort Bragg coastal community. One of Fort Bragg's most popular thrift shops for over thirty years!

California

Fullerton

Geez Louise
Vintage Clothing
111 E. Commonwealth Avenue
Fullerton, California 92832

Store Hours:
Monday-Friday 11:30am-7pm
Saturday 11am-6pm
Sunday 12pm-5pm

Phone: 714-871-4375
Fax: 714-871-0643
e-mail: geezlouise@aol.com
Web site: http://members.aol.com/
geezlouise

Vintage clothing for men &
women circa 1890-1970 &
accessories
Accepts cash, credit cards &
ATM cards

Store Policy: Buy, trade or consign

Gardena

TR Trading Company
15604 S. Broadway
Gardena, California 90248

Store Hours:
Monday-Friday 8:30am-5:30pm
Saturday 10am-5pm

Contact: Toni Ziff
Phone: 310-329-9242
Fax: 310-329-0789

Over 65,000 square feet of gently
used office furniture
Accepts Mastercard & Visa

Garden Grove

Denim Blue
9678 Chapman Garden Grove
Garden Grove, California
92841

Store Hours:
Monday-Saturday 10am-7pm
Sunday 11am-5pm

Contact: William Bowman
Phone: 714-534-7800

Gently used Levis & vintage
clothing
Accepts cash & checks

Store Policy: Cash paid for gently
used Levis & vintage clothing

Store Specials: Discounts for large
quantity purchases

Grass Valley

Linda's Kiddie Trade &
Mom's Boutique
128 E. Main Street
Grass Valley, California
95677

Second Location:
5895 Pacific Street
Rocklin, California 9677

Store Hours:
Monday-Friday 10am-5pm
Saturday 10am-4pm

Phone:
916-273-9246 Grass Valley
916-632-8830 Rocklin

Quality brand name clothing for
women & children, maternity
wear, baby equipment & furniture

Consignment Policy:
50/50 split

Store Specials: Markdowns on
select items

Guerneville

Seconds First
16365 Main Street
Box 1047
Guerneville, California
95446

Store Hours: Daily 11am-6pm

Contact: Arrow Olesky
Phone: 707-869-2211
Fax: 707-887-1832

Clothing for women & men,
featuring natural fibers (cotton,
silk, wool & linen)
Accepts cash, check, Visa &
Mastercard

Store Policy: Purchases clothing
outright, some trades

Hollywood

Aunt Bee's Out of the
Closet Thrift Store
1408 Vine Street
Hollywood, California 90028

Store Hours:
Monday-Sunday 10am-7pm

Phone: 213-468-0747

Clothing for the entire family,
high quality gently used books &
much more

Store Policy: Donations accepted

Proceeds from the shop benefit
people with AIDS.

Huntington Beach

Borne 2 Shoppe
18822 Beach Blvd #108
Huntington Beach,
California 92646

Phone: 714-962-2962
Fax: 562-459-4684

Store Hours:
Monday-Friday 11am-6pm
Saturday 11am-5pm
Sunday 12pm-4pm
Closed on major holidays

Clothing & accessories for
women, gift & decorative items,
housewares & furniture
Accepts cash, checks & credit
cards

Store Specials: Triple mark down
sale the last Saturday of the
month & frequent shopper
rewards

Second Location:
322 Pine Street
Long Beach, California 90802

Store Hours:
Monday-Friday 11am-5:30pm
Saturday 11am-5pm
Closed on major holidays

California

Phone: 562-436-1503

Clothing & accessories for men & women, gift & decorative items, housewares & furniture

Store Specials:
Triple markdown sale the first Saturday of the month & frequent shopper rewards

My Secret Place
18862 Beach Blvd #116
Huntington Beach,
California 92648

Store Hours:
Tuesday-Friday 12pm-6pm
Saturday 10am-4pm

Contact: CC Swenson & Daris Birt
Phone: 714-963-4743
Fax: 714-963-0333
Web site:
www.theclothestree.com/shops/
MySecretPlace/

Specializing in upscale gently used clothing & accessories sizes 14 & up
Accepts cash, checks & major credit cards

Consignment Policy: Consign ments accepted by appointment only

20

The shop accepts fine jewelry, vintage collectibles, antiques & other items on consignment. For a full list inquire within the shop.

Store Specials: "Secret Service" have your items picked- up at your home. Inquire in the shop for details. On premises estate sales.

Lafayette

Rosie's Consignment Shop
1020 Brown Avenue
Lafayette, California 94549

Store Hours:
Tuesday-Friday 10am-4:30pm
Saturday 11am-5pm

Contact: Sherissa Heiser
Phone: 925-283-6540

Upscale name brand & designer label clothing for women & accessories
Accepts cash, local checks, Visa & Mastercard

Consignment Policy: Items must be clean, on hangers & preferably 2-3 years old or newer
50/50 split
Items consigned for 60 days

Store Specials: Monthly color tag sale & Bi-annual 50% off sale at the end of each season

Laguna Beach

Tippe Canoes
648 S. Coast Highway
Laguna Beach, California
92651

Store Hours:
Monday-Sunday 10am-6pm

Vintage clothing, Levis 501 &
accessories
Accepts cash, checks, all major
credit cards & ATM cards

La Jolla

"Your Favorite Things"
Consignment Boutique
5645 La Jolla Boulevard
La Jolla, California 92037

Store Hour:
Monday-Saturday 10am-6pm

Contact: Diane Hart
Phone: 619-459-0311

Upscale clothing accessories for
men & women
Accepts cash, checks, Visa &
Mastercard

Consignment Policy:
50/50 split
Items consigned for 60 days

Store Specials: Check with the
shop for special sales

Present this coupon at
"Your Favorite Things"
Consignment Boutique
5645 La Jolla Blvd
La Jolla, California
& save $25.00
off any $100.00 purchase
Expiration Date: 12/31/99

Livermore

Tiny Tot's Closet
167 S. "P" Street
Livermore, California 94550

Store hours:
Tuesday-Friday 10am-5pm
Thursday until 7pm
Saturday 11am-5pm

Contact: Linda Doyle
Phone: 925-294-5881
e-mail: tnyttsclst@aol.com
Web site: http://members.aol.com/
tnyttsclst

Gently used clothing for children
sizes 0-14, furniture, toys &
accessories
Accepts cash & checks

Consignment Policy:
Consignor receives 50% of the
selling price for clothing & 60%
for furniture, toys & accessories

Store Specials:
At time of purchase inquire about
special discounts for seniors &
foster parents

California

With friendly service, great selection and a play area for children you are sure to have a pleasant shopping experience here!

Lomita

Encore Resale Boutique
1939 Pacific Coast Highway
Lomita, California 90717

Store Hours:
Tuesday-Friday 11am-6pm
Saturday 11am-5pm
& Sunday 12pm-5pm

Phone: 310-530-0196

Women's designer clothing & accessories, shoes, handbags, maternity wear, costume & vintage jewelry

Accepts cash, checks, Visa, Mastercard & Discover

Consignment Policy: Consignments accepted by appointment only

Long Beach

Ragtime Vintage Clothing
& Furnishings
3138 E 7th Street
Long Beach, California 90804

Store Hours:
Monday-Friday 12pm-6pm
Saturday 11am-6pm
Sunday 12pm-5pm

Phone: 562-438-5433

Vintage wear & furniture through the 1970's
Accepts cash, Visa, Novus, Mastercard

Consignment Policy: 60/40 split on furniture only

Los Altos

Round Robin
146 Main Street
Los Altos, California 94022

Store Hours:
Tuesday-Saturday
10:30am-5:30pm

Contact: Jodie Jensen
Phone: 415-948-0955

Apparel & accessories for women
Accepts cash & checks

Consignment Policy:
Consignments accepted by
appointment

Store Specials: Half price rack

Present this coupon
at *Round Robin*
146 Main Street
Los Altos, California
& save 20% off one purchase
Expiration Date: 12/31/99

Los Angeles

Aaardvark's Odd Ark Inc.
7579 Melrose Ave.
Los Angeles, California
90046

Store Hours:
Monday-Friday 11am-9pm

Phone: 213-655-6769

Gently used clothing
Accepts cash, checks, Amex,
Visa, Mastercard, Discover &
Debit cards

Store Specials: Wholesale
discounts & seasonal sales

Come To Mama
4019 West Sunset Blvd.
Los Angeles, California
90029

Store Hours:
Thursday-Sunday 12pm-6pm

Contact: Terri Mussatti
Phone: 213-953-1275

Specializing in vintage clothing &
accessories

Store Specials: On-going 25% &
50% off select color tags

Present this coupon at
Come To Mama
4019 West Sunset Blvd
Los Angeles, California &
save 25% off minimum
purchase of $25.00 on
vintage clothing only

Coupon not valid with any other
offers or discounts
Expiration Date: 12/31/99

Entre Nous
8430 West Third Street
Los Angeles, California
90048

Store Hours:
Monday-Saturday 11am-6pm

Contact: Carolyn Reyes &
Stephanie Magid
Phone: 213-655-9096
Fax: 213-655-9097
e-mail: sirens@earthlink.net

LA's newest resale boutique
featuring top designer clothing,

23

accessories & shoes

Consignment Policy:
50/50 split
Items consigned for two months

Decades Inc.
8214 Melrose Avenue
@ Harper
Los Angeles, California 90046

Store Hours:
Monday-Saturday 11:30am-6pm
or by appointment

Contact: Cameron Silver
Phone: 213-655-0223
Fax: 213-655-0172
e-mail: decadescouture@msn.com
Web site: www.decadesinc.com

Decades specializes in high-end
vintage couture clothing
primarily from the 1960's &
1970's for men & women. Top
European & American designers
are found here. Most items are
one of a kind!
Accepts cash, checks & most
major credit cards

Store Policy: Decades purchases
merchandise at fair market prices

Store Specials: Check with
Decades for occassional specials
& discounts

Decades has been featured on
TV & in major international
magazines. A favorite stop
among movie & TV personalities.

Ozzie Dots
4637 Hollywood Blvd.
Los Angeles, California 90027
Store Hours:
Monday-Saturday 11am-6pm

Sunday 12pm-6pm

Contact: Dan Hazen
Phone: 213-633-2867
Fax: 213-663-0501

Vintage clothing, hats, jewelry,
hosiery, gloves, makeup,
costumes, wigs, sunglasses & Levis
501's
Accepts cash, Mastercard, Visa,
American Express & ATM

Store Policy: Purchase merchandise outright

Store Specials: The first Saturday
of each month dollar sale!
Discounts available on large
quantity merchandise

PJ London
11661 San Vicente Blvd.
Los Angeles, California
90049

Store Hours:
Monday-Saturday 10:30am-6pm
Sunday 12pm-5pm

Phone: 310-826-4649
Fax: 310-826-7237
e-mail: PJLondon@aol.com
Web site: www.PJLondon.com

Gently used designer clothing "hot
off the runway" at great savings,
featuring designers such as
Armani, Chanel, Calvin Klein, Jil
Sander, Richard Tyler, Romeo
Gigli, Dolce & Gabbana!

Consignment Policy:
Consignor receives 40% of the
selling price
Items consigned for 90 days
After 60 days items are reduced
20%

PJ London receives merchandise daily from some of the world's best known celebrities & some of the best dressed women in Los Angeles.

Present this coupon at
P.J. London
11661 San Vicente Blvd.
Los Angeles, California
& save 10% off purchase
Expiration Date: 12/31/99

The Place & Company Resale
8820 South Sepulve Blvd.
Los Angeles, California
90045

Store Hours:
Monday-Saturday 10am-6pm

Phone: 310-645-1539

Top designer clothing for men & women from the rich & famous

Menlo Park

New Life Boutique
879 Santa Cruz Ave.
Menlo Park, California 94025

Store Hours:
Monday-Friday 11am-5pm
Saturday 10am-4pm

Phone: 650-325-3333
Contact: Carol Domingo

Designer clothing & accessories for women & children
Accepts cash, checks, Visa, Mastercard & American Express

Store Specials: On-going 20% discount on select items

Present this coupon at
New Life Boutique
879 Santa Cruz Ave.
Menlo Park, California & save 10% off entire inventory not previously discounted
Expiration Date: 12/31/99

Moreno Valley

True Wonders
24875-10 Alessandra Blvd
Moreno Valley, California
92553

Store Hours:
Monday-Saturday 9am-7pm
Sunday 9am-6pm

Contact: Maria Agramon
Phone: 909-780-3857

Clothing for the entire family
Accepts cash & checks

Store Specials:
Lay-a-way available

Napa

4 Kid's Sake
1556 Silverado Trail
Napa, California 94559

Store Hours:
Monday-Saturday 11am-5:30pm
Sunday 12pm-4pm

25

California

Contact: Robin Sisemore
Phone: 707-257-3657

Children's clothing & accessories, equipment & furniture. New Stride-Rite shoes too!
Accepts cash, checks, Visa, Mastercard American Express & Novus

Consignment Policy: 50/50 split
Items are consigned for 60 days

Store Policy: Great half price rack available at the beginning of each month

```
┌ ─ ─ ─ ─ ─ ─ ─ ┐
│  Present this coupon at      │
│       4 Kid's Sake           │
│    1556 Silverado Trail      │
│   Napa, California 94559     │
│    & save $5.00 off any      │
│   purchase over $20.00       │
│    Expiration Date: 12/31/99 │
└ ─ ─ ─ ─ ─ ─ ─ ┘
```

Newport Beach

Chez Elle Boutique
3601 Jamboree Road #7
Newport Beach, California
92660

Phone: 714-757-1555
Fax: 714-752-7068

Store Hours:
Monday-Friday 10am-7pm
Saturday 10am-5pm
Sunday 12pm-4pm

Designer fashions for women & men, sports wear to black tie, furs & evening wear

Consignment Policy:
50/50 split
Items consigned for forty-five days

Store Specials: On-going 50% off sale rack!

Oakland

Amercian Cancer Society
Discovery Shop
127 41st Street
Oakland, California 94611

Store Hours:
Monday-Saturday 10am-5pm

Contact: Linda Payne
Phone: 510-601-0100

Clothing for the entire family, furniture, bric-a-brac & jewelry
Accepts cash, checks, Visa & Mastercard

Store Policy: Donations welcome & proceeds benefit the American Cancer Society in the fight against cancer

New To You shops are located in Northern California. The Children's Hospital in Oakland, California was established in 1912. It is the largest and most comprehensive pediatric medical center for children located between Los Angeles & Seattle. Proceeds benefit children from the entire west coast in need of medical care.

Featured in the shops are new & gently used clothing for the entire family, jewelry, furniture, household items & much more!

Website: www.branches.org

New. To. You.
3271 Adeline Street
Berkeley, California 94703

Store Hours:
Monday-Saturday 11am-5pm

Phone: 510-428-3839

This location is stocked with over 3000 square feet of gently used & new merchandise for men, women & children, semi-formal dresses, beaded wedding gowns, furniture, jewelry, household items, toys, books & vintage items. Sharon, the store manager and her volunteer staff have created a pleasant at-home shopping atmosphere.

New. To. You.
5290 College Ave.
Oakland, California 94618
Phone: 510-658-7473

Store Hours:
Tuesday-Thursday 10am-3pm
Saturday 11am-3pm

This quaint boutique is located in Rockridge, one of Oakland's most electrifying shopping & dining areas. Items featured in this shop include clothing for the entire family, furniture, household items, vintage glassware, crystal & more. Donations are welcome during store hours.

Other Locations:
3219 MacDonald Ave
Richmond, California 94804
Phone: 510-234-4972

Featuring over 6,000 square feet of exquisite internationally consigned furniture, estate jewelry, books, china, crystal & collectibles. Over thirty-five dealer collections to peruse.

Consignment Policy: 50/50 split
Items are consigned for 90 days

Store Specials: Delivery & pick up services available throughout the state

California

Pacific Grove

Labels
157 Grand Avenue
Pacific Grove, California
93950

Store Hours:
Monday-Saturday 10am-5pm
Sunday 12pm-4pm

Contact: Grace Ashby
Phone: 408-372-4314
Fax: 408-649-8793

Upscale women's fashions
Accepts cash, checks, Mastercard
& Visa
Consignment Policy:
Consignor receives 40% of the
selling price for each item

Patrick's, Inc.
Fine Pre-owned Furniture on
Consignment
105 Central Avenue
Pacific Grove, California
93950

Store Hours:
Monday-Saturday 10am-5:30pm
Sunday 12pm-5pm

Phone: 408-372-3995

Fine furniture & home accessories

Reincarnation Vintage
Clothing
214 17th Street
Pacific Grove, California
93950

Store Hours:
Monday-Saturday 11am-5:30pm

Contact: Nancy Holland
Phone: 408-649-0689

Vintage clothing for men &
women, vintage costumes, jewelry,
hats, accessories & more!

Accepts cash, checks & major
credit cards

Palo Alto

Timeless
532 Bryant Street
Palo Alto, California 94301

Store Hours:
Monday-Saturday 11am-6pm
Thursday 11am-8pm

Contact: Monica Negri
Phone: 650-473-0201

Designer clothing for women
including vintage items too!
Accepts cash, Mastercard & Visa

Consignment Policy:
Items consigned by appointment

Paradise

Elegant Rose
5675 Almond Street
Paradise, California 95969

Store Hours:
Monday-Friday 10:30am-5:30pm
Saturday 11am-5pm

Contact: Gail Caldwell
Phone: 530-877-6136

Quality used clothing & accessories
Accepts cash, local checks, Visa & Mastercard

Store Specials: Select merchandise 75% off

• • • • • • • • • • • • • •
•   •
•   Present this coupon   •
•   *Elegant Rose*   •
•   *5675 Almond Street*   •
• *Paradise, California 95969* •
• & save 25% off any purchase •
• Coupon may only be used one time only and •
•   must be presented at purchase   •
•   Expiration Date: 12/31/99   •
•   •
• • • • • • • • • • • • • •

Pasadena

Something For Baby
1359 N. Hill Avenue
Pasadena, California 91104

Store Hours:
Monday-Saturday 11am-6pm

Contact: Sharon Moses
Phone: 626-791-3314

Top quality gently used clothing
for children
Accepts cash, checks, Visa,
Mastercard, Discover &
American Express

Consignment Policy: 50/50 split

Store Specials: Select tags 20% to
60% savings monthly

The Huntington Collection
766 South Fair Oaks Avenue
Pasadena, California 91105

Store Hours:
Monday, Tuesday, Wednesday &
Friday 10am-4pm,
Thursday 12pm-6pm

Phone: 626-397-3078

The Huntington Collection sells
donated, consigned and estate
items such as antiques, furniture,
fine china, crystal, silver, jewelry,
clothing, appliances & bric-a-brac
in its 12,000 square foot facility.

Accepts cash, checks & credit
cards

Store Policy: Donations are
welcome during store hours. A
free pick-up service for large
items is available within a fifty
mile radius. A receipt is provided
for tax purposes for all donations.

Consignments are accepted on all
items appraised for more
than $100.00 except clothing.

Call ahead to make an appointment

Items are consigned for three months with a contract & the split is 40/60.

Store Specials: The last Saturday of each month from 8am-1pm in the Annex, all white tag items are half price.
"Price & Pack" all-inclusive service is available for the appraisal, removal & sale of your personal property. Full-service estate sales are available

Proceeds from The Huntington Collection help support the Huntington Memorial Hospital S Senior Care Network. The shop is run by a small staff and extremely dedicated volunteers.

Paso Robles

**One More Time-
Recycled Rags
815 Spring Street
Paso Robles, California 93446**

Store Hours:
Monday-Thursday 11am-5pm
Friday 11:30am-5:30pm
Saturday 12pm-3pm

Phone: 805-239-3364

Contemporary clothing & accessories for women
Accepts cash & personal checks

Consignment Policy:
50/50 split
Items are consigned for 60 days
Consignments accepted by appointment only

Store Specials: Regular markdowns

Petaluma

**Vicki's Secret-Designer
Consignments
108 Petaluma Blvd. No.
Petaluma, California 94952**

Store Hours:
Monday-Friday 11am-5:30pm
Saturday 11am-5pm
Sunday 12pm-5pm

Contact: Vicki or Leah
Phone: 707-765-2807

Specializing in couture designer Japanese & American designer clothing. One of the largest selections of designer labels anywhere west of Chicago. Accepts cash, checks, Visa, Mastercard & Discover

Consignment Policy: Call for information

Placentia

**Consigment Ali
2370 Rose Drive
Placentia, California 92870**

Store Hours:
Tuesday, Wednesday & Friday
10am-5pm

Saturday 10am-4pm

Contact: Alison Drown
Phone: 714-572-6154

Clothing for women & children

Consignment Policy: Consignors
receive 40%
Items are consigned for 60 days

Store Specials: Grandparents
receive a 10% discount off
children's clothing & clearance
sales held the last Friday &
Saturday of each month

Pleasanton

Re-Runs for Little Ones
3037 Hopyard Road
Suite I
Pleasanton, California 94566

Store Hours:
Tuesday, Wednesday & Friday
10am-5pm
Thursday 10am-7pm
Saturday 12pm-5pm

Contact: DeAnn Taylor
Phone: 510-461-1260
e-mail: d.taylor@home.com

Children's clothing sizes 0-8,
maternity wear, toys, equipment
& baby furniture
Accepts cash, checks, Mastercard,

Visa & Discover

Rancho Cordova

Ritzy Rags
A Consignment Boutique
10947 Olson Drive
Suite 408

Rancho Cordova, California
95670
Located in Mervyn's Center

Phone: 916-638-9300

Clothing for the entire family,
jewelry & collectibles

Consignment Policy: 50/50 split
Items are consigned for 60 days

Red Bluff

Act II
368 South Main Street
Red Bluff, California 96080

Store Hours:
Monday-Friday 10am-5:30pm,
Saturday 10am-3pm

Contact: Carol A. Wood
Phone & Fax: 530-527-4227

Specializing in women's clothing
and accessories

Rocklin

Uptown Clothing Co.
Women's & Children's
Designer Consignment
Clothing
5050 Rocklin Road
Rocklin, California 95677
Located across from Sierra
College

Store Hours:
Monday, Wednesday & Friday
10am-5:30pm
Tuesday & Thursday 10am-7pm
Saturday 11am-5pm
Sunday 12pm-4pm

Designer clothing for women &
children

California

Accepts cash, checks, Visa, Mastercard, American Express

Store Specials: Markdowns from 25% to 50%

Sacramento

Act II For Her
2625 Alta Arden
Sacramento, California 95825

Store Hours: Monday-Friday
10am-6pm
Saturday 10am-5pm
Sunday 12pm-5pm

Contact: Leonard Salasky
Phone: 916-971-9977

All types of clothing for women
Accepts cash, checks, Visa, Mastercard, Discover, Amex & JCB

Consignment Policy:
An appointment is necessary to consign merchandise
60/40 split
Items consigned for 90 days

Store Specials: Periodic discounts through the mail

Auntie Mame's
2598 21th Street
Sacramento, California 95818

Store Hours: Monday-Saturday
10am-5:30pm

Contact: Barry & Carol Fyffe
Phone: 916-456-1719
Fax: 916-392-2125

Woman's clothing & accessories
Accepts cash, checks, Visa,

Mastercard & ATM

Consignment Policy:
Items consigned for 90 days
Discounted after 30 days

Store Specials: Select color tags discounted 25% to 50%

Bloomingdeals
Consignment Boutique
2228 J Street
Sacramento, California 95816

Store Hours:
Monday-Friday 11am-6pm
Saturday 11am-4pm

Contact: Susan Tiesing
Phone & Fax: 916-444-3668

Women's upscale fashions & accessories, all current styles including designer and better labels only
Accepts cash, personal checks, Visa, Mastercard, Discover & American Express

Consignment Policy:
New consignments accepted by appointment only
Items consigned for 90 days
60/40 cash out at the end of the contract
50/50 split when using a store credit

Store Specials: Receive a 5% discount with a cash payment

California

Sac's of Fruitridge
4220 Fruitridge Avenue
Sacramento, California 95820

Store Hours:
Monday-Saturday 9am-7pm

Phone: 916-391-2402

Second hand clothing for the entire family, houswares, electrical appliances, accessories & odds and ends
Accepts cash, Visa, Mastercard, Discover & ATM

Other Locations:

Generations
30200 Mission Blvd
Hayward, California 94544
Phone: 510-487-6212

Sac's of Carmichael
5733 Marconi Ave.
Sacramento, California 95608
Phone: 916-481-6592

The Outlet
1212 E Harding Way
Stockton, California 95205
Phone: 209-465-6323

The Value Center
490 Redwood Street

Vallejo, California 94590
Phone: 707-557-0238

The Bunny Patch
3200 Folsom Blvd.
Sacramento, California 95816

Store Hours:
Monday, Tuesday, Wednesday & Saturday 10am-6pm
Thursday & Friday 10am-7pm
Sunday 11am-5pm

Contact: Diane Watkins
Phone: 916-452-8669

Children's clothing, furniture, maternity clothing & great new gifts
Accepts cash, checks, credit cards, ATM & Itex

Salinas

Terri's Secrets
934 Main Street
Salinas, California 93901

Store Hours:
Monday, Tuesday, Wednesday, Friday & Saturday 11am-5pm
Thursday 11am-8pm

Contact: Terri Sally
Phone & Fax: 408-758-9090

California

Evening gowns, accessories, lingerie including plus sizes
Accepts cash, ATM, Visa, Discover & Bank Americard

Consignment Policy:
50/50 split

Store Specials: Markdown rack

This coupon entitles the bearer to save 15% off an item at
Terri's Secrets
934 S. Main Street
Salina, California
Expiration Date: 12/31/99

San Anseimo

Second Hand Land
703 San Anseimo Ave
San Anseimo, California
94950

Store Hours:
Wednesday-Saturday 11:30am-6pm

Phone: 415-454-5057
Website:
www.secondhandland.com

Gently used furniture, clothing, collectibles, vinyl records & lots of bric-a-brac
Accepts cash, check with ID, Visa, Mastercard & Discover

Store Policy: Buy, sell or trade

Store Specials: Prop rental & lay-a-way available

Present this coupon at
Second Hand Land
703 San Anseimo Avenue
San Anseimo, California
& save 15% off one regular priced item

Expiration Date: 12/31/99

San Diego

All Baby Needs
10615 B Tierra Santa Blvd.
San Diego, California 92124

Store Hours:
Monday-Friday 9am-6pm
Saturday 10am-6pm
Sunday 12pm-5pm

Contact: Cheri Lalone
Phone: 619-292-8226
Fax: 619-292-8602

Clothing for children sizes 0-14, maternity wear, toys, books, baby equipment, bedding & baby furnishings
Accepts cash, checks, Visa & Mastercard

Store Special: Join the mailing list & receive notification of special sales

This coupon entitles the bearer to save $5.00 off a purchase of $20.00 or more at
All Baby Needs
10615 B Tierra Santa Blvd.
San Diego, California
Limit one coupon per customer
Expiration Date: 12/31/99

Cream Of The Crop
4683 Cass Street
San Diego, California 92109

Store Hours:
Monday-Saturday 10am-6pm
Sunday 1pm-5pm

Contact: Cynthia Bassett
Phone: 619-272-6601

Accepts cash, local checks,
Mastercard & Visa

Other Location:
Cream Of The Crop
4672 Cass Street
San Diego, California 92109

Top quality men's clothing &
accessories

Dress To Impress
4242 Camino Del Rio N #9
San Diego, California 92108

Store Hours:
Monday-Friday 10am-6pm
Saturday 10am-5pm

Contact: Kathy Cramer
Phone: 619-528-9797

Designer label clothing &
accessories for women

Accepts cash, checks, Visa,
Mastercard, Discover & American
Express

Consignment Policy:
Consignor receives 40% o

Store Specials: Discounts
everyday!

Indigo way, Corp.
437 Market Street

San Diego, California 92101

Store Hours:
Monday-Saturday 11am-7pm
Sunday 12pm-5pm

Contact: Pascal Loupias
Phone: 619-338-0173
Fax: 619-338-0578
e-mail: indigoway@webtv.net

Vintage American sportswear,
work wear & gently used Levis
from all over the country!

St. Paul's Thrift Shop
3505 5th Ave.
San Diego, California 92103

Store Hours:
Monday-Saturday 10am-4pm

Contact: Jill Gibbs
Phone: 619-298-3098

Vast array of unique items
including furniture, curios,
housewares, clothing, collectibles
& books all displayed beautifully
for the discerning customer

Store Policy: Donations welcome

Store Specials: Annual storewide
half price sale the last week in
December & the first week in
January

San Francisco

CrossRoads Trading Company
1901 Fillmore
San Francisco, California
94115

Phone: 415-775-8885

Second Location:

**2231 Market Street
San Francisco, California
94114**

Phone: 415-626-8989

Store Hours: Monday-Friday
11am-7pm, Saturday 11am-6pm
& Sunday 12pm-5pm

Contemporary sportswear for
women, men & accessories

Store Policy: Buy, sell or trade
most merchandise
Some consignments accepted for a
50/50 split

**Heather's Consignment
Boutique
2249 Clement Street
San Francisco, California
94121**
Store Hours:
Tuesday-Saturday 11am-5pm
Sunday 12:30pm-4:30pm

Contact: Heather Thompson
Phone: 415-751-5511
Website: www.theclothestree.com/
shops/Heathers/

Contemporary designer clothing
for women & accessories
Accepts cash, checks, Mastercard
& Visa

Consignment Policy: Accepts
excellent quality upscale clothing
for women
Consignor receives 40% of the
selling price
Items consigned for 90 days

**Top Drawer
1781 Church Street
San Francisco, California
94131**

Store Hours:
Open daily from 10am-6pm
except on Tuesday

Contact: William Peecher
Phone: 415-695-0578

Clothing, furniture & lots of bric-
a-brac
Accepts cash, checks, Visa &
Mastercard

Consignment Policy:
50/50 split
Items consigned for 90 days

San Jose

**Our Secret
1357 Lincoln Avenue
Willow Glen
San Jose, California 95215**

Store Hours:
Monday, Tuesday, Wednesday,
Friday & Saturday 10am-5:30pm
Thursday 10am-7pm
Sunday 11am-3pm October
through December only

Phone & Fax: 408-289-9290
Web site: www.sanjose.org

Specializing in designer labels such
as Ellen Tracy, Dana Buchman,
St. John, Escada & more, designer
label handbags & accessories

Consignment Policy:
Items consigned for 60 days

Store Specials: Two annual end of
season clearance sales

Over one hundred new items
arriving daily! The shop has been
featured in the *San Jose Mercury
News.*

Member of The National Association of Resale & Thrift Shops

San Marcos

Antique Village Mall
983 Grand Ave
San Marcos, California 92069

Store Hours:
Monday-Sunday 10am-5:30pm

Contact: Sandy Dorian
Phone: 760-744-8718

Lots of great antiques, collectibles, furniture, bears, dolls, primitive & country items
Accepts cash, Mastercard, Visa, Discover & American Express

Store Specials: 10% offered to dealers with purchase over $25.00

San Mateo

Rags & Riches
715 South B Street
San Mateo, California 94401

Store Hours:
Monday-Saturday 10am-4pm

Phone: 605-348-3590

Clothing for the entire family, household goods, jewelry, books & small furniture
Accepts cash & checks

Store Policy: Donations welcome & a receipt may be given for tax purposes

Proceeds from the shop benefit the scholarship fund for Notre Dame High School.

Present this coupon at
Rags & Riches
715 South B Street
San Mateo, California & save
25% off any item
Expiration Date: 12/31/99

Santa Barbara

Jessica
2012 De La Vina Street
Santa Barbara, California
93015

Store Hours:
Sunday 11am-4pm
Monday 10am-5pm

Tuesday-Saturday 11am-5:30pm

Contact: Jessica Cashman
Phone: 805-687-2755

Women's fine designer apparel
Accepts cash, checks, Mastercard & Visa

Consignment Policy:
50/50 split
Appointments necessary to consign merchandise
Items consigned for two months

Store Specials: Special 50% off rack, merchandise changes every Monday

Play It Again Sam
1021 State Street
Santa Barbara, California
93101

Store Hours:
Monday-Thursday 10am-6pm
Friday & Saturday 10am-7pm

Sunday 11:30pm-6pm

Phone: 805-966-9989

Brand name clothing & accessories for women at a great savings!

Store Policy:
Sell, trade or consign items
Consignments accepted by appoinment only
50/50 split

Voted *"Best of Santa Barbara"* by the *Independent Newspaper!*

Santa Cruz

41st Avenue Vintage
881 41st Avenue
Santa Cruz, California 95012

Store Hours: Call for store hours

Phone: 408-476-1220

800 square feet of clothing circa 1920 to present, Levi's 501's & large selection of classic Hawaiian shirts

One of a kind items, great music & location near the beach are a great enticement to shop here!

R.A.G.E. (Recycled American Garment Exchange)
1349 Pacific Ave.
Santa Cruz, California 95060

Store Hours:
October-May:
Sunday-Thursday 11am-6pm
Friday & Saturday 11am-9pm

June-September:
Monday-Saturday 11am-9pm
Sunday 11am-6pm

Contact: Tracy Layne Boyd & Steve Boyd
Phone: 408-457-1031
e-mail: ultrab@pacbell.net

Over 5000 items from vintage to trendy retro styles specializing in the 1940's to the 1970's for men & women, accessories galore, shoes, handbags & more.
New items are available too!
Accepts cash, checks, Visa, Mastercard & American Express

Store Policy:
Appointment is necessary to trade or sell items.
Receive 40% in cash or 60% in store trade for each item

Store Specials:
Rage Club Card, $1.00 rack & special 35%-50% storewide sale yearly in March (one day only)

Walnut Avenue Resale Shop
303 Walnut Avenue
Santa Cruz, California 95060

Store Hours:
Tuesday-Friday 12:30pm-4:30pm
& Saturday 10am-2pm

Contact: Bunny Littlejohn
Phone: 408-426-3062

Featuring women's career clothing
Accepts cash & checks

Santa Maria

Family Thrift Store
1460 S Broadway
Santa Maria, California 93454

Store Hours:

Monday-Saturday 8am-7pm
Sunday 8am-6pm

Phone: 805-922-3006

Clothing for the entire family & more!

Santa Monica

Mo's Frugal Brits.. with alot of style
3004 Lincoln Boulevard
Santa Monica, California
90405

Store Hours:
Tuesday-Saturday 1pm-6:30pm
Sunday 1pm-5pm

Contact: Ms. Mo Potok
Phone: 310-392-7740
e-mail: frugalbrit@webtv.net

Top designer quality clothing & accessories-modern to vintage, gowns, hats, vintage costume jewelry & more
Accepts cash, checks, letter of credit & bank drafts

Consignment Policy:
Items consigned for 60 days

The shop is well-known for its vast array of hats.

The Great Name
Designer Resale Fashions
311 Wilshire Boulevard
Santa Monica, California
90401

Store Hours:
Monday-Saturday 11am-6pm

Phone: 310-395-2217

Top designer label clothing for women
Accepts cash, checks, Visa, Mastercard, American Express & Discover

Consignment Policy: Looking for designer label clothing

Store Specials: Mailing list coupons

Established twenty-four years ago by the Frost sisters, the shop specializes in great buys (50%-80%) off retail on most current designer labels & accessories. A bright cheerful resale shop featuring private dressing rooms and sales staff eager to help.

```
• • • • • • • • • • • • •
•  Present this coupon at    •
•     The Great Name         •
•     311 Wilshire Blvd      •
•  Santa Monica, California  •
•  & save 20% off one item   •
•     Expiration Date: 12/31/99  •
• • • • • • • • • • • • •
```

The Address Inc.
1116 Wilshire Blvd.
Santa Monica, California
90401

Store Hours:
Monday-Saturday 10am-6pm
Sunday 12pm-5pm

Contact: Maureen Clavin
Phone: 310-394-1406
Fax: 310-394-6171

Superb new & resale designer fashions & accessories at fabulous prices! Chanel, Prada, Valentino

& much more.
Accepts cash, checks, American Express, Visa & Mastercard

Store Specials: Ships nationwide & lay-a-way available

The Address boutique offers only the best in top name designer merchandise & is a favorite among celebrities

Vintage Vintage
1611 Montana Avenue
Santa Monica, California
90405

Store Hours:
Monday-Saturday 10am-6pm

Phone: 310-393-5588

Excellent quality vintage clothing circa 1930's to the 1960's, costumes, jewelry, accessories & featuring some new reproductions
Accepts cash, checks, Visa, Mastercard & American Express

Store Specials: Dealer discount

Seaside

Alberta's Place
1198 Broadway
Seaside, California 93955

Store Hours:
Monday-Saturday 10am-5pm

Phone: 408-393-0479

Clothing for the entire family, jewelry, housewares, records & more!

Cloud Nine By Barbarina
Upscale Resale

1958 Fremont Blvd.
Seaside, California 93955

Store Hours: Tuesday-Saturday
10:30am-5pm

Phone: 408-394-4595

New & nearly new clothing for women including bridal wear & rhinestone jewelry
Accepts cash, checks & major credit cards

Consignment Policy:
50/50 split

Solana Beach

The Treasure Chest
243 North Pacific Coast
Highway #3
Solana Beach, California
92075

Store Hours:
Monday-Sunday 10am-6pm

Contact: Kimberly Henderson
Phone: 619-481-1002

Clothing for women & men, gift items, household items, shoes, handbags, jewelry & more

Consignment Policy:
Consignor receives 40% of the selling price
Items are consigned for 90 days

Studio City

Lauras Designer Resale
Boutique
12426 Ventura Boulevard
Studio City, California 91604

Store Hours:
Tuesday-Saturday 10am-6pm
Phone: 818-752-2835

Couture designer clothing for
women
Accepts cash, checks, Visa,
American Express, Mastercard &
Discover

Store Specials: Twice a year half
price sale

Lis Resale Boutique
3949 Laurelgrove Avenue
Studio City, California 91605

Store Hours:
Tuesday-Saturday 11am-6pm
Monday-Sunday 12pm-5pm
*Store hours may vary during
the summer

Contact: Lissette Kivotos
Phone: 818-985-3003

Upscale American & European
designer women's clothing such as
DKNY, Ann Taylor, Bebe, Ann
Klein & more, shoes, jewelry &
accessories
Accepts cash, check with proper
ID & credit cards

Sunland

Sun Thrift Store
8800 Foothill Blvd
Sunland, California 91040

Store Hours:
Monday-Saturday 9am-6pm

Over 16,000 square feet of
clothing, household items,
furniture and lots more
Accepts cash, Visa, Mastercard,
Discover, American Express &
ATM

Store Specials:
Seniors receive a 30% discount on
Tuesday
Wednesday & Saturday don't miss
the morning madness sale

Sunnyvale

The Upstairs Gallery
Consignment Store
182 So. Murphy Avenue
Sunnyvale, California 94086
**Located in historic downtown
Sunnyvale**

Store Hours:
Wednesday-Saturday 10am-6pm

Contact: Brenda Klocker
Phone: 408-992-0277

California

Upscale clothing for women, jewelry, accessories, collectibles, small furniture & handcrafted gift items
Accepts cash & checks

Consignment Policy:
An appointment is necessary to consign merchandise
50/50 split

Store Specials: 50% off sale on clothing & shoes the last Saturday of each month

---

Present this coupon at
The Upstairs Gallery
Consignment Store
182 So. Murphy Ave
Sunnyvale, California
with $25.00 or more purchase
on clothing save
20% off original price
Expiration Date: 12/31/99

Sun Valley

What's New?
8311 San Fernando Road
Sun Valley, California 91352

Located in the Los Angeles area near Interstate 5

Store Hours:
Monday-Saturday 9:30am-6pm

Contact: Sharon Pereida
Phone & Fax: 818-768-3165
e-mail: sharon@thrift-store.com
Web site: www.thrift-store.com

Gently used furniture, books, household items, clothing, appliances & much more!

Accepts cash & checks

Many items from What's New have been featured on TV.
The shop rents items to movie studios.

Store Specials: Dealer friendly!

What's New invites everyone to "stop & shop"

Thousand Oaks

Fabulous Finds Designer Resale Apparel
La Siesta Plaza
1378 Thousand Oaks Blvd
Thousand Oaks, California 91362

Store Hours:
Monday-Saturday 11am-5:30pm

Contact: Jennifer Kramer

Phone: 805-496-7313
Fax: 805-493-4354

Fine women's designer clothing & accessories

Consignment Policy:
Consignor receives 40% of the selling price
Items consigned for 60 days
Some items purchased outright

Mention this coupon in
The Ultimate Consignment & Thrift Store Guide at
Fabulous Finds
Designer Resale
1378 Thousand Oaks Blvd,
Thousand Oaks, California
& save 20% off one purchase
Expiration Date: 12/31/99

Tiburon

The Second Generation
1 Blackfield Drive
Tiburon, California 94920

Store Hours:
Monday-Saturday 10am-5pm
Sunday 12pm-4pm

Phone: 415-388-8313
Website: www.theclothestree.com/
shops/SecondGeneration

Women's clothing, shoes &
jewelry
Accepts cash, Mastercard & Visa

Consignment Policy:
Consignments accepted Monday-
Saturday 10am-3pm
Items consigned for 60 days

Store Specials: Items marked down
after one month

Torrance

Gentlemen's Exchange
24066 Neece Avenue
Torrance, California 90505

Store Hours:
Tuesday-Saturday 11am-5pm

Contact: Patricia A. Benson
Phone: 310-375-4148
e-mail: MensCloths@aol.com

New & gently used designer
clothing & accessories for men
Accepts cash & checks

Consignment Policy: Items are
consigned by appointment

Store Special: Store sale every two
weeks

Tujunga

Ad-Mart
9937 Commerce Ave.
Tujunga, California 91042

Store Hours:
Monday-Saturday 9am-5pm

Contact: Bud & Margie
Hagemeyer
Phone: 818-353-1447

Clothing for the entire family,
household items, knick-knacks,
baby items

Consignment Policy: 50/50 split

Tulare

Jolly Good's Quality
Consignment For Women
304 E. King
Tulare, California 93274

Store Hours:
Monday-Friday 10am-5pm
Saturday 10am-3pm

Contact: Susan Sims
Phone: 209-688-5855

Quality clothing for women &
accessories, household items
Accepts cash, checks, Visa,
Mastercard, Discover & Debit
cards

Store Specials: Specific color tags
half price

California

Ukiah

Encore Fashions
109 N. Church Street
Ukiah, California 95482

Store Hours:
Tuesday-Friday 10am-5pm
Saturday 10am-2pm

Contact: Jana Bernard
Phone: 707-463-5590

New & nearly new designer label
clothing for women including
casual, professional, formal wear
& wedding gowns
Accepts cash, checks, Visa,
Mastercard & Debit cards

Consignment Policy:
Consignor receives 40% of the
selling price
Items consigned for 8 weeks

Venice

Pockets Resale Boutique
140 Lincoln Blvd.
Venice, California 90291

Store Hours:
Tuesday-Friday 12pm-7pm
Saturday 12pm-5pm

Phone & Fax: 310-452-1372
Designer & Vintage clothing,
jewelry, collectibles & small
furniture
Accepts cash & checks

Consignment Policy: 50/50 split
Items are consigned for
45 to 60 days

Store Specials: Lay-a-way
available for items over $75.00.
Every four months select items
are discounted 20% to 75%.

Ventura

Wear It Again Sam
Resale Boutique
1978 E. Main
Ventura, California 93001

Store Hours:
Monday-Saturday 10am-5:30pm

Contact: Karen Abel
Phone: 805-643-3989
New & gently used clothing, shoes
& jewelry
Accepts cash, checks, Mastercard,
Visa & American Express

Consignment Policy:
50/50 split
Items consigned for 60 days

Vista

**Garment Gourmet
Resale Shop
831 Williamston Street
Vista, California 92084**

Store Hours:
Monday-Saturday 10am-5pm
Thursday until 6pm

Phone: 760-630-6630

Women's clothing including bridal
& accessories
Accepts cash, checks, Visa &
Mastercard

Consignment Policy: Consignor
receives 40% of the selling price

Store Specials: 50% off clearance
racks & special coupons
Lay-a-way available

Walnut Creek

**Les Armoires
1688 Locust Street
Walnut Creek, California
94596**

Store Hours:
Tuesday-Friday 11am-6pm
Saturday 11am-4:30pm

Contact: Sharon Minch &
Diane Smith
Phone: 925-937-8110

Upscale women's clothing &
accessories

Consignment Policy: 50/50 split
Store Specials: Quarterly postcards
offering discounts up to 10%

Whittier

**Seven Year Itch
Vintage Clothing
7044A Greenleaf
Whittier, California 90602**

Store Hours:
Monday-Friday 1:30pm-7:30pm
Saturday 12pm-5pm
Sunday 2pm-6pm

Contact: Helen Hansen
Phone: 562-698-1867

California

Vintage clothing, accessories & collectibles
Accepts cash, checks, Mastercard & Visa

Store Specials: Costume rentals

Yuba City

YMCA Thrift Shop
628 Plumas
Yuba City, California 95991

Store Hours:
Monday-Friday 10am-4pm
Saturday 10am-3pm
Phone: 530-673-8478

Clothing for the entire family, household, bric-a-brac

Accepts cash, checks & travelers checks

Store Policy: Donations welcome

Colorado

Colorado Springs

The Consignment Gallery, Ltd.
Consigned Home Furnishings
715 Brookside
Colorado Springs, Colorado
80906

Store Hours:
Monday-Saturday 10am-6pm

Contact: Philip Yannias
Phone: 719-635-1746

Beautiful furniture & home accessories

Consignment Policy: Items are consigned for 90 days

Craig

Community Budget Center
552 Russell
Craig, Colorado 81625

Store Hours:
Monday-Saturday 10am-5pm

Phone: 970-824-7898

Clothing for the entire family, housewares & antiques

Store Policy: Donations welcome & a receipt may be provided for tax purposes

Community Budget Center proceeds benefit those in need in the community.

Denver

Flo's Elite Repeat
2725 South Colorado Blvd.
Denver, Colorado 80222

Store Hours: Monday-Saturday
10am-6pm
Sunday 12pm-5pm

Contact: Flo Salz
Phone: 303-753-6003

Clothing from Denver's best dressed women including furs & accessories

Consignment Policy:
Items consigned for 3 months
Consignor receives 50% of the selling price for the item

Store Specials: Extra 10% off after every season & the the sales lasts for 1 1/2 months!

With over twenty-three years of experience in the resale field, Flo offers customers some of the best clothing available in Colorado!

Member of The National Association of Resale & Thrift Shops

Colorado

Second-Hand Rose-Ann
3426 East 12th Ave
Denver, Colorado 80206

Store Hours:
Tuesday, Wednesday & Thursday
12pm-6pm
Friday & Saturday 10am-5pm

Contact: Judy Hill
Phone: 303-321-5530

Clothing for plus sizes 12 and up
Accepts cash, checks, Visa,
Mastercard & Novus

Consignment Policy:
Consigments accepted by
appointment
Items must be in season
Items consigned for 90 days
Consignor receives 50% of the
selling price for the item

Store Specials: Items marked down
after 60 days

Fountain

Bargain Hut
406 Royality Place
Fountain, Colorado 80817

Store Hours:
Tuesday-Saturday 10am-6pm

Phone: 719-382-9664

Clothing for the entire family,
furniture, books, videos, appliances, jewelry
Accepts cash & checks

Store Policy:
Donations & consignments
accepted

Present this coupon at
Bargain Hut
406 Royality Place
Fountain, Colorado
& save 15% off one purchase

Expiration Date: 12/31/99

Fort Collins

Raggedy Ann & Andy's
For Kids
107 West Monroe Drive
Ft. Collins, Colorado 80525

Store Hours:
Monday-Friday 9:30am-5:30pm
Saturday 10am-4pm

Phone: 970-223-2985
Contact: Brenda C. Yocom

New & consigned preemie, infant
and children's clothing to size 16,
maternity apparel, toys, furniture
& equipment

Store Specials:
Weekly and special Wednesday-
only sales
Wish list for those special items
that you are seeking

Excellent staff always available to
assist customers.

Lakewood

Cajun's Closet
5785 W. 6th Ave.
Lakewood, Colorado 80214

Store Hours:
Thursday & Friday 10am-5pm
Saturday 9am-4pm

Gently used clothing, collectibles,
books & more!
Accepts, cash, checks, Visa &
Mastercard

The proceeds from Cajun's Closet
help to support the Cat Care
Society, a cageless shelter for
homeless, abandoned cats.

Loveland

Mother Goose & Me
265 29th Street
Loveland, Colorado 80537

Store Hours:
Monday-Saturday 10am-5pm
(From January-April 7)
Monday-Saturday 10am-6pm

Contact: Brenda Saint
Phone: 970-962-9749

Gently used & new children's &
maternity clothing, toys, furniture
& other children's accessories

Consignment Policy:
50/50 split
Items are consigned for 90 days

Connecticut

Cheshire

**Children's Treasure
Chest LLC
186 S. Main Street
Cheshire, Connecticut 06410**

Store Hours:
Monday-Saturday 10am-5pm
Thursday until 7pm

Contact: Carol Doheny &
K. Hansell Markoja
Phone: 203-272-1870

Children's clothing from newborn
to size 14, maternity, baby
equipment, toys & videos

Consignment Policy:
50/50 split
Items consigned for 90 days

Store Specials: Special discounts
for new Moms!
Gift certificates available &
frequent shopper cards

```
This coupon entitles
the bearer to save
$5.00 off your first purchase
at
Children's Treasure Chest
186 S. Main St.
Cheshire, Connecticut
Expiration Date: 12/31/99
```

**Consignment
"Originals", Inc.
154 Main Street
Cheshire, Connecticut 06410**

Store Hours:
Monday, Tuesday, Wednesday
& Saturday 10am-5pm
Thursday & Friday 10am-8pm
Sunday 12pm-4pm

Contact: Jean M. Thompson
Phone: 203-271-0475
Fax: 203-271-2418
e-mail: Consign@snet.net
Web site: www.consignit.com

Other Locations:
**2399 Black Rock Turnpike
Fairfield, Connecticut 06430**
Phone: 203-372-8840
Fax: 203-372-1412

**320 Boston Post Road
Orange, Connecticut 06477**
Phone: 203-799-8075
Fax: 203-721-1527

**2139 Silas Deane Highway
Rocky Hill, Connecticut
06067**
Phone: 860-257-3224
Fax: 860-721-1527
Upscale designer clothing &
accessories for women

Enfield

One More Time
Consignment Boutique
634 Enfield Street
Enfield, Connecticut 06082

Store Hours:
Monday-Friday 12pm-7pm
Saturday 10am-3pm

Phone & Fax: 860-741-7520

e-mail: NEWMEL@juno.com

Clothing for men & women
including plus sizes & accessories

Consignment Policy:
Consignor receives 40% of the
selling price
Items are consigned for 60 days

Store Specials: After 30 days,
most items are reduced 25%

Glastonbury

Brides To Be
351 New London Turnpike
Glastonbury, Connecticut
06033

Store Hours:
Monday-Saturday 10am-6pm
Tuesday & Thursday 10am-8pm

Contact: Shirley Warren &
Phyllis Kelley
Phone: 860-633-3639

Wedding gowns, bridesmaids,
mother-of-the-bride, flower girl
apparel, jewelry, headpieces, veils,
gloves & petticoats

Consignment Policy:
Items consigned for one year

Granby

"Classics" Consignment
Boutique
257 Salmon Brook Street
Jct. Rtes 10/202 & 189
Granby, Connecticut 06035
Located next to Stony Hill Village
Granby Center

Store Hours:
Tuesday, Wednesday & Friday
10am-5pm
Thursday 10am-5:30pm &
Saturday 10am-3pm

Phone: 860-653-7953

Upscale clothing for women,
jewelry, scarfs, great gifts & more

Consignment Policy:
50/50 split
Items are consigned for 60 days

Phone & Fax: 203-230-2910

New & gently used designer labels
& vintage clothing for the entire
family, antiques, collectibles, toys
& furniture
Accepts cash, checks, Visa &
Mastercard

Store Policy: Donations welcome
during business hours & tax
receipts may be provided
Store Specials: Weekly specials &
50% off rack

Connecticut

Greenwich

Sophia's Great Dames
1 Liberty Way
Greenwich, Connecticut
06830

Store Hours:
Monday-Saturday 10am-5:30pm

Contact: Sophia Scarpelli
Phone: 203-869-5990

Vintage clothing circa 1880 to
1970, jewelry, antiques, collectibles, glassware, decorative
accessories, linens & antique
furniture
Accepts cash, checks, Visa,
Mastercard & American Express

Czech, Victorian & signed pieces,
pottery, porcelain, crystal,
depression glass, Hummels,
Limoge, art glass, cookie jars, tea
cups, roseville, furniture,
handbags, hats, linens & lace,
antiques & collectibles galore.
Inventory changes daily!!!

Hamden

The Hamden Goodwill Store
2369 Dixwell Avenue
Hamden, Conneticut 06514

Store Hours:
Monday-Saturday 10am-6pm
Sunday 12pm-5pm

Phone: 203-230-2910

Contemporary & vintage designer
label clothing, antiques, collectibles, toys, furniture & more
Accepts cash, checks, Visa &

Phone: 203-230-2910

Contemporary & vintage designer
label clothing, antiques, collectibles, toys, furniture & more
Accepts cash, checks, Visa &
Mastercard

Store Specials: Seniors receive a
20% discount every Wednesday,
weekly & holiday special sales,
preferred customer discounts
(check the store for details)

Proceeds from the shop benefit
the Easter Seals Rehabilitation
Center in New Haven,
Connecticut.

Manchester

A Vintage & Jewels
Collectible
190 West Middle Turnpike
Manchester, Connecticut
06040

Store Hours:
Wednesday-Saturday 10am-5pm
Thursday until 6pm or by special
appoinment

Contact: Deborah Robinson
Phone: 860-645-1525

860-533-9529
e-mail: Vinjewels@aol.com
Website: http://
www.theplace2b.com/
VintageJewels/

Specializing in all types of jewelry
including vintage, estate, forties,
collectibles, glassware, decorative
accessories, linens, antique
furniture
Accepts cash, checks, American

Express, Visa & Mastercard

Milford

Play It Again Pam
155 New Haven Ave
Milford, Connecticut 06460

Store Hours:
Monday & Saturday 10am-5pm
Tuesday, Wednesday & Friday
10am-6pm
Thursday 10am-7pm & Sunday
12pm-4pm

Phone & Fax: 203-876-7202
e-mail: pmorgan628@aol.com
Web site:
www.theclothestree.com/shops/
PlayItAgainPam/

Upscale clothing for women &
men
Accepts cash, Visa & Mastercard

Store Specials: Frequent buyer
cards

New Canaan

New Canaan Thrift Shop
2 Locust Avenue
New Canaan, Connecticut
06840

Store Hours:
Monday-Friday 12pm-4pm
Saturday 10am-1pm

Phone: 203-966-2361

Clothing for the entire family,
small furniture, household items,
bric-a-brac & jewelry
Accepts cash & checks

Store Policy: Donations welcome
Store Specials: Select items on sale
weekly

New Milford

Kangaroo Kids
34 B Dodd Road
New Milford, Connecticut
06776

Store Hours:
Wednesday-Saturday 10am-4pm

Phone: 860-354-7919

Children's clothing sizes 0-16,
maternity clothing, baby
equipment & toys
Accepts cash & checks

Consignment Policy: 50/50 split

Store Specials: On-going
reductions on merchandise from
25% to 50%

This coupon entitles the
bearer to save $5.00 off any
purchase over $15.00 at
Kangaroo Kids
34 B Dodd Road
New Milford, Connecticut

Expiration Date: 12/31/99

Connecticut

Shelton

Baby Behr's
477 Howe Avenue
Shelton, Connecticut 06484

Store Hours:
Tuesday-Saturday 10am-5pm
Thursday 10am-7pm

Phone: 203-924-8300

Children's clothing & accessories

Stamford

"A Woman's Exchange"
236 Bedford Street
Stamford, Connecticut 06901

Store Hours:
Monday, Tuesday, Wednesday,
Thursday & Friday 10am-6pm
Saturday 10am-5pm

Contact: Gabriela Czaja
Phone: 203-323-2595

Designer clothing for women,
unique jewelry, shoes &
accessories
Accepts cash, Visa, Mastercard &
Discover

Consignment Policy:
50/50 split
Items consigned for 60 days

Store Specials: Save 75% to 90%
off select items in the basement
level & on-going 25% to 50% off
discounts everyday!
Lay-a-way available

The Warehouse
425 Fairfield Avenue
Stamford, Connecticut 06902

Store Hours:
Monday, Thursday, Friday &
Saturday 10am-5pm
Sunday 11am-5pm
Closed Tuesday & Wednesday

Phone: 203-975-7177
1-800-578-8390
e-mail: ejkuhn@aol.com

The Warehouse specializes in
American manufactured furniture
circa 1890-1950. Choose from
dining room sets, bedroom sets &
upholstered pieces. Offering a
large selection of desks, dressers,
occasional tables, prints, mirrors
& accessories. New merchandise
arrives daily!
Accepts cash, checks, Visa,
Mastercard & Discover

Store Specials: Trade welcome

Waterbury

Consignment Boutique
835 Wolcott Street
Waterbury, Connecticut
06705

Store Hours:

Monday-Saturday 10am-7pm
Thursday until 8pm

Contact: Maria Civitello
Phone: 203-754-9108

Clothing for the entire family,
housewares & much more!
Accepts cash, checks, Mastercard,
Visa & American Express

Consignment Policy:
50/50 split
Items consigned for 60 days

Store Specials: Lay-a-way
available
Most items marked down 50%
after 30 days

This coupon entitles the bearer
to save 20% off a regular priced
item at the
Consignment Boutique
835 Wolcott Street
Waterbury, Connecticut
Expiration Date: 12/31/99

West Hartford

Clothes Horse
175 Park Road
West Hartford, Connecticut
06119

Store Hours:
Tuesday, Wednesday & Friday
10am-5pm
Thursday 10am-8pm &
Saturday 10am-4pm

Clothing for the entire family,
household items & books
Accepts cash & checks

Consignment Policy: Consignments accepted from Junior
League members only

Store Specials: On Wednesdays
seniors receive a 50% discount on
white ticket items
Holiday toy & gift events during
the month of December

Since 1928 the shop has been
owned & operated by
The Junior League of Hartford as
an on-going fund-raiser for several
community outreach programs.
The Junior League is a womens
organization committed to
voluntarism in the greater
Hartford area.

This coupon entitles the
bearer to save 50% off
a white ticket item when
presented at
The Clothes Horse
175 Park Road
West Hartford, Connecticut
Expiration Date: 12/31/99

Westport

Designer Label
Consignments
1344 Post Road East
Westport, Connecticut 06880

Store Hours:
Monday, Tuesday, Wednesday &
Saturday 10am-5pm
Thursday & Friday 10am-6pm
Saturday 10am-5pm & Sunday
12pm-5pm

Phone: 203-255-9099

Upscale designer consignment

clothing for women, men & children featuring designs by Armani, Donna Karan, Ralph Lauren, Chanel, Prada & much more! Elegant furs including mink coats, luxurious cashmeres & merino wool designer sweaters at great prices. Rothschild coats & Polo jumpers in abundance.

Consignment Policy: Consignments accepted seven days a week Free pick-up service is provided to suit the individual needs of each consignor

Bear

Second Time Around
Fox Run Around
Fox Run Shopping Center
Bear, Delaware 19701

Store Hours: Call for store hours

Clothing for women & children, accessories, baby equipment & toys
Accepts cash, checks, Mastercard & Visa

Phone: 302-836-5630

Fine women's designer clothing size 2-3x, including after five-wear, casual wear, suits & more!
Home decor items, limited fine & costume jewelry & accessories

With over 2400 consignors on their books, Second Time Around has lots of great merchandise to choose from.

Rehoboth Beach

All Saints Parish Thrift Shop
Ames Shopping Center
Rehoboth Beach, Delaware 19971
Located off Highway One

Store Hours:
Tuesday & Thursday 12pm-5pm
Saturday 10am-4pm

Contact: Ellen C. Smith
Phone: 302-226-3123

Clothing for the entire family, household items, books, furniture, appliances & more!
Accepts cash & checks

Store Policy: Donations welcome

Store Specials: Semi annual dollar bag sale

Bearly Worn
803C Rehoboth Ave
Rehoboth Beach, Delaware 19971

Store Hours:
Monday-Saturday 10am-5pm
Wednesday 10am-7pm

Consignment Policy:
50/50 split
Items consigned for 90 days, discounted 25% after 30 days & 50% after 60 days

Store Specials: Always featuring 25% to 75% off select merchandise & special store promotions during winter months

Wilmington

Better Furniture & Bargains, Inc.
401 Philadelphia Pike
Wilmington, Delaware 19809

Store Hours:
Monday-Thursday 10am-5pm
Friday 10am-8pm
Saturday 10am-4pm
Sunday 11am-3pm

Delaware

Contact: Elliott Pottock
Phone: 302-764-3777

Excellent quality fine traditional
& contemporary furniture
including many new pieces

Consignment Policy:
50/50 split
Items consigned for 60 days

The Resale Boutique
818 Philadelphia Pike
Wilmington, Delaware 19809

Store Hours:
Monday-Friday 10am-5pm
Saturday 10am-4pm

Contact: Meryl Pottock
Phone: 302-764-3646

An upscale consignment shop for
women and children. Featuring
Delaware's largest selection of
bridal gowns selling for a fraction
of their original cost

Consignment Policy: Call for an
appointment to consign
merchandise

Boca Raton

**Adolph & Rose Levis Jewish
Community Thrift Shop
2 SE 1st Street
Boca Raton, Florida 33432**

Store Hours:
Monday-Friday 9:30am-4:30pm
Saturday 10am-4pm

Phone: 561-368-3665
Fax: 561-368-9328
Web site: www.levisjcc.org

Featuring the largest selection of
resale merchandise in the Palm
Beach area and the Gold Coast of
Florida. Over 5000 square feet of
gently used, quality furniture,
housewares and clothing for the
entire family. Shop for great
bargains at "The Home
Center" for housewares, "The
Vintage Shoppe" for the finest
antiques & clothing,
"The Kids Korner" for lots of
great clothing, toys, books, shoes,
equipment & supplies for all ages
(infant through teens) & "The
Designer Square" for new & gently
used designer label clothing.

Store Policy: Donations welcome.
Furniture pick-up free of charge

Store Specials: College students
with proper ID receive a 25%
discount at all times

The JCC Thrift Shops proceeds
benefit the Adolph & Rose Levis
JCC Financial Aid program which
enables families in need to
participate in the early childhood
programs, after school programs
& summer camp.

**A Consignment Gallery
Fine Furnishings and Accessories
251 N. Federal Highway
Boca Raton, Florida 33432**

Store Hours:
Monday-Friday 10am-7pm
Saturday 10am-6pm
Sunday 12pm-4pm

Phone: 561-338-4706

Elegant home furnishings &
accessories

Consignment Policy:
60/40 split
Items consigned for 90 days

**Razamataz
140 NW 20th Street
Boca Raton, Florida 33427**

Store Hours:
Monday-Saturday 10am-5pm

Contact: Linda Ritzer
Phone: 561-394-4592
High quality clothing &
accessories for women
Accepts cash, checks, Visa &
Mastercard

Other Locations:

**The Catwalk
Mizner West Plaza
555 North Federal Highway
Boca Raton, Florida**
Located opposite Mizner Park in
downtown Boca Raton

Phone: 561-750-8424

Top designer apparel & accessories for women, Chanel, Armani &
Escada just to name a few.

Florida

118 North County Road
Palm Beach Island, Florida
Located near The Breakers Hotel

Phone: 561-655-2135

Featuring top designer clothing & accessories with labels designed by Chanel, Armani, Escada & many more!

Second Childhood, Inc.
5909 North Federal Highway
Boca Raton, Florida 33487

Store Hours:
Tuesday-Saturday 10am-4:30pm

Excellent quality clothing for children sizes infants to 14, shoes, toys, books & nursery equipment

Consignment Policy:
Consignments accepted by appointment only
Items consigned for 90 days

Store Specials: Frequent shopper rewards

Bonita Springs

Act II Ladies Consignment
8951 Bonita Beach Road #605
Bonita Springs, Florida 33923

Store Hours:
Monday-Saturday 10am-5pm

Contact: Cathy Appelbaum
Phone: 941-495-6647

Women's casual, career & cruise wear, sizes petite to plus
Accepts Cash, check, Visa & Mastercard

Store Specials: Frequent buyer discount, with purchase $250.00 worth of merchandise receive a $25.00 gift certificate

```
┌ ─ ─ ─ ─ ─ ─ ─ ─ ┐
│  This coupon entitles the  │
│  bearer to save 25% when you  │
│  purchase $50.00 or more at  │
│  Act II Ladies Consignment  │
│  8951 Bonita Beach Road #605 │
│  Bonita Springs, Florida  │
│  Expiration Date: 12/31/99  │
└ ─ ─ ─ ─ ─ ─ ─ ─ ┘
```

Boynton Beach

Act II of Boynton Beach
805 North Federal Highway
Boynton Beach, Florida 33435

Store Hours:
Monday-Saturday 10:30am-5pm

Contact: Donna Quintavlle
Phone: 561-737-4657

Quality consignment clothing for women & accessories

Consignment Policy:
50/50 split
Items are consigned for 90 days

Store Specials: Featuring on-going markdowns of 25% & 50% off select merchandise

Bradenton

Kid's Care-O-Sell
6600 Manatee Ave W
Bradenton, Florida 34209

Store Hours:
Monday-Saturday 10am-5pm
Friday 10am-8pm
Contact: Sharon L. Madsen

Phone: 941-761-8405

Children's clothing, furniture, toys, scout uniforms, books & maternity clothing

This coupon entitles the bearer to save 20% off one item at
Kid's Care-O-Sell
6600 Manatee Ave W
Bradenton, Florida 34209
Expiration Date: 12/31/99

Casselberry

Rutherfords Resale
1050 Semoran Blvd.
Casselberry, Florida 32707

Store Hours:
Monday-Saturday 10am-6pm
Sunday 12pm-5pm

Contact: Paul Rutherford
Phone: 407-834-2208
e-mail: Resale407@aol.com

Clothing & accessories for women & decorative home accessories
Accepts cash, checks, Visa, Mastercard, Discover & American Express

Consignment Policy:
No appointment necessary to consign merchandise
50/50 split

Store Specials:
Featuring daily specials

Present this coupon
at *Rutherfords Resale*
1050 Semoran Blvd
Casselberry, Florida & save
an extra 20% off already
reduced merchandise
Expiration Date: 12/31/99

Clearwater

Denise's Pieces Boutique
4100 East Bay Drive
Suite B-30
Clearwater, Florida 33764

Store Hours:
Monday-Friday 10am-6pm
Saturday 10am-4pm

Phone: 813-538-2972

Second Location:
Denise's Pieces Boutique
1238 S. Highland Ave.
Clearwater, Florida 33756

Store Hours:
Monday-Friday 10am-5:30pm
Saturday 10am-4pm

Phone: 813-443-1909

Designer apparel & accessories for women, jewelry & gifts
Accepts cash, checks, check card, Mastercard & Visa

Consignment Policy:
50/50 split
Items consigned for 90 days

$5.00 one time set-up fee to consign items

Store Specials:
After 30 days items reduced 20%
After 60 days items reduced 40%
Lay-a-way available

Cocoa Beach

Melodys 2nd Generation Children's Consignment
34 N. Brevard Ave
Cocoa Beach, Florida 32931

Store Hours: Monday-Friday
10am-5pm
Saturday 10am-4pm
Closed on Sunday

Contact: Jenny Hoffman &
Gina Homer
Phone: 407-784-4777
Fax: 407-799-2395

Children's clothing, shoes, furniture, toys, books. Featuring a unique selection of gift items from Arizona
Accepts cash & checks

Consignment Policy:
Items are consigned for 60 days

Store Specials: Items are marked down half price after 30 days

Coconut Creek

ReRuns Fashion Consignment
4419 W. Hillsboro Road
Coconut Creek, Florida 33073

Store hours:
Monday-Friday 10am-6pm
Saturday 11am-4pm

Contact: Karen Wade
Phone: 954-426-3091

Upscale women's designer labels from casual to sportswear

Consignment Policy:
50/50 split
Items consigned for 90 days & must be in current style, in excellent condition, clean, pressed & on hangers

Deerfield Beach

Hanky Panky's
3280 Hillsboro Blvd.
Deerfield Beach, Florida
33442

Store Hours:
Monday-Saturday 10am-5pm

Contact: Hank Phillips
Phone: 954-480-9495
Fax: 954-480-4868

Furniture, antiques & bric-a-brac

Consignment Policy: Items are
marked down 20% after 30 days
& 50% after 60 days
Hanky Panky's has been featured
on *Good Morning America.*

**What A Deal
Consignment, Inc.**
3312 W. Hillsboro Road
Deerfield Beach, Florida
33442
Located in Southern Florida
between West Palm Beach & Fort
Lauderdale

Store Hours:
Monday-Friday 10am-6pm
Saturday 11am-5pm

Phone: 954-428-1646

Upscale women's clothing from
casual wear to after-five with
designer labels by Liz Claiborne,
Donna Karan & many more.
Great purses, shoes &
fantastic costume jewelry.

• • • • • • • • • • • • • •
Present this coupon at
What A Deal Consignment
3312 W. Hillsboro Road,
Deerfield Beach, Florida
& receive 10% off all
merchandise
Expiration Date:12/31/99
• • • • • • • • • • • • • •

Delray Beach

**Labels Consignment
Boutique
1191 N. Federal Highway
Delray Beach, Florida 33483**

Phone: 561-278-8323

Store Hours:
Monday-Saturday 9am-5pm

Second Location:
**Lantana Center
S.W. Corner of U.S. 1 &
Ocean Ave.
Lantana, Florida 33462**

Phone: 561-582-7102

Store Hours:
Monday-Saturday 9am-5pm

Women's fine clothing, jewelry &
accessories

Fernandina Beach

**Buy-Gones
1122 South 14th Street
Eight Flags Center
Fernandina Beach, Florida
32034**

Store Hours:
Monday-Friday 10am-6pm
Saturday 10am-5pm

Florida

Contact: Kerry Smith Woods
Phone: 904-277-4071

Quality women's clothing at great prices! Vast array of sizes & new selections arrive daily. Vintage clothing, jewelry & costume sales & rental too!
Accepts cash, check, Visa, Mastercard & Discover

Consignment Policy:
50/50 split

```
This coupon entitles
the bearer to save 10%
off one purchase at
Buy-Gones
1122 S. 14th Street
Fernandina Beach, Florida
Expiration Date: 12/31/99
```

Fort Myers

Perennials
7051 Crystal Drive
Fort Myers, Florida 33907
Located behind KFC

Store Hours:
Tuesday-Thursday 10am-6pm
Friday & Saturday 10am-5pm

Contact: Gerri Ellis &
Barbara Andrasik
Phone: 941-275-8838

Designer label women's & children's clothing, furniture & home accessories
Accepts cash, check, Mastercard & Visa

Consignment Policy: Items

consigned for 3 months
50/50 split

Fort Pierce

The Watermelon Patch
2814 S US 1 #D1
Fort Pierce, Florida 34982

Store Hours:
Monday-Friday 10am-5pm
Saturday 10am-3pm

Phone: 561-465-6682
Fax: 561-461-8545
e-mail:
jillsteve.todd@mci2000.com

Brand name clothing for girls sizes newborn to Juniors & boys sizes newborn to 12. Featuring labels from Oshkosh, Gap, Carters, Guess, Gymboree & many more! Lots of baby accessories including cribs, walkers, swings, beds & more. Labels like Liz & Carole Little for women & maternity wear.
Accepts cash, checks, Mastercard, Visa & Discover

Consignment Policy:
Consignments are accepted during business hours & no appointment is necessary

50/50 split
Items are consigned for 90 days
Items are reduced 25% after
60 days & 50% after 90 days
Consignments accepted by mail!

Store Specials: Select color tickets
on sale every month!
Grandparents receive a 20%
discount off regular priced
merchandise every Wednesday

```
Present this coupon at
The Watermelon Patch
2814 S US 1 #D1
Fort Pierce, Florida 34982
& save $5.00 off any
purchase of $25.00 or more!
Expiration Date: 12/31/99
```

Gainesville

Fifi's Fine Resale Apparel
3501 SW 2nd Avenue
Suite P
(Creekside Shopping Center)
Gainesville, Florida 32607

Store Hours:
Monday-Friday 10am-6pm
Saturday 10am-5pm
Sunday: Call the shop for hours

Phone: 352-378-5020

Upscale designer clothing for
women sizes 2-24, accessories,
jewelry & shoes

```
Save 15% off non-sale items
when you present this coupon
at Fifi's Fine Resale Apparel
3501 SW 2nd Avenue Suite F
Gainesville, Florida
Expiration Date: 12/31/99
```

Jacksonville

The Snob
1936 San Marco Blvd.
Jacksonville, Florida 32207

Store Hours:
Monday-Friday 11am-6pm
Saturday 10am-5pm

Contact: Rula Carr
Phone: 904-396-2249
e-mail: thesnob&angelfire.com
Web site:
http://www.angelfire.com/biz/
thesnob

Upscale women's new & nearly
new designer clothing & accessories. Designs by Chanel, Gucci,
DKNY, Hermes, Anne Klein,
Prada, Dana Buchman, Ungaro
and many more!

Jensen Beach

Affordable Consignment
Furniture Inc.
869 Jensen Beach Blvd.
Jensen Beach, Florida 34957

Store Hours:
Tuesday-Saturday 10am-5pm

Phone: 561-334-9066

Excellent quality gently used
furniture

Lantana

Adopt-A-Family Thrift Shop
221 S. Third Street
Lantana, Florida 33462

Florida

Store Hours:
Wednesday-Saturday
10am-3pm (Hours may vary
depending on the season)

Phone: 561-586-7519

Gently used clothing for the entire
family, home accessories,
furniture, small appliances,
antiques, toys, lots of books &
much more!

Store Policy: Donations welcome
& receipt provided for tax
purposes

Proceeds benefit needy individuals
in the Palm Beach area.

Lauderdale Lakes

**Academy Thrift Avenue
Shoppes
3615 NW 19th Street
Lauderdale Lakes, Florida
33311**

Store Hours:
Monday-Saturday 10am-6pm
Sunday 12pm-5pm

Contact: Sandy Wasserman &
Steve King

Phone: 954-733-7557
954-917-8666
Accepts, cash, checks, Mastercard,
Visa, American Express &
Discover

Gently used clothing & household
items

All proceeds benefit the South
Florida Children's Scholarship
Fund.

Margate

**Academy Consignment
Furniture Galleries**

Gently Used Furniture™

**334 South State Road 7
Margate, Florida 33068**

Store Hours:
Monday-Saturday 10am-6pm
Sunday 12pm-5pm

Contact: Steve Kind &
Sandy Wasserman
Phone: 954-917-3444

Fine gently used furniture for the
living room, dining room,
bedroom sets in cherry,
mahogany, pecan, oak, birch,
zebra & other fine woods. Exports
worldwide!
Accepts cash, checks, Mastercard,
Visa, American Express &
Discover

Miami

**Beatnix
1149 Washington
Miami, Florida 33139**

Store Hours:
Open Daily 12pm-9pm

Phone: 305-532-8733

Vintage clothing specializing in
the 1970's & original store designs
Accepts cash

The Salvation Army
Thrift Stores
90 N.W. 23rd Street
Miami, Florida 33127

Store Hours:
Monday-Saturday 9am-5pm
Phone: 305-573-4200

Clothing for the entire family,
furniture, appliances & lots of
household items

Store Policy: Donations welcome
& receipt is provided for tax
purposes

Other Locations:

7802 N.W. 103rd Street
Hill Gard, Florida 33106
Store Hours:
Monday-Saturday 9am-8:30pm
Phone: 305-819-4146

5600 N.W. 7th Avenue
Miami, Florida 33127
Store Hours:
Monday-Saturday 9am-5pm
Phone: 305-757-1316

9790 S.W. Bird Road
Miami, Florida 33165
Store Hours:
Monday-Saturday 9am-8:30pm
Phone: 305-554-9669

8001 N.W. 27th Avenue
Miami, Florida 33147
Store Hours:
Monday-Saturday 9am-8pm
Phone: 305-836-8088

28610 S.W. 157th Avenue
Miami, Florida 33033
Store Hours:
Monday-Saturday 9am-8pm
Phone: 305-247-5477

Quality 2nd Hand Shop
6958 Collins Drive
Miami, Florida 33141

Store Hours:
Monday-Friday 10am-7pm
Saturday 1pm-7pm

Contact: Fredy Chavano
Phone: 305-864-7623

Furniture, jewelry & miscellaneous
items
Accepts cash, checks & credit
cards

Store Specials: Lay-a-way
available

Present this coupon at
Quality 2nd Hand Shop
6958 Collins Drive
Miami, Florida & save
$5.00 off any $50.00 purchase
Expiration Date: 12/31/99

Middleburg

Diane's Thrift Store
Black Creek Plaza
Suite #8
2554 Blanding Blvd.
Middleburg, Florida 32068

Store Hours:
Monday-Saturday 10am-6pm

Contact: Diane Webster
Phone: 904-282-1205
Fax: 904-213-9708
e-mail: dianesthrift@juno.com

Top quality clothing for the entire
family, shoes, handbags, belts,
hats, jewelry, lots of great gifts,
furniture & appliances

Accepts cash, checks & all major credit cards

Store Policy: Buy, sell & trade

N. Miami Beach

Again With Pizzazz
1791 NE 162 Street
N. Miami Beach, Florida
33162

Store Hours:
Monday, Tuesday & Wednesday
11am-5pm
Thursday, Friday & Saturday
10am-5pm

Phone: 305-940-3212

Women's designer clothing & accessories

Consignment Policy: 50/50 split
Items are consigned for 90 days

Store Specials: Select color tag sales & $5.00 items available everyday

Palm Beach Gardens

Bears Repeating
4509 PGA Blvd
Palm Beach Gardens, Florida
33418

Store Hours:
Monday-Friday 10am-6pm
Saturday 10am-5pm

Phone: 561-775-5727
Web site: www.bearsrepeating.com

Children's clothing for girls and boys sizes newborn to 10, maternity clothing & new gift

items
Accepts cash, checks, Mastercard, Visa & Discover

Consignment Connection
Promenade Plaza
9810 Alt A1A Suite 109B
Palm Beach Gardens, Florida
33410

Phone: 561-624-5217
Fax: 561-790-5886

Other Location:

Consignment Connection
Jupiter West Plaza
6689 W. Indiantown Road
Suite 48
Jupiter, Florida 33458

Phone: 561-745-8141
Fax: 561-790-5886

Store Hours:
Monday-Saturday 10am-6pm

Both shops feature 1800 square feet of designer name labels for women sizes 2-24, great accessories including shoes, belts, purses & scarves. New designer look-a-like sunglasses & jewelry at fantastic prices!

Consignment Policy: No appointment necessary
50/50 split
"Drop & run" service available

Pembroke Pines

It's A Blooming Deal
204 N. University Drive
Pembroke Pines, Florida
33024

Store Hours:

Saturday & Sunday 11am-5pm
Tuesday-Friday 11am-6pm

Contact: Anne Bogner
Phone: 954-421-3020
Fax: 954-433-0443
e-mail: ANIBGOOD@aol.com

Furniture, antiques, clothing, art,
collectibles & more
Accepts cash, checks, Visa &
Mastercard

Consignment Policy:
Items consigned for 90 days

Safety Harbor

Alison's Annex
(A Consignment Cafe)
470 2nd Street North
Safety Harbor, Florida 34695

Store Hours: Open 7 days a week

Phone: 813-669-0592

Offering a great selection of
excellent quality, brand name
new & gently used clothing for
women, men & children

Consignment Policy: 50/50 split
Items consigned for 60 days

Store Specials: Monthly sidewalk
sales & open house sales

Conveniently located in the
quaint town of Safety Harbor,
Alison's Annex offers a light
lunch and gourmet ice cream to
enhance your shopping experience. Browse through great
selections of gently used books
while you relax with a cup of
coffee or tea.

Our Little Secret
176 Fifth Avenue North at
Second Street N.
Safety Harbor, Florida 34695
Located behind the gazebo

Store Hours:
Wednesday, Thursday & Friday
10am-5pm
Saturday 10am-3pm

Contact: Edna Kirkirt
Phone: 813-724-0191

Elegant home decor items,
collectible & great gift items

Store Policy: Some items
purchased outright or
consignments accepted for a
50/50 split

This quaint shop's ambiance will
make you feel "at home".

Present this coupon at
Our Little Secret
176 Fifth Avenue North
Safety Harbor, Florida & save
10% on a purchase
Expiration Date: 12/31/99

St. Petersburg

Kiddy Korner
49th Street No.
Saint Petersburg, Florida
33710

Store Hours:
Monday, Tuesday, Thursday,
Friday & Saturday
10am-5pm
Wednesday 10am-6pm

Florida

Featuring over 3000 square feet of gently used furniture, antiques, clothing, art & collectibles
Accepts cash, checks, Visa & Mastercard

Consignment Policy:
Items consigned for 90 days
After 30 days, items are reduced 20%

Store Specials: Check with the shop for ongoing sales & specials

Royal Palm Beach

**Kid's Consignment World
1143 Royal Palm Beach Blvd.
Royal Palm Beach, Florida
33412**

Store Hours:
Monday-Saturday 9:30am-5pm

Phone: 561-798-0208
Fax: 561-798-8089

Children's clothing & accessories from newborn to teens, furniture, toys, equipment & personalized story books for children

Consignment Policy: No appoinment neccessary

The shop features an entertainment corner for children.

St. Petersburg

**Kiddy Korner
3618 49th Street North
St. Petersburg, Florida 33710**

Sunday 11am-4pm

Contact: Kelly Kress Miller
Phone: 813-527-3600

Quality clothing sizes newborn to teens, maternity wear, nursery furniture, baby items & accessories, toys, furniture & equipment rentals

Store Specials: First week in Jan. & July big 50% off sale!

Present this coupon at
*Kiddy Korner
3618 49th Street North
St. Petersburg, Florida*
& save 20% on your first visit
Expiration Date: 12/31/99

Stuart

**Racks Thrift Avenue
Consignment Boutique
5563 US 1-Salerno
Village Square
Stuart, Florida 34997**

Store Hours:
Monday-Friday 10am-5pm
Saturday 10am-4pm

Contact: Terri & Dick Noren
Phone: 407-283-3565

Upscale clothing & accessories for women & men

Consignment Policy:
50/50 split
Items are consigned for 60 days

Florida

Tallahassee

Elite Repeats
3840 N. Monroe #301
Tallahassee, Florida 32303

Store Hours:
Monday-Friday 10am-6:30pm
Saturday 10am-5pm

Contact: Sharon M. Brewer
Phone: 850-562-9380
Fax: 850-894-0325

Clothing for the entire family &
small household items
Accepts cash, checks, Visa &
Mastercard

Second Glance
1660-9 Monroe Street
Tallahassee, Florida 32303

Store Hours:
Monday-Saturday 10am-6pm
Sunday 1pm-5pm
Phone: 904-224-2962

Clothing & accessories for women

Tavares

Accent Consignment Shop
1270 S. Duncan Drive
Highway 19 S.
Tavares, Florida 32778

Store Hours:
Monday-Friday 10am-4pm
Saturday 11am-3pm

Contact: Diane Curth
Phone: 352-343-4015
Fax: 352-383-9012

Clothing for the entire family,
pageant dresses, household items,
baby items rental & much more!

Accepts cash, American Express
& Discover

Store Policy: All sales final

Store Specials: Dollar & half price
rack

Tequesta

Again and Again Apparel Inc.
Ladies Consignment
Clothing Boutique
175-A US Highway 1
Tequesta, Florida 33469

Store Hours:
Monday-Friday 10am-6pm
Saturday 10am-5pm

Phone: 561-745-3073

Upscale clothing & accessories
for women

Consignment Policy: 50/50 split
Items are consigned for 60 days

Store Specials: On-going 50% off
sales

Vero Beach

Vero Consignments
1605 10th Avenue
Vero Beach, Florida 32960

Store Hours:
Monday-Saturday 10am-4pm

Contact: Rita Sprague
Phone: 561-778-3726

Fine women's apparel
Accepts cash, checks & credit

Florida

cards

Store Specials: Check for current specials

West Palm Beach

Red Balloon
1800 Forest Hill Blvd
West Palm Beach, Florida
33406

Store Hours:
Monday-Saturday 10am-5:30pm
Thursday until 7pm

Contact: Pat or Dick Snayd
Phone: 561-966-7956
Fax: 561-582-1754
e-mail: RedBalloon@msn.com

Over 7000 square feet of children's & women's clothing including maternity & accessories Accepts cash, checks, Visa & Mastercard

Consignment Policy:
Consignments accepted Monday, Wednesday & Friday 10am-3:30pm and Thursday 4pm-7pm
50/50 split
Items kept consigned for three calendar months

Store Specials: Items half price after two calendar months

Decorative items displayed at
Our Little Secret in
Safety Harbor, Florida

Albany

Then & Now Boutique, Inc.
2401 B-8 Dawson Road
Albany, Georgia 31707

Store Hours:
Monday-Saturday 10am-6pm

Contact: Robert Keeffe
Phone: 912-435-3213

Upscale clothing for the entire
family including formal wear &
wedding dresses

Consignment Policy: 50/50 split
except when items are acquired
through liquidation the split is
60/40

Americus

The Second Look
Resale Boutique
218 W. Lamar Street
Americus, Georgia 31709

Store Hours:
Tuesday-Friday 10am-5:30pm
Saturday 10am-3pm

Phone: 912-928-9535
e-mail: LPGOVE@GNAT.NET

Clothing for women, men &
children, accessories

Store Policy: Purchase merchandise outright or by store credit

Store Specials: Offering 30% and
70% off merchandise every 30
days

Located in the heart of Americus,
a quaint Southern Georgia town,
The Second Look was the first
consignment shop to open in
town.

Atlanta

Best Dressed
220 Sandy Springs Circle
Suite 141
Atlanta, Georgia 30328

Store Hours:
Monday, Tuesday, Wednesday &
Friday 10am-6pm
Thursday 10am-7:30pm
Saturday 10am-5pm

Contact: Sharon Hartnett
Phone: 404-256-5100

Clothing for the entire family &
accessories

Consignment Policy: 50/50 split

Fantastic Finds
220 Sandy Springs Circle
Suite 189
Atlanta, Georgia 30328

Store Hours:
Monday, Tuesday, Wednesday,
Friday & Saturday 10am-6pm
Thursday 10am-8pm
Sunday 1pm-6pm

Contact: Selma Sax
Phone: 404-303-1313

Upscale top designer label &
couture clothing, accessories &
furs

Consignment Policy:
50/50 split
Items are consigned for 60 days

Store Specials: Individualized wardrobe consultation is available free of charge

Fantastic Finds was voted "*Best of Atlanta*" by *Atlanta Magazine* & *Creative Loafing Magazine*

Bogart

The Crowded Closet
3701 Atlanta Highway #17
Bogart, Georgia 30622

Store Hours:
Tuesday-Friday 11am-7pm
Saturday 11am-4pm

Contact: Peggy Rockwell
Phone: 706-354-6560

Women's clothing & accessories
Accepts cash, checks, Mastercard, Visa & Discover

Columbus

Second Time Around
3732 Woodruff Road
Columbus, Georgia 31904

Store Hours:
Monday-Friday 10am-6pm
Saturday 10am-4pm

Phone: 706-327-7065

Gently used clothing for women & children, shoes & accessories
Accepts cash, personal checks, Visa & Mastercard

Consignment Policy:
Items accepted by appointment

Decatur

Chickibea, Inc
2130 N. Decatur Place
Decatur, Georgia 30033

Store Hours:
Monday-Friday 10am-6pm
Saturday 11am-6pm

Contact: Chicki Lipton
Phone: 404-634-6995

Couture women's clothing
Accepts cash, checks & credit cards

Consignment Policy: 50/50 split

Store Specials: Offering special discounts throughout the year

Douglasville

Act II Your
Consignment Store
9459 Q Highway 5
Douglasville, Georgia 30315

Store Hours:
Monday, Wednesday, Thursday, Friday & Saturday 10am-6pm
Tuesday 10am-7pm
Sunday 1pm-5pm

Contact: Deborah Thompson
Phone: 770-920-2168

Clothing for the entire family, accessories & baby equipment

Consignment Policy: Consignor receives 40%
Store Specials: Referral card for store discounts & merchandise

Consignors receive a special discount

Member of The National Association of Resale & Thrift Shops

Lilburn

Back By Popular Demand
97 Main Street
Lilburn, Georgia 30247

Store Hours:
Monday-Saturday 10am-5pm

Contact: Dorothy C. York
Phone: 770-923-2968

Clothing & accessories for women & children

Marietta

"I Do" Consignments
2800 Canton Road
Piedmont Village
Marietta, Georgia 30066

Store Hours:
Wednesday, Thursday & Saturday 10am-6pm
Tuesday & Friday 10am-8pm

Phone: 770-592-3904
Web site:
www.theclothestree.com/shops/I DO/

Specializing in bridal & formal wear, bridesmaids, mother-of-the bride, flower girl, prom, pageant & after-five wear, unique hand crafted bridal accessories, custom made & consigned veils (all under $100.00)

Consignment Policy:
50/50 split

Newnan

Disabled American Veterans Community Thrift Store
72-10 Greenville Street
Newnan, Georgia 30263

Store Hours:
Monday, Tuesday, Thursday, Friday & Saturday 9am-6pm
Wednesday 9am-4pm

Contact: Mike Gowdy
Phone: 770-502-0000

Clothing for the entire family & much more!

Store Specials:
Select items half price
Wednesday seniors receive a 20% discount

Norcross

A Baby's Closet, Inc.
4650 Jimmy Carter Blvd.
#116-A
Norcross, Georgia 30092

Store Hours:
Monday-Saturday 11am-5pm

Phone: 770-491-0666

Clothing for children sizes infants to 6 & maternity clothing

Consignment Policy: 50/50 split
Items are consigned for 60 days
Some items purchased outright

Store Specials: Items are discounted 20% after 30 days

Georgia

Roswell

The Board of Trade
964 Alpharetta Street
Roswell, Georgia 30075

Store Hours:
Monday-Saturday 10am-5:30pm
Sunday 1pm-5pm

Contact: Sharon Boatwright
Phone: 770-640-7615

Antiques, fine furniture, artwork,
silver, china & jewelry

Consignment Policy:
Items automatically discounted
after 30 days

Sandy Springs

Second Chance Thrift Shop
205 Hilderbrand Drive
Sandy Springs, Georgia 30328

Store Hours:
Wednesday, Thursday & Friday
10am-4pm
Saturday 10am-1pm

Phone: 404-303-0364

Clothing for the entire family &
houseware items
Accepts cash

Store Policy: Donations welcome

Proceeds benefit community
outreach projects.

Snellville

Carriage House Furniture
Factory Outlet &
Consignment Gallery
Snellville Oaks
Shopping Center
2135 East Main Street
Highway 78
Snellville, Georgia 30078

Phone: 770-736-1600
Fax: 770-736-1666

Town & Country Shopping
Center
1355 Roswell Road
Marietta, Georgia 30062
Phone: 770-973-7100
Fax: 770-973-0674

Store Hours:
Monday, Tuesday, Wednesday &
Friday 10am-6pm,
Thursday 10am-8pm
Saturday 10am-5pm
Sunday 1pm-5pm

New & gently used high quality
furniture and antiques
Accepts cash, checks Mastercard
& American Express

Consignment Policy: 50/50 split

Over 31,000 square feet of
showroom space new & gently
used furniture & antiques
Accepts cash, checks, Visa,
Mastercard, American Express &
Discover

Hawaii

Honolulu

Consignment Closet
2970 E. Manoa Road
Honolulu, Hawaii 96822

Store Hours:
Tuesday-Saturday 11am-6pm
Sunday 9am-2pm

Contact: Sheena L. Turnball
Phone: 808-988-7442

Women's clothing, jewelry,
handbags & shoes

Consignment Policy:
50/50 split
Items are consigned for 90 days

Store Specials: Items marked down
50% after 30 days

Jan's Secret Closet
3427-A Waialae Avenue
Honolulu, Hawaii 96816

Store Hours:
Monday-Friday 11am-5:30pm
Saturday 10am-5pm

Contact: Jan HackBarth
Phone: 808-739-1774

Upscale designer fashions for
women
Accepts cash & all major credit
cards

Consignment Policy:
Items consigned for 90 days
Consignor receives 40%

Store Specials: Look for daily
store specials & sales

Present this coupon at
Jan's Secret Closet
3427-A Waialae Ave.
Honolulu, Hawaii & save
off all items
Expiration Date: 12/31/99

PZAZZ
1419 Kalakaua Ave
Honolulu, Hawaii 96826

Store Hours:
Monday-Saturday 10am-6pm

Contact: Judy Joseph
Phone: 808-955-5800

Women's designer clothing &
accessories
Accepts cash, checks & all charge
cards

Store Specials: Periodic sales

This coupon entitles the
bearer to save 20% off
an item at
Pzazz 1419
Kalakaua Ave.
Honolulu, Hawaii
Expiration Date: 12/31/99

Hawaii

The Ultimate You
1020 Auahi Street
Honolulu, Hawaii 96814

Store Hours:
Monday-Saturday 10am-6pm

Contact: Kelsey Sears
Phone: 808-591-8388

Upscale designer clothing for women such as Dior, Chanel, Missoni, Liz, Escada, Ralph Lauren & more! Jewelry & accessories galore

Consignment Policy:
Consignments accepted by appointment
Consignor receives 40%
Items are consigned for 90 days

New arrivals everyday previously owned by socialites & celebrities from New York, California & Europe.

Kauai

T.L.C. Consignment Boutique
1592 Kuhio Highway
Kapaa, HI 96746

Store Hours:
Monday-Saturday 10am-6pm

Contact: Terri Schield &
Lisa Breen
Phone: 808-828-1988
e-mail: neptoon@aloha.net

Exceptional clothing with "experience"
Accepts cash, Mastercard, Visa & American Express

Consignment Policy:
Looking for current style or exotic & interesting clothing
50/50 split
Items consigned for days

Store Specials: Beauty & fashion consulting services available

Maui

The Rainbow Attic
1881S. Kihei Road B-5
Kihei, Maui
Hawaii 96752

Store Hours:
Monday-Sunday 9am-9pm

Phone: 808-874-0884

Trendy clothing for women, furniture, antiques, collectibles & home deco items

Consignment Policy:
50/50 split

Over 1000 items arriving weekly!

Arlington Heights

Suitsmart Mens Clothing
388 E. Golf Road
Arlington Heights, Illinois
60005

Store Hours:
Monday-Friday 10am-7pm
Saturday 10am-5pm & Sunday
12pm-5pm

Contact: Philip Colomise
Phone: 847-290-8008
Fax: 847-290-0660

Finest quality contemporary
designer wear exclusively for men.
Many items previously owned
by famous Chicago celebrities
Accepts cash, checks & credit
cards

This coupon entitles the bearer
to save $20.00 off any suit
purchase at
Suitsmart Mens Clothing
388 E. Golf Road, Arlington
Heights, Illinois
Expiration Date: 12/31/99

Bensenville

The Society Shop
26 S. Center Street
Bensenville, Illinois 60106

Located approximately 4 miles
from O'Hare airport

Store Hours:
Monday-Friday 10am-4pm
Saturday 9am-3pm

Phone: 630-766-3240

Gently used clothing for the entire
family, housewares, jewelry,
collectibles, antiques, toys & small
furniture

Store Policy: Donations welcome

Proceeds are donated to the
Lifelink/Bensenville Home
Society, which benefits life
care residents in the Anchorage
Nursing Home & the Head Start
program for children.

Chicago

Beatnix Vintage Clothing
3400 N. Halsted
Chicago, Illinois 60657

Store Hours:
Open daily 12pm-9pm

Phone: 773-281-6933

Vintage clothing specializing in
the 1970's & original store designs
Accepts cash, Mastercard & Visa

Buy Popular Demand
2629 N. Halsted
Chicago, Illinois 60614

Store Hours:
Monday-Saturday 11am-7pm
Sunday 11am-5pm

Phone: 773-868-0404

Upscale women's designer clothing

Consignment Policy:
50/50 split
Items consigned for 60 days

Store Specials: In January & July
half price sales

Illinois

Chicago Fur Outlet
777 W. Diversey
Chicago, Illinois 60614

Store Hours:
Monday & Thursday 11am-7pm
Tuesday, Wednesday & Friday
11am-6pm
Saturday 11am-5pm
Sunday 12pm-4pm from October
to February

Contact: Howard & Eve Bresnik
Phone: 773-348-3877
Fax: 773-348-3833

New & resale furs, leather &
shearlings

Store Specials: Discounts available
on multiple purchases

Designer Resale Of Chicago
658 N. Dearborn Street
Chicago, Illinois 60610

Phone: 312-587-3312

Store Hours:
Monday, Tuesday & Saturday
11am-6pm
Wednesday, Thursday & Friday
11am-7pm
Sunday 11am-5pm

Second Location:
6522 Lincolnwood Avenue
Lincolnwood, Illinois 60645
Phone: 847-674-7989

Store Hours:
Monday-Saturday 11am-6pm
Sunday 12pm-5pm

Featuring top designer label
clothing such as Chanel, Armani,
Versace, Escada, Donna Karan,

vast array of jewelry, shoes, bags,
scarfs & belts.
Accepts cash, Visa & Mastercard

Consignment Policy:
50/50 split
Items are consigned for 90 days
After 90 days items reduced
50% to 80% off original
marked price

Store Specials: Designer Resale of
Chicago provides items for
fashion shows. Private shopping
for groups is available in addition
to workshops on "Dressing Better
For Less".

Interiors On Consignment
2150 N. Clybourn Avenue
Chicago, Illinois 60614

Store Hours:
Tuesday, Wednesday, Friday
Saturday 10am-6pm
Thursday 11am-7pm
Sunday 12pm-5pm

Contact: Kenneth V. Kohn
Phone: 773-868-0797
Fax: 773-868-0897

Fine furniture & accessories for
the home

Present this coupon at
Interiors on Consignment
on Consignment
2150 N. Clybourn Street
Chicago Illinois
& save 10% off one item
Coupon cannot be combined
with other offers &
discounts
Expiration Date: 12/31/99

The Time Well
2780 N. Lincoln Ave.
Chicago, Illinois 60614

Store Hours:
Monday, Thursday, Friday,
Saturday & Sunday 10am-5pm
Wednesday 10am-9pm

Phone: 773-549-2113
Fax: 773-528-9211
e-mail: Mort97@Flash.net

Great antiques & furniture
Accepts cash, check, Visa &
Mastercard

■■■■■■■■■■■■■■
■　Present this coupon at　■
■　　　*The Time Well*　　　■
■　　*2780 N. Lincoln Ave.*　■
■　　*Chicago, Illinois* &　　■
■　　save 5% off an item　　■
■　　　　　　　　　　　　　　■
■　　Expiration Date: 12/31/99　■
■■■■■■■■■■■■■■

Danville

Castaways
113 N. Vermilion Street
Danville, Illinois 61852

Store Hours: Monday-Friday
10am-5pm, Saturday 10am-3pm

Phone: 217-442-3795

Women's apparel & accessories

Store Policy: Items purchased
outright

Elk Grove Village

Twice Is Nice, Ltd.
780 S. Arlington Heights
Road

Elk Grove Village, Illinois
60007

Located one block north of
Biesterfield

Store Hours:
Monday-Friday 10am-6pm
Thursday 10am-7pm
Saturday 10am-5pm
Sunday 12pm-5pm

Contact: Kathi Mode
Phone: 847-228-5338
Fax: 847-981-1163
e-mail: kathi_mode@juno.com

Upscale clothing for women
Accepts cash, checks, Visa,
Mastercard, American Express &
Novus

Consignment Policy:
Annual $3.00 consignment fee
Items consigned for 60 days

Store Specials: Special charity
$3.00 charity rack on Fridays,
$2.00 rack on Saturday & $1.00
rack on Sunday

This coupon entitles the
bearer to save $5.00
off an item at
Twice Is Nice
780 South Arlington Heights
Road Elk Grove Village Illinois
Expiration Date: 12/31/99

Elmhurst

Elm Classic Consignment
Shoppe, Inc.

Store Hours:
Tuesday & Thursday 12pm-8pm
Wednesday & Friday 12pm-6pm
Saturday 11am-5pm

Contact: Patricia L. Lucchesi
Phone: 630-832-8187
Web site: www.webgo.com/vintage

Fine women's fashions including
evening & after-five, retro
clothing & lots of new accessories
Accepts cash, checks & credit
cards

Consignment Policy:
Consignments accepted by
appointment
50/50 split

Eclectic shop with festive window
displays

Galesburg

Cottage Corner Thrift Shop
444 E. Main Street
Galesburg, Illinois 61401

Store Hours:
Monday-Saturday 9am-5pm

Contact: Joan Carlson
Phone: 309-342-9018

Fabulous clothing for the entire
family, jewelry, housewares,
books, furniture & collectibles
Accepts cash, travelers checks,
personal checks with local ID

Store Policy:
Donations welcome & appreciated

Store Specials: Seniors over 60
receive a 10% discount every
Wednesday

Proceeds benefit the Cottage
Hospital Service Guild.

Present this coupon at
Cottage Corner Thrift Shop
444 East Main Street
Galesburg, Illinois and
receive half off any one item
in the shop
(Limit one coupon per customer)
Expiration Date: 12/31/99

Lake Forest

Mais Encore, Inc.
1361 Western Ave.
Lake Forest, Illinois 60045

Store Hours:
Monday, Tuesday, Thursday,
Friday & Saturday 10am-4pm

Contact: Kathy Early
Phone: 847-234-4696

Upscale designer clothing for
women, men & children &
accessories
Accepts cash & personal checks

Consignment Policy: Items
consigned for 60 days
Consignor receives 60% of the
selling price

Store Specials: Half price racks all
year round

Normal

BroMenn Thrift Shop
1203 S. Main
Normal, Illinois 61761

Store Hours:
Monday-Friday 10am-5pm
Saturday 10am-4pm

Phone: 309-454-7074

Clothing for the entire family,
household items, small knick-
knacks & much more

Store Policy: Donations welcome

Olney

The Garage Sale
630 West Chestnut
Olney, Illinois 62450

Store Hours:
Monday-Saturday 9am-5pm
Sunday 12pm-5pm

Phone: 618-392-2440
e-mail: runyon@wworld.com

Wide selection of gently used
clothing for men, women &
children sizes infants to plus.
Large selection of toys, dishes,
crafts, tools & lots of baby
supplies

Consignment Policy:
Consignors receive 60% of the
selling price

Peoria

The Clothe Line
3025 N. Sterling Ave
Peoria, Illinois 61604

Store Hours:
Tuesday-Thursday 10am-5pm
Friday 10am-6pm
Saturday 10am-4pm

Phone: 309-685-2150
e-mail: carebear@davesworld.net

Clothing for women & children,
jewelry & beanie babies
Accepts cash & checks

Consignment Policy:
$5.00 per year handling fee
to consign items
50/50 split

Store Specials: Select color tickets
reduced 50% the first week of
every month

The Corner Closet
2818 N University
Peoria, Illinois 61604
Located on the lower level of the
church

Store Hours:
Wednesday & Friday 10am-4pm
Thursday 10am-5pm
Saturday 10am-12:30pm
Closed July & the last half of
December

Contact: Barbara Gurtler &
Beth Ziegele
Phone: 309-688-8113
Fax: 309-688-4576

Clothing for the entire family,
shoes & jewelry
Accepts cash & personal checks

Illinois

Rochester

The Kids Closet
130 S. John Street
Rochester, Illinois 62563

Store Hours:
Monday, Tuesday, Wednesday &
Thursday 9am-6pm
Friday 9am-8pm
Saturday 9am-5pm
Sunday 10am-5pm

Contact: Kitty Boyce
Phone: 217-498-9434
888-537-2578
e-mail: kdsclst@cybercityusa.net
Website: www.springfieldil.net/
kidscloset/

Fabulous children's clothing-sizes
newborn to 16 for girls, up to size
20 for boys, infant accessories,
furniture, toys, shoes & maternity
wear
Accepts cash, checks, Mastercard,
Visa, Discover & Debit cards

Consignment Policy:
50/50 split
Items consigned up to six months
$1.00 per year account fee
Markdowns at the end of each
season or after 90 days (which-
ever comes first)
Items must be freshly cleaned, in
good condition, in style &
seasonal
Jan 1 to June 20 accepts Spring &
Summer, July 1 to December 20
accepts Fall & Winter
Consignments accepted everyday

Store Specials:
Drop & Run service
Frequent shopper cards-receive

$25.00 in free merchandise after
$200.00 in purchases
Wish list

The Kids Closet is Illinois largest
children's resale store featuring
over 7500 square feet of terrific
merchandise.

Present this coupon next
time you visit the
Kids Closet
130 South John Street
Rochester, Illinois &
receive $2.00 off your next
purchase of $10.00 or more
Expiration Date: 12/31/99

Schaumburg

Precious Gift Thrift Shop
Schamburg Towncenter
1108 S. Roselle Road
Schamburg, Illinois 60193

Store Hours:
Monday, Tuesday, Wednesday &
Thursday 10am-8pm
Friday & Saturday 10am-3pm
Sunday 12pm-4pm

Contact: Georgia Scarpa
Phone: 847-891-0978

Clothing for the entire family,
knick-knacks & furniture
Accepts cash, Visa & Mastercard

Store Specials: Sales daily

Store Policy: Donations welcome

Proceeds from Precious Gift Thrift Shop benefit the mental health program and meals-on-wheels for the elderly at the Kenneth Young Center in Illinois assisting seniors to remain independent.

West Chicago

Designer's Discount
33W624W. Roosevelt Road
West Chicago, Illinois 60815

Store Hours:
Monday-Friday 10am-6pm
Saturday 10am-5pm,

Contact: Paula Dunlap
Phone: 630-232-9345

Women's apparel
Accepts cash, personal checks,
Mastercard & Visa

Consignment Policy: 50/50 split
Items consigned for 60 days

Store Specials: Half price rack

Winnetka

For Kids Only
1048 Gage Street
Winnetka, Illinois 60096

Store Hours:
Tuesday, Wednesday & Thursday
9am-4pm
Friday 10am-5pm
Saturday 10am-4pm

Phone: 847-441-6640
Fax: 847-441-6648

Designer European boutique featuring clothing for infants to size 14, toys & equipment
Accepts cash, checks, ships out of state with payment by money order or certified check

Store Specials:
New items discounted 25% to 50%

This coupon entitles the
bearer to save $5.00 off
one $25.00 purchase at
For Kids Only
1048 Gage Street
Winnetka, Illinois
(Tax not included and excludes sale items)
Expiration Date: 12/31/99

Indiana

Beach Grove

Kiddie Klothes
615 Main Street
Beach Grove, Indiana 46107

Store Hours:
Monday, Wednesday, Friday &
& Saturday 10am-4pm
Tuesday & Thursday 10am-7pm

Phone: 317-781-8260
Website:www.theclothestree.com/
shops/KiddieKlothes/

Clothing for children sizes infant
to 14, maternity clothing,
furniture for kids & toys

Chestertown

Buttons & Bows
1457 Broadway
Chesterton, Indiana 46304

Store Hours:
Monday, Tuesday, Wednesday
& Friday 9am-5pm
Thursday 9am-6pm
Saturday 9am-4pm

Phone: 219-926-2332

Top quality clothing for children,
maternity wear, baby furniture,
toys & accessories

Consignment Policy:
40/60 split

Fort Wayne

Cameo Consignment
5958 Stellhorn Road
Ft. Wayne, Indiana 46815

Store Hours:
9:30am-6pm

Phone: 219-486-7890
e-mail: rmuldoon@aol.com

High quality new & gently used
clothing for women, sizes 3 petite
to 28 & men, all sizes. Accessories galore including handbags,
shoes & jewelry

Consignment Policy:
Call ahead before bringing items
to consign
Items are consigned for 90 days

Present this coupon at
Cameo Consignment
5958 Stellhorn Road
Fort Wayne Indiana & save
$5.00 off your total purchase
of $20.00 or more

Expiration Date: 12/31/99

Concordia High School
Thrift Shop
3319 North Anthony Blvd.
Fort Wayne, Indiana 46805

Store Hours:
Monday-Friday 10am-5pm
Saturday 9:30am-3:30pm

Contact: Lou Linnemeier
Phone: 219-482-1403

Clothing for the entire family,
jewelry, shoes, household goods,
small appliances & books
Accepts cash & checks

Store Specials: Offering monthly
sales

Proceeds from the shop benefit
Concordia Lutheran High School

Francisco

**Eagle's Nest Consignments
R #1 Box 21400
Highway 64
Francisco, Indiana 47694**

Store Hours:
Monday-Friday 9am-5pm
Saturday 9am-8pm
Phone: 812-782-3745

Antiques, collectibles & knick
knacks

Store Specials: Dealer discount

Indianapolis

**Consignor Clothes
Ladies Upscale Resale
8055 Madison Ave
Indianapolis, Indiana 46227**

Store Hours:
Monday-Friday 10am-6pm

Contact: Jackie Barker
Phone: 317-887-6787

Women's clothing & accessories
Accepts cash, checks, Visa,
Mastercard & Discover

Store Specials: Layaway available

Marion

**Country Kids
209 E. 33rd
Marion, Indiana 46953**

Store Hours:
Tuesday-Friday 11am-5pm
Saturday 11am-3pm
Closed on Sunday & Monday

Phone: 317-662-3870

Clothing for children, accessories

Consignment Policy: 50/50 split
Annual $5.00 fee to consign
merchandise

Store Specials: Foster parents in
Grant Co. inquire in the shop
about special program for clothing

Nappanee

**The Alternative Choice, Inc
Children's Resale
159 South Main
Nappanee, Indiana 46550**

Store Hours:
Monday-Friday 10am-5pm
Saturday 10am-3pm

Phone: 219-773-2884

Clothing for children & maternity
wear & toys

Consignment Policy: 50/50 split

Indiana

New Castle

**Classic Collections
Consignment Boutique
1701 Riley Road
New Castle, Indiana 47362**

Store Hours:
Monday-Saturday 10am-5pm
Sunday 12pm-5pm

Women's clothing, accessories &
close out jewelry
Accepts cash, checks,
Visa & Mastercard

Classic Collections is known for
their friendly atmosphere in
addition to their great merchandise.

Terre Haute

**The Children's Path
4408 S. 7th Street
Terre Haute, Indiana 47802**

Store Hours:
Monday-Saturday 10am-6pm

Phone: 812-299-7284

Clothing for children, handmade
items, shoes, toys & furniture

Consignment Policy: 50/50 split
Items are consigned for 90 days

Bettendorf

The Growing Years
2395 Cumberland
Square Drive
Bettendorf, Iowa 52722

Store Hours:
Monday-Friday 10am-6pm
Saturday 10am-5pm

Phone: 319-355-1301

Children's clothing

Consignment Policy: 50/50 split
Items are consigned for 90 days

Cedar Rapids

Elegant Repeats
An Exclusive Ladies'
Consignment
Boutique & Discount Bridal
Outlet
3531 Mt. Vernon Road SE
Cedar Rapids, Iowa 52403

Store Hours:
Monday, Tuesday, Wednesday &
Friday 10am-6pm
Thursday 10am-7pm
Saturday 10am-5pm
Sunday 12pm-4pm (Except from
Memorial Day to Labor Day)

Contact: Kathy Kamberling
Phone: 319-365-1070
e-mail: Eleganrep@aol.com

Designer women's clothing &
accessories from jeans to
professional attire, bridal &
formal wear

Consignment Policy: Consignments accepted by appoinment

Davenport

Kids Crew And Moms Too
1606 West Locust Street
Davenport, Iowa 52804

Store Hours:
Monday-Saturday 9am-6pm
Sunday 12pm-6pm

Contact: Becki Menart
Phone: 319-324-0301

Children's clothing, maternity
wear & baby furniture

Consignment Policy:
Items are consigned for 3 months
Some merchandise bought outright
for cash

Ritzi Reruns
220 W. 3rd
Davenport, Iowa 52801

Store Hours:
Monday-Friday 10am-5pm
Saturday 10am-3pm

Contact: CJ Bock
Phone: 319-322-8684

Women's designer label clothing &
accessories

Consignment Policy: Consignments accepted by appointment
50/50 split
Items are consigned for 90 days
Items marked down after 60 days

De Moines

Fashion Junction
2921 Ingersoll Avenue
Des Moines, Iowa 50312

Saturday 9am-5pm &
Sunday 12pm-4pm (August-May)

Phone: 515-255-5453
Fax: 515-255-8196
e-mail: FJCONSIGN@aol.com
Web site: http://members.aol.com/
fjconsign/index.html

Top designer clothing for the
entire family, labels such as
DKNY, Dana Buchman, Ellen
Tracy & more. Formal & bridal
wear, new clothing items too,
gifts, cards & lots of great jewelry
Accepts cash, Mastercard, Visa &
Discover

Store Specials: Special on going
color ticket sale & Lay-a-away
available

Consignment Policy: Consignor
receives 40% of the selling price
Consignments accepted Tuesday
& Thursdays from 9:30am-
11:30am & 3pm-6pm
Drop & Run service available

Newton

Children's Recycling Shop
2617 1st Ave E
Newton, Iowa 50208

Phone: 515-791-7779

Second Location:
25 S. First Street
Marshalltown, Iowa 50158
Phone: 515-753-5255

Store Hours:
Monday-Saturday 10am-5pm

Contact: Joni Recinos

New & pre-loved clothing for
children, women & men (Men's
clothing available in Marshalltown
location, baby furniture & toys

The Dressing Room
322 South 2nd Avenue W.
Newton, Iowa 50208

Store Hours:
Monday 10am-8pm
Tuesday-Saturday 10am-4pm
Sunday 12pm-4pm

Contact: Shirley Jones
Phone: 515-792-0783

Clothing for the entire family

Consignment Policy:
50/50 split

Concordia

Mr. Thrifty's
514 Washington
Concordia, Kansas 66901

Store Hours:
Monday-Saturday 10am-7pm

Phone: 913-243-7360

Clothing & lots of collectibles

Copeland

The Mark Down Shop
Highway 56 & Stanley Street
PO Box 234
Copeland, Kansas 67837

Store Hours:
Wednesday, Thursday & Friday
10am-5:30pm & Saturday 10am-3pm

Clothing, accessories, kitchenware, bedding & much more

El Dorado

Twice Is Nice
109 N. Main
El Dorado, Kansas 67042

Store Hours:
Monday, Tuesday, Wednesday &
Friday 10am-6pm & Thursday
until 7:30pm
children, jewelry including new
earrings & great children's gifts
Accepts cash, checks, Mastercard
& Visa

Consignment Policy: Cash paid
for children's clothing & women's
clothing. Baby furniture accepted
on consignment.

Contact: Pam Gull &
Connie Darnell
Phone: 316-321-2187
e-mail: pam@southwind.net
Web site: www.theclothes.com/
shops/TwiceIsNice

Over 3400 square feet of gently
used clothing for women &
Store Specials:
Lay-a-way available
Discounted items always available!
First Friday in August "Fantastic
Finds" preview clothing for
children. Change of season sales
on children's clothing twice a
year.

Present this coupon at
Twice Is Nice
109 N Main
El Dorado, Kansas &
receive a free pair of earrings
when you stop by to say hello!

Hays

The Arc Thrift Shop
116 E. 11th Street
Hays, Kansas 67601

Store Hours:
Monday-Thursday 9:30am-4:30pm
Friday & Saturday 9:30am-3:30pm

Phone: 785-628-8831

Clothing for the entire family,
toys, books, knick-knacks &
seasonal items

Kansas

Store Policy: Donations welcome

What started out as a basement sale in order to raise funds for the ARC of Central Plains has blossomed into one of the best thrift shops in the central plains. Proceeds from the shop benefit ARC (Association for Retarded Citizens) various programs such as The Children's Center, a day care center for mentally retarded children, the Homer Training Center for mentally retarded adults, special olympics, recreational & community activities & much more.

Lawrence

Lasting Impressions Consignment Boutique 711 W. 23rd Street Suite 22 Lawrence, Kansas 66046

Store Hours:
Monday-Saturday 10am-6pm
Thursday until 8pm

Contact: Carol Broman
Phone: 785-749-5122

Gently used clothing for women, men & children, accessories, furniture, wall & home decor items

Consignment Policy: Items consigned Monday-Saturday 10am-2:30pm
Consignor receives 40%
Items are consigned for 90 days & reduced after two months

Store Specials: Bimonthly newsletter that includes coupons. Sales on the first Thursday of every quarter in Jan., April, July & October.

■ Present this coupon at
Lasting Impressions
Consignment Boutique
711 W. 23rd St, Suite 22,
Lawrence, Kansas and receive
10% off any purchase

(Not valid with other offers)
Expiration Date: 12/31/99

Manhattan

Grandma's Trunk Thrift Shop 1304 Pillsbury Drive Manhattan, Kansas 66502

Store Hours:
Monday-Saturday 10am-6pm

Phone: 913-537-2273

Clothing, furniture, knick-knacks, antiques & much more!

Store Policy: Items bought outright

Store Specials: Dealer discounts

Overland Park

Plus Size Consignment Shop 95th & Nall Nalls Hills Shopping Center Overland Park, Kansas 66207

Store Hours:
Monday-Saturday 10am-6pm
Thursday until 8pm

Contact: Robbie Williams
Phone: 913-642-1989
Upscale one-of-a-kind plus size clothing for women &

formal wear rental
Some new items too!

Consignment Policy:
Items consigned for 90 days
Consignor receives 40%

Sacks on Santa Fe
8025 Santa Fe
Overland, Kansas 66212

Store Hours:
Monday-Saturday 10am-4:30pm

Phone: 913-642-6061

Clothing for the entire family,
accessories, household goods &
more

Topeka

Mommy & Me
1707 SE 29th #400
Topeka, Kansas 66605

Store Hours:
Monday-Friday 10am-6pm,
Saturday 9am-5pm

Contact: Karen Shaffer
Phone: 785-266-0375

Maternity & children's clothing,
baby accessories
Accepts cash, checks, Visa,
Mastercard & Discover

Store Policy:
Items accepted on Monday,
Tuesday, Thursday & Saturday
between 10am to 3pm

the first Tuesday of every month

Fashion Exchange Ltd.
Consignment   Boutique
Foxcross Shopping Center
5967 SW 29th Street
Topeka, Kansas 66614

Store Hours:
Monday-Friday 10am-6pm
Thursday until 8pm
Saturday 10am-4pm

Phone: 913-271-8500

Upscale resale designer fashions
for women

Consignment Policy: 50/50 split
Items are consigned for 90 days

Wichita

Kid Stuff
818 W. 53rd North
Wichita, Kansas 67204

Store Hours:
Wednesday, Thursday & Friday
11am-6pm
Saturday 10am-5pm
Phone: 316-838-6500

Clothing for children, toys & baby
furniture
Accepts cash & checks

Consignment Policy: 50/50 split

Kentucky

Adairville

Tina's Treasures
110 W. Gallatin Street
"On The Square"
Adairville, Kentucky 42202

Store Hours:
Tuesday-Friday 11am-5pm
Saturday 11am-3pm

Contact: Tina Smith
Phone: 502-539-3563
e-mail: treasure@logantele.com

Gently used clothing for women
sizes 2-28, accessories, costume
jewelry, handbags, scarfs, books,
housewares, crafts & gifts,
children's clothing size 0-18,
maternity clothing, items for baby
needs, formal & pageant wear
including new pageant dresses,
socks, hair bows & toys
Some new items too!
Accepts cash, check, Visa &
Mastercard

Consignment Policy:
Consignments by appointment
only
50/50 split
Items consigned for 90 days with
a 50% reduction after 45 days

Store Specials:
Gift wrapping & lay-a-way
available
Seniors receive a 15% discount
Half price sales & $1.00
clearance rack everyday!

Present this coupon at
Tina's Treasure
Consignment Shop
110 W. Gallatin Street
Adairville, Kentucky and
save 10% off one
entire purchase
Expiration Date: 12/31/99

Brandenburg

Fashionable Alternatives
Consignments
2615 Brandenburg Road
Brandenburg, Kentucky
40108

Store Hours:
Monday-Saturday 10am-5pm

Phone: 502-422-5828

Clothing for the entire family,
household decor, furniture,
appliances, jewelry & much more!

Consignment Policy: 50/50 split
Consignments accepted by
appointment

Store Specials: Twice a year 75%
off clothing sale

Campbellsburg

Campbellsburg
Consignment & Gift Shop
Highway 421 &
8839 Main Street
PO Box 54
Campbellsburg, Kentucky
40011

Located one mile from Exit 34
off I-71 between Louisville and

Cinncinnati, Ohio

Store Hours:
Monday-Saturday 9am-5pm

Contact: Sue Kelley

Phone: 502-532-6596

Excellent quality clothing for the entire family, shoes, small household items including dishes, linens and much more.
The gift shop carries beautiful handmade items such as dolls, flowers and candles.
Accepts cash

Consignment Policy:
50/50 split
$3.00 per year fee to consign merchandise

Present this coupon at
Campbellsburg Consignment & Gift Shop
Hwy 421-8839 Main Street
Campbellsburg, Kentucky
& save 20% off any item

Expiration Date: 12/31/99

Edgewood

**Clothes Call
Consignment Shop
148 Barnwood Drive
Edgewood, Kentucky 41017**

Store Hours:
Monday-Friday 10am-5pm
Saturday 10am-4pm

Phone: 606-341-3536
Clothing for women & men, furniture & home accessories

Florence

**Decorate With What
You Have
268 Main Street
Florence, Kentucky 41042**

Store Hours:
Monday-Friday 10am-6pm
Saturday 10am-4pm

Phone: 606-525-1661

Furniture, household accessories, crafts, antiques, window treatments, fabrics & more

Consignment Policy:
$7.00 annual registration fee to consign merchandise

Lexington

**Double Exposure
3122 Richmond Road
Lexington, Kentucky 40509**

Store Hours:
Monday-Friday 10am-8pm
Saturday 10am-6pm

Phone: 606-269-3103

Excellent quality clothing & accessories for women

Consignment Policy:
50/50 split

Store Specials: Serious bargain hunters look for the $2.00 dollar & half off bargain rack

**Sassy Fox
3101 Richmond Road**

Suite 312
Lexington, Kentucky 40509

Store Hours:
Monday, Tuesday, Wednesday,
Friday & Saturday
10am-6pm
Thursday 10am-8pm & Sunday
12pm-5pm

Phone: 606-266-5138

Second Location:
628 University Shopping
Center
Richmond, Kentucky 40509

Store Hours:
Monday-Friday 10am-5:30pm &
Saturday 10am-4pm
Phone: 606-624-2253

Designer clothing for women &
children & wedding dresses

Consignment Policy: 50/50 split
Items consigned for ten weeks

Walk N' Closet
1545 Alexandria Drive
Lexington, Kentucky 40504

Store Hours:
Monday-Friday 10am-6pm
Saturday 10am-5pm & Sunday
1pm-5pm

Contact: Juanita Ryker
Phone: 606-277-3898

Clothing for men & women &
jewelry

Consignment Policy:
50/50 split
Items consigned for 90 days
Store Specials: Lay-a-way
available

Member of The National
Association of Resale & Thrift
Shops

Unique Consignment
1020 Industry Road
Suite 38
Lexington, Kentucky 40505

Store Hours:
Monday-Saturday 10am-5pm

Contact: Cleta Howard
Phone: 606-233-3410

Clothing for women & men &
accessories

Member of The National
Association of Resale & Thrift
Shops

Louisville

Baby Bargains
Consignment Shop
5715-A Bardstown Road
Louisville, Kentucky 40299

Store Hours:
Monday-Friday 11:30am-6pm &
Saturday 12pm-4pm

Phone: 502-231-0025

Baby clothing sizes newborn to 6,
maternity wear, baby furniture,
toys & much more

Consignment Policy: 50/50 split
No appointment necessary to
consign merchandise

Store Specials: Seasonal sales

Better Ladies Consignment
2916 Frankfort Avenue
Louisville, Kentucky 40206

Store Hours:
Monday-Friday 10am-6pm
Saturday 10am-5pm

Phone: 502-893-6577

Women's designer clothing &
accessories

Cachet
2505 Hermitage Way
Louisville, Kentucky 40242

Store Hours:
Tuesday-Saturday 10am-5pm

Phone: 502-426-3334

Upscale designer clothing for the
entire family, household items,
antiques, furniture & toys

Store Specials: Semi-annual half
price sale in January & July

Encore Consignment
9301 New La Grange Road
Louisville, Kentucky 40242

Store Hours:
Monday-Thursday 10am-6pm
Friday & Saturday 10am-5pm

Phone: 502-423-8375

Upscale clothing for women &
children, wedding dresses & formal
wear
Accepts cash, checks, Visa &
Mastercard
Consignment Policy:
$5.00 registration fee to consign

50/50 split

Store Specials: Year round special
sales

Foster Duerr's
Consignments, Inc.
1961 Brownsboro Road
Louisville, Kentucky 40206

Store Hours: Call for store hours

Phone: 502-893-6500

Clothing for the entire family,
jewelry, accessories & collectibles
Accepts cash, checks, Visa,
Mastercard & Discover

Store Specials: Lay-a-way
available

Save 20% off any one
non-sale item when you
present this coupon at
Foster Duerr's Consignments
1961 Brownsboro Road,
Louisville, Kentucky

Expiration Date: 12/31/99

Kentucky

Goodwill Industries
of Kentucky
909 E. Broadway
Louisville, Kentucky 40204

Store Hours:
Monday-Saturday 9am-6pm
Sunday 1pm-6pm

Phone: 502-584-8821

Clothing for the entire family,
shoes, handbags, furniture, toys,
jewelry & more

Store Policy: Donations welcome
& a receipt may be provided

Piccadilly Plaza
5324 Bardstown Road
Louisville, Kentucky 40291
Phone: 502-491-9336

2315 Nashville Road
Bowling Green, Kentucky
42101
Phone: 502-781-4301

4101 Taylorsville Road
Louisville, Kentucky 40220
Phone: 502-456-4735

655 U.S. Highway 31-W.
Bypass
Bowling Green, Kentucky
42101
Phone: 502-781-5464

Whipps Mill Shopping Center
9321 New LaGrange Road
Louisville, Kentucky 40242
Phone: 502-429-6758

Shoppers Village
316 Versailles Road
Frankfort, Kentucky 40601

Phone: 502-695-1100

110 Edgewood Plaza
Nicholasville, Kentucky
40356
Phone: 606-887-1818

2208 Ft. Campbell Blvd.
Hopkinsville, Kentucky 42240
Phone: 502-887-9024

469-B Eastern Bypass
Richmond, Kentucky 40475
Phone: 606-623-7173

124 W. Mulberry Street
Lebanon, Kentucky 40033
Phone: 502-692-4808

201 Tradewind Shopping
Center
Somerset, Kentucky 42501
Phone: 606-678-4429

Meadowthorpe Shopping
Center
1441 Leestown Road
Lexington, Kentucky 40511
Phone: 606-233-0222

Laurel Plaza Shopping
Center
1809 N. Main Street
London, Kentucky 40741
Phone: 606-877-1138

Stonewall Shopping Center
3101 Clays Mill Road
Lexington, Kentucky 40503
Phone: 606-223-4550

2005 N. Dixie Highway
Elizabethtown, Kentucky
42701
Phone: 502-737-7162

Judy's Finest Consignment
11604 Main Street

Louisville, Kentucky 40243

Store Hours:
Monday-Saturday 10:15am-5pm

Phone: 502-245-5425
e-mail:jh814@aol.com
Web site: www.judys-finest.com

Specializing in designer & better
apparel for women, accessories,
jewelry, hats & furs in season
Accepts cash, Visa, Mastercard &
Discover

Consignment Policy:
$2.00 fee to consign items
Consignor receives 50% of the
selling price for items under
$100.00 & 55% of the selling
price for items over $100.00

Store Specials: End-of-season
sales on overstocked items

Paducah

**Cotton Tails Children's
Consignment Shop
2201 Broadway
Paducah, Kentucky 42001**

Store Hours:
Tuesday-Saturday 10am-5pm

Phone: 502-449-9727

Children's clothing & accessories

Somerset

**Dress For Less
5454 South Highway 27
Somerset, Kentucky 42501**

Store Hours:
Monday-Saturday 9am-6pm

Phone: 606-561-4645

Clothing for the entire family

Consignment Policy:
50/50 split
Items consigned for 90 days

Louisiana

Alexandria

Act II Resale Boutique
1305 Metro Drive Suite 7
Alexandria, Louisiana 71301

Store Hours:
Monday-Friday 10am-5:30pm
Saturday 10am-4pm

Phone: 318-445-2720

One of the areas finest consignment shops featuring gently worn
clothing for women & children,
shoes & accessories
Accepts cash, Visa, Mastercard,
Discover & American Express

Consignment Policy:
50/50 split
Items consigned for 90 days

Baton Rouge

Lots For Tots
12330 Florida Blvd.
Suite 10
Baton Rouge, Louisiana
70815-2720

Store Hours:
Tuesday-Saturday 10am-5pm

Contact: Ellen S. Miller
Phone: 504-273-1262

Children's clothing sizes infants to
14, shoes, toys, books, nursery
items, baby furniture & maternity
clothing

Consignment Policy: Items are
consigned for 120 days

Store Specials: Special sales
Lot's For Tots is Baton Rouge's
largest & oldest resale shop.

Lafayette

Rags To Riches
3216 Johnston Street
Lafayette, Louisiana
70503-3744

Store Hours:
Monday-Saturday 10am-5:30pm

Contact: Joanna Oliver
Phone: 318-988-4679
e-mail: Rag3216@aol.com

Excellent quality clothing for
women, men & children
Accepts cash, checks & credit
cards

Consignment Policy:
No appointment needed to
consign clothing
Items consigned for 60 days
50/50 split
After you becoming a consignor
the drop & run service may be
utilized

Store Specials: Discounted color
tags daily

Rags to Riches specializes in high
quality items and excellent
customer service.

Upscale Resale
102 Rena Drive
Lafayette, Louisiana 70503

Store Hours:
Monday-Saturday 10am-5:15pm

Phone: 318-988-5700

Clothing for the entire family,

furniture, jewelry, shoes & knick-knacks
Consignment Policy: 50/50 split
Items are consigned for 60 days

Metairie

The Book Rack
2305 Metairie Road
Metairie, Louisiana 70001

Store Hours:
Monday-Saturday 10am-6pm
Sunday 12pm-4pm

Gently used paperback books

Store Policy: Buy & sell paperback books

New Orleans

Paisley Babylon
1319 Decatur Street
New Orlean, Louisiana 70116

Store Hours:
Monday-Thursday 12pm-6pm

Contact: Valerie
Phone: 504-529-3696

Vintage clothing & accessories
circa 1920's to 1970's
Accepts cash, major credit cards
& travelers checks

Store Policy: Buy, sell or trade
Call the shop for an appointment

Store Specials: Specializing in
vintage leather & Levi's at
low to moderate prices

Providing many items for movie
& video wardrobes, Paisley

Babylon is a favorite among rock
stars & bands such as Lenny
Kravitz, White Zombie & more!

The Blind Cat, Inc.
Resale Boutique
714 Adams Street at Maple
New Orleans, Louisiana
70118

Store Hours: Call for store hours

Phone: 504-862-0073
Contact: Stacy Fahm Peterson &
Sally Fahm

Men's, women's, children's
clothing & furniture

Slidell

Fashion Reborn, Inc.
163 Northside Plaza
Slidell, Louisiana 70460

Store Hours:
Monday-Saturday 10am-6pm
Thursday 10am-8pm

Phone: 504-641-8748

Clothing for the entire family &
bridal outlet

Consignment Policy: 50/50 split
Items consigned for 90 days

Maine

Auburn

Punkins Inc.
Children's Resale Shoppe
Women's Consignment
Shoppe
20 Union Street Bypass
Auburn, Maine 04210

Store Hours:
Winter hours:
Monday-Saturday 10am-5pm
Summer hours:
Monday, Wednesday & Friday
11am-6pm
Tuesday & Thursday 11am-8pm
Saturday 10am-2pm

Phone: 207-784-1407

Gently used clothing for children,
accessories, furniture, small toys,
wedding & prom gowns

Consignment Policy: 50/50 split

Store Specials: Frequent buyer
cards

Bangor

Repeat Performance
Resale Boutique
60 Main Street
Bangor, Maine 04401

Store Hours:
Monday-Friday 10am-5pm
Saturday 10am-4pm

Phone: 207-990-4300

Elegant, trendy, professional
fashions for women

Consignment Policy:
50/50 split
Items are consigned for 60 days
102

Brewer

Sylvia's Resale Shop
86 S. Main Street
Brewer, Maine 04412

Store Hours:
Monday-Saturday 10am-5pm

Contact: Sylvia Pomroy
Phone: 207-989-6441

Clothing for entire family &
vintage jewelry
Accepts cash & checks

Consignment Policy:
50/50 split
Consignment by appointment
only

Store Specials: Dollar rack,
bargain basket

Located in an antique house built
in 1884, Sylvia has been
successfully offering great unique
items at fabulous prices for over
twenty-six years! A play area is
available for children.

Unique Boutique
The Resale Shop with More!
575 Wilson Street
Brewer, Maine 04412

Store Hours:
Monday-Saturday 10am-4pm

Phone: 207-989-1900

Clothing for the entire family,
jewelry, wedding gowns

Consignment Policy: 50/50 split

Store Specials: Half price items

every day!!

Ellsworth

**Hodge Podge Oldies N'
Goodies
The Mill Mall
RT. 1A
Ellsworth, Maine 04065**

Store Hours:
Monday-Saturday 9am-5pm

Phone: 207-667-2221

Glassware, furniture, jewelry,
vintage items, knick-knacks and
much more

Store Policy: Consignments and
donations accepted

Greene

**Kids Kloset
103 West Main Street
Greene, Maine 04236**

Store Hours:
Monday-Saturday 10am-4pm

Phone: 207-946-5098

Children's clothing to size 14

Kennebunk

**The Budget Box
St. David's Episcopal Church
1 High Street
Kennebunk, Maine 04043**

Store Hours:
Monday-Friday 10am-4pm
Saturday 10am-1pm

Phone: 207-985-3544

Clothing for the entire family,
giftware, housewares, toys &
appliances

Store Specials: Twice-a-year sales
in March & August

Proceeds from the shop are
donated to St. Davids Church.

Machias

**Bags O' Rags Thrift Store
28 Main Street
Machias, Maine 04654**

Store Hours: By appointment or
call ahead of time

Contact: Sandi Bryand
Phone: 207-255-4649
       207-454-0347

Recycled clothing, household
goods, books, toys & lots of
treasures

Store Specials: Donations
welcome

Store Specials:
Items available for 25 cents and
over
$3.00 bag sale & items provided
free for those in severe need

Millinocket

**Another Time Around
Consignment Boutique
153 Penobscot Ave
Millinocket, Maine 04462**

Store Hours:
Monday-Friday 9am-5pm

Saturday 10am-3pm
Sunday-By appointment only

Phone: 207-723-8523
e-mail: joncamp@ime.net
Web site: http://w3.ime.net/
~joncamp/atacb.htm

Excellent quality clothing for
women, men & children, antiques,
jewelry & formal wear

Consignment Policy:
Items for consignment may be
dropped off during business hours
50/50 split
Items consigned for 60 days

Store Specials: Frequent shopper
card

Portland

Laurel's Rich Rags
463 Stevens Avenue
Portland, Maine 04102

Store Hours:
Monday-Saturday 10am-6pm

Contact: Laurel Schuttle Worth
Phone: 207-761-2955

Brand name clothing for women
men & children, bridal gowns
Accepts cash & checks

Store Specials: 50% off all
merchandise

Present this coupon at
Laurel's Rich Rags
463 Stevens Avenue
Portland Maine when you
purchase $25.00 in merchandise
receive a $5.00 coupon
Expiration Date: 12/31/99

Van Buren

Main Street Consignment
80 Main Street
P.O. Box 493
Van Buren, Maine 04785

Store Hours:
Wednesday & Saturday 10am-5pm
& by appointment

Phone: 207-868-2969
Antiques, collectibles, books,
magazines & clothing

Store Specials: Dealer discounts &
lay-a-way available

Winthrop

Becky's Second Time Around
41 Main Street
Winthrop, Maine 04364

Store Hours:
Monday-Friday 10am-4pm
Saturday 10am-2pm

Contact: Wendy or Becky
Phone & Fax: 207-377-9494

Women's clothing
Accepts cash, checks, Mastercard
& Visa

Consignment Policy: Items
consigned for 90 days

Annapolis

Annapolis Consignors, Inc.
55 West Street
Annapolis, Maryland 21401

Store Hours:
Monday-Friday 11am-5pm

Phone: 410-263-7476

Clothing for women & men

Consignment Policy:
Items consigned for 60 days
Consignor receives 40%

Baltimore

The Zone
813 N. Charles Street
Baltimore, Maryland 21201

Store Hours:
Monday-Saturday
12:30pm-6:30pm

Contact: Donna Jenkins
Phone: 410-539-2817

Vintage & local designer clothing,
vast array of sterling silver
imported from Nepal, Mexico &
Indonesia
Accepts cash & credit cards

Store Policy: Buy, sell or trade

- - - - - - - - - - - - -
Present this coupon
at
The Zone
813 N. Charles Street
Baltimore, Maryland & save
20% off all vintage apparel
Expiration Date: 12/31/99
- - - - - - - - - - - - -

Vogue Revisited
4002 Roland Avenue
Baltimore, Maryland 21211

Store Hours:
Monday, Wednesday & Friday
11am-5:30pm
Tuesday & Thursday
11am-6:30pm
Saturday 10am-5pm

Contact: Chris Anderson
Phone: 410-235-4140

Women's clothing & accessories
Accepts cash, Visa & Mastercard

Consignment Policy:
50/50 split
Items consigned for 90 days
After 30 days items are marked
down 20% & 50% after 60 days

Bel Air

Country Britches
2111 Conowingo Road
Bel Air, Maryland 21014

Store Hours:
Monday-Saturday 10am-4pm
Thursday 10am-7pm

Phone: 410-893-8552

Excellent quality new and nearly
new children & maternity
clothing, toys, books,
baby equipment, infant furniture,
handmade Amish wood furniture,
handmade children's clothing,
American doll furniture &
clothing, candles, handmade
jewelry, crafts and much more!
Accepts cash & checks

Store Specials: Lay-a-way
available & call for current sales

& discounts

Bethesda

Second Chance
7702 Woodmont Ave.
Bethesda, Maryland 20814

Store Hours:
Tuesday-Saturday 10am-6pm
Sunday 12pm-4pm
Monday 12pm-5pm

Contact: Tobe Kingsley &
Charlotte Kingsley
Phone: 301-652-6606
e-mail: cybermaxed@aol.com

Designer clothing & accessories
for women. Labels such as
Chanel, Donna Karan, Escada &
more!
Accepts: cash, Mastercard, Visa &
American Express

Consignment Policy:
Call for an appointment
Items must be designer or better
label, in-style & in good condition

Established over twenty years ago,
Second Chance is well known for
designer label merchandise at
great prices.

Frederick

M & S Consignments & Gifts
10 Hillcrest Drive
Frederick, Maryland 21703

Store Hours:
Tuesday-Friday 9am-4pm
Saturday 9:30am-5pm
Phone & Fax: 301-846-4227

Clothing for the entire family,
bridal gowns, prom gowns &

costume jewelry

Consignment Policy:
50/50 split
Items consigned for 30 days

Store Specials: End of the season
bag sales

The Consignment Shop
15 East Patrick Street
Frederick, Maryland 21701

Store Hours:
Monday, Tuesday, Thursday &
Friday 10am-5pm
Saturday 10am-6pm & Sunday
12pm-6pm

Phone: 301-695-9674

Antiques, beautiful decorative art,
architectural & garden items &
jewelry

Vast array of merchandise from
over two hundred consignors!

Kensington

A.B.'s Consignment &
Collectibles
3734 Howard Avenue
Kensington, Maryland 20895

Store Hours:
Tuesday-Saturday 10am-6pm
Sunday 12pm-5pm

Phone: 301-946-9646

Excellent quality china, crystal,
silver & knick-knacks

Consignment Policy:
50/50 split
Items are consigned for 90 days

As Kids Grow Consignments
10303 Kensington Parkway
Kensington, Maryland 20895

Store Hours:
Tuesday-Friday 9:30am-4:30pm
& Saturday 10am-5pm

Phone: 301-933-1152

Clothing for children sizes
newborn to 16, preteen &
maternity clothing, furniture,
toys & infant accessories

Consignment Policy:
Consignments accepted daily

Store Specials: After 60 days
items are reduced 50%

Specializing in excellent prices &
friendly service.

Kensington Caboose
10508 Connecticut Avenue
Kensington, Maryland 20895

Store Hours:
Monday-Friday 9am-5pm
Sunday 12pm-5pm
Check for special summer &
holiday hours

Phone: 301-929-0178

Children's clothing, toys, books &
baby equipment

Consignment Policy:
An appointment is necessary
50/50 split

Store Specials: Half price sales

at the end of each month

Sunflowers Consignment
Boutique
10307 Kensington Parkway
Kensington, Maryland 20895

Store Hours:
Monday-Friday 9:30am-4:30pm
& Saturday 10am-5pm

Phone: 301-946-6721

Women's designer clothing &
accessories

Consignment Policy:
50/50 split
Items are consigned for 60 days

Store Specials: $5.00 dollar bag
sale

Laurel

RePeats Consignment
Super Store
13919 Baltimore Avenue #9
Laurel, Maryland 20707

Store Hours:
Monday-Friday 10am-7pm
Saturday 10am-6pm & Sunday
12pm-5pm

Phone: 301-604-2400
e-mail:
michael.goldstein&mcione.com
Web site: www.repeats.com

Clothing for the entire family,
home furnishings, antiques,
collectible computers, jewelry &
much more!

Consignment Policy:
50/50 split
Items are consigned for 60 days

Maryland

Rockville

Carousel Consignments, Inc.
12168 Nebel Street
Rockville, Maryland 20852

Store Hours:
Monday-Saturday 10am-6pm

Phone: 301-230-1300
Fax: 301-230-1970

Women's designer clothing,
jewelry, accessories, furs &
collectibles

Consignment Policy: Items
consigned for 90 days
50/50 split

Established in 1993, Carousel
Consignments is an upscale shop
offering a vast array of designer
labels from the traditional to the
unique. Many items with original
tags may be found here.

Consignment Furniture
Gallery
11722 Nicholson Lane
Rockville, Maryland 20852

Store Hours:
Tuesday, Wednesday, Friday &
& Saturday 10am-6pm
Thursday 10am-8:30pm

Sunday 12pm-5pm
Closed on Monday except on
holidays
Phone: 301-770-4402

Excellent quality furniture &
decorative accessories

Severna Park

Mary's Designer
Resale Boutique
554 B & A Boulevard
Severna Park, Maryland
21146

Store Hours:
Monday-Friday 10:30am-7pm
Saturday 10am-6pm
Sunday 12pm-5pm

Contact: Mary Feeley
Phone: 410-647-1142
Toll Free: 1-800-293-3910 to
order a fantastic find
Fax: 410-647-0232
Website: www.marys.com

Beautiful collection of new &
previously owned contemporary
business & casual apparel, wedding
gowns, antique & estate jewelry
& one of a kind keepsakes &
vintage fashions

Consignment Policy:
50/50 split
Items consigned for 60 days

Store Specials: Personal shopping,
expert alterations & personal
closet audits available.
Free gift packing, gift registry &
gift certificates available & Mary's
ships worldwide!

Timonium

Clearing House Ltd.
200 W. Padonia Road
Timonium, Maryland 21093

Store Hours:
Tuesday-Saturday 10am-5pm
Sunday 12pm-4pm

Phone: 410-561-4546

Fabulous home furnishings &
accessories
Accepts cash, checks, Mastercard,
Visa & Discover

Consignment Policy: Consignor
receives 2/3 of the selling price
Items reduced 15% every 30 days

The Clearing House was named
"Baltimore's Best Pick"1997 in
Baltimore Magazine.

Towson

Once Again Boutique, Inc.
501 York Road
Towson, Maryland 21204

Store Hours:
Monday-Saturday 10am-6pm
Closed on Mondays after July 4th
until the third week of August

Contact: Bernyce Brothers
Phone: 410-337-7174

Women's designer clothing for all
occasions & accessories

Consignment Policy: 50/50 split

Woodbine

Hannah's Child
Consignment Boutique
The Woodbine Shopping
Center
7627 Woodbine Road
Woodbine, Maryland 21797

Store Hours:
Monday, Tuesday & Saturday
10am-6pm
Friday 5pm-8pm

Phone: 410-549-4755

Maternity & children's clothing,
nursery furniture & equipment,
toys & books
Accepts cash & checks

Consignment Policy:
50/50 split

Present this coupon at
Hannah's Child
Consignment Boutique
7627 Woodbine Road
Woodbine, Maryland
& save 10% off any
purchase of $10.00 or more

Expiration Date: 12/31/99

Massachusetts

Acton

Ms. To Maternity
170 Great Road
Rte. 2A
Acton, Massachusetts 01720

Store Hours:
Monday-Saturday 10am-6pm
Thursday until 7pm
Sunday 1pm-5pm

Phone: 978-266-9939

Excellent quality women's career
& casual clothing & maternity
Accepts cash, Visa & Mastercard

Consignment Policy:
No appointment needed to
consign merchandise
55/45 split

Tables To Teapots, Distinctive
Furniture and Accessories on
Consignment, Inc.
452 Great Road (Rt. 2A)
Acton, Massachusetts 01720

Store Hours:
Tuesday, Wednesday & Friday
10am-6pm, Thursday 10am-7pm,
Saturday 10am-5pm
Sunday 12pm-5pm

Phone: 978-266-1115

Fine furniture-contemporary to
antique and home accessories,
china, crystal/stemware, flatware,
kitchen accessories, collectibles,
lamps, small appliances, books,
jewelry, linens, CD's, VCR's, audio
tapes and much more
Accepts cash, in state checks,
Mastercard & Visa

Consignment Policy:

Consignor receives 60% of the
selling price for the item
Items consigned for 90 days
Consignment by appointment or
may be dropped off

Store Specials: In December at the
Junior Citizens Sale, children 16 &
under receive a 10% discount

Tables To Teapots offers 5000
square feet of excellent quality
merchandise!

Ashland

Two-Way Boutique
61 Pond Street
Ashland, Massachusetts
01721

Store Hours:
Tuesday, Wednesday, Friday &
Saturday 10am-5pm
Thursday 10am-8pm

Contact: Joanne Kaufman
Phone: 508-872-5731

Upscale clothing new & gently
used clothing for women &
accessories

Consignment Policy:
50/50 split
Store Specials: Frequent buyer
cards

Save 10% off an item
when this coupon is presented
at *Two-Way Boutique*
61 Pond Street
Ashland, Massachusetts

Expiration Date: 12/31/99

Auburn

Consigning Women
850 Southbridge Street
West Side Plaza
Auburn, Massachusetts 01501

Store Hours:
Monday, Tuesday, Thursday &
Friday 10am-6pm
Wednesday 10am-7pm
Saturday 10am-3pm

Phone: 508-832-9005

Quality clothing for women &
children, jewelry, small furniture,
baby & household items

Consignment Policy: 50/50 split
Items are consigned for 60 days

Boston

Boomerangs
60 Canal Street
Boston, Massachusetts 02114

Store Hours:
Monday-Friday 11am-6:30pm
Saturday 10am-5pm
Sunday 12pm-5pm

Phone: 617-450-1500
e-mail: boomerangs@aac.org
Website: http://www.aac.org/
support/boomer/boomer.htm

A great variety of high quality
"previously owned" merchandise
at bargain prices!

Store Policy: Donations welcome

All proceeds benefit the AIDS
Action Committee's programs for
AIDS prevention, care &
advocacy.

The Closet Upstairs
223 Newbury Street
Boston, Massachusetts 02116

Store Hours:
Monday-Saturday 11am-6pm
Sunday 12pm-6pm

Phone: 617-267-5757

Vintage & funky clothing
Accepts cash, checks, Mastercard,
Visa & Discover

Consignment Policy:
Consignor receives 45%

Chic Repeats
117 Newbury Street
Boston, Massachusetts 02116

Store Hours:
Monday-Friday 10am-6pm
Thursday 10am-8pm
Saturday 10am-6pm
Sunday 12pm-8pm

Phone: 617-536-8580

Women's designer clothing &
accessories

Consignment Policy: 50/50 split
Items consigned for 60 days

Brockton

Amvets Thrift Store
189 Oak Street
Brockton, Massachusetts
02401

Store Hours:
Monday-Saturday 9am-6pm
Sunday 12pm-6pm

Phone: 508-580-2973
General merchandise & bric-a-brac

Massachusetts

Store Policy: Donations welcome

Brookline

Beth Israel Deaconess Thrift Shop
25 Harvard Street
Brookline, Massachusetts
02146

Store Hours:
Monday-Saturday 10am-5:30pm
Wednesday & Saturday 10am-4pm
for donation drop off

Phone: 617-566-7016

All inclusive department store selections including small appliances & electronic equipment
Accepts cash, Mastercard & Visa

Store Policy: Donations welcome

Store Specials: Daily $1.00 clothing, three books for $1.00 & 10% off your purchase for first time customers

```
Present this coupon at
Friends of Beth Israel
Deaconess Thrift Shop
25 Harvard Street
Brookline, Massachusetts
& save 10% off one item
for first time customers only

Expiration Date: 12/31/99
```

Silk Road Consignerie
1382 Beacon Street
Brookline, Massachusetts
02146

Store Hours:
Monday-Saturday 11am-6pm,
Thursday until 7pm & Sunday 12pm-5pm

Contact: Gail Mauriello
Phone: 617-739-3399

Quality pre-owned designer and better clothing

Cambridge

Christ Church Thrift Shop
17 Farwell Place
Harvard Square
Cambridge, Massachusetts
02138

Store Hours:
Tuesday, Wednesday, Thursday 10am-4pm
Saturday 11:30am-2:30pm

Clothing, household items, bric-a-brac & lots of great treasures
Accepts cash & checks

Thrift Policy: Donations welcome and appreciated

Great Eastern Trading Company
49 River Street
Cambridge, Massachusetts
02139

Store Hours:
Monday-Friday 12pm-7pm
Saturday 11am-6pm
Sunday 1pm-5pm

Phone: 617-354-5279
Unique vintage clothing for men & women, jewelry, accessories, lamps & furniture
Accepts cash, checks, Visa, Mastercard & Discover

Store Specials: Merchandise is marked down after one month

Oona's
Experienced Clothing
1210 Mass. Ave.
Cambridge, Massachusetts
02138

Store Hours: Monday-Friday
10am-7pm & Sunday 12pm-6pm

Phone: 617-491-2654

Established in 1972, Oona's carries vintage clothing circa 1920 to the 1970's
Accepts cash & credit cards

The Garment District
200 Broadway
Cambridge, Massachusetts
02139

Store Hours:
Monday-Friday & Sunday
11am-7pm
Saturday 9am-7pm

Phone: 617-876-5230
Fax: 617-547-8477
e-mail: webslacker@garment-district.com
Web site: www.garment-district.com

Large selection of clothing for men & women including vintage 60's, 70's & 80's, contemporary, jeans, cords, shoes, hats, seasonal clothing, accessories, jewelry, boa's, manic panic makeup, records, CD's's & much more!

Consignment Policy:
50/50 split
Clothing accepted by appointment only

Store Specials: Discount section-clothing, bric-a-brac & more are sold by the pound

For over thirteen years, The Garment District has been offering a vast array of merchandise for sale at fantastic prices! "You must see it to believe it!"

Fall River

Once Is Not Enough
234 Stafford Road
Fall River, Massachusetts
02721

Store Hours:
Tuesday-Saturday 10am-4pm
Clothing for women & children & accessories
Accepts cash & checks

Consignment Policy: Items are consigned for eight weeks

25% markdown after four weeks

Store Specials: Daily discounts of 25% to 50% off select items & $1.00 rack

---

Present this coupon at
Once Is Not Enough
234 Stafford Road
Fall River, Massachusetts &
save 25% off any item

Expiration Date: 12/31/99

Feeding Hills

Trunk 'N Attic
1325 Springfield Street
Feeding Hills, Massachusetts
01030

Store Hours:
Monday & Saturday 10am-7pm
Tuesday, Wednesday & Friday
10am-5:30pm
Thursday 10am-7:30pm

Designer label clothing for women, jewelry, designer handbags, scarfs & fine jewelry Accepts cash, checks with the proper ID, Mastercard, Visa, Discover & American Express

Store Specials:
Clearance corner & twice-a-year major clearance sales, Wish list

Trunk 'N Attic offers fashion advice including skin care & cosmetic consultations.

Member of the National Associa-

tion of Resale & Thrift Shops

Framingham

CeCe's Maternity Resale
419 Worcester Road
Rt. 9 West
Framingham, Massachusetts
01701

Store Hours:
Tuesday, Thursday, Friday
Saturday 10am-5pm &
Wednesday 11am-5pm

Women's maternity clothing

Consignment Policy: Items consigned for 90 days

Gloucester

Cape Ann Gift Shop
70 Middle Street
Gloucester, Massachusetts
01930

Store Hours:
Tuesday-Friday 10am-2pm

Phone: 508-283-2767

Clothing for the entire family & bric-a-brac

Consignment Policy: 50/50 split

Hingham

Children's Corner
Consignment Shop
24 North Street
Hingham, Massachusetts
02043

Store Hours:
Monday-Friday 10am-5pm
Saturday 11am-4pm

Contact: Mary Flaherty
Phone: 781-740-8135
e-mail: ccconsign@aol.com

Children's clothing from infant to
size 14, maternity, toys, juvenile
furniture and equipment & new
books for children
Accepts cash, checks, Visa,
Mastercard

Consignment Policy:
Items consigned for 60 days
Automatic markdowns on
children's clothing
Equipment is purchased outright

Store Specials: Children's clothing
marked down 25% after 30 days
& 50% after 60 days

Hyannis

**Alchemy and Lace Bridal
Consignments
59 Center Street
Hyannis, Massachusetts
02601**

Store Hours:
Tuesday, Wednesday, Friday &
Saturday 11am-5pm
Thursday 11am-7pm

Phone: 508-771-1166

Bridal & formal wear

Consignment Policy: 50/50 split
Items consigned for 60 days

Lexington

The Acorn Shop

**8 Muzzey Street
Lexington, Massachusetts
02173**

Store Hours:
Monday-Saturday 11am-5pm

Phone: 781-861-9646

Women's better label clothing &
accessories
Accepts cash & checks

Store Policy: Items bought
outright

Store Specials: Discounts offered
at the end of each season

Marion

**Elegance Renewed
3 Wells Road
Marion, Massachusetts 02738**

Store Hours:
Tuesday-Friday 10am-4pm
Saturday 10am-3pm

Phone: 508-748-3166

Upscale clothing for women &
children

Consignment Policy: Consignments accepted Tuesday-Thursday
10am-12pm by appointment

Millbury

**Blue Moon Enterprises
26 Main Street
Millbury, Massachusetts
01527**

Store Hours:

Monday-Friday 9am-5pm
Wednesday & Thursday until 6pm
Saturday 9am-3pm

Contact: Loretta Young
Phone: 508-865-8615

Vintage to modern clothing for
women, men & children, furniture,
household items, collectibles,
antiques, jewelry, baby
furniture, toys & costumes for
kids

Located in the quaint town of
Millbury, Massachusetts the shop
has new arrivals daily!!

Natick

Charitable Heart
691 Worcester Road
Natick Massachusetts 01760

Store Hours:
Monday-Saturday 9:30am-5:30pm
Sunday 1pm-5pm

Contact: Lee O'Neil
Phone: 508-655-2460

Clothing for the entire family,
vintage wear, furniture,
housewares, collectibles, antiques,
jewelry & much more!
Accepts cash & checks

Store Policy: Donations welcome

Store Specials: Weekly specials

Present this coupon at
Charitable Heart
691 Worcester Road
Natick, Massachusetts
& save 20% off furniture
or clothing

Expiration Date: 12/31/99

The Peanut Gallery
45 South Main Street
Natick, Massachusetts 01701

Store Hours:
Monday-Saturday 10:30am-5pm

Contact: Joan McMahon
Phone: 508-655-9440

Brand name maternity &
children's fashions, baby
equipment, toys & novelty items

Consignment Policy:
Consignments accepted by
appointment only
50/50 split
Items consigned for 90 days
Items reduced 25% after 60 days
& 50% after 90 days

Well-known for their great
merchandise, *The Peanut Gallery*
has been featured in *"Mr Cheaps
Boston"* & was voted
"Best of MetroWest" by the
Middlesex News & winner of the
"1996 Readers Choice Award" by
Tab Newspaper.

Norwell

Beach Plums
293 Washington Street
Norwell, Massachusetts 02061

Store Hours:
Sunday & Monday 12pm-6pm
Tuesday & Saturday 10am-6pm
Wednesday & Friday 10am-7pm
Thursday 10am-9pm

Phone: 781-659-0561
Contact: Susan Johnson

Women's & men's clothing,
jewelry & accessories
Accepts cash, personal checks &
all major credit cards

Consignment Policy:
50/50 split

Store Specials: $5.00 room

Salem

Samantha's
Consignment Boutique
205 Essex Street
Salem, Massachusetts 01970

Store Hours:
Monday-Saturday 10am-5pm
Sunday 11am-4pm

Phone & Fax: 978-745-7909
Website: http://members.aol.com/
samssalem/samanthas.html

Excellent quality clothing for
women & men, jewelry &
accessories. Visit Samatha's
Costume Shop located next
to the consignment boutique.
Over three hundred original
costumes for sale & rental. The
costume shop is open, Tuesday-
Saturday11am-5pm.

Sandwich

The Children's Gallery
4 Merchant Square
Sandwich, Massachusetts
02561

Store Hours:
Monday-Saturday 10am-5pm

Phone: 508-833-9129

Clothing for children, accessories
& furniture

South Easton

Barbara's
Consignment Boutique
49 Belmont Street
South Easton, Massachusetts
02375

Store Hours:
Wednesday-Saturday 10am-5pm

Contact: Barbara Kempf
Phone: 508-238-1513

Designer clothing for women,
accessories & jewelry
Accepts cash, checks, Visa &

Massachusetts

Mastercard

Consignment Policy:
50/50 split

Store Specials: Weekly markdowns
on certain items

This coupon entitles
the bearer to save 20%
off any one item
at
*Barbara's Consignment
Boutique*
49 Belmont Street
South Easton Massachusetts

Expiration Date: 12/31/99

Springfield

The Kiddie Kloset
392 Dickinson Street
Springfield, Massachusetts
01108

Store Hours:
Monday-Saturday 10am-5pm
Sunday 12pm-4pm

Contact: Andrea Martin
Phone: 413-788-4395

Discounted new & gently used
children's clothing, toys & baby
equipment
Accepts cash, checks, Mastercard,
& Visa

Store Policy: Items bought
outright at Kiddie Kloset or
at your door

Over 4000 square feet of great
merchandise!

Sturbridge

Now & Again
Consignment Boutique
538 Main Street
Sturbridge, Massachusetts
01518

Store Hours:
Monday, Wednesday, Thursday,
Friday, Saturday & Sunday
11am-6pm

Phone: 508-347-1955

Casual & career apparel for
women

Consignment Policy: 50/50 split

Sudbury

Classic Consignment
730 Boston Post Road
Sudbury, Massachusetts
01776

Store Hours:
Tuesday-Saturday 10am-5pm
Sunday 12pm-5pm

Contact: Helene Guski &
DJ Layhe
Phone: 978-443-9149
e-mail:treaspedlr@aol.com

Quality furniture & decorative
accessories from antique to
contemporary, fine jewelry &
vintage linen
Accepts cash, personal checks,
Visa & Mastercard

Consignment Policy:
Consignments accepted by
appointment only

Consignor receives 60%
Items are consigned for 90 days
Items are reduced 10% at 30 days
& 15% at 60 days

Store Specials: Estate sales

Vineyard Haven

Hellie's Closet
3 Centre Street
Vineyard Haven,
Massachusetts 02568

Located on the quaint island of
Martha's Vineyard

Store Hours: Summer hours:
Monday-Saturday 10:30am-5pm
& Sunday 11am-4pm
Spring & Winter hours:
Wednesday-Saturday 11am-5pm

Contact: Helen Neumann
Phone: 508-693-5828
e-mail: hellie@vineyard.net

Apparel for women & children,
accessories including jewelry,
shoes, handbags, wedding & party
dresses. Hellie's Closet is the only
exclusive consignment shop on
the Vineyard. All items are
offered at great prices!

Consignment Policy: Items
reduced 25% after 30 days & 50%
after 60 days

Present this coupon at
Hellie's Closet
3 Centre Street
Vineyard Haven, Massachusetts
& save 10% off any purchase

Expiration Date: 12/31/99

Watertown

The Laughing Rainbow
222 Waverley Ave.
Watertown, Massachusetts
02172

Store Hours:
Monday, Wednesday & Friday
9am-6pm
Tuesday & Thursday 10am-7pm
& Sunday 12pm-6pm

Phone: 617-924-4555
e-mail:
JEDIRRAN@MCIONE.COM

Beautiful array of new & gently
used children's clothing, toys,
furniture & accessories
Accepts cash & checks

Consignment Policy:
Items consigned by appointment
only
Consignor paid with a store credit
or cash

Store Specials: Half price rack,
Visit the information center
for the latest happenings &
events

Present this coupon at
The Laughing Rainbow
222 Waverley Ave.
Watertown, Massachussetts
& save 25% off a clothing
purchase

Expiration Date: 12/31/99

119

Massachusetts

Webster

Kattie's Korner
105 School Street
Webster, Massachusetts
01570

Store Hours:
Tuesday, Wednesday, Thursday
& Friday 10am-4pm
Saturday 10am-2pm
Accepts cash & local checks

Women's clothing & accessories.
A full service hair salon is on the
premises.

Consignment Policy:
50/50 split

West Concord

Reflections
Consignment Shop
101 Commonwealth Avenue
W. Concord, Massachusetts
01742

Store Hours:
Monday-Saturday 9:30am-5:30pm
& Thursday 9:30am-8pm
Consignment Hours: Monday-
Friday 10am-3pm & Thursday
10am-7pm during the first two
weeks of the month

Quality clothing & accessories
for women
Accepts cash, checks, Mastercard
& Visa

Consignment Policy:
50/50 split
Items are discounted 25% after
four weeks & 50% after seven
weeks

Ann Arbor

Klothes Kloset
2410 E. Stadium Blvd.
Ann Arbor, Michigan 48104

Store Hours:
Monday-Friday 10am-6pm
Saturday 10am-4pm

Phone: 313-971-6211

Women's clothing & accessories

Consignment Policy: 50/50 split
Items are consigned for 60 days

Birmingham

Suzann's Emporium
33255 Woodward Ave
Birmingham, Michigan 48009

Store Hours:
Monday-Saturday 11am-6pm
Special hours by appointment

Phone: 248-594-4545

New & gently used casual, career,
glitz & glamour designer clothing
for women, accessories & furs
Accepts cash, checks & all major
credit cards

Consignment Policy:
Items consigned for 90 days

Present this coupon at
Suzann's Emporium
3325 Woodward Ave
Birmingham, Michigan
and receive 10% off one item
(coupon cannot be used for 50% off items)
Expiration Date: 12/31/99

Detroit

Peek-A-Boo
19431 Livernois
(The Avenue of Fashion)
Detroit, Michigan 48221

Store Hours:
Monday, Tuesday, Thursday,
Friday & Saturday 10am-6pm

Contact: Johnnie R. Miller
Phone: 313-863-2323

Children's clothing sizes 0-16,
educational books, toys, baby
shower gifts & more!
Accepts cash, Visa, Mastercard &
American Express

Consignment Policy: 50/50 split

Store Specials: Foster mother's
receive a 10% discount

Grand Rapids

Boutique Elan
717 Bagley S.E.
Grand Rapids, Michigan
49506

Store Hours:
Monday-Friday 12am-6pm
Wednesday until 8pm
Saturday 10am-5pm

Phone: 616-454-5355

Designer clothing for men &
women & accessories

Consignment Policy: Consignor
receives 45%

Store Specials: Personal shopping
services, private shopping parties
& corporate account programs

Good-As-New
5280 Northland Drive N.E.
Grand Rapids, Michigan
49505

Store Hours:
Monday-Friday 10am-6pm
Saturday 10am-5pm

Phone: 616-363-6622

Designer clothing for women &
children & accessories

Consignment Policy:
Items are consigned for 60 days

Grosse Point

Samira's Family Fashion of
Grosse Point
21027 Mack Ave
Grosse Point, Michigan 48236

Store Hours:
Monday-Saturday 10am-5pm
Thursday 10am-7pm

Contact: Samira Fayad
Phone & Fax: 313-886-5043

Top designer clothing for women,
men & children sizes 2-26, handbags, shoes, accessories & furs.
Labels such DKNY, Dior, St. John
& more!
Accepts cash & credit cards

Consignment Policy:
Items consigned by appointment
only on Thursdays
50/50 split
Items consigned for 90 days

Store Specials: Gift certificates
available & customer birthday
specials

Samira's is an elegant consignment
boutique offering excellent quality
service and upscale clothing at
great prices!

Jackson

Bougain Villea
1228 Greenwood
Jackson, Michigan 49203

Store Hours:
Monday-Friday 10am-5pm
Saturday 10am-3pm

Phone: 517-788-6279

Clothing for the entire family &
accessories

Consignment Policy: 50/50 split
Items are consigned for 90 days

Keego Harbor

Bloomfield Keego Resale
3425 Orchard Lake Road
Keego Harbor, Michigan
48320

Store Hours: Monday, Tuesday,
Wednesday, Friday & Saturday
10am-5pm
Thursday 10am-7pm

Phone: 248-681-5424

Women's clothing
Accepts cash, checks, Visa &
Mastercard

Store Specials: Monthly $1.00
sale

Just Plum $mart Women's

Boutique & Kinderware
Resale Boutique
2141 Cass Lake Road
Keego Harbor, Michigan 48323

Store Hours:
Monday-Friday 10am-6pm
Saturday 10am-4pm
Phone: 248-682-1866

Kinderware carries new & gently
used children's clothing. Just Plum
$mart features women's clothing
& maternity wear.

Present this coupon at
Kinderware & Just Plum $mart
2141 Cass Lake Road
Keego Harbor, Michigan
& save 10% off a second
purchase over $25.00

Expiration Date: 12/31/99

Lake Orion

2nd Hand Ann's
678 S. Lapeer Road
Lake Orion, Michigan 46382

Store Hours: Tuesday, Wednesday
& Thursday 10am-6pm, Friday
11am-6pm & Saturday 10am-3pm

Contact: Ann Swanson
Phone: 248-814-9631

Large variety of clothing for men,
women and children (to size 6x
for children) and more
Accepts cash or personal checks
All sales are final

Consignment Policy: Some items
purchased outright or 60/40 split

Store Specials: Seasonal and
monthly sales

Livonia

Reruns
Consignment Boutique
33666 Five Mile Road
Livonia, Michigan 48154

Store Hours:
Monday, Wednesday & Friday
10am-6pm
Tuesday & Thursday 10am-7pm
Saturday 10am-4pm

Contact: Nancy Reaume
Phone: 734-522-2868

Excellent quality career, casual &
after-five designer clothing for
women, men & children,
accessories, jewelry, furs &
vintage items

Consignment Policy:
50/50 split
Items consigned for 60 days

Store Specials:
Year round discounts from
25% to 50%
Preferred customer punch card

Reruns has been voted the
number one shop by bus
tour shoppers!

Member of The National
Association of Resale & Thrift
Shops

Northville

Baby Baby
153 E. Main Street
Northville, Michigan 48167

Store Hours:
Monday-Saturday 10am-6pm

Phone: 248-347-2229

Clothing for children including
teens, maternity wear & baby
equipment
Accepts cash, checks, Visa,
Mastercard & Discover

Consignment Policy:
50/50 split for items under $30.00

60% for items over $30.00

Store Specials: Consignors receive
10% off all merchandise

Piconning

Morgan's Bargain Barn
300 N. Huron
Piconning, Michigan 48650

Store Hours:
Monday-Saturday 9am-6pm
Sunday 10am-5pm

Phone: 517-879-2873

Bric-a-brac

Rochester

Heart O The Hills
Resale Shop
402 East Street
Rochester, Michigan 48307

Store Hours:

Tuesday & Wednesday 12pm-5pm
Thursday, Friday & Saturday
10am-3:30pm

Contact: Gertrude Riethmeier
Phone: 810-651-4010

Women's clothing, jewelry,
household items, small furniture
& more!
Accepts cash & checks

Store Specials: Clothing discounted after one month &
household items after six months

Shelby Twsp

Elite Repeat Resale
45553 Mound Road N. of M59
Shelby Twsp., Michigan 48317

Store Hours:
Tuesday & Thursday 11am-7pm
Wednesday, Friday & Saturday
11am-5pm

Phone: 810-997-0331
Contact: Marega DeLizio

Top brand women's casual,
professional and after-five
apparel, jewelry, shoes &
accessories, men's designer casual
and some domestic items.
Featuring brands from Express,
Dayton-Hudson, Jacobens, Lord &
Taylor, Gantos & The Limited &
more. New clothing too!
Accepts cash, checks, Visa &
Mastercard

Consignment Policy:
50/50 split
$5.00 fee per anniversary year to
consign items
Items consigned for 60-75 days

Elite Repeat has been offering stylish better made clothing at great bargain prices for over twenty years!

Southgate

Molly's Closet
15040 Fort Street
Southgate, Michigan 48195

Store Hours:
Monday-Saturday 10am-5pm
First Sunday of each month
12pm-4pm

Contact: Ann Richardson
Phone: 313-282-3782

Women's clothing & accessories
Accepts cash, checks, Mastercard
& Visa

Store Specials: On-going sales

Waterford

Kelley's Consignments
4260 Dixie Highway
Waterford, Michigan 48329

Store Hours:
Monday, Wednesday & Friday
10am-5pm
Thursday 10am-7pm & Saturday
10am-3pm

Contact: Laura Kelley
Phone: 248-674-8232

Clothing for women, men &
children & household items

Present this coupon at
Kelley's Consignments
4260 Dixie Highway
Waterford, Michigan
& receive 10% off
any purchase

Expiration date: 12/31/99

Westland

Nicole's Revival Designer
Resale Clothier
958 N. Newburgh Road
Westland, Michigan 48185

Located N. of Cherryhill-
S. of Ford

Store Hours:
Monday, Tuesday & Friday
10am-6pm
Wednesday 1pm-6pm
Thursday 11am-7pm
Saturday 10am-5pm

Contact: Nicole Christ
Phone: 734-729-1234
Fax: 734-729-5678
e-mail: sales@nicolesrevival.com
Web site: www.nicolesrevival.com
Web shopping available!

Over 3000 square feet of fine quality couture apparel such as Armani, Chanel, Escada to items from the Gap for men, women & children. Many items featured have been worn by models in the Detroit Auto Show and worldwide! A vast array of fabulous accessories. The largest selection of upscale merchandise for men in the state of Michigan.

Michigan

Accepts all major credit cards

Store Policy: Items purchased outright

Store Specials:
Join the mailing list to receive a free quarterly newsletter "Smart Shopper Tidings" with the latest information on events & specials at Nicole's Revival.
Sponsors New York style fashion shows. Fun resale bus tours of stores in Michigan & European shopping tours.
Resale party nights!
Spend $500.00 in one shopping visit at Nicole's Revival & receive door to door limo service as a thank you!

Nicole Christ owner of Nicole's Revival in Westland Michigan

Austin

Country Thrift & Gift Shop
Highway 218 South
Austin, Minnesota 55912

Store Hours:
Tuesday-Friday 1pm-5pm
Saturday 12:30pm-3pm

Clothing for the entire family,
household items & knick-knacks

Consignment Policy: 50/50 split
Items are consigned for 90 days

Burnsville

Second Edition
13765 Nicollet Ave South
Burnsville, Minnesota 55337

Store Hours:
Monday, Wednesday & Friday
10am-6pm
Tuesday & Thursday 10am-8pm
Saturday 10am-5pm
Sunday 12pm-5pm

Contact: Nancy McGlone
Phone: 612-898-1515

Clothing for men & women, bridal
& formal wear, maternity wear,
samples & gifts
Accepts Visa, Mastercard &
Discover

Consignment Policy: 50/50 split

Store Specials: On-going discounts

Cannon Falls

Char's Twice But Nice
105 North 4th Street
Cannon Falls, Minnesota
55009

Store Hours:
Tuesday-Friday 9am-5pm
Saturday 9am-4pm

Contact: Char Figg
Phone: 507-263-4090

Clothing for the entire family,
housewares, jewelry, antiques &
much more!
Accepts cash & checks

Consignment Policy:
40/60 split
Items consigned for 90 days

Store Specials: 25% to 50% off
select items daily

> Present this coupon at
> *Char's Twice But Nice*
> *105 North 4th Street*
> *Cannon Falls, Minnesota*
> & save 10% off an item
> (up to $5.00)
>
> Expiration Date: 12/31/99

Crystal

Repeat Boutique
3542 Douglas Drive North
Crystal, Minnesota 55422

Store Hours: Call for store hours

Phone: 612-533-8956

Women's designer label clothing & accessories

Consignment Policy:
50/50 split

Duluth

Lots For Tots
2910 West 3rd Street
Duluth, Minnesota 55806

Store Hours:
Monday-Thursday & Saturday
10:30am-5pm
Friday 10:30am-6pm

Phone: 218-624-1227

Second Location:

4921 Matterhorn Drive
Village Mall II
Duluth, Minnesota 55811

Store Hours:
Monday-Friday 10am-6pm
Saturday 10am-5pm

Phone: 218-722-2028

e-mail: ladybear@cp.duluth.mn.us

Resale children's clothing, toys, furniture, equipment & accessories, maternity items
Accepts cash & checks

Store Policy:
Items purchased outright

Store Specials:
Frequent Buyer Program
Boy's tuxedo rentals
& "Santa" rentals during Christmas.

Eden Prairie

Encore
An Upscale Designer
Consignment Boutique
8264 Commonwealth Drive
Eden Prairie, Minnesota
55344

Store Hours:
Monday, Tuesday, Wednesday &
& Friday 10am-6pm
Thursday 10am-8pm & Saturday
10am-4pm

Phone: 612-944-9290

Upscale designer clothing for women

Consignment Policy:
Items consigned for 90 days

Hackensack

Consignment Plus
Rte 1 Box 9E
Hackensack, Minnesota
56452

Store Hours: Tuesday-Saturday
9am-5pm-October 15-March 15
Saturday 10am-4pm

Phone: 218-675-6263

New & gently used sail boats, motor boats & more!

Moorhead

Center of Fashion
11 9th Street
South Moorhead, Minnesota
56560

Store Hours:
Monday-Friday 10am-6pm
Saturday 10:30am-4:30pm
(Summer until 2pm)

Contact: Kim Fischer
Phone: 218-236-6937

Women's clothing & accessories,
bridal gowns, formal wear, shoes
and much more!

Accepts cash, checks & credit
cards

Store Specials: One month lay-a-
way plan

This coupon entitles the
bearer to save 10% off
an item at
Center of Fashion
11 9th Street
Moorhead, Minnesota

Expiration Date: 12/31/99

New Hope

Down "on 42nd Ave."
7180 42nd Ave.
New, Hope, Minnesota 55427

Store Hours:
Monday, Friday & Saturday
10am-5pm
Tuesday, Wednesday & Thursday
10am-8pm
Sunday 12pm-4pm

Phone: 612-537-3374

Upscale designer fashions for
women & accessories

Consigment Policy: 50/50 split
Items consigned for 90 days

Value Village Thrift Store
4223 Winnetka Ave. N.
New Hope, Minnesota 55428

Store Hours:
Monday-Friday 9am-9pm
Saturday 9am-6pm
Sunday 12pm-6pm

Phone: 612-535-7972

Second Location:
6528 Penn Ave S
Richfield, Minnesota 55423

Phone: 612-866-9550

Great selection of retro & vintage
clothing & accessories, antiques &
collectibles

Store Policy: Donations welcome
during store hours

Store Specials: Seasonal tag sales

Richfield

Designer Wardrobe
6628 Penn Ave
Richfield, Minnesota 55423

Store Hours:
Monday-Friday 10am-6pm
Saturday 10am-5pm
Sunday 12pm-5pm

Contact: Sheree &
Dolores Swanson
Phone: 612-861-1460

Women's clothing
Accepts cash, checks, Visa &
Mastercard

Store Specials: Items reduced after 60 days

**Turn Style
Consignment Shops
Highland Shopping Center
Cleveland & Ford Parkway
Richfield, Minnesota 55423**
Phone: 612-690-3438

Other Locations:
**Southdale Square
Shopping Center
66th Street & Xerxes
Richfield, Minnesota 55423**
Phone: 612-798-0343

**Park Square
Shopping Center
Brooklyn Blvd. & Highway 81
Richfield, Minnesota 55423**
Phone: 612-315-4727

Store Hours
Monday-Friday 10am-8pm
Saturday 10am-6pm
Sunday 12pm-5pm

Outstanding quality designer clothing & accessories for men, women & children

Consignment Policy:
Appointment is necessary
Items must be in excellent condition, clean, pressed & on hangers
50/50 split
Items consigned for 90 days
Items reduced 50% after 60 days

St. Cloud

**Fashion Exchange
540 N 25th Ave
St. Cloud, Minnesota 56301**

Store Hours:

Monday-Friday 10am-6pm
Saturday 10am-5pm

Phone: 320-656-1525

Second Location:
**Fashion Exchange
Thomas Lake Center
1565 Cliff Road
Eagan, Minnesota 55122**

Store Hours:
Monday-Thursday 10am-8pm
Friday 10am-6pm
Saturday 10am-5pm
Sunday 12pm-5pm

Eagan: 612- 686-5177

Women's & children's clothing & accessories
Accepts cash & all credit cards

Consignment Policy:
Consignments accepted by appointment only

Store Specials: Frequent shopper cards

Cary

Cary Christian Center Shop
1 Cottonwood Street
PO Box 54
Cary, Mississippi 39054

Store Hours:
Monday-Saturday 9:30am-5pm

Phone: 601-873-4602

Clothing, furniture, household items

Gulfport

Re-Threads Quality
Consignment Res-Sale
1008 East Pass Road
Gulfport, Mississippi 39507

Store Hours:
Monday, Tuesday, Wednesday,
Friday & Saturday 10am-5pm
Thursday 10am-8:30pm
Sunday 1pm-5pm

Contact: Teena Richardson
Phone: 601-896-3850

Clothing for the entire family including including maternity, baby equipment, toys & name brand home furnishings

Consignment Policy: Consignor receives 40% of the selling price on most items; 67% on baby equipment

Store Specials:
On-going sale on clothing!
Items reduced 25% every 30 days

This coupon entitles the
bearer to save 10% off
a purchase at
Re-Threads
1008 East
Gulfport, Mississippi

Expiration Date: 12/31/99

Natchez

Four Korners
107 Jeff Davis Blvd.
Natchez, Mississippi 39210

Store Hours:
Monday-Saturday 10am-5pm

Phone: 601-445-6018

Clothing for the entire family sizes infants to 6x, maternity wear & more

Store Policy: Items purchased outright

Petal

Penny Pincher &
The Bookworm
920 Highway 11
Petal, Mississippi 39205

Store Hours:
Tuesday-Saturday 9am-5pm

Contact: Jo Doherty
Phone: 601-543-0297

Featuring new & gently used merchandise & a book exchange

Accepts cash, checks, Visa & Mastercard

Mississippi

Ridgeland

Kid's Kloset
554 Highway 51, Suite C
Ridgeland, Mississippi 39157

Store Hours:
Tuesday-Saturday 10am-5:30pm

Phone: 601-853-6930
Clothing for women & children
including maternity wear

Consignment Policy: 50/50 split
No appointment is neccessary to
consign merchandise

Southaven

Designer Exchange
775 Goodman Road Suite 23
Southaven, Mississippi 38671

Store Hours: Monday, Tuesday,
Wednesday & Friday 10am-6pm
Thursday 10am-7pm &
Saturday 10am-5pm

Contact: Cindy Williams
Phone: 601-349-2003

Resale clothing for junior &
misses, formal rentals for women

This coupon entitles the bearer
to save $10.00 off a purchase
of $40.00 or more at
Designer Exchange
775 Goodman Road Suite 23,
Southaven, Mississippi
(Coupon not valid with any other offers)
Expiration Date: 12/31/99

Starkville

Treasure Chest
Consignments
106 E. Main Street
Starkville, Mississippi 39759

Store Hours:
Monday-Saturday 10am-5:30pm

Phone: 601-324-0969

Gently used clothing for the entire
family & accessories

Consigment Policy: Consignor
receives 40%
Items are consigned for 90 days

Summit

Second Act
820 Robb Street
Summit, Mississippi 39666

Store Hours: Tuesday-Friday
10am-5pm, Saturday 10am-2pm

Phone: 601-276-9275

Clothing for the entire family &
formal wear

Consignment Policy: 50/50 split

Ballwin

Aunty's Attic
15260 Manchester Road
Ballwin, Missouri 63011

Store Hours:
Monday, Friday & Saturday
10am-5pm
Tuesday, Wednesday & Thursday
10am-8pm

Phone: 314-227-2279
Website: www.theclothestree.com/
shops/AuntysAttic/
Furniture, home accessories &
more

Consignment Policy: 50/50 split
Items are consigned for 60 days

DAV Thrift Shops

The DAV Thrift Shops are owned
and operated by the St. Louis
Chapter No. 1 Disabled Ameri-
cans.
All proceeds assist war disabled
veterans throughout the St. Louis,
Missouri area.
All shops are open Monday-
Saturday 10am-6:30pm & Sunday
11am-6:30pm.
Accepts cash, checks, Mastercard,
Visa & Discover.
The shops carry a great selection
of gently used clothing,
housewares, bric-a-brac, furniture,
antiques, collectibles and much
more!
Donations are welcome everyday
during store hours. All shops
feature daily tag sales, seasonal
clearances and other special sales.

Bridgeton

Best Value Thrift Store
11444 St. Charles Rock Road
Bridgeton, Missouri 63044
Phone: 314-298-2750

Hazelwood

Best Value Thrift Store
8780-A Pershall Road
Hazelwood, Missouri 63042
Phone: 314-522-9072

St. Louis

Veterans Village Thrift Store
3617 Delmar Avenue
St. Louis, Missouri 63108

Veterans Village Thrift Store
4236 Natural Bridge
St. Louis, Missouri 63115
Phone: 314-531-7454

Belton

Plus Size Consignment Shop
417 Main
Belton Missouri 64012

Store Hours:
Monday-Friday 10am-7pm
Saturday 10am-5pm

Contact: Robbie Williams
Phone: 816-322-1987

Upscale one of a kind plus
size clothing for women &
formal wear rental
Some new items too!

Consignment Policy:
Items consigned for 90 days
Consignor receives 40% of the
selling price for the item

133

Missouri

Cape Girardeau

Carol's Closet
1020 N. Kings Highway
Cape Girardeau, Missouri
63701

Store Hours:
Monday-Friday 10am-6pm
Saturday 10am-5pm

Phone: 573-335-7533

Clothing for the entire family &
accessories
Accepts cash, Visa, Mastercard,
American Express & Discover

Consignment Policy: 50/50 split

Store Specials: On-going half price
rack

Chesterfield

One More Time
55 Forum Center
Olive & 141
Chesterfield, Missouri 63017

Store Hours:
Monday-Thursday 10am-8pm
Friday & Saturday 10am-5pm

Phone: 314-878-0581

Clothing for women

Columbia

New Beginning
Consignment Clothing
7 South Tenth Street
Columbia, Missouri 65201

Store Hours:
Tuesday-Saturday 10am-5pm
Thursday 10am-6:30pm

Contact: Shannon Thompson
Phone: 573-449-5722
Web site:
www.theclothestree.com/shops/
NewBeginning

Excellent quality name brand
gently used clothing & accessories
for the entire family
Accepts cash, local checks,
Mastercard, Visa, Discover &
American Express

Consignment Policy:
Consignments accepted by
appointment
Consignor receives 40% to 45%
Items are consigned for three
months

Store Specials: Special 10%
discount card the month of your
birthday
After hours shopping parties!

Present this coupon at
New Beginning
Consignment Clothing
7 South Tenth Street
Columbia, Missouri
& save 10% off your total
purchase
Expiration Date: 12/31/99

Joplin

My Sister's Closet
524 Main Street
Joplin, Missouri 64804

Store Hours:
Tuesday-Friday 9:30am-5pm

Saturday 10am-4pm

Phone: 417-781-6311

Women's clothing & accessories

Kansas City

Act II, Inc For Men & Women
1507 West 47th Street
Kansas City, Missouri 64112

Store Hours:
Monday-Saturday 10am-5:30pm

Contact: Gloria Everhart
Phone: 816-531-7572

Upscale consignment clothing & accessories
Accepts cash, checks and all credit cards

Second Fiddle Thrift Shop
7140 Wornall Road
Kansas City, Missouri 64114

Store Hours:
Monday-Saturday 9am-5pm
Thursday 9am-7pm

Phone: 816-822-2285

Clothing for the entire family, small furniture, housewares, artwork, collectibles & more

Proceeds from the shop benefit the Kansas City Symphony.

Springfield

Fashion Revue Resale
Shoppe-Rental & Sales
723 N. Glenstone
Springfield, Missouri 65802

Store Hours:

Monday-Saturday 10am-6pm
Contact: Shirley Voelker
Phone: 417-862-0723

New & gently used casual clothing sizes 4 to 30, formal-wear, prom & party dresses, bridesmaid dresses and a great selection of current stylish bridal gowns
Accepts cash & checks

Consignment Policy: 50/50 split

Store Specials: Markdowns after 45 to 60 days
Lay-a-way plan
Gown rentals for bridesmaids and brides at very reasonable prices!

Present this coupon at
Fashion Revue Resale Shoppe
723 N. Glenstone
Springfield, Missouri
receive $5.00 off a $25.00
purchase or
$10.00 off a $50.00
purchase or
$20.00 off a $100.00 or more
purchase
Expiration Date: 12/31/99

St. Louis

Kotton Kandy
A Children's Resale Shop
13836 Manchester Road
St. Louis, Missouri 63011

Store Hours:
Monday, Tuesday, Thursday & Friday 10am-5pm

Phone: 314-394-1938

Clothing for children, maternity wear, baby equipment, tuxedo rentals for boys & more!

Consignment Policy:
Items are consigned for 90 days

Second Sitting Consignments
10404 Manchester Road
St. Louis, Missouri 63122

Store Hours:
Monday-Saturday 10am-5pm
Phone: 314-965-4949

Fine home furnishings
Accepts cash, checks, Visa & Mastercard

Consignment Policy: Consignments accepted by appointment only

Store Specials: Items discounted 10%-30%

The Velvet Rabbit Shop
3329 Lemay Ferry Road
63125 North of So. Co.
Shopping Center
St. Louis, Missouri 63125

Store Hours
Monday-Saturday 10am-5pm

Phone: 314-894-7349

Children's clothing, baby equipment, toys, books, videos & maternity wear
Accepts cash, checks, Mastercard, Visa, Discover
Consignment Policy: 50/50 split
An appointment is necessary to consign merchandise
Items are consigned for 90 days

Store Specials: End of the season tag sales

Upscale Resale
Warson Woods Shopping Center
9993A Manchester Road
St. Louis, Missouri 63122

Store Hours:
Monday, Tuesday, Friday & Saturday 10am-5pm
Wednesday & Thursday 10am-7pm

Better label clothing for women
Accepts cash, checks, Mastercard, Visa & Discover

Consignment Policy:
50/50 split
Items consigned for 60 days

Store Specials: End of the season tag sales

Belgrade

Sacks of Belgrade
31 E. Main
Belgrade, Montana 59714

Sacks of Bozeman
138 W. Mendenhall
Bozeman, Montana 59715

Store Hours:
Monday-Saturday 9:30am-6pm

Contact: Linda Gipp
Phone: 406-587-7283
Fax: 406-587-5056
e-mail: baglady@gomontana.com

Clothing for the entire family,
housewares, furniture, books,
jewelry, antiques, domestics &
collectibles
Accepts cash, checks, Visa &
Mastercard

Store Policy: Donations welcome

Store Specials:
Weekly drawings for $5.00 off a
purchase
Receive your dollar buck with a
purchase over $10.00
Weekly color tag sales offering
50% to 75% off select items
$1.00 bag every Friday &
Saturday

Proceeds benefit the Help Center,
a free crisis & counseling center
for those in need.

Missoula

Goodwill Industries of
Missoula
1020 North Avenue West
Missoula, Montana 59801

Store Hours:
Monday-Friday 9am-6:30pm
Saturday 10am-6pm
Sunday 12pm-5pm

Phone: 406-549-6969
Fax: 406-549-2166

Clothing for the entire family,
housewares, home furnishings,
jewelry & much more!

Store Policy: Donations welcome

Store Specials: Seniors &
University students receive a 10%
discount

Nebraska

Blair

Thrifty Kids
1670 Washington Street
Blair, Nebraska 68008

Store Hours
Monday-Friday 9am-5:30pm
Saturday 9am-3pm

Contact: Diane Carson
Phone: 402-426-9711

Children's clothing to size 14,
maternity, women's clothing &
infant furniture
Accepts cash

Consignment Policy: Items must
be clean, on hangers or folded
neatly

Store Specials: 10% discount to
consignors who spend their
consignment checks at the shop

Kearney

Fashion Encore
2217 First Avenue
Kearney, Nebraska 68847

Store Hours:
Monday-Saturday 9:30am-5pm
Thursday 9:30am-7pm

Phone: 308-234-3636

Clothing for the entire family

Consignment Policy: 50/50 split
Items are consigned for four
months

Store Specials: Daily discounts

Goodwill Industries

Goodwill Industries offer several
shopping locations throughout
Nebraska. Goodwill stores
carry a variety of gently used
clothing for the entire family,
housewares & furniture.
Donations are welcome and a
receipt for tax purposes is
provided. Proceeds from
the shop benefit programs for
those in need.

Goodwill
1820 North 6th Street
Beatrice, Nebraska 68310

Phone: 402-228-2660

Store Hours:
Monday-Wednesday, Friday &
Saturday 9am-5pm
Thursday 9am-7pm
Sunday 1pm-5pm

Goodwill
5500 South 56th Street
Suite #3
Lincoln, Nebraska 68516
Phone: 402-421-2669

Store Hours:
Monday-Friday 9am-9pm
Saturday 9am-6pm
Sunday 1pm-5pm

Goodwill
3910 North 27th Street
Lincoln, Nebraska 68521

Phone: 402-465-4663
Store Hours:
Monday-Thursday 8am-7pm
Friday & Saturday 8am-6pm
Sunday 12pm-6pm

Goodwill
1338 South Street
Lincoln, Nebraska 68502

Phone: 402-438-1109
Store Hours:
Monday-Thursday 8am-6pm
(Summer until 7pm)
Friday & Saturday 8am-5pm
(Summer until 6pm)
Sunday 12pm-5pm

Goodwill
4555 Vine Street
Lincoln, Nebraska 68503

Phone: 402-466-3223
Store Hours:
Monday-Friday 9am-9pm
Saturday 9am-6pm
Sunday 12pm-5pm

Goodwill
512 Grant Avenue
York, Nebraska 68467

Phone: 402-362-6206
Store Hours:
Monday-Friday 9am-6pm
Saturday 9am-5pm

Lincoln

Junior League
Consignment & Thrift Shop
2201 O Street
Lincoln, Nebraska 68510

Store Hours:
Monday-Saturday 10am-5pm

Contact: Gwen Gies
Phone: 402-435-7506

Women's, men's & children's
clothing, housewares & jewelry

Consignment Policy: Consignments accepted by appointment

50/50 split
Consignor pays $1.00 processing
fee

Store Specials: The shop offers
seniors and students a 20%
discount on Mondays.

Established in 1921 as a garage
sale, all profits support local
community projects which help
youths at risk.

One More Time Furniture
850 N. 27th Street
Lincoln, Nebraska 68503

Store Hours:
Tuesday-Saturday
10am-6pm & Sunday 12pm-5pm

Fine consignment furniture &
home decorative items

Phone: 402-474-2065

Consignment Policy: 50/50 split
Items are consigned for 90 days

One More Time Clothing
1725 Van Dorn Street
Lincoln, Nebraska 68502

Store Hours: Tuesday-Saturday
10am-6pm, Thursday until 8pm
& Sunday 12pm-5pm

Contemporary clothing &
accessories for women & men

Phone: 402-423-2066

Consignment Policy: 50/50 split
Items are consigned for 90 days

Nebraska

Omaha

Deja Vu-
The Children's Edition
246 No. 114th Street
Omaha, Nebraska 68154

Store Hours:
Monday, Wednesday & Friday
10am-6pm
Tuesday & Thursday
10am-7:30pm
Saturday 10am-5:30pm
Sunday 12pm-4pm

Phone: 402-334-2496

Clothing for the entire family,
toys & accessories

Consignment Policy: Items
consigned for 90 days

York

Backstage Consignment
116 South Lincoln Avenue
York, Nebraska 68467

Store Hours:
Monday-Friday 10am-6pm
Saturday & Sunday 10am-5pm

Phone: 402-362-6484

Furniture, housewares, clothing &
accessories for the entire family

Consignment Policy: 50/50 split

Carson City

Encore Consignment
108 E. John Street
Carson City, Nevada 89701

Store Hours:
Tuesday-Friday 11am-6pm
Saturday 11am-5pm

Contact: Beth Walsh
Phone: 702-885-2595

Contemporary women's clothing,
large selection of wedding gowns,
mother-of-the-bride & bridesmaid
dresses

Consignment Policy: Items
consigned for 60 days
50/50 split

Store Specials: On-going 50% off
select merchandise

Save $5.00 off any purchase
of $25.00 or more at
Encore Consignment
108 E. John Street
Carson City, Nevada

Expiration: 12/31/99

Fallon

Fallon Thrift Store
1520 S. Maine Street
Fallon, Nevada 89407

Store Hours:
Monday-Friday 10am-4:30pm

Phone: 702-423-4760

Clothing for the entire family,
household items & furniture

Store Policy: Donations welcome
& a receipt may be provided for
tax purposes

Store Specials: Bag sales every
four months

Proceeds benefit the Association
for Retarded Citizens.

Las Vegas

Exclusively Mens
Consignment
3675 S. Decatur #6
Las Vegas, Nevada 89103

Store Hours:
Monday-Friday 10am-5:30pm
Saturday 10am-3pm

Phone: 702-222-1792

Men's clothing from casual to
formal wear & accessories.
Specializing in business wear.
Exclusively Mens Consignment is
the only resale shop in Las Vegas
specializing in men's items.

Plus Size Resale
3675 S. Decatur #11
Las Vegas, Nevada 89103

Store Hours:
Monday-Saturday 10am-5:30pm

Contact: Ellen Miner
Phone: 702-365-6795

Featuring plus size fashions
16 to 5x, casual to after-five

Nevada

Opportunity Village
921 South Main Street
Las Vegas, Nevada 89101

Store Hours:
Monday-Sunday 9am-5pm

Phone: 702-383-0903

Second Location:

583 South Boulder Highway
Henderson, Nevada 89015

Gently used clothing for the entire
family, furniture & household
items

Reno

Changes   Consignment
Clothing
467 Ralston
Reno, Nevada 89503

Store Hours:
Tuesday-Friday 10am-5pm
Saturday 11am-4pm

Contact: Gloria Eastland
Phone: 702-322-4614

Contemporary clothing for
women, men & children
Accepts cash & checks

Consignment Policy: Consignor
receives 40%
Items consigned for 90 days

Store Specials: Offering monthly
half price items on specific
color tickets

Echo
Lakeridge Pointe Center
6135 Lakeside Drive
Reno, Nevada 89511

Store Hours:
Monday-Friday 9:30am-5pm
Saturday 10am-4pm

Contact: Genie Kocher
Phone: 702-827-4227

Upscale resale clothing for women
& new unique jewelry
Accepts cash, check, Visa &
Mastercard

Consignment Policy:
60/40 split
Items consigned for 60 days

Store Specials: Check in store for
special sales

```
Present this coupon at
        Echo
   6135 Lakeside Drive
   Reno, Nevada & save
$5.00 off a purchase of $20.00

     Expiration Date: 12/31/99
```

Labels
Consignment   Boutique
3350 Lakeside Court
Reno, Nevada 89509

Store Hours:
Monday-Friday 10am-6pm
Saturday 10am-5pm

Contact: Janice Lubra
Phone: 702-825-6000

Ladies' designer apparel
Accepts cash, checks, Visa &
Mastercard

Consignment Policy: 50/50 split

Store Specials: Merchandise
discounted after 30 days,
four storewide sales per year

Present this coupon and
receive $5.00 off one item at
Labels Consignment Boutique
3350 Lakeside Court
Reno, Nevada

(No restrictions apply)

Nearly New Shoppe
405 W. Fifth Street No.3
Reno, Nevada 89503

Store Hours:
Tuesday-Friday 10:30am-5pm
Saturday 11am-4pm

Phone: 702-323-2980

Upscale excellent quality women's
& children's clothing & accessories

Consignment Policy: 50/50 split
Items are consigned for 60 days

Play IT Again Kids
4040 Kietzke Lane
Reno, Nevada 89502

Store Hours:
Monday-Friday 10am-7pm
Saturday 10am-6pm
Sunday 12pm-5pm
Phone: 702-825-4448

Children's apparel, furniture &
accessories
Accept cash, Visa, Mastercard,
Discover & ATM

Store Policy: Pay immediately

Washoe Association For Retarded Citizens

Washoe Association for Retarded
Citizens Thrift Shops carry
clothing, new gifts & closeout
items and lots of great bric-a-
brac. Donations are welcome &
appreciated.

Store Hours:
Monday-Saturday 9am-5:45pm
Sunday 12pm-4:45pm

Store Locations

790 Sutro Street
Reno, Nevada 89512
Phone: 702-333-8262

201 Keystone Ave
Reno, Nevada 89503
Phone: 702-324-1992

570 Gentry Way
Reno, Nevada 89502
Phone: 702-825-1972

406 Pyramid Way
Reno, Nevada 89510
Phone: 702-358-1972

Sparks

Ms. LaRue's
Consignment Boutique
1196 Rock Blvd.
Sparks, Nevada 89431

Nevada

Store Hours:
Monday-Friday 10am-5:30pm
Saturday 10am-5pm

Contact: Kathleen LaRue
Phone: 702-359-4290
e-mail:
mslaruesconsign@pyramid.net

Women's clothing, accessories &
exquisite vintage jewelry
Accepts cash, American Express,
Visa & Mastercard

Consignment Policy:
Consignors receive 40%
Items are consigned for 60 days

Store Specials: Items reduced
50% after 30 days

Amherst

**My Sister's Closet
Consignment Boutique
101A Amherst Plaza
Amherst, New Hampshire
03031**

Store Hours:
Monday-Friday 10am-5pm
Sunday 12pm-5pm

Phone: 603-881-3366

Fabulous clothing for women sizes
2 to 28

Consignment Policy:
Consignors receive 40%
Items are consigned for 60 days

Store Specials: Unique one of a
kind pieces created by using
recycled earrings & buttons

**Proms To Weddings
Consignment Formal Shop
131 101-A Amherst Plaza
Amherst, New Hampshire
03031**

Store Hours:
Wednesday, Friday & Saturday
10am-5pm
Thursday 12pm-7pm
Sunday 12pm-4pm
Evenings available on Monday &
Tuesday

Contact: Jan Lemay
Phone: 603-881-5766

Vast array of prom gowns, wedding
gowns, cocktail & cruise wear,
mother-of-the-bride, groom &
flower girl dresses, veils, shoes,
jewelry, glasses, garters and much
more. Some new gowns too!
Accepts cash, personal checks,
Mastercard, Visa & Discover

Consignment Policy: 50/50 split
Wedding gowns consigned for nine
months, other items for six
months

Store Specials: Proms to Weddings
offers alterations & wedding
invitations

Bradford

**Reaching Hands Thrift Shop
18 Ring Hill Road
PO Box 478
Bradford, New Hampshire
03221**

Store Hours:
Monday, Tuesday & Wednesday:
By chance
Thursday, Friday & Saturday
10am-4pm

Gently used clothing for the entire
family & household items
Accepts cash

Store Policy: Donations welcome

Store Specials: Weekly advertised
specials

This coupon entitles the
bearer to save 10% off at
Reaching Hands Thrift Shop
18 Ring Hill Road
Bradford, New Hampshire

Expiration Date: 12/31/99

New Hampshire

Campton

Sweet Charity
Campton Plaza
P.O. Box 801
Campton, New Hampshire
03223

Store Hours:
Tuesday-Saturday 10am-6pm
Sunday 12pm-5pm

Phone: 603-726-4312

Clothing for the entire family

Consignment Policy: Items
consigned for 120 days

Canaan

LISTEN
(Lebanon In Service
To Each Neighbor)
Route 4
Canaan, New Hampshire
03741
Phone: 603-632-5331
Located east of Mascoma
High School

Other Locations:
60 Hanover Street
Lebanon, New Hampshire
03766
Phone: 603-448-1294

Store Hours: Monday-Saturday
10am-5pm
Sunday 12pm-5pm

Clothing for the entire family,
housewares, bric-a-brac &
furniture
Accepts cash, checks & credit
cards

Store Specials: 10% membership
discount

Listen Thrift Stores proceeds
benefit many community service
programs.

Guild

Mary's Little Lamb
16 Hale Street Routes 11/103
Guild, New Hampshire 03754

Store Hours:
Tuesday-Saturday 10am-4pm

Phone: 603-863-3027

Childrens's clothing, toys &
equipment

Consignment Policy: 50/50 split

Hampton

Aged Elegance
882 Lafayette Road Route 1
Hampton, New Hampshire
03842

Store Hours:
Monday-Sunday 10am-5pm
Friday until 8pm

Phone: 603-926-4928

Clothing for women & men

Consignment Policy: 60/40 split
Items are consigned for 60 days

Store Specials: Senior citizen
discount available

Keene

St. James Thrift Shop

25 Lamson Street
Keene, New Hampshire 03431

Store Hours: Tuesday, Wednesday,
Thursday & Friday 10am-4pm
Saturday 11am-4pm

Phone: 603-352-3697

Clothing for the entire family,
housewares, small appliances,
books & more

Store Policy: Donations welcome

Nashua

**Mother & Child's Clothing,
Gifts & more
111 W Pearl Street
Nashua, New Hampshire
03060**

Phone: 603-886-2900
Toll Free in New Hampshire
1-800-546-6727

Second Location:
**Amherst Plaza
Rte 101-A
Amherst, New Hampshire
03031**

Store Hours:
Monday-Saturday 10am-5pm
Nashua location open until 8pm
*Call ahead for special hours

603-886-6727 Amherst
e-mail: motherand@aol.com
Web site: http://members.aol.com/
motherand

Excellent quality secondhand
clothing, accessories, equipment,
toys & furniture. Featuring
Lapdoodles, Cow & Lizard,

Zutano, Flap Happy & much
more! Including a variety of
natural health care products.
Accepts cash, debit/ATM cards,
major credit cards & checks
with ID
Mail order is available. Items must
be prepaid with a major credit card
or check with the proper ID.
Most items shipped withith 48
hours.

Consignment Policy:
No appointment is necessary to
consign items
Call ahead to inquire about
the stores acceptance policy
Consignor receives 40%
Items sold for $50.00 or more
Consignor receives 60% of the
selling price in cash or store credit

Store Specials: Half price sales in
January, February, June & July

Plymouth

**Shorts Subjects Clothes &
Toys For Boys & Girls
#594 Tenney Mountain
Highway Unit #4
Plymouth, New Hampshire
03264**

Store Hours:
Monday-Saturday 10am-5pm

Phone: 603-536-5655

Excellent quality gently used
clothing & accessories for
children

Store Policy: Most items
purchased outright

New Hampshire

Rochester

Family Warehouse
Thrift Shop
43 North Main Street
Rochester, New Hampshire
03867

Store Hours:
Monday-Wednesday 9am-3pm
Thursday & Friday 9am-5pm
Saturday 9am-3pm

Phone: 603-330-0093

Clothing for the entire family

Store Policy: Donations welcome

Absecon

**Kidsignments Resale and
Speciality Boutique
22 N. Shore Road
Abescon, New Jersey 08201**

Store Hours:
Monday 10:30am-3:30pm
Tuesday-Friday 10am-5pm
Saturday11am-4pm

Phone: 609-646-0860

Children's clothing from newborn
to 14/16, maternity, toys,
furniture & some new gift &
speciality items

Consignment Policy:
$5.00 one time fee to consign
An appointment is necessary to
consign more than twenty items
Items consigned for 60-120 days
by appointment

Store Specials: Select merchandise
reduced from 10% to 50%

Present this coupon
at *Kidsignments*
22 N Shore Road
Absecon, NJ &
save $5.00 off a
$25.00 purchase

Expiration Date: 12/31/99

Bergenfield

**Almost New Shops I & II
30 N. Washington Ave
Bergenfield, New Jersey
07621**

Store Hours:
Tuesday-Saturday 10am-5:30pm
Thursday until 7:30pm

Phone: 201-387-9591
Fax: 201-569-4209

Clothing for the entire family,
accessories, jewelry, artwork,
furniture and much more

Store Policy: Donations welcome
and appreciated
Tax receipts provided for
donations

Store Specials: Check for new sales
everyday!

Berkeley Heights

**Act II Consignment Shoppe
635 Springfield Ave
Berkeley Heights, New Jersey
07922**

Store Hours:
Tuesday-Saturday 10am-5pm
Thursday until 8pm

Contact: Diane Firestine
Phone: 908-464-8477
Fax: 908-668-1741

Clothing for the entire family,
housewares, linens, collectibles,
jewelry & antiques

149

Accepts cash, checks, ATM cards & all major credit cards

Store Specials: Seniors receive a 10% discount on Tuesday

Present this coupon at
Act II Consignment Shoppe
635 Springfield Avenue
Berkeley Heights, New Jersey
& save $2.00 off one $10.00
purchase or 10% off one
houseware purchase over $10.00

Coupon cannot be combined with any other offers and must be presented prior to purchase

Expiration Date: 12/31/99

Bernardsville

Encore Quality Consignments
123 Claremont Road
Bernardsville, New Jersey 07924

Store Hours:
Tuesday-Friday 10am-6pm
Thursday until 8pm & Saturday 10am-5pm

Contact: Carol MacArthur
Phone: 908-766-7760

Contemporary clothing, jewelry, antiques, furniture, furs & collectibles
Accepts cash, checks, Visa, Master card & American Express

Store Specials: On-going 50% to 75% off clothing & great bi-annual bag sales

Furnishings discounted 10% each month

Bloomfield

The Resale Rack
170 Broad Street
Bloomfield, New Jersey 07003

Store Hours:
Monday-Saturday 10am-6pm
Friday 10am-7pm

Contact: Sandy Shein
Phone: 973-743-1888

Clothing for the entire family
Accepts cash, checks & money orders

Consignment Policy: Consignments accepted Monday-Friday 10am-2pm by appoinment only 50/50 split

Store Specials: Specializing in estate clothing & jewelry
Pick-ups available for estates
Weekly 20% off & half price sale

Bogota

Resale Brigade
Consignment Boutique
42 Queen Anne Road
Bogota, New Jersey 07603

Store Hours:
Tuesday-Friday 10:30am-6pm
Saturday 12:30pm-5pm

Phone: 201-487-6232

Featuring contemporary fashions & accessories for women including juniors & unique gift items

Accepts cash and all major credit cards

Consignment Policy:
50/50 split
Items half price after 30 days

Store Specials: Big sales promotions year round

Califon

Carly's Closet
438 Rt 513 @Victorian
Square Mall
Califon, New Jersey 07830

Store Hours:
Tuesday-Saturday 10am-5pm

Phone: 908-832-6799
Contact: Carolyn Sunday

Children's clothing, toys, furniture, equipment & gifts

Consignment Policy:
50/50 split
Items consigned for ten weeks

Secrets@Victorian Square
A Very Special
Consignment Shop
438 Rt. 513 Victorian Square
Califon, New Jersey 07830

Store Hours:
Tuesday-Saturday 10am-6pm
Hours may vary slightly during the year

Contact: Kathy Cook
Phone: 908-832-9777
Website: www.theclothestree.com/shops/Secrets

New & consigned clothing for women, great gift items, furniture & collectibles. Special "new" Secrets Room with new clothing designs
Accepts cash, checks & all credit cards

Consignment Policy: 50/50 split on clothing consigned for two months
60% for household items, consigned for three months

Collingswood

Elite
742 Haddon Ave.
Collingswood, New Jersey
08108

Store Hours:
Monday-Thursday & Saturday
11am-6pm
Frday 11am-7pm
Phone: 609-858-4121

Clothing for the entire family &
accessories
Accepts cash & checks

Consignment Policy:
$5.00 yearly fee to consign
merchandise
Items are consigned for 60 days
50/50 split

Store Specials: Items reduced 20%
every 30 days

Second Showing
685 Haddon Avenue
Collingswood, New Jersey
08108

Store Hours:
Tuesday-Friday 11am-4:30pm
Saturday 11am-4pm

Phone: 609-854-0520

Upscale consignment clothing for
women & men
Accepts cash only

Consignment Policy:
$3.00 yearly service fee to
consign merchandise
50/50 split

Second Showing has been
successfully selling consignment
clothing for over twenty four
years!

The Plus Closet
602 Haddon Ave
Collingswood, New Jersey
08108

Store Hours:
Tuesday-Friday 10am-5pm
Saturday 10am-4pm

Contact: Sandra Barletta
Phone: 609-854-8828

Plus size women's clothing &
accessories
Accepts cash or checks

Consignment Policy: 50/50 split
$5.00 fee per year to consign
merchandise

Store Specials: Select color tags
on sale the first of the month

Present this coupon at
The Plus Closet
602 Haddon Avenue
Collingswood, New Jersey
& save $5.00
off one purchase

Expiration Date: 12/31/99

East Brunswick

**Karen's
Consignments Boutique
336 Highway 18
East Brunswick, New Jersey
08816**

Store Hours:
Monday-Tuesday 11am-6pm
Wednesday-Saturday 10am-6pm
Thursday until 8pm
Sunday 12pm-4pm

Contact: Karen Kaufman
Phone: 908-254-3584
e-mail: kskgirl@aol.com

Women's designer & better brand
sportswear, outerwear &
accessories

Store Specials:
25% off merchandise on select
days, bring in a new customer &
receive 10% off an item

This coupon entitles the bearer
to save 25% off one total
purchase at
Karen's Consignment Boutique
336 Highway 18
East Brunswick, New Jersey

Excluding furs, jewelry & special sale days

Expiration Date: 12/31/99

Edgewater

**Rags To Riches
8915-17 River Road
Edgewater, New Jersey 07020**

Store Hours: Call for store hours

Contact: Sheila Gross
Phone: 201-941-3121
Web site:
www.theclothestree.com/
shops/RagsToRiches/

Unique, creative, vintage clothing,
accessories including hats, bags,
jewelry & more. Furniture,
antiques & fun, funky, one-of-a-
kind items! Shopping at Rags To
Riches is a magical experience.

Store Policy: Open to all
agreements

Present this coupon at
Rags To Riches
8915-17 River Road
Edgewater, NJ
& save 20% off of one
item or 10% a total purchase

Expiration Date: 12/31/99

Englewood

**Gentlemen's Agreement Inc.
20 North Van Brunt Street
Englewood, New Jersey 07631**

Store Hours:
Tuesday-Saturday 10am-6pm
Thursday until 7pm

Phone: 201-568-5511

New Jersey

Featuring gently used men's designer clothing

Consignment Policy: 50/50 split
Items are consigned for 60 days

Ewing

"Re-Runs"
246 Scotch Road
Glen Rock Shopping Center
Ewing, New Jersey 08628

Store Hours:
Monday, Tuesday,
Wednesday, Friday & Saturday
11am-4pm
Thursday 12pm-6pm

Contact: Judi DePula
Phone: 609-882-6653

All items for women from "head to toe"
Accepts cash, checks, Visa, Mastercard & Novus

Store Specials: Check for frequent sales

Ewing

Re-Runs
246 Scotch Road
Ewing, NJ 08628

Store Hours:
Monday, Tuesday, Wednesday,
Friday & Saturday 11am-4pm
Thursday 12pm-6pm

Phone: 609-882-6653

Women's gently used fashions from head to toe

Flanders

Karengale's Consignment &
Creative Gifts, LLC
286 Route 206 South
Flanders, New Jersey 07836

Store Hours:
Tuesday-Friday 9:30am-3pm
Tuesday 7pm-9pm
Thursday 5pm-9pm
Saturday 10am-4pm

Contact: Gale Rooney &
Karen Schneeberg
Phone: 973-927-7990

Children's gently used clothing & accessories, maternity wear & hand crafted items
Accepts cash, checks, Mastercard, Visa & American Express

Store Specials: Select merchandise reduced 10% to 50%

■■■■■■■■■■■■■■■■
Present this coupon at
Karengale's Consignment
& Creative Gifts. LLC
286 Rt. 206 South
Flanders, New Jersey &
save 20% off total sale

(Excluding white tickets
& sale merchandise)
Expiration Date: 12/31/99
■■■■■■■■■■■■■■■■

Flemington

Consignment   Collections
9 Central Ave
Flemington, New Jersey
08822

Store Hours:
Wednesday-Saturday 10am-5pm
Sunday 12pm-4pm

Contact: Ruth J. Hall
Phone: 908-788-0103

Home furnishings & decorative items

Consignment Policy: Furniture consigned for six months
Items reduced 10% after 30 days
Dealer discount available

```
┌ ─ ─ ─ ─ ─ ─ ─ ─ ─ ┐
│   Present this coupon at    │
│   Consignment Collections   │
│        9 Central Ave        │
│       Flemington, NJ        │
│      & save $5.00 off       │
│   an item $50.00 or more    │
│      Expiration Date: 12/31/99      │
└ ─ ─ ─ ─ ─ ─ ─ ─ ─ ┘
```

Unforgettable Consignments
7 Mine Street
Flemington, New Jersey
08822

Store Hours:
Monday-Thursday 10am-3:30pm
Friday & Saturday 10am-5pm
Sunday 1:30am-4:30pm

Phone: 908-788-8806

Clothing & accessories for the entire family

Consignment Policy:
50/50 split
Items consigned for six weeks

VHSS Consignment Shop
117 Broad Street
Flemington, New Jersey
08822

Store Hours:
Monday-Saturday 11am-3pm

Phone: 908-788-4017

Clothing for women & children

Consignment Policy: 50/50 split
Items consigned for four weeks
$20.00 yearly registration fee

Freehold

CentraState Medical Center Thrift Shop
45 Throckmorton Street
Freehold, New Jersey 07728

Store Hours:
Monday-Saturday 10am-2:30pm

Phone: 732-462-3437

Clothing, household items & toys
Accepts cash

Store Policy: Donations welcome

Store Specials: Mailing list customers receive discount coupons

```
• • • • • • • • • • • • •
•   Present this coupon    •
•  CentraState Medical Center  •
•        Thrift Shop        •
•    45 Throckmorton Street    •
•  Freehold, NJ & save 20% on  •
•      total purchase       •
•  (Coupon cannot be used on half price  •
•     items or bag sale days)     •
•     Expiration Date: 12/31/99     •
• • • • • • • • • • • • •
```

Deja Vu
15 W. Main Street
Freehold, New Jersey 07728

Store Hours:
Monday-Saturday 10am-5pm

Phone: 908-431-2001
Website: www.theclothestree.com/
shops/DejaVu

Designer clothing for the entire
family, accessories, furniture,
china & vintage clothing

Consignment Policy: 50/50 split
Items are consigned for 60 days

Store Specials: Wish list

Second Turn Around
14 W. Main Street
Freehold, New Jersey 07728

Store Hours:
Monday-Saturday 10am-4:30pm

Phone: 908-431-7667

Clothing & accessories for
women & children

Consignment Policy:
50/50 split

Haddonfield

All My Children
4 Mechanic Street
Haddonfield, New Jersey
08033

Store Hours: Daily 10am-5pm

Phone: 609-429-9000

Children's clothing, maternity
wear & equipment
Accepts cash, checks & credit
cards

Consignment Policy:
50/50 split
Items consigned for 90 days

Store Specials: Half price sales in
January, February, June & July

Kearny

Karyn's Consignment
Boutique & Bridal Salon
264 Kearny Avenue
Kearny, New Jersey 07032

Store Hours:
Tuesday-Saturday 11am-6pm
Friday 11am-7pm
After hours by appointment

Contact: Karen
Phone: 201-998-8710

Women's apparel, after-five,
evening wear, beautiful bridal
gowns, mother-of-the-bride,
accessories, coats & furs
Accepts cash, Visa, Mastercard &
American Express

Consignment Policy: 50/50 split
High ticket items negotiable

Store Specials:
Lay a-way available
Cash & carry discount

This coupon entitles the
bearer to save 10% cash &
carry at
Karyn's Consignment
Boutique & Bridal Salon
264 Kearny Avenue
Kearny, New Jersey
(Coupon excludes sale items)
Expiration Date: 12/31/99

Livingston

**Duet Designer
Consignment Boutique
79 South Livingston Avenue
Livingston, New Jersey 07029**

Store Hours:
Monday-Saturday 10am-6pm
Thursday until 8pm
Sunday 12pm-5pm

Contact: Lynn Meisler
Phone: 973-535-1133
Fax: 973-535-1183

Upscale designer clothing for women, accessories & designer bridal gowns
Accepts cash, checks & all major credit cards

Consignment Policy: Items must be in pristine condition

Lyndhurst

**Small Change
508 Valley Brook Ave
Lyndhurst, New Jersey 07071**

Phone: 201-935-9061

Second Location:
**118-A Midland Ave.
Kearny, New Jersey 07032**

Phone: 201-991-9049
Website: www.SmallChange.com

Store Hours:
Monday-Friday 11am-6pm
Thursday until 8pm
Saturday 11am-5pm

Contact: Carolyn Oberndorf

Fabulous children's clothing & equipment
Accepts cash, checks, Mastercard & Visa

Store Policy: Items purchased outright

Store Specials:
January & July-Buy one item get second item for a penny
Easter egg hunt in April offering discounts from 10%-50%
Grandparents Day

This coupon entitles the bearer to save $5.00 off purchase of $15.00 or more on clothing at
*Small Change Consignment Shop
508 Valley Brook Ave
Lyndurst, NJ or
118-A Midland Ave
Kearny, N.J.*

Coupon cannot be combined with other promotions or sales)
Expiration Date: 12/31/99

New Jersey

Madison

**New Leaf Consignment
Boutique
16 Park Avenue
Madison, New Jersey 07940**

Store Hours: Monday, Wednesday
& Friday 10am-6pm
Tuesday & Thursday 10am-7pm
Saturday 10am-5pm
Sunday 12pm-5pm

Contact: Arleen J. Gaetani
Phone: 973-377-2422

Women's designer label clothing,
accessories, jewelry, leather
goods, maternity wear, children's
clothing, furniture pieces,
beautiful crystal, lamps, giftware
& other household items

Consignment Policy:
Items consigned for 90 days

Store Specials: On-going sales

Manville

**The Closet Quality
Consignments
45 South Main Street
Manville, New Jersey 08835**

Store Hours:
Monday-Friday 9am-6pm
Saturday 9am-3pm

Contact: Victor Bukovecky
Phone: 908-725-3858

Clothing, jewelry, collectibles,
antiques & vintage wear

Maple Shade

**Designer Consignments
Kingsway Plaza
Kings Highway &
Lenola Road
Maple Shade, New Jersey
08052**

Store Hours:
Monday-Thursday 10am-7:30pm
Friday 10am-9pm
Saturday 10am-8pm
Sunday 12pm-6pm

Phone: 609-231-1500
Fax: 609-797-0773

Second Location:
**Center Point Plaza
Route 9 & Tilton Road
Northfield, New Jersey 08825**

Store Hours
Monday, Tuesday, Thursday &
Saturday 10am-6pm
Wednesday & Friday 10am-8pm
Sunday 11am-5pm

Phone: 609-646-7022
Fax: 609-484-8618
Website:
www.designerconsignments.com

Top designer women's attire
featuring labels such as Donna
Karan, Ann Taylor, Escada,
Armani & many more.
Mens-wear including designs by
Zenga, Escada, Armani, Marzotto,
Mondo & Polo. Children's wear,
accessories galore, jewelry,
collectibles & more! One-of-a-
kind formal wear rental.

Martinsville

**Time & Again Quality
Consignment Boutique
1938 Washington Valley Road
Martinsville, New Jersey
08836**

Store Hours:
Tuesday, Wednesday & Thursday
11am-6pm
Friday 10:30am-5pm
Saturday 10am-4pm

Phone: 908-805-9222

Designer apparel & accessories
for women, jewelry, collectibles,
antiques & more

Consignment Policy:
50/50 split
$6.00 annual registration fee
to consign merchandise

Maywood

**The Barter Place
Consignment Store
42 W Pleasant Avenue
Maywood, New Jersey 07607**

Store Hours:
Tuesday-Saturday 10am-6pm
Thursday until 8pm

Phone: 201-843-5650

Clothing for the entire family,
collectibles, bric-a-brac, jewelry,
antiques, household items
Accepts cash, Visa, Mastercard &

Consignment Policy: 50/50 split
Consignments are consigned for
60 days

Store Specials: Seniors receive a
discount on Wednesday

• • • • • • • • • • • • • • •
•   •
•   Present this coupon at   •
•   The Barter Place   •
•   Consignment Store   •
•   42 W Pleasant Ave   •
•   Maywood, New Jersey &   •
•   save 25% off one item   •
•   •
•   Expiration Date: 12/31/99   •
• • • • • • • • • • • • • • •

Morristown

**Nearly New Shop
7 King Place
Morristown, New Jersey
07960**

Store Hours:
Monday-Saturday 10am-4pm

Phone: 973-539-4274

Clothing & accessories for the
entire family, houswares & linens
Accepts cash & checks

Consignment Policy:
50/50 split
Annual registration fee of $10.00

Store Specials: Automatic
markdowns after three weeks
Check for occassional dollar rack

Nearly New Shop was established
by the Junior League of
Morristown. Proceeds benefit
the following organizations, Arts
Council of the Morris Area,
Marrow Donor Program & many
more.

New Jersey

The Bargain Box
A "Thrift Boutique"
102 Mt. Kemble Ave
Route 202 S.
Morristown, New Jersey
07960

Store Hours:
Monday 12:30pm-4pm
Tuesday-Friday 10am-4pm
Saturday 10am-3pm
Open during the Summer too!

Phone: 973-267-1334

Established over thirty years ago, the Bargain Box offers everything from designer clothing for the entire family, housewares, bric-a-brac & much more!
Accepts cash, NJ personal checks, Visa & Mastercard

Store Policy: Donations welcome

┌─────────────────────────┐
│ Present this coupon at │
│   *The Bargain Box*   │
│   *102 Mt. Kemble Ave.* │
│   *Morristown, NJ* & save │
│ $5.00 off   │
│ any purchase of $20.00 or more │
│   │
│   Expiration Date: 12/31/99 │
└─────────────────────────┘

Mount Holly

Liz's Unique Boutique
1690 Rt. 38
Mt. Holly, New Jersey 08015

Store Hours:
Monday-Friday 10am-7pm
Saturday 10am-5pm & Sunday 12pm-5pm

Contact: Patti Pudlo

160

Phone: 609-265-8508

Clothing for the entire family, accessories, maternity wear, Bridal gowns, formal wear & furs.
Expert watch & jewelry repair.
Accepts: cash, checks, Visa, Mastercard, American Express, Discover & MAC

Consignment Policy: 50/50 split
Items consigned for three months

Store Specials:
Lay-a-way available
Seasonal markdowns

The Children's Home
Thrift Shop
1735 Route 38
Mount Holly, New Jersey
08060

Store Hours:
Monday-Sunday 9am-3:30pm

Phone: 609-265-8788
Fax: 609-261-5672
e-mail: thriftshop@chbc.org
Website: www.childrens-home.org/thriftshop.html

Clothing for the entire family, furniture, computers, books & much more!
Accepts cash, checks, Mastercard & Visa

The Children's Home, a non-profit agency established in 1864, provides special education and residential services to disadvantaged youths. The thrift shop provides the children with an introduction to the "World of Work." Proceeds from the shop are used to support all services at The Children's Home.

Neptune City

Forever Chic
Consignment Boutique
Route 35 and 3rd Avenue
Neptune City, New Jersey
07753

Store Hours:
Monday-Saturday 10am-6pm

Phone: 908-775-7781

Designer label clothing for the entire family

New Brunswick

Golden Opportunities
Outreach
Thrift Outlet
133 French Street
New Brunswick, New Jersey
08901

Store Hours: Monday-Saturday
10am-5pm

Contact: Carol Hennessey &
Gail Maund
Phone: 732-448-9789

Clothing for the entire family,
toys, housewares & furniture
Accepts cash

Store Specials: $3.00 bag of
clothing

Proceeds benefit those in need.

Newton

Beehive Thrift Shop
123 Spring Street
Newton, New Jersey 07860

Store Hours:
Tuesday-Friday 10am-4pm
Saturday 10am-2pm

Phone: 201-383-1288

Gently used clothing, toys,
household items & furniture

North Plainfield

Apparel Revisited
320 Somerset Street
North Plainfield, NJ 07060

Store Hours:
Monday-Saturday 10am-6pm
Thursday until 8pm

Contact: Mim McGrath
Phone: 908-757-4470
Website: www.theclothestree.com/
shops/ApparelRevisited

Featuring over 2000 square feet
of clothing for the entire family,
accessories, great jewelry,
housewares, furniture, toys &
much more!

Consignment Policy:
Consignments accepted by
appointment
50/50 split

Store Specials: Discounted baby
basket!

New Jersey

Great play area for kids!

Palisades Park

Connie's Place
Your Consignment Boutique
520 Bergen Blvd.
Palisades Park, New Jersey
07650

Store Hours:
Tuesday-Saturday 10am-6pm
Wednesday 11am-8pm

Contact: Connie Selleck
Phone: 201-947-7320

Designer clothing for women,
jewelry & furs
Accepts cash, checks, Mastercard,
Visa & American Express

Consignment Policy: 50/50 split
Items consigned for 60 days

Pennington

The Discovery Shop-
An American
Cancer Society Shop
The Pennington
Shopping Center
25 Route 31
Pennington, New Jersey
08534

Store Hours:
Monday-Friday 11am-6pm
Saturday 10am-4pm

Phone: 609-737-2211

Upscale clothing for the entire
family, jewelry & collectibles

Store Policy: Donations welcome
& a receipt may be provided
for tax purposes

Second Time Around
14 N. Main St.
Pennington, New Jersey

Store Hours:
Tuesday-Friday 10:30am-4:30pm
Saturday 10am-4pm

Phone: 609-737-2828

Clothing for the entire family &
jewelry

Consignment Policy: 50/50 split

Pennsauken

Debra's Closet
2673 Haddonfield Road
Hargrove Plaza
Pennsauken, New Jersey

Store Hours:
Monday, Tuesday, Wednesday &
Thursday 10am-5pm
Friday 10am-7pm
Saturday 12pm-4pm

Phone: 609-486-9636

Fantastic clothing for women,
jewelry & handbags

Consignment Policy: 50/50 split
No appointment is necessary

Store Specials: Bag sales &
clearance rack

Perth Amboy

Sales By The Bay Thrift Store
315 State Street
Perth Amboy, New Jersey
08861

Store Hours:
Monday 11am-2:20pm
Tuesday & Wednesday
10:30am-2:30pm
Friday 10:30am-1pm

Phone: 737-442-8933

New & gently used clothing,
housewares, furniture, toys,
books, tools, costume jewelry
Accepts cash

Store Policy: Donations welcome

Store Specials: $5.00 bag sale

Pompton Plains

The Wise Old Owl
Thrift Shop
599 Newark Pompton
Turnpike
Pompton Plains, New Jersey
07444

Store Hours:
Monday-Saturday 10am-4pm
Closed on Monday in July &
August

Contact: Judy B. Less
Phone: 973-839-9431

Clothing, household items & small
appliances
Accepts cash

Store Policy: 50/50 split
Items accepted on Wednesdays
between 10am-3pm

Rahway

Repeat Performance
88 E. Cherry Street
Rahway, New Jersey 07064

Store Hours:
Tuesday-Friday 11am-5pm
Saturday 11am-4pm

Phone: 732-382-3322

Upscale clothing & accessories
for women
Accepts cash, Visa & Mastercard

Consignment Policy: 50/50 split

Raritan

Kidz Klozet
30 Thompson Street
Raritan, New Jersey 08869

Store Hours:
Tuesday-Friday 10am-6pm
Saturday 10am-5pm

Phone: 908-231-6677

Gently used clothing for tots
to teens, baby furniture &

Rosemont

Sweat Repeats
Intersection of Route 519 &
Route 604
Rosemont, New Jersey 08556
Located six miles north of
Lambertville & nine miles west of
Flemington

Store Hours:
Wednesday-Friday 10am-5pm
Saturday 10am-4pm
Sunday 12pm-4pm

Closed on Sundays-January
through March

Contact: Mary Hartom-Alley
Phone: 609-397-9383
Fax: 609-397-0880

Over 2200 square feet of
exceptional clothing & accesso-
ries for women.
Featuring labels designed by
BlueFish, Liz, Jones, Talbots,
Coach, Dooney & Bourke &
much more!
Accepts cash, Mastercard & Visa

Consignment Policy: Consignments accepted by appointment
only

Salem

Society To Protect Animals
Thrift Shop
192-194 East Broadway
Salem, New Jersey 08079

Store Hours:
Monday-Saturday 8am-3pm

Phone: 609-935-7042

Antiques, clothing & lots of bric-
a-brac

Store Policy: Donations welcome

Proceeds are donated to the
animal shelter.

Sea Bright

Upscale Resale
1088 Ocean Avenue
Sea Bright, New Jersey 07760

Store Hours:
Monday-Saturday 10am-5pm

Contact: Anna Marie Paneck
Phone: 732-741-5527

Women's apparel & accessories

Consignment Policy:
Consignments accepted without
an appointment every month
from the 1st to the 15th
on Wednesday, Thursday &
Saturday
50/50 split
Items are consigned for 90 days

Store Specials: $5.00 rack
proceeds donated to various
charities

Present this coupon at
Upscale Resale
1088 Ocean Avenue
Sea Bright, New Jersey & save
10% off one purchase

Expiration Date: 12/31/99

Sea Girt

The Exchange
Consignment Boutique
501 Washington Boulevard
Sea Girt, New Jersey 08750

Store Hours:
Thursday & Friday 12pm-5pm
Saturday & Sunday 11am-6pm

Contact: Beth Insabella &
Laurie Pilling
Phone: 732-449-9007

Upscale gently used designer label
clothing, accessories & vintage
items too!

Consignment Policy:
Consignments accepted by
appointment
50/50 split
$5.00 annual fee to consign
merchandise
Items are consigned for eight
weeks
Limit six seasonal items

Beautiful classic decor & the soft
sounds of Billy Holiday add to a
delightful shopping experience!

Present this coupon at
The Exchange
Consignment Boutique
501 Washington Blvd.
Sea Girt, New Jersey &
save 20% off one
entire purchase
(Sale items not included)
Expiration Date: 12/31/99

New Jersey

Somerville

New Start Consignment Shop
26 West Main Street
Somerville, New Jersey 08876

Store Hours:
Wednesday-Friday 11am-5pm
Saturday 11am-3pm

Contact: Thomas Babcock

Phone: 908-429-0588
Apparel for women & men,
Accepts cash & checks
No fee
50/50 split
Accepts in-season clothing with a
twenty item limit
Items are consigned for 60 days

Established in 1993, New Start
offers 1000 square feet of well
organized exquisite pre-owned
items. Including JNY, Liz, Chaus,
Picone & Carol Little for her &
Levis, Gap, Aeropostale &
Banana Republic for him. Over
1000 consignors, hundreds of new
items arrive daily.

Store Specials: 50% off end of
the season sales & clearance racks

South Plainfield

Twice Is Nice
175 Front Street
South Plainfield, New Jersey
07080

Store Hours:
Monday-Friday 10am-5pm
Saturday 10am-4pm

Contact: Darlene Pinto
Phone: 908-561-6151
Fax: 908-561-9889

Apparel for women & children,
accessories, craft & gift items
Accepts cash & checks

Store Specials: Biannual bag sales

South River

Designer Consignor Boutique
60 Main Street
South River, New Jersey
08882

Store Hours:
Tuesday-Saturday 10am-4pm &
Friday 10am-7pm

Phone: 908-432-0433

Clothing for the entire family,
knick-knacks & more!

Spring Lake

Foxy Ladies Consignment
219A Morris Ave.
Spring Lake, NJ 07762

Store Hours:
Daily 11am-5pm

Phone: 908-449-4066

Designer clothing & accessories,
antiques, fur & more

Teaneck

Ava's Seek & Find Boutique
"A Classy Consignment
Shop"
202 W. Engelwood Avenue
Teaneck, New Jersey 07020

Store Hours:
Wednesday-Saturday
10:30am-5pm

Contact: Ava Sharpe
Phone: 201-833-1213

Clothing for women & accessories

Consignment Policy: 50/50 split

Store Specials: Merchandise
discounted everyday & gift
certificates available

Council Thrift Shop
1386 Queen Anne Road
Teaneck, New Jersey 07666

Store Hours:
Monday-Friday 10am-5:30pm
Thursday until 8pm

Contact: Lillian Loving
Phone: 201-837-4415

Clothing for the entire family,
accessories, housewares, furniture
& antiques
Accepts cash & checks

Toms River

Second Time Around
Consignment Shop
200 Corporate Circle
Toms River, New Jersey 08755

Store Hours:
Monday-Saturday 10am-4pm
Tuesday 6pm-9pm

Phone: 732-341-5191

Clothing for the entire family &
housewares
Accepts cash

Consignment Policy:
$5.00 annual fee
Consignor receives 60%
Consignments accepted by
appointment

Proceeds from the shop benefit
the Community Medical Center.

Silk Purse Consignments
602 Clifton Avenue
Toms River, New Jersey 08753

Store Hours:
Tuesday-Saturday 10am-5pm
Thursday until 7pm

Contact: Pam Waller
Phone: 908-914-1413
e-mail: PWaller@IBM.NET

Apparel & accessories for women
& children

Consignment Policy:
Consignments accepted by

167

appointment only

**Time After Time
Consignment Boutique
117 Route 37 East
Toms River, New Jersey 08753**

Store Hours:
Monday-Saturday 10am-5pm

Phone: 732-473-0906

Women's designer fashions &
accessories, formal wear, evening
gowns, bridal gowns, mother-of-
the-bride & bridesmaid dresses &
bridal accessories
Accepts cash, checks & Visa

Voorhees

**Kim's Consignment
1225 Haddonfield-Berlin Rd.
Southgate Plaza
Voorhees, New Jersey 08043**

Store Hours:
Tuesday, Thursday & Friday
10am-5pm
Wednesday 10am-7pm
Saturday 12pm-5pm

Phone: 609-753-4334

Apparel & accessories for women
& children, handmade craft items
& more

Wall

**Career Women's
Consignment Boutique
1818 Highway 35
Wall, New Jersey 07719**

Store Hours:
Tuesday-Friday 10am-5pm
Thursday 12pm-7pm
Saturday 10am-4pm

Contact: Gayle Redepenning-Turi
Phone: 732-280-2855

Excellent quality women's career
& casual clothing and accessories

Consignment Policy:
50/50 split
$15.00 registration fee to consign
items
Consignments by appointment
only, limit 15 items

Store Specials: Colored tags offer
35%-50% off select merchandise
every week!
End of the season bag sales-fill a
bag for only $5.00 from the sales
rack

New Jersey

Warren

The Great & Small Shop®
184 Mt. Bethel Road
Warren, N.J. 07059

Store Hours:
Tuesday-Friday 10:30am-6pm
Thursday 10:30am-8pm
Saturday 10am-5pm
Sunday 12pm-4pm

Contact: Cindy Bogan &
Erin Bogan
Phone: 908-647-9009
Website: www.greatandsmall.com

Gently used maternity & infant
wear sizes newborn to 4 toddler
Accepts cash, checks, Visa &
Mastercard

Store Specials: Discount coupons
available on website

Sell your maternity clothing
at
The Great & Small Shop
184 Mt. Bethel Road
Warren, New Jersey
& receive a Great & Small
Shop gift certificate.
Value is 10% of the amount
Great & Small pays for your
maternity clothing only.
Gift certificate is fully
transferable & may be
combined with other discounts
No expiration date

Westfield

American Cancer Society
Discovery Shop
311 South Ave.
Westfield, N.J. 07090

Store Hours:
Monday-Saturday 10am-4pm

Phone: 908-232-3332

Upscale clothing, household items
& knick-knacks

Store Policy: Donations welcome

Consign With Me Sheila
329 South Avenue West
Westfield, New Jersey 07090

Store Hours
Tuesday, Wednesday,
Thursday & Friday
10:30am-5:30pm
Saturday until 3pm
Evening appointments available
by request

Contact: Sheila Nurin Pollack
Phone: 908-232-0779

Gently used clothing for women &
men, accessories & specializing in
plus sizes for women

Consignment Policy: 50/50 split
Items are consigned for six weeks

Store Specials: Bag sales

New Jersey

West Milford

Treasures Thrift Store
196 Lincoln Ave
West Milford, New Jersey
07480

Store Hours:
Monday, Tuesday, Thursday,
Friday & Saturday 9am-5pm
Wednesday 9am-8pm
Sunday 10am-4pm

Phone: 973-728-2506
Fax: 973-728-7664
e-mail: ssisters@warwick.net

Clothing for the entire family,
accessories, jewelry, housewares,
furniture, baby items, toys, books,
collectibles, records & appliances

Store Policy: Donations welcome

Store Specials: $5.00 bag sale
Double bag sales occasionally

All proceeds benefit Strengthen
Our Sister, a battered women's
shelter in West Milford, New
Jersey.

West Orange

Debby's New To You
Consignment Boutique
640 Eagle Rock Avenue
West Orange, New Jersey
07052

Store Hours:
Monday, Tuesday, Wednesday &
Friday 10am-6pm
Thursday 10am-8pm
Saturday 10am-5:30pm

Contact: Debby Brill
Phone: 973-731-0304
e-mail: DEBBYSNTU@aol.com

Specializing in an impressive
selection of contemporary
apparel for women, shoes,
handbags, jewelry, leather outwear
and furs. Featuring preferred
department store & designer label
fashions.

Consignment Policy:
50/50 split
60 day contract
Special programs for charity fund-
raisers

Store Specials:
Twice a year estate fur sales
featuring over 180 furs coats &
jackets
Women's fashions & accessories
marked down 25% every 30 days

Woodbury

**Charlotte's Threads
Consignment Boutique
417 Salem-Kings Highway
Woodbury, New Jersey 08090**

Store Hours:
Tuesday-Saturday 10am-6pm

Contact: Susanne Dennis
Phone: 609-845-0900
Website: www.theclothestree.com/
shops/Charlottes/

Women's apparel & accessories,
wedding gowns, formal wear,
lingerie, leather & furs, fad
clothing & costumes, lots of
knick-knacks & decorative items
for the home. Lots of new items
too!

Consignment Policy:
No appointment necessary
50/50 split
Items consigned for 90 days
Items reduced 20% after 30 days
& 50% after 60 days

Store Specials
$1.00 rack & advertised discounts

*Elegant wedding gown & formal
attire from Karyn's Kloset in
Kearny, New Jersey*

*Trendy clothing & accessories
from New Leaf Consignment
Boutique in Madison, New Jersey*

*The latest clothing displayed
in an organized fashion at
New Start Consignment Shop
in Somerville, New Jersey*

New Jersey

Festive window display adds to
the ambiance at Secrets in
Califon, New Jersey

Chic suits featured at Debby's
New To You in West Orange,
New Jersey

Fine children's clothing
displayed at
Small Change in Lyndhurst,
New Jersey

Convenient play area designed
for children at Apparel Revisited
in North Plainfield, New Jersey

Albuquerque

**Albuquerque Nob Hill
Thrift Store
3701-370 S Central N.E.
Albuquerque, New Mexico
87109**

Store Hours:
Summer hours: 11am-6pm
Winter Hours: 11am-5pm

Phone: 505-262-9677

Clothing for the entire family,
furniture, books & more!

**Ritzy Rags Resale
1200 Yale Blvd. S.E.
Albuquerque, New Mexico
87106**

Store Hours:
Monday-Saturday 9:30am-6pm

Contact: Dian & Norman Bazient
Phone: 505-255-6251

Upscale clothing & accessories
for women

Store Policy:
Items purchased outright

Store Specials:
Discount coupons twice a year
by mail

Moriarty

**Bethel Community
Storehouse
400 Center Street
Moriarty, New Mexico 87035**

Store Hours:
Tuesday-Saturday 12pm-4pm

Phone: 505-832-6642
Fax: 505-832-4249

Clothing, furniture, books, toys,
jewelry & bric-a-brac
Accepts cash & local checks

Store Specials:
Seniors receive a 10% discount
on Wednesday & $2.00 bag sale
twice per year

Present this coupon at
*Bethel Community
Storehoure
400 Center Street
Moriarty, New Mexico* &
save 10% off one purchase

No restrictions apply

Santa Fe

**Act 2
410-B Old Santa Fe Trail
Santa Fe, New Mexico 87501**

Store Hours:
Monday-Saturday 10am-6pm
Sunday 11am-4pm

Phone: 505-983-8585

Apparel for women & men,
contemporary to vintage

Consignment Policy:
Consignor receives 40%

New York

Marjuree's Consignment Boutique in Lancaster, New York shows their fine array of accessories

Well tailored outfits displayed at Peninah's Treasures in Brooklyn, New York

Tokio 7, a fine vintage boutique in New York City

Albany

The Church Mouse
109 State Street
Albany, New York 12207

Store Hours:
Wednesday-Friday 10am-2pm

Phone: 518-465-5382

Clothing for the entire family & more

Store Policy: Donations welcome

Store Specials: Periodic bag sales

Beacon

As Good As New
500 Main Street
Beacon, New York 12508

Store Hours:
Wednesday-Sunday 11am-5pm
(May vary depending
on the season)

Phone: 914-838-3031
800-566-3031
Fax: 914-831-3923
e-mail: asgood@earthlink.net
Website:http://
www2.webyellowpages.com/
webyellowpages/asgood.htm

Children's clothing sizes newborn
to 14/16, furniture, books, toys,
videos & more

Store Specials: Select color tags
$5.00 annual fee to consign
merchandise
Items consigned for 60 days
Frequent shopper discount cards:
Automatic markdowns: After

Chappaqua

Elegance II Ltd.
75 S. Greeley Avenue
Chappaqua, New York 10514

Store Hours:
Monday-Saturday 10am-5pm
Thursday until 6:30pm

Phone: 914-238-3341

Upscale designer apparel for women

Store Specials: Monthly discounts from 20% to 50%
End of the season sales-75% off select merchandise

Cicero

Fine Things Boutique
8319 Rt. 11
Cicero, New York 13039

Store Hours:
Monday-Friday 10am-6pm
Saturday 10am-4pm

Phone: 315-698-6860

Contact: Mary Beth Kendig & Terese Melfi

Women's casual & career clothing, children's clothing sizes newborn to 8, shoes, accessories, jewelry, wedding gowns, decorative housewares and crafts
Accepts cash, checks with a New York State drivers license, Mastercard, Visa & Discover

Consignment Policy:
No appointment necessary

three weeks items reduced 20%, Store Specials: After five weeks items reduced 40%

This coupon entitles the bearer to save 25% off your consignment purchase at Fine Things Boutique
8319 Rt. 11
Cicero, New York.
Present this coupon at checkout.
(Not valid for craft purchases)

Dobbs Ferry

Affordables
10 Main Street
Dobbs Ferry, New York 10522

Store Hours:
Monday-Saturday 10am-4pm
Thursday until 6pm

Contact: Linda Cronquist & Pat Kolbay
Phone: 914-693-3610

Apparel for children sizes 0 to 14, maternity wear, baby equipment, toys, books, games, ice skates, roller blades & cleats
Accepts cash, local checks, Visa, Mastercard & Discover

Affordable Elegance
117 Main Street
Dobbs Ferry, New York 10522

Store Hours:
Tuesday-Friday 12pm-6pm
Saturday 10am-6pm
Evenings by appointment

New York

Phone: 914-693-5798

Bridal gowns, mother-of-the-bride, flower girl dresses, headpieces and veils, gloves & petticoats
Accepts cash & checks

Consignment Policy:
$5.00 fee to consign
50/50 split

Store Specials: Lay-a-way available

Fairport

Lu's Back Door
19 Jefferson Avenue
Fairport, New York 14450
Located on the outskirts of Rochester

Store Hours: Open ten months a year except in July & February
Monday, Wednesday & Friday
10am-6pm
Tuesday 10am-8pm
Thursday 10am-9pm
Saturday 10am-5pm

Top label fashions for women, men & children, decorative household items, new gift items & salesman & craft samples

Lou's Back Door is a spacious, well organized boutique in which to shop.

Fort Covington

Calico Cat Whatnot Shop
High & Blanchard
Fort Covington, New York
12937

Store Hours:
Monday-Sunday 9am-5pm

Phone: 518-358-4560

Vintage clothing, antiques & collectibles

Kingston

Clothes Friends
337 Washington Avenue
Kingston, New York 12401

Store Hours:
Tuesday-Friday 11am-5pm
Saturday 9am-1pm

Contact: Carol Dolan & Lucia Reich
Phone: 914-334-9008

Women's designer clothing & accessories

Consignment Policy:
50/50 split
Items consigned for 60 days

Store Specials:
Holiday raffles
Bag sales at the end of Summer &
Winter season

Lancaster

**Marjuree' Consignment
Shoppe & Boutique
4729 Transit Road Suite #5
Lancaster, New York 14043**

Store Hours:
Tuesday, Wednesday & Friday
10am-5pm
Thursday 10am-7pm
Saturday 10am-4pm

Contact: Marjorie Long
Phone: 716-656-9377

Designer clothing for women
from casual to evening wear &
select men's clothing, jewelry,
reproduction designer purses,
scarfs, shoes & much more

Consigment Policy: Consignor
receives 40%
Items are marked down after 60
days

Store Specials: Mailing list specials

Marjuree's features items
previously worn by many TV
personalites.

Long Island

Baldwin

**A to Z Thrift Shop
584 Seaman Ave
Baldwin, New York 11510**

Store Hours:
Winter hours: 10am-5pm daily
Summer hours: 12pm-7pm

Contact: Felix Meyer
Phone: 516-868-9557

Home furnishings, appliances,
knick-knacks and much more
Accepts cash or checks

Store Policy:
Donations accepted or
Buy, sell or trade your items

Present this coupon to
save 10% off a purchase over
$50.00
at
*A to Z Thrift Shop at
584 Seaman Ave,
Baldwin, New York*

Expiration Date: 12/31/99

Cedarhurst

**A Consignor's Showcase
126 Cedarhurst Avenue
Cedarhurst, New York 11516**
Store Hours:
Monday-Saturday 11am-6pm,
Thursday until 8pm & Sunday
12pm-5pm

Phone: 516-295-2147

Upscale clothing for women, children's clothing, furs & accessories

Consignment Policy:
Consignor receives 40% of the selling price for the item
Items marked down after 60 days

Glen Cove

Family Service Association Thrift Shop
190 Glen Cove Avenue
Glen Cove, New York 11542

Store Hours:
Monday, Tuesday, Thursday
10am-5pm
Wednesday & Friday
10am-5:30pm
Sunday 12pm-4pm

Phone: 516-671-7929

Gently used clothing for the entire family & bric-a-brac

Store Policy: Donations welcome

Great Neck

The Discovery Thrift Shops
741 Middle Neck Road
Great Neck, New York 11029

Store Hours:
Monday-Thursday 10am-4pm
Friday & Saturday 10:30am-4pm
& the last Sunday of every month
12pm-3pm

Phone: 516-482-3004

Upscale designer clothing & jewelry
Accepts cash, Visa, Mastercard & Discovery

Store Policy: Donations welcome & a receipt may be provided for tax purposes

Huntington

The Community Thrift Shop
8 E. Carver Street
Huntington, New York 11743

Store Hours:
Monday-Saturday 10am-4pm

Contact: Harriet Miller
Phone: 516-271-4883

Gently used clothing for the entire family including a special designer boutique, jewelry, china, glassware, small appliances, housewares, small furniture, artwork, books & linens

Store Policy: Donations welcome & are tax deductible

Store Specials: On-going specials & seasonal sales

The shop is run by volunteers who represent non-profit agencies such as the American Red Cross, Family Service League, Health Services at Home, Huntington Hospital & others. Proceeds benefit the community.

N. Bellmore

A.C.S. Discovery Shop
1194 Oakfield Avenue
N. Bellmore, N.Y. 11710

Store Hours:
Monday-Friday 10am-4pm
Saturday 11am-3pm

Phone: 516-785-9436

"Nearly new" designer clothing & accessories, housewares, knick-knacks & more!

Store Policy: Donations welcome & a receipt may be provided for tax purposes

Rockville Center

Curtain Call, Inc.
88A N. Village Avenue
Rockville Center, New York 11570

Store Hours:
Monday 11am-5:30pm
Tuesday, Wednesday & Saturday 10am-5:30pm
Thursday 10am-9pm
Sunday 11am-3pm

Contact: Mary Batus
Phone: 516-766-7664

Clothing for women

Consignment Policy:
60/40 split on clothing
50/50 split on furs

Store Specials: Five sales per season & weekly specials

Present this coupon at
Curtain Call, Inc.
88A N. Village Ave
Rockville Center, New York &
save 10% off any non-sale item

(Excludes furs)
Expiration Date: 12/31/99

Sag Harbor

Around Again Inc.
P.O. Box 1004
Long Wharf Promenade
Sag Harbor, New York 11963-0029
Located on the Long Wharf in Sag Harbor, Long Island

"Our Inventory Is As Varied As The Lifestyles Of Our Consignors." (And We've Got GREAT Consignors!)

Store Hours:
Monday-Thursday 10am-5:30pm
Friday-Sunday: Call for extended store hours

Contact: Marjorie Scanlon
Phone: 516-725-4067

Top label designer clothing for the entire family, accessories, fine pieces of furniture, prints & pictures
Accepts cash, Visa, Mastercard & Discover

New York

New York City

Brooklyn

D & G Thrift Shop
873 Broadway (Between
Lewis Ave. & Belvidere St.)
Brooklyn, New York 11206

Store Hours:
Monday-Saturday 10am-5pm

Contact: David Becker
Phone: 718-452-5686

Everything imaginable including
clothing, furniture, household
items & much more!
Accepts cash & credit cards

Store Specials: Free delivery on
furniture

```
........................
.                      .
.  Present this coupon at  .
.     D&G Thrift Shop      .
.      873 Broadway        .
.    Brooklyn, New York    .
.      & save 10% off      .
.      all merchandise     .
.                          .
.   Expiration Date: 12/31/99  .
........................
```

Peninahs Treasures
1632 Coney Island Ave
(Corner of Avenue M)
Brooklyn, New York 11230

Store Hours:
Monday, Tuesday, Thursday
10am-6pm
Wednesday until 8pm
Friday 11:30am-check with shop
Sunday 10:30am-2:30pm

Phone: 718-338-6175
24 Hour Consignor Hotline:
718-377-9550
Website: www.theclothestree.com/
shops/PeninahsTreasures/

Contact: Rachel Kaplan

Peninahs Treasures offers upscale
women's sizes 2-24, girl's sizes 5-
preteen, maternity, clothing and
accessories. Choose from an
elegant selection of labels such
as DKNY, Escada, Fendi, Mondi,
Ralph Lauren and much more.

Consignment Policy:
Consignor receives 40%
Items consigned for 90 days
Drop and Run service available

Merry Go Round
177 Court Street
Brooklyn, New York 11201

Store Hours:
Wednesday-Friday 12pm-6pm
Saturday 11:30am-4pm

Phone: 718-596-1639

Upscale designer apparel,
accessories & furs for women
Accepts cash

Store Specials:
Lay-a-way available

```
Present this coupon at
    Merry Go Round
    177 Court Street
   New York, NY 11201
  & save 20% one item

  Expiration Date: 12/31/99
```

Manhattan

A Repeat Performance
156 1st Avenue
New York, New York 10009

Store Hours: Monday-Saturday
12pm-8pm & Sunday 2pm-8pm
Friday until midnight

Specializing in European
lampshades
Accepts cash, Mastercard, Visa &
American Express

```
Save 15% when this
coupon is presented at
A Repeat Performance
156 1st Avenue
New York, New York

Expiration Date: 12/31/99
```

A Second Chance
1133 Lexington Avenue
New York, New York 10021

Store Hours:
Monday-Friday 11am-7pm
Saturday 11am-6pm
Sunday (October-May)
12pm-5pm

Contact: Maria Ridolfi &
Nelida Leichtung
Phone: 212-744-6041

Upscale designer clothing &
maternity wear

Consignment Policy:
50/50 split
Items consigned for 90 days
Items reduced 20% after 30 days
& 50% after 60 days

Store Specials: End of the season

Allan & Suzi
416 Amsterdam Ave
New York, New York 10024
Located on the corner of 80th
Street

Store Hours:
Monday & Saturday 11am-7pm
Tuesday-Friday 12pm-8pm
Sunday 12pm-6pm

Phone: 212-724-7445
Fax: 212-724-6483

Fabulous designer new & vintage
clothing & accessories
A favorite among celebrities!
Accepts all major credit cards

Store Specials: Always available!

Canal Street Jean Company
504 Broadway
New York, New York 10012

Store Hours
Monday-Sunday 10am-8pm

Contact: Mett Gilliam
Phone: 212-226-1130

Great vintage clothing & military
surplus from around the world
Accepts cash, checks with ID &
all major credit cards

Store Specials:
Weekly sales & special 25 cent
rack

Cancer Care Thrift Shop
1480 3rd Avenue
New York, New York 10036

Store Hours:
Monday, Tuesday & Friday
11am-6pm
Wednesday & Thursday
11am-7pm
Saturday 10am-4:30pm

Phone: 212-879-9868

Clothing for the entire family,
clothing sizes infant-10, toys, car
seats, strollers, portable cribs &
much more!

Consignment Policy:
No appointment necessary

Consignments accepted during
regular business hours

Crocodile Computers
360 Amsterdam Avenue
New York, New York 10023

Store Hours:
Monday-Friday 11am-7pm
Saturday 11am-5pm

Phone: 212-769-3400

After donating merchandise

Secondhand computers, monitors
& accessories at a great savings!

Cheap Jack's
Vintage Clothing
841 Broadway (Between 13th
& 14th Street)
New York, New York 10003

Phone: 212-777-9564
212-995-0403

Over 15,000 square feet of the
best vintage clothing in the world
from the 1800's to the 1970's.
Thousands of items to choose
from.

Store Specials: Pay cash at Cheap
Jack's & receive a 50% discount
on merchandise priced from $5.00
to $50.00

Church Street Surplus
327 Church Street
New York, NY 10013

Store Hours:
Monday-Saturday 10:30am-6pm

Phone: 212-226-5280

Vintage & gently used military
clothing

Children's Resale
303 East 81st Street
New York, New York 10028

Store Hours:
Monday-Friday 11am-7pm
Saturday 10am-6pm
Sunday 12pm-5pm

Phone: 212-734-8897

Upscale children's gently used
clothing & accessories

Designer Resale
324 East 81st Street (Between
1st & 2nd Avenue)
New York, New York 10028

Store Hours:
Monday-Friday 11am-7pm
Thursday until 8pm
Saturday 10am-6pm
Sunday 12pm-5pm

Contact: Myrna Skoller
Phone: 212-734-3639

Upscale clothing & accessories for women

Consignment Policy:
Consignments accepted during regular business hours, no appointment necessary
Items consigned for 90 days
After 30 days items are reduced 20%, after 60 days items are reduced 50%

Dress For Success® New York

135 W. 4th Street
New York, New York 10012

Phone: 212-545-DSNY
Store Hours: Monday-Friday
10am-5pm
Saturday 12pm-3pm
Web site: http://
www.dressforsuccess.org

Dress For Success® (DSNY) provides interview appropriate clothing to low income women seeking employment.
Dress For Success accepts donations of skirts, pantsuits, blouses, scarves and other interview appropriate clothing and accessories. Larger size clothing is especially appreciated.

include your name and address and a receipt will be mailed to you for tax purposes.
Donations must be in excellent condition and ready to use i.e., laundered and ironed or dry-cleaned or pressed.
Menswear, sportswear and other items are not accepted. Garments that Dress For Success cannot use are donated to charities.
Dress For Success is a national grass-roots effort dedicated to helping disadvantaged women overcome one obstacle to rejoin the workforce. It is staffed almost entirely by volunteers. All clients are referred by member organizations, including domestic violence programs, homeless shelters and incarcerated women's groups.
Dress For Success sister programs have begun in Brookhaven, New York, Mid Fairfield County-Hartford, Conneticut, St. Louis, Missouri and New Orleans with more groups opening soon.

Ellen Christine & Company
151 Ludlow Street
New York, New York 10002

Store Hours:
Tuesday-Saturday 1pm-8pm
Sunday 12pm-6pm

Phone: 212-979-9370
e-mail:
ellenalamode@memefashion.com
Web site: www.memefashion.com

A vast collection of 1940's fashions & accessories.
Choose from a unique selection of fanciful millinery, textiles &

183

accessories that sets the mood for a glamourous experience.

Encore
1132 Madison Ave
New York, New York 10028
Located between 84th & 85th Street

Store Hours:
Monday, Tuesday, Wednesday & Friday 10:30am-6:30pm
Thursday 10:30am-7:30pm
Saturday 10:30am-6pm
Sunday 12pm-6pm
*Except in July & August

Phone: 212-879-2850

Women's designer & couture clothing & accessories
Accepts cash & checks

Store Specials: Special sales

Established in 1954 as the first consignment shop in New York City, Encore offers two floors of celebrity designer clothing at great prices!

Fialka Boutique
324 E. 9th Street
New York, New York 10003

"The best little shop in the East Village"
Store Hours:
Monday-Saturday 1pm-8pm

Phone: 212-460-8615

Featuring casual, business & evening wear from labels such as Christian Dior to the Gap
Accepts cash

Goddard-Riverside
Thrift Shop
647 Columbus Avenue
New York, NY 10025

Store Hours:
Monday-Saturday 12 noon-5pm

Phone: 212-873-6608

Clothing for women, men & children, housewares, art, glassware, china, linen & novelties
Accepts: Cash only

Store Policy: Donations welcome & appreciated

Store Specials: Weekly Specials & Special Shopper's Card

Godmothers' League
Thrift Shop
1459 Third Avenue
Between 82nd & 83rd Streets
New York, New York 10028

Store Hours:
Monday-Saturday 10am-6pm
Sunday 12pm-5pm

Phone: 212-988-2858

Lots of assorted merchandise & bric-a-brac

Gentlemen's Resale
322 E. 81st Street
New York, New York 10028

Contact: Gary Scheiner
Phone: 212-734-2739

Store Hours:
Monday-Friday 11am-7pm
Saturday 10am-6pm
Sunday 12pm-5pm
Upscale designer clothing & accessories for men

Accepts cash & all major credit cards

Store Specials:
Items discounted 20% after 30 days, 50% after 60 days

Housing Works Thrift Shops
202 East 77th Street
Between 2nd & 3rd Avenue
New York, New York 10021
Web site: www.housingworks.org

Store Hours:
Monday-Saturday 10am-6pm
Sunday 12pm-4pm
Phone: 212-772-8461

Other Locations:

143 West 17th Street
Between 6th & 7th Avenue
New York, New York 10011

Store Hours:
Monday-Saturday 10am-6pm
Sunday 12pm-4pm
Phone: 212-366-0820

306 Columbus Ave.
Between 74th & 75th Street
New York, New York 10023

Store Hours:
Monday, Tuesday, Wednesday & Friday 11am-7pm
Thursday until 8pm
Saturday 10am-6pm
Sunday 1pm-5pm
Phone: 212-579-7566

Used Book Cafe
126 Crosby Street
South of Houston
New York, New York 10012

Store Hours:
Monday-Thursday 10am-8pm
Friday 10am-9pm
Saturday 12pm-9pm
Sunday 12pm-7pm
Phone: 212-334-3324

Voted the best thrift shop in New York City, Housing Works Thrift Shop features designer clothing, accessories & an eclectic array of antiques & home furnishings. The shop's "boutique type atmosphere" has caught the attention of *The New York Times, The New York Post, Good Morning America & Fox News.* All shops accept cash, Mastercard, Visa & American Express

Store Policy: Donations welcome & appreciated or call 212-366-0820 ext. 2 for pick-up information

Store Specials:
Many events throughout the year include, "Beach Ball" on June 23 featuring a wide variety of summer wear & items at the 17th Street shop. Fall preview 98 on Sept. 1, 1998 from 5pm-8pm at the 17th Street location; September 8th at the Columbus Ave location & September 15th at the 77th Street location. "Annual Thanksgiving Food Drive" from Nov. 1st-24th. "Annual Christmas Toy Drive" from November 17th-December 15th. December 1 1998-World Aids Day & December 2, 1998 "World Aids Day" Thrift Store Holiday Bargain Kick-Off".

All proceeds benefit homeless & formerly homeless men, women & children with HIV & AIDS.

Irvington Thrift Shop
1534 Second Avenue
New York, New York 10021

Store Hours:
Monday, Tuesday, Friday &
Saturday 10am-6pm
Wednesday & Thursday
10am-8pm
Sunday 12pm-5pm

Contact: Ned Brody
Phone: 212-879-4555

Clothing for the entire family,
furniture, silver, china, artwork &
much more
Accepts cash, Visa, Mastercard,
Discover, NYCE ATM cards

Store Policy: Donations Welcome

Store Specials: Periodic special
sales & promotions

Jane's Exchange
Children's Resale &
Consignment Shop
107-109 Avenue B (7th Street)
New York, New York 10009

Store Hours: Monday-Saturday
10am-6pm

Phone: 212-674-6268

Clothing for children, toys,
furniture & much more!

Consignment Policy:
50/50 split

La Boutique
1045 Madison Avenue
(Between 79th & 80th Street)
New York, New York 10021

Store Hours:
Monday, Tuesday, Wednesday,
Friday & Saturday 10am-7pm
Thursday 10am-8pm
Sunday 12pm-6pm

Contact: Jonathan Tse
Phone: 212-517-8099
e-mail: jon@laboutique.com
Website: www.laboutique.com

Located on New York's upper east
side, La Boutique carries over 100
pieces of couture & designer label
clothing. Featuring a vast
selection of the most current style
fashions, all in pristine condition.

Present this coupon at
La Boutique
1045 Madison Ave.
New York, NY & save
10% off one regular price item

Limit one coupon per customer only
(Coupon not valid with any other offer
or any sale item)
Expiration Date:12/31/99

Animal Care Thrift Boutique
247 East 81th Street
New York, New York

Store Hours:
Monday-Friday 11:30am-7:30pm
Saturday 11am-7pm
Sunday 12pm-6pm

Phone: 212-327-4878

Clothing for men & women

Lincoln Business Machines, Inc.
111 W. 68th Street
New York, New York 10023

Store Hours:
Monday-Friday 8:30am-6pm
Saturday 10am-4pm

Phone: 212-769-0606
Fax: 212-787-4246

Gently used computers, office equipment & supplies. Featuring an interesting collection of antique typewriters.

Lincoln Business Machines has been featured in *The Wall Street Journal*.

Memorial Sloan-Kettering Thrift Shop
1440 Third Avenue at 82nd Street
New York, New York 10028

Store Hours:
Monday, Tuesday, Wednesday & Friday 10am-5:30pm
Thursday 10am-8pm
Saturday 10am-5pm

Phone: 212-535-1250

Clothing for the entire family, furniture & bric-a-brac
Accepts cash, Visa, Mastercard & American Express

Store Policy: Donations welcome

Michael's, the Consignment Shop for Women and Brides
1041 Madison Ave
Second Floor
New York, NY 10021

Store Hours:

Monday-Saturday 9:30am-6pm
Thursday until 8pm
Closed on Saturdays in July and August

Phone: 212-737-7273
e-mail: zfluhr@bway.net

Setting the standard in the ladies' consignment industry for over forty years, Michael's offers a "white-glove" selection of couture and designer fashions and accessories.
Chanel, Prada, YSL, Donna Karan, Hermes & Moschino are among the fine list of items to choose from which arrive from the finest homes on "Park Avenue" in New York City.
Michael's also offers an outstanding selection of "delicately worn" designer wedding gowns sizes 2-14.
Please call for an appointment at the wedding salon.

Consignment Policy:
50/50

New & Almost New Shop
65 Mercer Street
New York, NY 10012

Store Hours:
Tuesday-Friday 12pm-6:30pm
Saturday 1pm-6pm

Contact: Maggie Poon
Phone: 212-226-6677

Designer label clothing and vintage
Accepts cash, American Express, Mastercard, Visa & ATM cards
All sales are final

Store Specials: On-going sales

New York

Once Upon A Time
171 East 92nd Street
New York, New York 10128

Store Hours:
Monday-Saturday 10am-6pm
Monday-Friday July-August
10am-6pm

Contact: Ronnie Mann
Phone: 212-831-7619

Spectacular children's resale
clothing & new items too!

Consignment Policy: Consignor
receives 40%
Items consigned for six months

Store Specials: January & July
special 30%-50% off select items

Pretty Plus Plus
1309 Madison Avenue
New York, New York 10128

Store Hours:
Monday & Friday 11am-6pm
Wednesday & Thursday
11am-7pm
Saturday 10am-5pm

Contact: Helen Norton &
Jeanne File
Phone: 212-427-4724

Specializing in plus size clothing
for women sizes 14 & up
Accepts cash, checks, Visa &
Mastercard

Store Specials: Lay-a-way
available & special sales twice a
year

Ritz Furs
107 West 57th Street
New York, NY 10019

Monday-Saturday 9am-6pm
November to January: Sundays
11am-5pm

Phone: 212-265-4559

Established over 50 years ago,
Ritz Furs offers the best luxurious
furs at affordable prices.
"No one beats the Ritz." Known
as New York's department store
for fabulous furs, Ritz Furs also
offers an "ever changing variety
of new, one of a kind designer
furs, shearling, fur-lined and fur-
trimmed outerwear".
Accepts cash, Visa, Mastercard,
Diners, Discover & American
Express

Store Specials: Necessary
alterations available at no charge
& free summer storage for
garments purchased at the Ritz

Spence Chapin Thrift Shop
1430 Third Ave
New York, New York 10028

Store Hours:
Monday-Friday 10am-7pm
Thursday until 8pm
Saturday 10am-5pm
Sunday 12pm-5pm

Phone: 212-737-8448

1850 Second Ave
New York, NY 10128

Store Hours:
Tuesday-Friday 10am-6pm
Saturday 9am-5pm
Sunday 12pm-5pm

Phone: 212-426-7643

Clothing for the entire family, furniture, bric-a-brac, paintings, antiques and much more!

Store Policy:
Donations welcome &a tax receipt provided

Store Specials:
New sales daily!

St. George's Thrift Shop Annex
209 East 16th Street
New York, New York 10003

Store Hours:
Tuesday-Saturday 11am-5:30pm

Phone: 212-475-5510

Specializing in furniture, housewares, books, jewelry & children's items

Store Policy: Donations welcome

St. Lukes Thrift Shop
487 Hudson Street
New York, New York 10014

Store Hours:
Monday, Tuesday & Wednesday
11am-6pm
Thursday, Friday & Saturday
11am-7pm

Phone: 212-924-9364

Clothing for the entire family, china, jewelry, furniture & bric-a-brac
Accepts cash, Mastercard, Visa & American Express

Store Policy: Donations welcome

Store Specials: Seniors receive a 20% discount
Look for special holiday sales!

St. Luke's Thrift Shop is "pet friendly."

Stella Dallas
Vintage Clothing
218 Thompson Street at
Bleecker
New York, New York 10012

Store Hours:
Open every day from 12pm-7pm

Contact: Carol Atkin
Phone: 212-674-0447

Classic vintage clothing for women & men. Specializing in the 1930's, 40's & 50's era, accessories, linens & drapes
Accepts cash, travelers checks, Visa, Mastercard & American Express

Celebrating their twenty-fifth anniversary this year!

The Bridal Garden
122 East 29th Street
New York, New York 10016
Located off Park Ave South

Store Hours:
Monday-Friday 10am-4pm

Contact: Geraldine Brower & Ginine Mohamad
Phone: 212-252-0661

The Bridal Garden is New York City's most exclusive elegant bridal boutique. At the shop couture bridal gowns are available

189

for a fraction of their original cost.

Featuring designs by Vera Wang, Carolina Herrera, Marissa, Yumi Kastura & Priscilla of Boston. A great way to save "thousands" for that special day.

Accepts cash, Visa & American Express

Store Policy: Donations welcome & appreciated. Tax receipt provided if requested.

Store Specials: Dry cleaning & slip/petticoat discount

The Bridal Garden is sponsored by Sheltering Arms Services, New York City's premier non-profit organization which has been helping disadvantaged children since 1823. Proceeds benefit over 3000 children and their families each year for day care, foster care, adoption, special education and after school programs.

The Family Jewels
Vintage Clothing
832 Sixth Avenue
New York, New York 10001

Store Hours:
Monday-Sunday 11am-7pm

Contact: Lillyan Peditto
Phone & Fax: 212-679-5023

Marvelous vintage clothing for men, women & children

Store Policy: Consignment offered on hard to find pieces from the 20's, 30's & 40's

Thousands of unique items bring

shoppers from all over the US, Europe & Japan to the Family Jewels. Items from the shop are often featured in magazines such as *Vogue, In Style, W & Details*. A favorite among photographers, costume designers & design houses.

Tokio 7
64 E 7th Street
New York, New York 10003

Store Hours:
Monday-Sunday 11:30am-8:30pm

Phone: 212-353-8443
Contact: Makoto Watanabe

Lots of fantastic funky & designer vintage clothing
Accepts cash, Visa, Mastercard, American Express & Debit cards

West Shop of The Bridge Inc.
642 Amsterdam Ave &
91th St.
New York, New York 10024

Store Hours:
Monday-Sunday 9:15am-4:20pm

Phone: 212-874-1340

Clothing for the entire family, furniture & bric-a-brac

Store Policy: Donations welcome & a receipt may be provided for tax purposes

Store Specials: $1.00 bin
Fill a bag of basement books for $3.00

Proceeds from the shop benefit the mentally ill.

What Comes Around Goes Around
351 Broadway
New York, New York 10013
Located in Soho between Broome & Grand Street

Store Hours:
Sunday-Wednesday 11am-8pm
Thursday-Saturday 11am-Midnight

Phone: 212-343-9303
Fax: 212-966-7130
e-mail:
Website: www.nyvintage.com

Fine collection of pieces from the Victorian era to the 1970's. Specializing in over a thousand pieces of denim including Levi's. The shop has been featured in *The New York Times, The Daily News, New York Magazine, Rolling Stone Magazine & ABC TV*. Many models, movie & rock stars have worn clothing from this shop. The staff's expertise, vast selection & reasonable prices makes this shop a definite stop.

Wholesale Location:

Buckleback Jack
Laigh Street
New York, New York

Phone: 212-274-8340
Fax: 212-274-8449

e-mail:
buckleback@nyvintage.com

Thousands of wholesale vintage items!

Queens

Antonett's
106-05 Metropolitan Avenue
Forest Hills, New York 11375

Store Hours:
Wednesday-Saturday 12pm-6pm

Phone: 718-520-8272

Upscale new & gently used clothing & accessories for women

Staten Island

Every Thing Goes Clothing
140 Bay Street
Staten Island, New York 10301

Store Hours:
Tuesday-Saturday 11am-6pm

Phone: 718-273-7139
Fax: 718-448-6842
e-mail: ganas@well.com

Clothing for the entire family including vintage & handmade items

Every Thing Goes Art & Antique Gallery
123 Victory Blvd.
Staten Island, New York 10301

Store Hours:
Tuesday-Thursday 11am-6:30pm
Friday & Saturday 11am-7:30pm

Phone: 718-815-9724

A vast array of antiques & beautiful art work

191

New York

Every Thing Goes Furniture
17 Brook Street
Staten Island, New York
10301

Phone: 718-273-0568

Store Hours:
Tuesday-Thursday 11am-6:30pm
Friday & Saturday 11am-7:30pm

Excellent quality gently used
furniture at reasonable prices

Every Thing Goes Original
208 Bay Street
Staten Island, New York
10301

Phone: 718-447-8256

Store Hours:
Tuesday-Saturday 11am-6pm

Gifts, collectibles, jewelry, toys,
household furnishings, small
appliances, dishes, cookware,
linens, curtains, books, records &
much more!

Store Specials: Cash & carry
discount for furniture
Monthly discounts from 10% to
25% off select merchandise as
advertised on the sidewalk signs in
front of the store
Flyers at the store with special
discounts

Repeat Performance
807 Castleton Ave
Staten Island, New York
10310

Store Hours:
Monday-Saturday
10:30am-4:30pm

Contact: Dorothea Dooley &
Lisa Cuevas
Phone: 718-442-1743

Children's clothing sizes newborn
to 14, baby equipment & toys
Consignment Policy: Items must
be consigned by appointment only
Items accepted for consignment
must be in season
Consignor receives 30%-50%

Store Specials: Grandparents
receive a 10% discount on
clothing

Time After Time
59 New Dorp Plaza
Staten Island, New York
10306

Store Hours:
Monday-Saturday 11am-5pm
Thursday 11am-6pm

Phone: 718-987-0853

Clothing & accessories for women
including costume & silver jewelry

Middletown

The Salvation Army
80 W. Main Street
PO Box 759
Middletown, New York 10940

Store Hours:
Monday-Saturday 9am-12pm
& 1pm-3pm

Contact: Lt. Tim Duperee
Phone: 914-343-0821

Clothing for the entire family &
small household items
Accepts cash

Store Policy:
Donations welcome

Monticello

Encore Fashions
126 E. Broadway
Monticello, New York 12701

Store Hours:
Tuesday-Saturday 10am-5:30pm
Closed on Sunday & Monday
during the winter

Phone: 914-791-6070

Clothing for the entire family,
accessories, household items,
books, records & much more!
Accepts cash only

Store Specials:
Items are marked down 25% after
30 days & 50% after 60 days

```
Save 10% off a purchase of
$150.00 when this coupon is
presented at
Encore Fashions
126 E Broadway
Monticello, New York
Expiration: 12/31/99
```

Mount Kisco

Consignor's Closet
36 S. Moger Ave.
Mount Kisco, New York 10549

Store Hours:
Monday-Saturday 10am-5pm
Thursday until 6pm

Contact: Nancy Swensen &
Rhoda Brown
Phone: 914-241-9462

Women's designer clothing &
accessories
Accepts cash & checks

Consignment Policy:
50/50 split
Items consigned for three months
Items reduced 20% after 30 days
& 50% after 60 days

New Rochelle

Humane Society Thrift Shop
311 North Ave
New Rochelle, New York
10801

Located only 25 minutes on
Metro North from Grand
Central Station. Parking is located
in the municipal lot on Garden
Street.

Store Hours:
Monday-Saturday 11am-5pm

Contact: Lucia Kim
Phone: 914-633-7683

"Nearly new" designer clothing,
toys, records, books, costume
jewelry, bric-a-brac, antiques,
furniture, sporting goods and
much more!
Accepts cash only

Store Policy: Donations welcome
& are tax deductible

Established in 1980, proceeds
from the thrift shop benefit
the New Rochelle Humane

Society. The Society houses hundreds of stray and unwanted pets. Twenty-four emergency ambulance service is provided for injured animals & wildlife rescue on the Long Island Sound. Many items have been donated by celebrities. There are lots of treasures waiting here to be discovered here.

Present this coupon at the *Humane Society Thrift Shop* *311 North Avenue* *New Rochelle, New York* & save 10% off one item

No expiration

Schenectady

Seconds Furniture Plus
715 State Street
Schenectady, New York 12307

Store Hours:
Monday-Friday 11am-4:30pm
Saturday 11am-2pm

Phone: 518-393-2914

Gently used furniture & appliances

Unadilla

Busy Bea's Lawn &
Cellar Sales
1020 State Highway 7
Unadilla, New York 13849

Store Hours:
Monday-Sunday 10am-5pm or call for an appointment

Consigment Policy: Items consigned for 60 days

Store Specials: Top name handbags (new) discounted
Lots of antiques & gently used furniture
Accept cash or checks

Store Policy: Consignments accepted

Westmoreland

Bittersweet Pines
Pre-Owned Furniture
4900 St. Rt. 233
PO Box 448
Westmoreland, New York
13490

Store Hours:
Tuesday-Friday 11am-4pm

Phone: 315-853-3677
Website: www.theclothestree.com/shops/Bittersweet/

Fine quality pre-owned furniture, decorative items, lamps, mirrors, books & some antiques
Accepts cash, Visa & Mastercard

White Plains

Marra's Treasures
369 Mamaroneck Ave
White Plains, New York
10605

Store Hours:
Tuesday & Wednesday 11am-6pm, Thursday & Friday 11am-7pm
Saturday 11am-5pm

Phone: 914-761-1110
Contact: Donna Vought

Women's quality consignment apparel
Accepts all forms of payment

Consignment Policy: Consignments by appointment only
After 30 days items marked down 25%, after 60 days items marked down 50%

Store Specials:
Lay-a-ways available
On-going discounts & seasonal

Williamsville

Village Exchange
Women's Designer Quality Clothing
5949 Main Street
Williamsville, New York 14221

Store Hours: Call for store hours

Phone: 716-632-6926

Better quality gently used designer clothing for women with discriminating taste! Buffalo's best kept secret.

North Carolina

Burnsville

Nancy's New & Nearly New
615 W. Main
Burnsville, North Carolina
28714

Store Hours:
Monday, Tuesday, Thursday &
Friday 10am-5pm
Saturday 10am-3pm

Phone: 704-682-7479

Clothing for women & children
Accepts cash & checks

Charlotte

A Closet Full
1729 Garden Terrace
Charlotte, North Carolina
28203

Store Hours:
Tuesday, Wednesday & Friday
10am-5:30pm
Thursday 10am-7pm
Saturday 10am-4pm

Contact: Linda Moneta
Phone: 704-372-5522

Plus size clothing and accessories
Accepts cash, checks, Mastercard,
Visa & Discover

Store Specials: Weekly markdowns

Brides House of Originals
2008 Commonwealth Ave
Charlotte, North Carolina
28205

Store Hours:
Monday-Friday 10am-5pm
Saturday 10am-4pm

Contact: Betty Ziegler
Phone: 704-333-1073

Everything for the bride including
gowns, veils, slips & jewelry
Accepts cash, checks & all major
credit cards

Store Specials: 20%-80%
discounts off select items
Invitation special: 100 invitations
for under $40.00!

Caswell House Ltd.
360 North Caswell Road
Charlotte, North Carolina
28204

Store Hours:
Monday 10am-3pm
Tuesday-Friday 10am-6pm
Saturday 10am-5pm

Phone: 704-331-0555

Vast selection of gently used &
new furniture, home accessories &
unusual gifts.

Classic Consignment
645 Albermarle Road
Charlotte, North Carolina
28212

Store Hours:
Monday-Friday 10am-5:30pm
Saturday 10am-5pm

Contact: Jana Basden
Phone: 704-535-5999

Women's new & gently used
clothing sizes 3 to 26
Accepts cash, local checks,

Mastercard, Visa & Novus

ClearingHouse
701 Central Avenue
Charlotte, North Carolina
28204

Store Hours:
Monday-Saturday 10am-4pm

Phone: 704-375-7708

Furniture, antiques, collectibles & more!

Consignment Policy: Consignor receives 60%

Fayetteville

Sacks Consigned Designs
2631 Raeford Road
Fayetteville, North Carolina
28303

Store Hours:
Monday-Saturday 10am-6pm

Contact: Judy Robinson
Phone: 919-485-3587

Clothing & accessories for women & children, household items & small furniture. Specializing in designer labels & better store brand labels.
Accepts cash, checks, Visa, Mastercard & Discover

Store Specials: Frequent buyer club & seasonal sales

Second Location:
3491 Lackey Street
Luberton, North Carolina
28358

Store Hours:
Monday-Friday 10am-6pm &
Saturday 10am-5pm

Contact: Brenda Richardson
Phone: 919-671-8623

Clothing for the entire family & accessories

Store Specials: Frequent buyers club & seasonal sales

Gastonia

C & J Discount Furniture &
Appliances
239 E. Main Street
Gastonia, North Carolina
28052

Store Hours:
Monday-Friday 9:30am-5pm
Saturday 9:30am-3pm

Contact: Kathy Jones
Phone: 704-868-2487

Furniture, appliances, dishes, pictures, bedding & antiques
All sales final

Store Specials: 30 day lay-a-way

North Carolina

Greensboro

Carolina Thrift Inc.
311 Creekridge Road
Greensboro, North Carolina
27406

Store Hours
Monday-Saturday 8am-8pm
Sunday 10am-6pm

Phone: 910-379-0844

Clothing for the entire family,
knick-knacks, furniture & more
Accepts cash, checks, Visa,
Mastercard & American Express

Store Policy: Donations welcome

Store Specials: Half price items
available

> Present this coupon at
> *Carolina Thrift Inc.*
> *311 Creekridge Road*
> *Greensboro, North Carolina* &
> save 10% off one item
> Expiration Date: 12/31/99

Replacements, Ltd.
1089 Knox Road
P.O. Box 26029
Greensboro, North Carolina
27420

Phone: 1-800-REPLACE
e-mail: ReplaceLtd@aol.com

Replacement's Ltd. offers the
world's largest selection of new &
discontinued china, crystal,
flatware, & collectibles. Replacements Ltd. offers a free identifica-
tion service, lay-a-way
program, Offer to Purchase &
Call Collect programs are among
some of the available services.
Visit their 12,000 foot showroom
& museum and you are sure to
find that perfect piece for your
collection.

Hillsborough

My Secret Closet
347 Ja Max Drive
Hillsborough, North Carolina
27278

Store Hours:
Tuesday-Friday 11am-6pm
Saturday 10am-5pm

Contact: Pam Sullivan &
Cindy Cheek
Phone: 919-732-1254
e-mail: mycloset@nutek.com

Fine women's consignment
clothing

Store Special: Secret sale every
week

> This coupon entitles the
> bearer to save 25%
> off one item at
> *My Secret Closet*
> *347 Ja Max Drive*
> *Hillsborough, North Carolina*
>
> Expiration Date: 12/31/99

Kernersville

Yesterday's
123 Pineview Drive
Kernersville, North Carolina
27284

Store Hours:
Monday-Friday 10am-8pm
Saturday 10am-4pm

Contact: Sonja Mitchell
Phone: 336-996-7007

Clothing for the entire family,
accessories & household items

Consignment Policy:
50/50 split
Items consigned for 60 days

Store Specials: Dot sales

Morgantown

Bloom Again
Consignment Boutique
120 N. Sterling Street
Morganton, North Carolina
28655

Store Hours:
Monday-Friday 10am-5pm
Saturday 10am-3pm

Contact: Sandy Cooper &
Becky Strauss
Phone: 704-439-9020

Clothing for women & children,
bridal gowns, formal-wear, prom
& maternity clothing
Accepts cash & checks

Consignment Policy: 50/50 split

Store Specials: On-going
markdowns

> Present this coupon at
> *Bloom Again*
> *Consignment Boutique*
> *120 N. Sterling Street*
> *Morganton, North Carolina* &
> save 20% off one regular
> priced item
>
> (Coupon only good for one visit)
> Expiration Date: 12/31/99

Mt. Airy

Mayberry Consignments &
Souvenirs
182 N. Main Street
Mt. Airy, North Carolina
27030

Store Hours:
Monday-Saturday 10am-5pm

Contact: Julie M. Teague
Phone: 336-719-2363

Clothing for the entire family,
accessories, household items,
furniture, gift items & sporting
goods
Accepts Visa, Mastercard,
Discover, cash & checks

Consignment Policy:
Items consigned for 60 days
50/50 split

Store Specials: Special discounts
according to color tickets

North Carolina

New Bern

Twice As Nice
Consignment Shop
504 Berne Square
New Bern, North Carolina
28562

Store Hours:
Monday-Friday 9am-6pm,
Saturday 9am-5pm
Sunday 12:30pm-5:30pm

Phone: 919-633-1868

Clothing for the entire family,
nursery items & books

Consignment Policy: 60/40 split
Items are consigned for 90 days

Store Specials: Senior discount

Raleigh

ARround Again Family
ConsignmentTM
4550 Capital Blvd.
North Boulevard Plaza/
Mini City
Raleigh, North Carolina
27604

Store Hours:
Monday-Friday 10am-7pm
Saturday 10am-6pm
Call for Sunday & holiday hours

Contact: Carol, Rick or Lucie
Phone: 919-USA-SAVE (872-
7283)-24 hour information

Featuring 4000 square feet of
Nice-As-NewTM & new clothing
and accessories for boys newborn
through teens, men & women
sizes petite to plus, casual to
elegant, 250 plus wedding gowns,
formal & maternity, cribs & baby
accessories
Accepts cash, Discover, Visa &
Mastercard

Consignment Policy:
All items must be better brands,
designer labels, in style (less than
3 years of old) & next season
(four seasons), freshly cleaned,
pressed & ready to wear, free of
spots, stains, odors, wear &
damage
Consignments by appointment &
there is no waiting when you
arrive
Call to reserve your appointment
before preparing your items

Store Specials: Offers select
merchandise up to 40% extra
savings & periodic special sales.
50% off normal retail prices on
new, first line merchandise every
day, including a great selection of
new wedding gowns.

ARound Again features over
12,000 items at any time. The
shop introduces 500-1000 items
each week! *Triangle Magazine*
voted ARound Again the "best
consignment store in the

Triangle".
The shop is well known for offering a large selection of merchandise, reasonable prices & attentive service by their helpful, knowledgeable staff.
Member of The National Association of Resale & Thrift Shops

Present this coupon for your free gift at
*ARound Again Consignments
4550 Capital Blvd.
Raleigh, North Carolina*

Name:_____

Address: _____

_____

City: _____ State ____

Zip: _____

Phone: (____) _____

Expiration Date: 12/31/99

Toy-Go-Round Inc.
6635 Falls of the Neuse Road
Raleigh, North Carolina
27615

Store Hours:
Monday-Saturday 10am-6pm

Contact: Lorraine Schlueter
Phone: 919-846-0350

Top quality name-brand gently used toys, books & baby equipment. Featuring toys for all ages & collectibles too!
Accepts cash, checks, Mastercard

& Visa

Store Policy:
Appointment necessary
Cash paid for toys
Toys must be clean & reusable

Present this coupon at
*Toy-Go-Round
6635 Falls of the Neuse Road
Raleigh, North Carolina &
save 10% off one purchase
over $25.00*

Expiration Date: 12/31/99

Wilmington

Repeat Performance
419 S.College Road Suite 33
Wilmington, North Carolina
28403

Store Hours:
Monday-Friday 10am-6pm
Saturday 11am-5pm

Contact: Vivian Vaughan
Phone: 910-799-9552

Upscale clothing for women, accessories & shoes
Accepts cash, checks, Mastercard, Visa & Discover

Winston Salem

Snob Shop
465 West End Blvd.
Winston-Salem, North
Carolina 27101
Store Hours:
Monday-Saturday 10am-6pm

Phone: 336-724-2547

North Carolina

Clothing for the entire family,
household items, antiques &
collectibles

Accepts cash, checks, Visa,
Mastercard & American Express

Store Specials:
On-going discounts
20% to 80%

*ARound Again Consignment
Boutique in Raleigh, North
Carolina features 4000 square
feet of excellent merchandise*

North Dakota

Bismarck

Repeat Performance
220 W. Front
Bismarck, North Dakota
58504

Store Hours:
Monday 10am-8pm
Tuesday 10am-7pm
Saturday 10am-6pm

Contact: Lorissa Birst
Phone: 701-255-0096

Clothing for the entire family,
bridal & formal wear sizes 0 to 28
Accepts cash, check, Visa &
Mastercard & Discover

Consignment Policy:
60/40 split on general items &
50/50 split on bridal & formal-
wear
Items consigned for 90 days

Fargo

The Arc Thrift Store
1206 3rd Avenue North
Fargo, North Dakota 58102

Store Hours:
Monday-Friday 9am-7pm
Saturday 9am-5pm

Phone: 701-232-6641

Clothing for the entire family &
bric-a-brac

Store Policy: Donations welcome

Valley City

The Arc Thrift-E-Shop
121 2nd Street N.E.
Valley City, North Dakota
58072

Store Hours:
Monday-Saturday 9:30am-5:30pm

Phone: 701-845-4189

Clothing for the entire family,
household goods, furniture &
costume rental

Store Policy: Donations
welcome

Ohio

Akron

Clothes Renaissance
639 E. Cuyahoga Falls Ave.
Akron, Ohio 44310

Store Hours:
Monday-Thursday 11am-7pm
Friday-Saturday 10am-6pm

Phone: 330-945-4407

Clothing for the entire family
Accepts cash, checks with proper
ID, Mastercard & Visa

Consignment Policy: 50/50 split
An appointment is necessary to
consign merchandise

Cincinnati

2nd Chance Upscale
Resale Shoppe
3670 Werk Road
Western Hills
Cincinnati, Ohio 45248

Phone: 513-451-1451

Springdale
11792 Springdale Pike
Cincinnati, Ohio 45248
Phone: 513-671-7162

Store Hours for Western Hills &
Springdale locations:

Monday, Tuesday & Saturday
10am-6pm
Wednesday, Thursday & Friday
10am-8pm
Sunday 12pm-5pm

White Oak
6845 Cheviot Road
Cincinnati, Ohio 45248
Phone: 513-385-8045

Store Hours for White Oak
location:
Monday-Saturday 10am-6pm
Sunday 12pm-5pm

Upscale women's & children's
clothing & decorative household
items (at Springdale location
only)

Consignment Policy:
50/50 split
Items consigned for ten weeks
No fee to consign merchandise
Accepts cash, checks & major
credit cards

Store Specials:
After 30 days discounted 30%,
After 60 days items discounted
60%

Present this coupon at
2nd Chance
3670 Werk Road
Cinncinnati, Ohio &
save 10% off a purchase

Expiration date: 12/31/99

Columbus

One More Time
1521 W. 5th Ave
Columbus, Ohio 43212

Store Hours:
Monday-Friday 11am-8pm
Saturday 10am-6pm

Contact: Chris Cowman
Phone: 614-486-0031
Consignment Information
Hotline: 614-486-2229
e-mail: omtcec@aol.com

Over 7000 square feet of upscale clothing & accessories for women & men including plus sizes, jewelry, small household items & more. Featuring labels such as Escada, Donna Karan, Ralph Lauren & more.
Accepts cash, checks, Mastercard, Visa & Discover

Consignment Policy: 50/50 split

Second Chance
1790 W 5th Ave
Columbus, Ohio 43212

Store Hours:
Tuesday-Friday 11am-6pm
Saturday 10am-6pm

Contact: Annette Hines
Phone: 614-488-3006

Gently used designer clothing for women & men and designer decorative

Consignment Policy:
No appointment necessary
Consignments accepted
Wednesday-Saturday 12pm-5pm
Items consigned for 60 days
50/50 split

$1.00 seasonal fee to consignors

Dayton

Eliza Doolittle's Boutique
6382 Far Hills Avenue
Dayton, Ohio 45459

Store Hours: Monday, Wednesday & Friday 10am-5:30pm
Tuesday-Thursday 10am-7pm & Saturday 10am-5pm

Contact: Beverly Faul
Phone: 937-434-6520

Clothing & accessories for women
Accepts cash, checks, Mastercard & Visa

Consignment Policy: 50/50 split

Store Specials: Golden Buckeye Senior Citizens receive a 10% discount

Elyria

New To You
625 W. Broad Street
Elyria, Ohio 44035

Store Hours:
Monday-Friday 10am-6pm
Thursday until 8pm
Saturday 11am-5pm

Contact: Bobbie Breen
Phone: 440-322-0755

Men's, women's & children's clothing & accessories, bridal, costume & vintage

Consignment Policy:
50/50 split
Most merchandise consigned for 60-90 days except formals & vintage consigned for one year

Store Specials:
On-going four color tags discounted 1/3
Special half price racks

Ohio

Greenville

Biddlestone Consignments
126 W. 4th Street
P.O. Box 236
Greenville, Ohio 45331

Store Hours:
Monday-Saturday 10am-5pm

Contact: Debbie Biddlestone
Phone: 937-548-3180
Fax: 937-548-3213

Clothing for the entire family,
baby furniture, knick-knacks,
small appliances & much more!
Accepts cash, checks, Visa,
Mastercard & Discover

Consignment Policy:
50/50 split on
clothing & miscellaneous items

Store Specials: Lay-a-way
available & on-going sales
After 45 days items are marked
down 50% & after 70 days items
are marked down to $1.00!

Hamilton

Extravagant Bargains
233 Dayton Street
Hamilton, Ohio 45011

Store Hours:
Monday, Wednesday & Friday
10am-5pm

Phone: 513-894-9010

Clothing for the entire family,
toys & furniture
Accepts cash

Independence

Affordables by Pat
7087 Brecksville Road
Independence, Ohio 44131

Store Hours:
Monday 11am-5pm
Tuesday-Friday 11am-6pm
Saturday 10am-5pm

Phone: 216-642-1144

Nearly new apparel for women
& children, antique jewelry &
collectibles

Consignment Policy:
50/50 split
Items are consigned for 60 days
Consignments accepted by
appointment

Kent

Main Montage
144 East Main Street
Kent, Ohio 44240

Store Hours:
Monday-Friday 12pm-6pm
Saturday 12pm-5pm & occasion-
ally on Sunday
*Often open later than posted
hours

Phone & Fax: 330-673-4005

Contemporary, retro & vintage
clothing for men & women, lots
of great accessories including hats,
gloves, feather boas, shoes &
handbags, small furniture, jewelry,
great gift items & home furnishings, books, greeting cards &
oddities of all kinds
Accepts cash, checks, Visa/
Mastercard, Discover & American
Express

Consignment Policy:
Consignments accepted by
appointment only
50/50 split
Items are consigned for 60 days

Store Specials: End-of-the season
sales, new customer coupon &
frequent Main Montager card

Established in 1996, Main
Montage is located in downtown
Kent close to Kent State
University. The shop features
items from the ordinary to the
extraordinary.

Mention this listing at
Main Montage
144 East Main Street
Kent, Ohio 44240
& save 10% off one single
purchase

Expiration Date: 12/31/99

Lakewood

Another Chance
12417 Madison
Lakewood, Ohio 44107

Store Hours:
Monday-Wednesday
11am-2:30pm
Thursday- Saturday 11am-6pm

Phone: 216-221-8733

Women's clothing & beanie babies

Accepts cash & checks

Store Policy: Items bought
outright

Store Specials: 50% to 75% off
select merchandise

Present this coupon at
Another Chance
12417 Madison
Lakewood, Ohio
& save 10% off one
clothing item

Expiration Date: 12/31/99

Ohio

Newark

Abby's Attic Consigned Clothing Etc.
126 B South 30th Street
Sanor Center
Newark, Ohio 43055

Store Hours:
Tuesday-Friday 11am-6pm
Saturday 10am-4pm

Contact: Judy Pearson Blair
Phone: 740-344-8171

Consignment clothing for women

Perrysburg

Change of Seasons
26597 N. Dixie Highway
Perrysburg, Ohio 43551

Store Hours:
Monday-Friday 10am-6pm
Saturday 10am-5pm

Contact: Betty Hill
Phone: 419-872-9300

Women's clothing & accessories
Accepts cash, checks, Mastercard
& Visa

Consignment Policy:
50/50 split
Items consigned for 90 days

Store Specials: Items reduced 25%
every 30 days

Rocky River

Sacks of WestLake
20350 Center Ridge Road
Rocky River, Ohio 44116

Store Hours:
Monday-Saturday 10am-6pm
Sunday 1pm-5pm

Contact: Vicki Britting
Phone: 216-333-3404

Upscale clothing & accessories for
women, men & children
Accepts cash, checks, Mastercard,
Visa & Discover

Consignment Policy:
Items must be clean, pressed, on
hangers & no older than two years

Stow

Sassy Seahorse
Consignment Shop
4958 Darrow Road
Stow, Ohio 44224

Store Hours
Monday, Tuesday, Friday &
Saturday 11am-5pm
Wednesday & Thursday
11am-7pm

Contact: Deb Willhite
Phone: 330-650-0073

Clothing for the entire family
& accessories, bridal apparel,
household items, new & estate
jewelry
Accepts cash, checks, Visa &
Mastercard
Store Specials: Lay-a-way
available

Toledo

Sandy's Stuff
Quality Women's
Consignment/Resale Shop
3820 West Alexis Road
Toledo, Ohio 43623

Store Hours:
Tuesday 5pm-8pm
Wednesday & Thursday
2pm-8pm
Friday & Saturday 10am-5pm

Phone: 419-472-8259
e-mail: pirwitz@aol.com

Women's clothing

Oklahoma

Enid

Mother & Child Again
224 W. Randolph
Enid, Oklahoma 73701

Store Hours:
Tuesday-Friday 10am-5:30pm
Saturday 10am-2pm

Contact: Cynthia Newman
Phone: 580-233-8787
Website: www.theclothestree.com/
MotherandChild/

Gently used fashionable clothing
for children, vast range of baby
equipment & hard-to-find items
Accepts cash, local checks, Visa &
Mastercard

Store Policy: Cash for items
accepted

Specializing in personalized
service!

Oklahoma City

Elite Repeat
7308 N. Western
Oklahoma City, Oklahoma
73116

Store Hours:
Monday-Friday 10:30am-6pm
Thursday until 8pm
Saturday 10am-5pm

Phone: 405-848-1595

Upscale designer clothing for
women

Consignment Policy: 50/50 split
Items are consigned for 60 days

Shawnee

In Vogue Consignment
735 E. Independence Street
Shawnee, Oklahoma 74801

Store Hours:
Monday-Friday 9am-5:30pm
Thursday until 6:30pm
Saturday 10am-5pm

Phone: 405-275-4326
Website: www.theclothestree.com/
shops/InVogue/

Clothing for the entire family in
all sizes, accessories including
brand name handbags
Accepts cash, local checks,
Mastercard, Visa, American
Express & Discover

Consignment Policy:
50/50 split
Items are consigned for 90 days

Store Specials: Select items
reduced 25% to 75% off

> Present this coupon at
> *In Vogue Consignment*
> *735 E. Independence*
> *Shawnee, Oklahoma* & save
> 25% off any one
> non-sale item
>
> Expiration Date: 12/31/99

Tulsa

Cherry Street Boutique
1548 E. 15th Street
Tulsa, Oklahoma 74120

Store Hours:

Wednesday-Friday 10am-2pm
Saturday 10am-5pm

Phone: 918-583-7467

Women's & children's clothing &
accessories

Store Policy: Donations welcome

**Consign It For Kids/Expecting
Again**
6064 S. Sheridan
Tulsa, Oklahoma 74145

Store Hours:
Monday, Tuesday, Wednesday &
Friday 10am-5:30pm
Thursday until 7pm
Saturday 10am-5pm

Phone: 918-496-2222

New & consigned clothing for
children, furniture, toys, accessories & maternity wear

The Clothes Line
6553 E. 71th Street
Tulsa, Oklahoma 74133

Store Hours:
Monday-12pm-6pm
Tuesday-Saturday 10am-6pm

Phone: 918-496-3361
Accepts cash, Visa & Mastercard

Clothing for women

Consignment Policy: 50/50 split

Store Specials:
End of the month $1.00 sale
Daily specials
Rainy days & Mondays extra
savings on new arrivals

The Re-Finery
7903 E. 50th Street
Tulsa, Oklahoma 74145

Store Hours:
Monday-Friday 10am-6pm
Saturday 10am-5pm

Phone: 918-627-1826
Website: www.Tulsapages.com

Women's designer clothing,
wedding & after-five-wear
Accepts cash, Mastercard, Visa &
Discover

Consignment Policy:
50/50 split
Items consigned for 60 days

Oregon

Baker City

Baker Exchange
3780 Tenth Street
Baker City, Oregon 97814

Store Hours:
Monday-Friday 9am-5pm
Saturday 9am-1pm

Contact: Ray & Kirsten Badger
Phone: 541-523-3104

Household items, furniture,
appliances, jewelry & gifts
Accepts cash, in state checks, Visa
& Mastercard

Store Specials: In store specials

```
┌ ─ ─ ─ ─ ─ ─ ─ ─ ┐
│   Present this coupon at   │
│      Baker Exchange        │
│      3780 Tenth Street     │
│   Baker City, Oregon &     │
│   save 10% off any item    │
│     in the gift section    │
│   Expiration Date: 12/31/99 │
└ ─ ─ ─ ─ ─ ─ ─ ─ ┘
```

Bend

Buffet Flat/The Funny Farm
64990 Deschutes Market Road
Bend, Oregon 97701

Store Hours:
Monday-Sunday 10am-6pm

Phone: 541-389-6391

Antiques & lots of unique items

Store Specials: Senior discount

Dallas

Green Valley Bargain Center
3535 Dallas-Kings
Valley Highway
Dallas, Oregon 97338

Store Hours:
Tuesday-Saturday 10am-5pm

Phone: 503-623-2807

Furniture, appliances, tools,
household goods, garden tools,
& much more!
Accepts cash & checks

Gresham

Child Of Mine
40 NW 2nd Street
Gresham, Oregon 97030

Store Hours:
Monday-Saturday 10am-5pm
(Winter Hours)
Call for Summer hours

Contact: Trish Moore
Phone: 503-667-2245

Children's clothing (including
infants) & maternity, accessories,
toys, books, infants
& children's furniture
Accepts cash, checks, Visa,
Mastercard & Discover

Consignment Policy:
50/50 split or trade for 30% store
credit

Store Specials:
Receive a baby buck with each
$15.00 purchase
50% off rack
25 cent table

Oregon

Portland

Here We Go Again
9519 SW Barbur Ave
Portland, Oregon 97219

Store Hours:
Monday-Saturday 10am-6pm
Thursday 10am-8pm
Sunday 12pm-4pm

Contact: Chris Gauger
Phone: 503-244-0855
e-mail: hwga@europa.com
Website: www.hwga.com

Women's clothing & accessories,
after-five & bridal
Accepts cash, checks, Visa,
Mastercard & Discover/Novus

Consigment Policy:
50/50split
Items other than bridal consigned
for 60 days
Bridal consigned for six months

Store Specials: Frequent Sales

Junior League of Portland
Bargain Tree
838 S.W. 4th Avenue
Portland, Oregon 97204

Store Hours:
Monday-Friday 10am-5:30pm
Saturday 10am-4pm

Phone: 503-227-7413

Upscale thrift store specializing in
designer label clothing

Store Specials: Sale merchandise
available each week

The Second Edition
12505 N.W. Cornell Road
Portland, Oregon 97229

Store Hours:
Tuesday-Saturday 10am-5pm

Contact: Charleen Mc Keehan
Phone: 503-644-6395
Website: www.cedarmill.org/
library/used.htm

Clothing for the entire family,
accessories, housewares, toys &
seasonal decorations
Accepts cash & checks

Store Policy: Donations welcome

Store Specials: Periodic holiday sales & twice yearly 50% off clearance sales known as M.E.S.S. (Miscellaneous Et Cetera Super Sale)

```
■ ■ ■ ■ ■ ■ ■ ■ ■ ■ ■ ■ ■
■                         ■
■    Present this coupon at    ■
■    The Second Edition Resale  ■
■           Shop           ■
■   12505 N. W. Cornell Road   ■
■       Portland, Oregon      ■
■       & save 50% off any     ■
■        one clothing item     ■
■       Expiration Date: 12/31/99   ■
■ ■ ■ ■ ■ ■ ■ ■ ■ ■ ■ ■ ■
```

The Silver Lining
7044 SE Milwaukee Avenue
Portland, Oregon 97202

Store Hours:
Monday-Friday 11am-6pm
Saturday 11am-5pm & Sunday 12pm-4pm

Contact: Karen Ripplinger
Phone: 503-238-5578
e-mail: GKRIPP@aol.com
Website: www.citysearch.com/pdx/silverlining

Upscale consignment apparel for women sizes 2-24, formal to casual wear

Established in 1983, The Silver Lining has an outstanding reputation among shoppers in Oregon. "Name brand clothing at these prices is like finding gold", raves a customer.

William Temple House
Thrift Store
2230 NW Glisan
Portland, Oregon 97210

Other drop off center for donations:
1910 NW 23rd Place
Portland, Oregon 97210

Donations accepted
Monday-Friday 8:30am-5pm
Donations accepted at
2230 NW Glisan on
Monday-Friday 9am-6pm
Saturday 9am-6pm
Sunday 12pm-6pm

Store Hours:
Monday-Friday 9am-8pm
Saturday 9am-6pm
Sunday 12pm-6pm

Phone: 503-222-3328
Fax: 503-222-0761
Web site: www.teleport.com/~wthts

Upscale thrift store located in trendy NW Portland featuring over 8400 square feet of antiques, collectibles, clothing, furniture & bric-a-brac

Store Policy: Donations welcome & appreciated. Tax receipts provided.

Proceeds from the thrift store benefit those in need.

Allentown

Abe's Furniture Shop
607 N. 7th Street
Allentown, Pennsylvania
18102

Store Hours:
Monday-Friday 12pm-6pm

Phone: 610-439-0057

Furniture, appliances & antiques

Consignment Policy: 50/50 split
Items consigned for 30 days

Bala Cynwyd

Second Editions
Consignment Shop
155 Bala Avenue
Bala Cynwyd, Pennsylvania
19004

Store Hours:
Monday-Friday 10:30am-6pm
Saturday 10:30am-5pm

Contact: Jeannette Siegel-Muller
Phone: 610-664-8508

Women's designer clothing

Beaver

Pretty Woman
Consignment Clothier
543 Third Street
Beaver, Pennsylvania 15009

Store Hours:
Monday-Saturday 10am-4pm
Thursday 10am-6pm

Phone: 724-728-7670

Apparel for women & children
including plus sizes & accessories

Bradford

Golden Baskets
419 E Main Street
Bradford, Pennsylvania 16701

Store Hours:
Monday-Saturday 9am-5pm

Contact: Linda Woodley
Phone: 814-368-8647
e-mail: linwood4@Juno.com

Clothing for women including
maternity & children's
Accepts cash & checks

Consignment Policy:
Consignments accepted Monday-
Saturday 9am-10am, others
by appointment
Items consigned for 60 days
50/50 split

Dallas

Deja Vu
66 Main Street
Dallas, Pennsylvania 18612

Store Hours:

Tuesday & Wednesday 10am-4pm
Thursday 11am-8pm
Friday 11am-7pm
Saturday 11am-5pm

Phone: 717-675-9301
Website: www.theclothestree.com/
shops/Dejavu/
Clothing & accessories for women
Accepts cash & personal checks

• • • • • • • • • • • • • •
• •
• Present this coupon at •
• *De Javu* •
• *66 Main St.* •
• *Dallas, Pennsylvania* & save •
• $5.00 off purchase of •
• $20.00 or more •
• •
• Expiration Date: 12/31/99 •
• •
• • • • • • • • • • • • • •

Danville

Abigail's Attic
329 B Ferry Street
Danville, Pennsylvania 17821

Store Hours:
Tuesday-Friday 10am-4pm
Saturday 9:30am-12pm

Contact: Linda Neddoff
Phone: 717-275-6372

Clothing for the entire family,
accessories, household items &
small pieces of furniture

Store Policy: Donations welcome
& appreciated

Abigail's Attic is a non-profit
thrift shop whose proceeds benefit
Penn State Geisinger Hospital.

Doylestown

Edison Furniture Store
1880 S. Easton Road
Doylestown, Pennsylvania
18901

Store Hours:
Monday-Saturday 9am-4pm

Established in 1949, Edison
Furniture Store offers gently used
personal property at reasonable
prices
Accepts cash

Easton

Nice As New
601 Village at
Stones Crossing
Easton, Pennsylvania 18045

Store Hours:
Monday-Friday 10am-8pm
Saturday 10am-5pm
Sunday 12pm-4pm

Phone: 610-253-7334
e-mail: nmccormi@fast.net
Website: http://www.csnet.net/
LehiVal/NiceAsNew

Clothing for women, sizes one to
plus, children's clothing sizes
newborn to 16 & boy's clothing to
size 12, lots of accessories,
costume jewelry, shoes, handbags,
hats & scarves
Accepts cash, checks with proper
ID, Visa, Mastercard, Discover,
American Express & Debit cards
Consignment Policy:
Call for an appointment to
consign mechandise
50/50 split

Store Specials:
After 30 days most
items reduced 25%
Customer punch card

• • • • • • • • • • • • • •
• Save 25% off any one •
• non-sale item when you •
• present this coupon at •
• *Nice As New* •
• *601 Village at Stones Crossing* •
• *Easton, Pennsylvania* •
•   •
• Expiration Date: 12/31/99 •
• • • • • • • • • • • • • •

Repeat Boutique
401 Northampton Street
Easton, Pennsylvania 18042

Store Hours:
Monday-Saturday
10am-5pm, Friday 10am-8pm
Sunday 12pm-5pm

Contact: Jean Corrigan
Phone: 610-258-5823

All items for children including
clothing sizes newborn to 14,
toys, baby furniture, strollers &
maternity wear
Accepts cash, checks, Visa,
Mastercard & Discover

Consignment Policy: 50/50 split
Items are consigned for eight
weeks

Store Specials: Select color tags
discounted 25%

┌─────────────────────────────┐
│ This coupon entitles the │
│ bearer to save 25% off │
│ any item at │
│ *Repeat Boutique* │
│ *401 Northampton Street* │
│ *Easton, Pennsylvania* │
│ │
│ Expiration Date: 12/31/99 │
└─────────────────────────────┘

Ephrata

Pass It On!
558 N. Reading Road
Ephrata, Pennsylvania 17522

Store Hours:
Monday, Wednesday, Thursday &
Saturday 10am-4pm
Tuesday & Friday 10am-8pm

Contact: Jane Rhoads &
Kelley Clark
Phone: 717-733-7232

Gently used clothing for the entire
family
Accepts cash, checks, Visa &
Mastercard

Consignment Policy:
50/50 split
Items are consigned for 90 days

Store Specials: Winter & Summer
clearance sales

Pennsylvania

Erie

City Mission Thrifty Shopper
1213 State Street
Erie, Pennsylvania 16501

Store Hours:
Monday-Friday 9:30am-5pm
Saturday 9am-4pm

Phone: 814-452-4421
Fax: 814-455-8825
e-mail: cmission@ncinter.net

Clothing for entire family,
jewelry, furniture, appliances,
toys, sporting goods, housewares,
antiques & collectibles

Store Policy: Donations welcome
& receipt provided for tax
purposes

Store Specials:
Senior discounts
Customer appreciation days
Fashion shows & special seasonal
discounts

Proceeds from The Thrifty
Shopper benefit the City

Mission Services which include
meals for men, women &
children, emergency food bags
for individuals & families, shelter
for the homeless & after school &
summer programs for inner city
children.

Fairless Hills

Serendipity Shoppe Inc.
96 Trenton Road
Fairless, Pennsylvania 19030

Store Hours:
Tuesday-Thursday 11am-5:30pm
Friday 11am-7pm
Saturday 10am-5pm

Contact: Alison Secoda
Phone: 215-943-2299

Upscale women's & children's
clothing & small collectibles
Accepts cash, checks, Visa,
Mastercard & Discover

Consignment Policy:
50/50 split for women's & 60/40
split for children's

Store Specials:
Special sales ranging from 20% to
50% off

Glenside

Act II
80 S. Keswick Avenue
Glenside, Pennsylvania 19038
Located at the corner of Keswick
& Glenside Avenue
Plenty of parking available on the
side of the building

Store Hours:
Tuesday-Friday 10am-6pm
Saturday 10am-5pm (Summer

hours 11am-5pm)

Contact: Christina Davidson
Phone: 215-887-7784

Specializing in business, semi-formal & casual attire for women, lots of great accessories including jewelry, scarfs, handbags, collectibles, china, crystal & silver, bric-a-brac, artwork & furniture
Featuring a new line of candle & frames, potpourri and cards, all for that perfect last minute gift.
Accepts cash, checks and all major credit cards

Consignment Policy:
50/50 split
Most items consigned for ten week period, some items may be consigned longer

Store Specials: Special sales every week!
Ask for your customer appreciation card for extra savings

Present this coupon at
Act II
80 S. Keswick
Glenside, Pennsylvania
and save $5.00 off
any purchase of $25.00 or
$10.00 off any purchase of
$50.00 or more.

Not valid for merchandise
already discounted more than 20%.
Copies of this coupon not accepted.
Expiration date: December 31, 1999

New To You
244 Keswick Avenue
Glenside, Pennsylvania 19038

Store Hours:
Monday-Saturday 10am-5pm
Wednesday 10am-7:30pm

Contact: Jody New
Phone: 215-884-8824

Children's clothing, maternity wear, baby equipment & furniture

New to You has been featured on *CBS & NBC News* as the best consignment store for children's & maternity clothing in Philadelphia.

Johnstown

Repeat Boutique
1222 Scalp Avenue
Johnstown, Pennsylvania
15904

Store Hours:
Monday-Friday 10am-6pm
Saturday 10am-4pm

Contact: Jessica Wingard
Phone: 814-269-3295

Clothing for the entire family
Accepts cash, checks, Visa, Mastercard & Discover

Consignment Policy:
50/50 split
Items are consigned for 90 days
Items accepted by appointment

Store Specials: Frequent buyer discounts

Pennsylvania

Kutztown

Clare's Closet
58 Noble Street
Kutztown, Pennsylvania
19530

Store Hours:
Tuesday, Wednesday & Saturday
10am-5pm
Thursday & Friday 10am-7pm

Contact: Janet Brito &
Barb O'Brien
Phone: 610-683-8112

Designer clothing for women-
juniors to plus sizes, men &
children sizes 4-16 including
casual, career & cocktail items,
large selection of costume & retro
wear

Store Specials:
Monthly tag sales offering savings
up to 75% off
Buy two items get the third free
several times per year

Consignment Policy:
Clothing accepted by appointment only
50/50 split
Items are consigned for 90 days

Store Specials:
The shop offers organizational
accounts for non-profit organizations.

Clare's Closet offers four spacious
rooms to shop in and a large play
area for children.

Present this coupon at
Clare's Closet
58 Noble Street
Kutztown, Pennsylvania &
save 50% off any one item

(Includes sale items,
excludes white tags)
Expiration Date: 12/31/99

Lansdale

West Main Consignment
305 West Main Street
Lansdale, Pennsylvania 19446

Store Hours:
Monday-Friday 10am-5pm
Saturday 10am-4pm
Sunday 12pm-4pm March-April
& October though Christmas,
Closed on holidays

Contact: Janice Tindall
Phone: 215-855-8533

Over 1700 square feet of clothing
for the entire family, jewelry,
accessories & household items.
Hundreds of items arrive daily!
Accepts cash, personal checks,
Visa & Mastercard

Consignment Policy: 50/50 split
Items are consigned for 60 days
Call for an appointment to
consign merchandise

Store Specials: Gift certificates
available

Lititz

Kidz Korner
Consignment Shop
Warwick Center
Lititz, Pennsylvania 17543

Store Hours:
Tuesday, Wednesday, Thursday &
Saturday 10am-4pm
Friday 10am-7pm

Phone: 717-627-2636
Website: www.theclothestree.com/
shops/KidzKorner/

Clothing for children sizes 0-16,
maternity wear, baby equipment &
furniture & toys

Manheim

Consignment Warehouse
339 S. Main Street
Manheim, Pennsylvania
17545

Store Hours:
Monday, Tuesday, Wednesday
& Friday 10am-5pm
Thursday 10am-7pm
Saturday 10am-3pm

Contact: Renee J. Martin
Phone: 717-664-5151

Clothing for the entire family
including maternity wear & plus
sizes, toys, nursery items &
household items

Consignment Policy:
50/50 split
No appointment is necessary to
consign merchandise
Items are consigned for 90 days

Store Specials:
Wacky Wednesday dollar rack
20% off select items weekly

Consignment Warehouse has a
play center for children. Their
motto is "You have shopped the
rest, now shop the best". The
shop was featured in *Women's
World Magazine* in August, 1996.

Monroeville

Second Chance
500 Garden City Drive
Garden City Plaza
Monroeville, Pennsylvania
15146
Located five minutes from the
Pennsylvania Turnpike

Store Hours:
Monday-Saturday 10am-5pm
Wednesday 10am-8pm

Phone: 412-372-4308

Clothing for the entire family,
small household items, linens,
knick-knacks
Accept cash, Visa, Mastercard &
Discover

Consignment Policy:
50/50 split
Items consigned for 60 days

Store Policy: Automatic
markdowns on tickets

Moon Township

Consignment Cottage
234 Moon Clinton Road
Moon Township, Pennsylvania
15108

Pennsylvania

Store Hours:
Tuesday-Saturday 10am-5pm
Thursday 10am-7pm

Contact: Terry Chesky &
Jean Maggio
Phone: 412-262-0833

Clothing for women & children
including maternity, baby
equipment & home decor items
Accepts cash, personal checks,
Visa, Mastercard & Discover

Consignment Policy:
Consignments accepted by
appointment only
50/50 split
Items are consigned for 60 days

Store Specials: Annual September
tent sale, fashion shows & private
evening shopping parties
Image consulting services
available
Select items always 50% off

Child & baby friendly shop which
includes a special play area for
kids.

```
Present this coupon at
Consignment Cottage
243 Moon Clinton Road
Moon Township, Pennsylvania
& save 10% off total
purchase & a free
sachet with purchase

Expiration Date: 12/31/99
```

Morrisville

Carousel
Consignment Shoppe
Giant Plaza
833 W. Trenton Ave

222

Morrisville, Pennsylvania
19067

Store Hours:
Monday-Thursday 10am-6pm
Friday 10am-7pm
Saturday 10am-5pm

Contact: Helen M. Noble
Phone: 215-295-2461

Clothing for the entire family,
small antiques, toys, books,
children's furniture & equipment
Accepts cash & personal checks

```
Present this coupon at
Carousel Consignment Shoppe
833 W. Trenton Ave
Morrisville, Pennsylvania
& save 10% off one
clothing item

Expiration Date: 12/31/99
```

Newton

The Thrift Shop of the Bucks
County Association
for the Blind
400 Freedom Drive
Newton, Pennsylvania 18940

Store Hours:
Monday-Thursday 10am-5pm
Friday 10am-8pm
Saturday 10am-4pm

Phone: 215-968-9400

Clothing for the entire family,
housewares. books, magazines,
toys, accessories & brooms made
by the blind
Accepts cash & personal checks

with the proper ID

Store Policy: Donations accepted (except for furniture & cars). Receipt provided for tax purposes

Store Specials: Storewide sales in February & August & half price clothing sales

Founded over 25 years ago the shop helps support the association's social service programs.

Norristown

Crossroad Gift & Thrift, Inc.
14 E. Main Street
Norristown, Pennsylvania
19401

Store Hours:
Monday-Friday 9:30am-4:30pm
Saturday 10am-4pm

Contact: Mae Reinford
Phone: 610-275-3772

All types of clothing, housewares, crafts, Ten Thousand Villages worldwide crafts, purses & shoes

Store Policy: Donations welcome

Philadelphia

Bird In Hand
Consignment Shop
8419 Germantown Avenue
Chestnut Hill
Philadelphia, Pennsylvania
19118

Store Hours:
Monday-Saturday 10am-4:30pm

China, crystal, antiques & collectibles
Accepts cash & checks

Consignment Policy: Consignments accepted Monday 9am-11pm, no appointment necessary & Tuesday & Wednesday 1pm-3pm & Friday 9am to 11pm by appointment only

Burholme Thrift Shoppe
7106 Rising Sun Ave
Philadelphia, Pennsylvania
19111

Store Hours:
Monday, Wednesday, Friday & Saturday 10am-3pm

Contact: Millie Schick
Phone: 215-742-8877

From the unusual to great vintage items, Burholme Thrift Shoppe has it all. A fun shop featuring children's clothing, jewelry, pottery, trains, collectibles, retro wear and much more!
Accepts cash

Store Specials: Lay-a-way
Weekend specials too!

O'Baby It's Just Like New
4040 Woodhaven Road
Philadelphia, Pennsylvania
19154

Store Hours:
Monday-Friday 10am-7pm
Saturday 10am-5pm

Phone: 215-612-5520

Children's clothing sizes 0 to 14, toys, books, furniture &

Pennsylvania

equipment

Consigment Policy: 50/50 split
Items are consigned for 90 days

Peek-a-Bootique
184 E. Evergreen Avenue
Philadelphia, Pennsylvania
19118

Store Hours:
Tuesday-Friday 9am-4pm
Saturday 9am-3pm

Phone: 215-248-4466

Clothing for the entire family,
maternity wear, baby equipment,
nursery equipment, toys & more

Consignment Policy:
Consignments accepted by
appointment only
50/50 split

Sophisticated Seconds
114-116 18th Street
Second Floor
Philadelphia, Pennsylvania
19103

Store Hours:
Monday, Tuesday, Thursday,
Friday & Saturday 10am-6pm
Wednesday 10am-8pm

Contact: Valori Zaslow
Phone: 215-561-6740

Couture new & gently recycled
designer clothing for women sizes
2-24, men sizes 36-52, accessories, shoes. Designer clothing
featured by Chanel, Donna Karan,
Escada, Moschino, Bob Mackie &
more for women.
For men featuring Giorgio
Armani, and more at reduced

prices. Children's clothing sizes
infant to 10, Wedgewood &
Lenox crystal pieces available.
Accepts cash, checks, Visa,
Mastercard & American Express

Consignment Policy: 50/50 split
An appointment is necessary to
consign merchandise

Store Specials: Consignment Club
cards & custom tailoring available

Voted *"City Paper Readers Choice
Awards"* in 1994.

The Bridal Exchange
An Upscale Consignment
& Discount Boutique
Society Hill
Philadelphia, Pennsylvania

Store Hours: By appointment
only, closed on Sunday & Monday

Contact: Debra Sitner &
Debra Bryce
Phone: 215-923-8515
e-mail: bridalx@aol.com
Website: www.modernbride.com/
bridalexchange
Upscale bridal gowns, head pieces
& veils. 100% silk gowns ranging
from $700.00 to $2500.00 &
head pieces ranging from $150.00
to $600.00
Accepts cash, checks, Visa &
Mastercard

Consignment Policy: 100% silk
gowns only-original price
minimum $1000.00 & must be in
good condition, no more than two
years old

Pittsburgh

Affordable Fashions

1047 Perry Highway
Pittsburgh, Pennsylvania
15237

Store Hours:
Monday 12pm-8pm,
Tuesday-Closed
Wednesday & Friday 12pm-5pm,
Thursday 10am-8pm
Saturday 10am-5pm

Contact: Lorri Miller
Phone: 412-364-3256

Upscale designer name clothing
for women, maternity & plus sizes
too!
Accepts cash, personal checks &
Discover

• • • • • • • • • • • • •
•   •
•   Present this coupon at   •
•   *Affordable Fashions*   •
•   *1047 Perry Highway*   •
•   *Pittsburgh, Pennsylvania*   •
•   and save 25% off   •
•   total purchase   •
•   •
•   Expiration Date: 12/31/99   •
• • • • • • • • • • • • •

Clothes Corner
1250 Old Freeport Road
Pittsburgh, Pennsylvania
15238

Store Hours:
Monday-Friday 10:30am-6pm

Phone: 412-963-0776

Upscale clothing for the entire
family, jewelry & home furnishings

Furniture Emeritus
101-26th Street at Smallman
Pittsburgh, Pennsylvania
15222-4635

Store Hours:
Monday-Saturday 10am-5pm
Sunday 12pm-4pm

Phone: 412-263-2626

Fine furniture on consignment
from the 1950's vintage to 1990's
contemporary
Accepts cash, Mastercard, Visa &
Discover

Consignment Policy:
50/50 split
Items consigned for six months

Store Specials: Items reduced 20%
after 91 days

Pottstown

Evergreen Consignment
Company
810 Spruce Street
Pottstown, Pennsylvania
19464

Store Hours:
Monday-Friday 9am-6pm
Saturday 9am-5pm

Contact: Faye Read
Phone: 610-970-9925

Variety of clothing, furniture,
baby equipment, jewelry, candles
& gifts
Accepts cash, checks, credit cards
& Mac cards

Store Specials: $1.00 clothing
sales & candle specials

Member of The National
Association of Resale & Thrift
Shops

Pennsylvania

The Second Hand Connection
RD 2 & Rt. 100
Pottstown, Pennsylvania
19465

Store Hours: Call for store hours

Phone: 610-469-1088

Gently used riding saddles,
clothing, boots, shoes &
equipment

Sewickley

Secondhand Rose, Inc.
411 Walnut Street
Sewickley, Pennsylvania
15143

Store Hours: Tuesday-Saturday
10am-4pm

Phone: 412-741-5909

Clothing for the entire family &
accessories

Consignment Policy:
Items consigned by appointment
only
50/50 split
Items consigned for 60 days

Skippack

Repeat Boutique
4072 Skippack Pike
Skippack, Pennsylvania
19474
Located in quaint Skippack Village
in SE Pennsylvania

Store Hours:
Wednesday, Thursday & Sunday

12pm-5pm
Friday 10am-7pm
Saturday 10am-5pm

Phone: 610-584-8887
e-mail: shop@repeatboutique.com
Website: www.repeatboutique.com

Two floors of clothing for women
& men sizes 4 to 22, jewelry,
accessories, collectibles, books &
more!

Consignment Policy: Consignments are accepted by appointment

Verona

Yesterday's Friends
719 Allegheny River Blvd.
Verona, Pennsylvania 15147

Store Hours:
Monday-Friday 10am-5pm
Thursday 10am-8pm
Saturday 10am-4pm

Contact: Betsy Monheim
Phone: 412-828-4552

Clothing for the entire family &
accessories
Accepts cash, checks & charge
cards

Consignment Policy: $10.00

yearly fee
50/50 split

Store Specials: Seasonal clearance
sales

This coupon entitles the bearer
to save $5.00 off one
purchase of $25.00
or more at
Yesterday's Friends
719 Allegheny River Blvd,
Verona, Pennsylvania
Expiration Date: 12/31/99

West Chester

The Growing Years
3 N. Five Points Road
West Chester, Pennsylvania
19380

Store Hours:
Monday-Saturday 10am-5pm
Wednesday until 6pm

Phone: 610-430-7601
e-mail: sasnol@aol.com
Web site: www.growingyears.com

Children's & maternity new &
"like new" clothing & worldwide
costume exchange for children

Second Location:
Kathleen's at the
Growing Years
100 Baltimore Pike
Chadds Ford, Pennsylvania
19342

Store Hours:
Monday-Saturday 10am-5:30pm
Wednesday until 6:30pm
Sunday 12pm-4pm

Apparel for women & children

West Reading

Memories
622 Penn Avenue
West Reading, Pennsylvania
19611
Located close to the Vanity Fair
Outlet Shopping Center on Rt 422

Store Hours:
Sunday-Wednesday by
appointment
Thursday 11am-7pm
Friday & Saturday 11am-5pm
Contact: Diane Impink
Phone: 610-374-4480

Vintage clothing, jewelry, antiques
& collectibles
Accepts cash, check, Visa, Novus
& Mastercard

Consignment Policy: 50/50 split

Store Specials: Monthly sales &
Discounts for theater

Present this coupon at
Memories
622 Penn Ave
West Reading, Pennsylvania
& save 10% on one item

(Coupon cannot be
combined with any
other coupons or sales)
Expiration Date: 12/31/99

Williamsport

American Rescue Workers
Thrift Store
643 Elmira Street
Williamsport, Pennsylvania
17701

Pennsylvania

Store Hours:
Monday-Friday 9am-5pm
Saturday 9am-4pm

Contact: Nancy Moser
Phone: 717-323-8401
Fax: 717-323-0980
e-mail: amercscwk@crslink.net
Web site: www.arwus.com

"Shop where your dollar buys
more"

Other Locations:

924 Funston Ave
Newberry, Pennsylvania
17701
Phone: 717-323-1837

16N. Main Street
Hughesville, Pennsylvania
17737
Phone: 717-584-4296

141-143 S. Main Street
Jersey Shore, Pennsylvania
17740
Phone: 717-398-4311

122 Maple Avenue
Milton, Pennsylvania 17847
Phone: 717-742-2141

109 E. Main Street
Lock Haven, Pennsylvania
17745
Phone: 717-748-6896

358 Chestnut Street
Mifflinburg, Pennsylvania
17844
Phone: 717-966-1992

118 N. Allegheny Street
Bellefonte, Pennsylvania
16823
Phone: 814-355-3871

9 South Main Street
Muncy, Pennsylvania 17756
Phone: 717-546-6987

200 S. Market Street
Selingsgrove, Pennsylvania
17870
Phone: 717-374-7908

339 Market Street
Sundbury, Pennsylvania
17801
Phone: 717-286-6518

R 534 N. Derr Drive
Lewisburg, Pennsylvania
17837
Phone: 717-523-1102

Clothing for the entire family,
household items, bedding,
furniture, books, collectibles,
jewelry, craft items, fabric, dishes,
shoes, small appliances & small
electronic items
Accepts cash

Store Policy: Donations welcome

Store Specials: Check the shop for
daily specials

All proceeds from the shops help
to provide the less fortunate with
all items necessary to setup
housekeeping.

York

Nearly New Boutique
2555 South Queen Street
Olde Tollgate Village
York, Pennsylvania 17401

Store Hours:
Monday, Tuesday, Wednesday
10am-6pm
Thursday & Friday 10am-8pm

Saturday 10am-5pm

Phone: 717-741-3385
e-mail: nnb@netrax.net
Website: http://www.narts.org/
nearlynew

Clothing for women & children,
accessories & bridal wear
Accepts cash, Visa, Mastercard &
Discover

Rhode Island

Barrington

The Stock Exchange TM
57 Maple Avenue
Barrington, Rhode Island
02806

Store Hours:
Tuesday-Saturday 10am-4pm
Thursday until 7pm
Sunday 12pm-4pm

Phone: 401-245-4170

Second Location:
232 Waseca Ave.
Barrington, Rhode Island
02806
Phone: 401-247-7774

Contact: Jennifer LaFrance

Excellent quality household items, furniture, sterling silver, crystal, jewelry, antiques, china & paintings.
Visit the new annex location featuring lots of great books & more contemporary items.

Accepts cash, checks & all major credit cards

Store Policy: Items must be in good condition & are consigned for 120 days

Store Specials: Items marked down 15% every 30 days

This coupon entitles
the bearer to save 10% off
any one item under $100.00 at
The Stock Exchange
57 Maple Ave,
Barrington, Rhode Island

Expiration Date: 12/31/99

Cranston

2nd Time Around
330 Atwood Avenue
Cranston, Rhode Island 02920

Store Hours:
Monday, Tuesday & Wednesday
10am-6pm
Thursday 10am-8pm
Friday 10am-6pm
Saturday 10am-5pm

Contact: Jeannine Mastrate
Phone: 401-942-5078

Women's, men's & children's gently used clothing, furniture & antiques

Consignment Policy:
50/50 split
Items consigned for 60 days

This coupon entitles the
bearer to save 20% off one
single women's clothing
item over $25.00 at
2nd Time Around
330 Atwood Ave.
Cranston, Rhode Island

(Furs not included)
Expiration Date: 12/31/99

Cumberland

The Clutter Queen's Closet
Resale Boutique
288 Broad Street
Cumberland, Rhode Island
02864

Store Hours:
Wednesday, Thursday & Friday

10am-5pm
Saturday 10am-4pm

Phone: 401-724-6661

Clothing for women & children
including vintage items,
housewares & bric-a-brac

Consignment Policy: 50/50 split
Items are consigned for 90 days

```
Present this coupon at
    Clutter Queens Closet
      Resale Boutique
       288 Broad Street
  Cumberland, Rhode Island
   & save $2.00 off any one
 purchase of $10.00 or more

    Expiration Date: 12/31/99
```

Middletown

Labels
238 East Main Street
Middletown, Rhode Island
02842
(Located corner of Valley & E.
Main)

Store Hours:
Monday-Saturday 10am-6pm
Sunday 12pm-5pm

Phone: 401-846-3343

Women's fine clothing, jewelry &
accessories

Consignment Policy:
50/50 split
Items consigned for 3 months

Narragansett

The Hope Chest Inc.
Fine Consignments
124 Point Judith Road
Narragansett, Rhode Island
02882

Store Hours:
Monday-Saturday 10am-5pm
Sunday 1pm-5pm

Phone: 401-783-8840

Collectibles, fine home furnishings
& antiques

Portsmouth

Wedding House
1408 W. Main Road
Portsmouth, Rhode Island
02871

Store Hours:
Tuesday, Wednesday & Friday
10am-2pm
Thursday 4pm-9pm

Phone: 401-624-6998
e-mail: weddinghse@meganet.net

New & pre worn designer wedding
gowns, antique gowns, bridesmaid
dresses, bride & groom's mother
dresses & flower girl dresses,
capes, petticoats & veils. Items
available for rental. Discount
service is available for
nationally advertised wedding &
bridesmaid dresses
Accepts cash

Consignment Policy: 50/50 split
Items consigned for 6 to 12
months

Store Specials: Cleaning &

preserving wedding gowns at discounted prices, discounted wedding invitations & professional bridal consultant is available

Providence

The Salvation Army
201 Pitman Street
Providence, Rhode Island
02906

Store Hours:
Monday-Saturday 9am-5:30pm

Phone: 401-421-5270

New & gently used clothing, furniture & bric-a-brac

Store Specials: Weekly half price sales

Smithfield

Upscale Resale
466 Putnam Park
Smithfield, Rhode Island
02828

Store Hours:
Monday-Saturday 10am-5pm
Thursday 10am-8pm

Contact: Andrea Robertson
Phone: 401-949-4480

Upscale women's clothing & accessories
Accepts cash, checks & credit cards

Consignment Policy:
Consignments accepted daily without an appointment
$5.00 annual registration fee to consign items

50/50 split
Items consigned 60 days
Items discounted 20% after 30 days

Wakefield

The Kiddie Kloset
329 Main Street
Wakefield, Rhode Island
02879

Store Hours:
Monday-Friday 10am-5pm
Saturday 10am-3pm

Phone: 401-783-8680

Children's clothing sizes 0-14, toys, books, baby equipment & furniture
Accepts cash, Visa & Mastercard

Aiken

**The Closet Collection
111 York Street SE
Aiken, South Carolina 29801**

Store Hours:
Tuesday-Saturday 10am-4pm
Friday 10am-5pm

Phone: 803-648-8686

Clothing for the entire family

Consignment Policy: 50/50 split
Items are consigned for 60 days

Charleston

**Consigning Women &
Furniture
19 Magnolia Road
Charleston, South Carolina
29407**

Store Hours:
Monday-Friday 10am-6pm
Saturday 10am-5pm

Phone: 803-556-1871

Clothing for women, accessories,
jewelry, furniture & home
accessories

Consignment Policy: Items are
consigned for 90 days

Columbia

**Revente
733 & 737 Saluda Ave.
5 Points
Columbia, South Carolina
29205**

Store Hours:
Monday-Saturday 10am-6pm

Contact: Debbie McDaniel
Phone: 803-256-3076
803-771-8860
Web site: http://www; colasc.com/
revente/

Clothing for women, bridal,
furniture & home accessories

Second Location:
**5339H Sunset Blvd.
Topspin Plaza
Lexington, South Carolina
29072**

Phone: 803-359-7005

Clothing for women & furniture

Consignment Policy:
Consignments accepted by
appointment only
Women's clothing is consigned for
eight weeks & the consignor
receives 40% of the selling price
Furniture is consigned for 90 days
& the consignor receives 50% to
60%

Store Special: Referral cards &
frequent shopper cards

Hilton Head

**Sacks
27 Arrow Road
Hilton Head, South Carolina
29928**

Store Hours:
Monday-Friday 10am-5:30pm
Saturday 10am-4pm

Contact: Mary Hiers &
Marie Ownes

South Carolina

Phone: 803-842-4222

Upscale designer clothing & accessories for women, men & children featuring labels such as St. John, Escada, Ralph Lauren, Fendi, Calvin Klein & many more!

Consignment Policy: 50/50 split

Located in the beautiful resort town of Hilton Head, Sacks offers the finest current fashions available.

Myrtle Beach

Around Again Bargains
219 W. Broadway
Myrtle Beach,
South Carolina 29577

Store Hours:
Monday-Friday 10am-5:30pm

Phone: 803-448-5998
e-mail: CARNUM21@aol.com

All types of furniture & antiques

Konsignment Korner
1118 N. Kings Highway
Myrtle Beach,
South Carolina 29577

Store Hours:
Monday-Thursday 10am-5pm
Friday & Saturday 10am-3pm

Contact: Sandra Griffin
Phone: 803-448-0861

Clothing for women, men & children & home decor items
Accepts cash, checks & all major credit cards

Store Specials: Different color tickets on sale daily

Surfside Beach

New For You
Consignment Shop
352-A Hwy. 17 North
Surfside Beach,
South Carolina 29575

Store Hours:
Monday-Saturday 10am-5pm

Contact: Vikki Miller
Phone: 803-238-2177

Clothing & accessories for women, formal wear, antiques & vintage jewelry
Accepts cash, local checks, Visa, Mastercard & Discover

Consignment Policy: 50/50 split
Items are consigned for 60 days

234

Brookings

Second Edition
509 Main Street
Brookings, South Dakota
57006

Store Hours:
Monday-Friday 10am-5pm
Saturday 10am-2pm

Phone: 605-697-6554

Gently used clothing for the entire family and household items
Accepts cash & checks

Store Specials: Weekly sales

Faith

Varlands Varieties
211 Main Street
Faith, South Dakota 57626
Located in ranch country 70 miles south of the North Dakota border

Store Hours:
Monday-Saturday 9:30am-5pm

Contact: Ann Varland
Phone: 605-967-2127

New & used household items, some furniture, saddles & tack equipment, tools, clothing & more!

Consignment Policy:
Consignor receives 25% of the selling price on most items

"Wear it again Sam", Inc.
402 East Fairmont Blvd.
Suite D

Rapid City, South Dakota
57702

Store Hours:
Monday-Friday 9am-6pm
Saturday 9am-5pm
Sunday 12pm-4pm

Phone: 605-342-8283

Clothing for women & men & costume rental

Consignment Policy: 50/50 split
Items are consigned for 60 days

Pierre

Hospice Thrift Store
1105 E. Sioux
Pierre, South Dakota 57501

Store Hours:
Tuesday-Friday 10am-5:30pm
Saturday 9am-5pm

Contact: Amy Fallis
Phone: 605-945-0150
Fax: 605-224-3308

All types of secondhand merchandise & collectibles
Accepts cash

Store Policy: Donations welcome

Store Specials: Clothing discounted the first Saturday of each month

Proceeds from the shop benefit the Hospice Inpatient Unit.

South Dakota

Sioux Falls

**Union Gospel Mission
Thrift Store
617 E. 7th Street
Sioux Falls, South Dakota
57102**

Phone: 605-334-6732

Clothing for the entire family, household items, furniture & more!

Store Policy: Donations welcome

Cookeville

**Annie's Trunk
Consignment Shop
142 S. Willow
Cookeville, Tennessee 38501**

Store Hours:
Monday-Saturday 10am-5:30pm

Contact: Lora Bohannon &
Claude Ann Burton
Phone: 931-528-7737

Women's casual clothing &
formal wear

Store Specials: On-going color tag
sale monthly

Goodlettsville

**Cream of the Crop
Repeat Shop
136 S. Main Street
Goodlettsville, Tennessee
37072**

Store Hours:
Monday-Saturday 10am-5:30pm

Phone: 615-851-6000

Clothing for women & children,
formal wear, furniture &
household items

Consignment Policy: 50/50 split

Knoxville

**Encores For Kids, Inc.
8807 Kingston Pike
Suite N1
Ten Mile Center
Knoxville, Tennessee 37901**

Store Hours:
Monday-Saturday 10am-5pm
Sunday 1pm-5pm

Phone: 423-539-9941

Gently used clothing for children

McKenzie

**Ashley & Codi's
Upscale Consignment
585 N. Main Street
McKenzie, Tennessee 38201**

Store Hours:
Monday-Saturday 9am-5pm

Phone: 901-352-6004

Consignment Policy: Consignor
receives 40%

Store Specials: Items marked down
after 30 days

Memphis

**Birth Right Bargains
3417 Summer
Memphis, Tennessee 38122**

Store Hours:
Monday-Saturday 10am-4pm

Phone: 901-324-2373

Clothing for the entire family,
housewares, shoes, toys, records &
books

Store Policy: Donations welcome

Store Specials: Dollar annex

Tennessee

Kids Corner/Montana Lamb
709 S. Mendenhall
Memphis, Tennessee
38117

Store Hours:
Monday-Saturday 10am-5:30pm

Phone: 901-766-0939

Children's clothing & maternity
wear, toys, baby swings & lamps

Consignment Policy: 50/50 split
No appointment is needed to
consign merchandise

Priscilla's Plus Sizes
Resale Consignment
301 E. McLemore Avenue
Memphis, Tennessee 38106-
2938

Store Hours:
Tuesday-Saturday 10am-6pm

Contact: Priscilla Collins
Phone: 901-774-4001

Specializing in women's plus sizes
& children's clothing too
Accepts cash & checks

Consigment Policy: Items are
consigned for 90 days

Store Specials: Special coupon
offers

Present this coupon at
Priscilla's Plus Sizes
Resale Consignment
301 East McLemore Ave.
Memphis, Tennessee
& save 20% off your
purchase over $50.00
Expiration Date: 12/31/99

Simply Divine Plus Sizes
713 S. Mendenhall Road
Memphis, Tennessee 38117

Store Hours:
Monday 12pm-6pm
Tuesday & Friday 10am-6pm
Saturday 10am-5pm

Contact: Barbara Askew
Phone: 901-684-1023

Women's plus clothing sizes
14-32

The Clothes Line
7095 S. Mendenhall
Memphis, Tennessee 38117

Store Hours:
Monday-Saturday 10am-5:30pm

Contact: Sandi Moore
Phone: 901-766-0900

Consignment clothing for women,
men & children
Accepts, cash & all major credit
cards

Consignment Policy:
50/50 split
Items are consigned for 90 days

Nashville

Designer Consignors
3702 Nolensville Road
Nashville, Tennessee 37135

Store Hours:
Monday-Saturday 11am-6:30pm

Phone: 615-834-4012

Upscale women's clothing &
accessories

Consignment Policy: 50/50 split
Items are consigned for 90 days

Designer Renaissance
2706 Hillsboro Road
Green Hills
Nashville, Tennessee 37215

Store Hours:
Monday-Saturday 10am-6pm

Phone: 615-297-8822

Designer clothing & accessories
for women & featuring a special
bridal room with upscale wedding
gowns

Consignment Policy: 50/50 split
Items are consigned for 60 days

DAV Thrift Store of Nashville
766 Two Mile Parkway
Nashville, Tennessee 37211

Store Hours:
Monday-Friday 9am-7pm
Sunday 1pm-6pm

Phone: 615-228-8624

Clothing for the entire family,
furniture & more!
Accepts cash, checks & major
credit cards

Store Specials: Seniors & DAV
members receive a 10% discount
On-going half price sales

Pieces
211 Louise Ave
Nashville, Tennessee

Store Hours: Call for store hours

Phone: 615-329-3537

Great vintage clothing &
accessories

Razzmatazz
Consignment Shop
3061 Brick Church Pike
Nashville, Tennessee 37207

Store Hours:
Tuesday-Friday 11am-7pm
Saturday 10am-6pm

Phone: 615-262-1133

Specializing in women's designer
clothing & accessories

The Fashion Connection
5115 Nolensville Road
Nashville, Tennessee 37211

Store Hours:
Monday-Thursday 10am-7pm
Friday & Saturday 10am-5pm

Phone: 615-333-2632

Quality resale apparel for men &
women & accessories
Accepts cash, checks, American
Express, Visa & Mastercard

Consignment Policy: Call for an
appointment
Accepts items in season

Second Location:

Fashion Connection Too
4734 Old Hickory Blvd.
Old Hickory, Tennessee 37138

Store Hours:
Tuesday 10am-6pm
Wednesday-Saturday 10am-5pm

Phone: 615-872-9746

Tennessee

Store Specials:
Clearance sales, bonus bucks &
50% to 75% off select merchandise

Oneida

Castaways & Company
271 Main Street
Oneida, Tennessee 37841

Store Hours:
Monday-Friday 10am-5pm
including the first Saturday
of each month

Phone: 423-569-1898
e-mail: Castaways@highland.net
Web site: www.geocities.com/
eureka/plaza/9156

Lots of great secondhand items
from antiques, crafts, collectibles,
great gifts and lots more

Union City

Fashion Network/Upscale
Resale
224 South First Street
Union City, Tennessee 38261

Store Hours:
Monday-Saturday 10am-5pm
Thursday until 7pm

Contact: Lyda Rice
Phone: 901-885-3988

New & gently used clothing &
accessories for the entire family

Store Specials: Bonus bucks

Present this coupon at
Fashion Network
Upscale Resale
224 South First Street
Union City,
Tennessee & save $3.00 off
your first purchase

Expiration Date: 12/31/99

Arlington

Western Wear Exchange
2538 E. Abram
Arlington, Texas 76010

Store Hours:
Tuesday-Saturday 10am-7pm
Sunday 1pm-7pm
Phone: 817-794-0216

Second Location:

Western Wear Exchange
2809 Alta Mere
Fort Worth, Texas 76116

Store Hours:
Monday-Saturday
10am-6pm
Phone: 817-738-4048

The only exclusive western wear consignment shop in the US, featuring top brand name western wear for the entire family, at great prices!

Consignment Policy:
50/50 split on western wear
Items consigned for 90 days & marked down after 60 days

Austin

Fashion Xchange
Resale Boutique
5114 Balcones Woods Drive
#304
Between 183 and
Jollyville Road
Austin, Texas 78759

Store Hours:
Monday-Saturday 10am-7pm
Sunday 12pm-4pm

Phone: 512-338-0200

Upscale apparel for women
Accepts cash & major credit cards

Consignment Policy:
50/50 split

A Time or Two
1748 W. Anderson Lane
Austin, Texas 78757

Store Hours:
Monday-Friday 10:30am-6pm
Saturday 10:30am-5:30pm

Phone: 512-452-6992
Fax: 512-451-2482
e-mail: TimeorTwo@aol.com
Website: www.citysearch.com/Aus/ATimeorTwo

Women's apparel & accessories

Accepts cash, checks,Visa, Mastercard, Discover & American Express

Consignment Policy: Items consigned for 90 days

Corpus Christi

Red Door Resale
4839 S. Staples
Corpus Christi, Texas 78411

Store Hours:
Tuesday-Saturday 11am-7pm

Contact: Beci Potter
Phone: 512-992-3440

Clothing for the entire family
Accepts cash, local checks, Visa, Mastercard, Discover & Amex

Dallas

Accent on Designers
7517 Campbell Road #602
Dallas, Texas 75248

Store Hours:
Monday-Friday 10:30am-6pm
Saturday 10am-5pm

Phone: 972-732-8770

Apparel for women

Champagne Taste
5211 Forest Lane
Suite #115
Dallas, Texas 75244

Store Hours:
Monday-Friday 10am-6pm
Thursday 10am-7pm
Saturday 10am-5pm

Phone & Fax: 972-233-9999

Designer & couture clothing for
women, shoes, purses, belts,
hats, scarves, jewelry (costume,
fine & antique), furs, accessories
& much more! Some samples,
petites & maternity too.
Sizes 4-44 plus!
Accepts cash, checks, Visa,
Mastercard & Discover

Consignment Policy:
Seasonal current better labels
accepted Monday-Thursday

90 day contract
50/50 split
Furs accepted year round

Store Specials: Lay -a-way
available

Champagne Taste has been the
"Rolls-Royce" of women's resale
since 1982.

■■■■■■■■■■■■■■■
■ Mention this listing at ■
■ *Champagne Taste* ■
■ *5211 Forest Lane* ■
■ *Suite 115* ■
■ *Dallas, Texas* ■
■ & save 10% off one ■
■ clothing item ■
■ ■
■ Expiration Date: 12/31/99 ■
■■■■■■■■■■■■■■■

Clotheshorse
Anonymous Inc.
1413 Preston Forest Square
Dallas, Texas 75230

Store Hours:
Monday-Saturday 10am-6pm
Thursday 10am-8pm
Sunday 12pm-6pm

Phone: 972-233-7005

Over 7000 square feet of upscale
clothing for women such
as Escada, DKNY, Calvin Klein,
Armani, shoes, accessories & gift
items

Consignment Policy: 50/50 split
on most items except couture
items which are 60/40

Store Specials: Complimentary
pick-up service

**Clothes Circuit Decidedly
Upscale Resale
6105 Sherry Lane
Preston Center
Dallas, Texas 75225**

Store Hours:
Monday, Tuesday, Wednesday &
Friday 10am-7pm
Thursday 10am-8pm
Saturday 10am-6pm
Sunday 12pm-6pm

Phone: 214-696-8634

Designer label & bridge wear for
women & bridal fashions

Consignment Policy: 50/50 policy
Items consigned for 60 days

Store Specials: Seasonal back
room sales in January & July

**Consignment Collection
5211 Forest Lane
#108 at Inwood Road
Dallas, Texas 75244**

Store Hours:
Monday-Saturday 10am-6pm

Phone: 972-788-4444

Furniture, antiques & decorative
items

Consignment Policy: Consignor
receives 55% of the sales price

**Consignment Galleries
5627 W. Lovers Lane
Dallas, Texas 75209**

Store Hours:
Monday-Saturday 10am-5:30pm

Phone: 214-357-3925

e-mail: congal@juno.com
Website: www.themetro.com/02/
consign

Antique & traditional furniture &
accessories
Accepts cash, checks, Mastercard
& Visa

Consignment Policy:
55/45 split

**Gent●ly Owned Men's
Consignery
17610 Midway Road #106
Dallas, Texas 75287**

Store Hours:
Monday-Friday 10am-7pm
Saturday 11am-5pm

Contact: Todd Shevlin
Phone: 214-733-1115
Website: www.metroplexweb.com

Upscale clothing & accessories for
men & European labels!

Consignment Policy:
50/50 split
Items are consigned for 90 days

**Kids Kloset
6138 Luther Lane
Dallas, Texas 75225**

Store Hours:
Monday-Saturday 10am-5pm
Sunday 12pm-4pm

Contact: Lynn Piranio
Phone: 214-369-2243

Designer children's clothing &
maternity
Accepts cash, check, Visa &
Mastercard

Items are consigned for 90 days

Store Specials: Lay-a-ways & alterations available

**Larger Than Life-
Rubenesque Resale
10233 East Northwest
Highway
Suite 435
Dallas, Texas 75238**

Store Hours:
Monday-Saturday 10am-6pm
Thursday 10am-8pm

Contact: Kat Krone
Phone: 214-342-8550
Fax: 214-342-3592

Featuring plus size clothing exclusively
Accepts cash, checks, Visa, Mastercard & Discover

Consignment Policy: Consignments accepted on Monday & Thursday only without an appointment

Store Specials: Automatic markdowns up to 30% on select items

**Second Hand Rose
1152 N Buckner
Dallas, Texas 75218**

Store Hours:
Monday-Friday 10am-6pm
Saturday 10am-5pm

Contact: Harriett Anderson
Phone: 214-324-8062

Better quality clothing for women & girls, bridal & after-five
Accepts cash, checks, Visa,

Mastercard & Discover

Consignment Policy:
50/50 split
Items consigned for 90 days

● ● ● ● ● ● ● ● ● ● ● ● ● ● ●
●   ●
●   Present this coupon at   ●
●   *Second Hand Rose*   ●
●   *1152 N Buckner*   ●
●   *Dallas, Texas* & save   ●
●   10% off one item   ●
●   ●
●   Expiration Date: 12/31/99   ●
●   ●
● ● ● ● ● ● ● ● ● ● ● ● ● ● ●

DeSoto

**Twice Is Nice
210 E. Beltline Road Suite 111
DeSoto, Texas 75115**

Store Hours:
Monday-Friday 10am-6pm
Saturday 10am-5pm
Sunday 12pm-5pm

Contact: Peggy Brown
Phone: 972-274-9900
e-mail:dbrown20@airmail.net

Upscale designer labels for women sizes 2 to 32 & accessories

Consignment Policy:
50/50 split
Items are consigned for 60 days

El Paso

**St. Clements Bargain Box
528 E Yandell
El Paso, Texas 79902**

Store Hours:
Tuesday-Friday 10am-4pm
Saturday 10am-1pm

Phone: 915-532-1731

Clothing furniture & collectibles
Accepts cash & checks

Fort Worth

Mudpuppy
5714 Locke Avenue
Ft. Worth, Texas 76107

Store Hours:
Monday-Saturday 10am-5pm

Contact: Jana Minter
Phone: 817-731-2581

Children's clothing, toys, shoes &
baby accessories

Consignment Policy:
50/50 split

Store Specials: Half price sales in
January & July

Galveston Island

The Queen's Attic, Inc
4501 Broadway
Galveston Island, Texas 77550

Store Hours:
Tuesday-Saturday 10:30am-
5:30pm
Open late the last Thursday of
every month

Phone: 409-765-7078
e-mail: TXJD22A@prodigy.com

Gently used clothing, housewares,
furniture & books

Best Kept Secret
13150 F.M. 529 #122
Houston, Texas 77041

Store Hours:
Tuesday-Friday 11am-5pm &
Saturday 12pm-5pm

Upscale clothing for women &
accessories, beautiful vintage
jewelry, wedding gowns & party
dresses for little girls

Phone: 915-532-1732

Clothing for the entire family,
furniture, small appliances,
& more

Consignment Policy: 50/50 split
Items are consigned for 90 days

Grand Prairie

Hannah's Hand-Me-Downs
513 West Marshall
Grand Prairie, Texas 75051

Store Hours:
Tuesday-Saturday 10am-6pm

Contact: Jan Agrusa
Phone: 972-642-1115

Clothing for the entire family &
much more!
Accepts cash

Store Specials: Donations
accepted

All proceeds support Brighter
Tomorrows, a local domestic
violence program.

Houston

Assistance League of Houston
1902 Commonwealth
Houston, Texas 77006

Texas

Store Hours:
Tuesday-Saturday 10am-3pm

Phone: 713-526-5425

Gently used clothing &
housewares

**Gentleman's Closet
Men's Upscale Resale
1212 Westheimer
Suite 102
Houston, Texas 77077**

Store Hours:
Monday-Saturday 10am-5pm
Wednesday 11am-7pm

Contact: Lori Carbone
Phone: 281-293-7020
Fax: 281-293-0668
e-mail: txemma@aol.com

Upscale clothing for men from
corporate to casual
Accepts cash, Mastercard, Visa,
American Express & Discover

Consignment Policy: 40/60 split
Items are consigned for 90 days

Store Specials: Discount rack

Gentlemen's Closet has been
featured in *The New York Times* &
USA Today.

**Sand Dollar Thrift Stores
7018 Harrisburg
Houston, Texas 77011**

Store Hours:
Monday-Saturday 9am-7pm

Sunday 10am-6pm

Phone: 713-923-1461
Fax: 713-923-3093

Other Locations:
**2300 N. Main Street
Houston, Texas 77011**

**1903 Yale Street
Houston, Texas 77011**

**2535 Spencer Highway
Pasadena, Texas 77504**

Clothing for the entire family,
shoes, books, housewares & much
more!

Store Policy: Donations welcome
and tax receipt may be provided

Store Specials: Seniors receive
50% discount on clothing once
a month

Proceeds benefit the Sand Dollar
Youth Service Center. Named
Houston Press Best Pick in 1996.

Lancaster

**BackRoom Raggs
129 Historic Town Square
Lancaster, Texas 75146**

Store Hours:
Tuesday-Friday 10am-5pm
Thursday 10am-8pm
Saturday 10am-5pm

Phone: 972-227-4600

Women's clothing
Accepts cash, Mastercard, Visa &
Discover

Consignment Policy:
Consignments accepted Tuesday
or Saturday

Leakey

Judy's Caboodle
Downtown Leakey
Leakey, Texas 78873

Store Hours:
Monday-Saturday 10am-6pm

Contact: Judy Adams
Phone: 830-232-5897

Fax: 830-232-5300
e-mail: dbjadams@hctc.net

Clothing for the entire family
including plus & maternity sizes,
antiques, collectibles & much
more!
Accepts cash, checks, Mastercard
& Visa

Store Specials:
Lay-a-way available, discounts on
overstocks & fun sales year round

• • • • • • • • • • • •
•
• Present this coupon at
• *Judy's Caboodle*
• *Downtown Leakey*
• *Leakey, Texas* &
• save 20% off a purchase
•
• Expiration Date: 12/31/99
• • • • • • • • • • • •

Mesquite

The Emporium of Big Town
Crafts & Consignments/
Antique Mall & Victorian
Garden Tea Room
950 Big Town Mall
Mesquite, Texas 75149

Store Hours:
Monday-Saturday 10am-8pm

Sunday 12pm-5:30pm
Tea Room Hours:
Tuesday-Saturday 11:30am-3pm

Antiques, jewelry, glassware &
collectibles, original crafts &
creations, furniture & quality
accessories

Portland

Lady Ds' Resale
1524 Wildcat Drive @
Highway 181/N Plaza
Portland, Texas 78374-2814

Store Hours:
Monday-Saturday 10am-6pm

Phone: 512-643-4491
Website: www.theclothestree.com/
shops/LadyDs/

Clothing for women & accessories

Consignment Policy: 50/50 split
Items are consigned for 90 days

Store Specials: Call or visit for
daily specials

Texas

San Antonio

Anew Again Boutique
1719 Babcock
San Antonio, Texas 78229

Store Hours:
Monday-Friday 10am-5:30pm
Saturday 10am-4pm

Phone: 210-342-3354

Top quality clothing for women,
accessories, antique jewelry &
collectibles

Consignment Policy: An
appointment is necessary to
consign merchandise

Encore For Women
2191 N.W. Military Highway
San Antonio, Texas 78213

Store Hours:
Monday, Tuesday, Wednesday &
Friday 10am-5:30pm
Thursday 10am-7pm
Saturday 10am-4pm

Phone: 210-341-0939
Contact: Barbara Allison

Upscale clothing for women
Accepts all cash, credit cards and
checks

Consignment Policy:
50/50 split
Items consigned for 60 days

Just For Kids Resale
1576 Babcock Road
San Antonio, Texas 78229

Store Hours:
Monday-Friday 10am-5:30pm
Saturday 10am-5pm

Contact: Kathleen Falkiewicz
Phone: 210-340-8949
e-mail: JUST4KIDS@juno.com
Website:
www.theclothestree.com/shops/
JustForKids/

Children's clothing, toys, infant wear, furniture & accessories & maternity clothing
Consignment Policy:
60/40 split
Items consigned for 60 days

Consignments accepted by appointment only

Store Specials: Grandparents receive a 10% discount on Wednesday

---

Present this coupon at
Just For Kids Resale
1576 Babcock Road
San Antonio, Texas &
save 20% off any regular priced item

Expiration Date: 12/31/99

Me & Mom Resale Boutique
13909 Nacogdoches Suite 100
San Antonio, Texas 78217

Store Hours:
Monday-Friday 10am-6pm
Saturday 10am-4pm

Phone: 210-590-2888

Over 1400 square feet of clothing for children to size 6X, maternity wear & more!

Bygone Better Homes & Bargains
Showroom @ Trend Setters
15679 San Pedro
San Antonio, Texas 78232

Store Hours:
Monday-Saturday 10am-6pm

Contact: Craig Farkas & Gene Weston
Phone: 210-490-9319
Fax: 210-490-9322

Second Location:
Annex @ Mil Encinos
2250 Thousand Oaks #102
San Antonio, Texas 78232

Phone: 210-495-3500

Quality pre-owned furniture & accessories, antiques, collectibles, silver, crystal, china, rugs, lamps, fine art, jewelry, patio furniture & estate liquidations. Save at least half off original cost!
Accepts cash, checks, Visa, Mastercard & Discover

Store Specials: 10% consecutive markdowns after three, five & seven weeks

The shop has been featured and received high ratings in *The Lady's Day Out* & *The Underground Shopper.*

Texas

Slaton

The Clothes Rack
215 W. Lubbock Street
Slaton, Texas 79364

Store Hours:
Monday 2pm-5:30pm
Tuesday, Wednesday & Friday
9am-5:30pm
Thursday 9am-6:30pm
Saturday 9am-4:30pm

Phone: 806-828-1455

Brand name clothing & accessories for the entire family & new items too!
Accepts cash & checks

Consignment Policy:
50/50 split
Items consigned for 60 days
Store Specials: Lay-a-way available

Sweetwater

Second Hand Rose Resale
122 Oak Street
Sweetwater, Texas 79556

Store Hours:
Monday-Saturday 12pm-6pm

Phone: 915-235-1504

Clothing for the entire family & featuring over 1500 hats!
Accepts cash & checks

Consignment Policy: 50/50 split

Store Specials: Seasonal sales from 20% to 60% off select items

Universal City

The Clothes Tree
Consignment Boutique
2326 Pat Booker Road
Universal City, Texas 78148

Store Hours:
Monday-Saturday 10am-6pm
Phone: 210-658-1205
Website: www.theclothestree.com

Top name clothing for the entire family, accessories, bridal wear & much more! Over 20,000 items on hand to choose from. The inventory changes daily! Shop on www.theclothestree.com and view thousands of items for sale at great prices. Visit the Virtual Tour of consignment & thrift shops at www.theclothestree.com, the first of its kind on the web. Vast array of items available from stores around the world at The Clothes Tree online auction & catalog!

Other Locations:
453 W. San Antonio Street
New Braunfels, Texas 78130

Store Hours:
Monday-Saturday 10am-6pm
Phone: 830-606-5544

715 E. Court Street
Seguin, Texas 78155

Store Hours:
Monday-Saturday 10am-5pm
Phone: 210-303-0999

Present this coupon at
The Clothes Tree
Resale Boutique
2326 Pat Booker Road
Universal City, Texas

Other Locations:
453 W. San Antonio Street
New Braunfels, Texas

715 E. Court Street
Seguin, Texas

& save 10% off one in-store purchase

*The Clothes Tree Reserves the right not to discount items or services according to our policies

Code: TCT1
Expiration Date: 12/31/99

Attention:
Consignment &
Thrift Store Owners

Join the fastest growing resale shopping site on the internet at www.theclothestree.com The Clothes Tree Virtual Tour of Consignment & Thrift Stores is the only virtual tour of consignment & thrift stores on the internet. This tour gives your business the opportunity to be viewed by millions of potential customers worldwide. Join the The Clothes Tree worldwide online auction.

If you already have a website, you may join the tour free of charge. Contact Bob Hauver with your website & e-mail address and you will receive the tour code to display on your site as a link. If you do not have a web page, let The Clothes Tree design a page for you for as little as $10.00.

Send the following information & include a check for $10.00 to The Clothes Tree.

1.Your business name, address, phone, fax, e-mail address.
2. A description about your store.
3. A description of how you would like your web page designed.
4. Any pictures you would like to include on your site.

* This is the minimum amount of information you need to be included on the tour.

Send all the information to:
Mr. Bob Hauver, Jr.
The Clothes Tree
Resale Boutique
2326 Pat Booker Road
Universal City, Texas 78148
or e-mail: bob@theclothestree.com

Code: TCT2
Expiration Date: 12/31/99

Utah

Provo

Community Thrift & Relief
515 N. University Avenue
Provo, Utah 84603

Store Hours:
Monday-Saturday 10am-5pm
Phone: 801-377-7676

Gently used clothing for the entire family & more!

Salt Lake City

Cassandra's Closet Inc.
4227 So. Highland Drive
Salt Lake City, Utah 84117

Store Hours: Monday-Saturday
11am-5:30pm

Contact: Suzi Berrett
Phone: 801-278-5446
Fax: 801-942-0265

Designer clothing for women
Accepts cash, checks & credit cards

Store Specials: 40% off select items every month, lay-a-way available

---

Save 15% off one item
with this coupon at
Cassandra's Closet
4227 So. Highland Drive
Salt Lake City, Utah

Expiration Date: 12/31/99

Swappers Market
427 East 3300 South
Salt Lake City, Utah 84115

Store Hours:
Monday-Sunday 10am-6pm

Phone: 801-486-0505

Household items, tools, appliances, electronics, furniture & more!

Consignment Policy: Consignor receives 60%

The Stork Exchange
3257 E. 3300 S.
Salt Lake City, Utah 85109

Store Hours:
Monday-Friday 10am-6pm
Saturday 10am-5pm

Phone: 801-485-8870

Gently used clothing for children up to size 10, books, toys & baby equipment

Consignment Policy: 50/50 split

South Jordan

Kid to Kid of South Jordan
10366 S. Redwood Road
South Jordan, Utah 84095

Store Hours:
Monday-Saturday 10am-8pm

Phone: 801-253-4436

Gently used clothing for children, toys & equipment

West Valley City

Silverwing USA, LLC
2983 West 3500 South
West Valley City, Utah 84119

Store Hours:
Monday-Friday 10am-7pm
Saturday 11am-6pm

Contact: Ali H. Sabbah
Phone: 801-963-4121

Featuring over 3000 pairs of
gently used jeans & name brand
casual clothing for the entire
family
Accepts cash, checks & credit
cards

Vermont

Bennington

Second Hand Rose
303 Depot Street
Bennington, Vermont 05201

Store Hours:
Monday-Saturday 9am-4pm
Friday 9am-6pm

Contact: Cindy Bastarache
Phone: 802-447-1563

New & gently used clothing for
the entire family, household items
& new accessories like gloves,
hats, mittens, scarves & jewelry
Accepts cash, checks, Visa,
Mastercard & Discover

Consignment Policy: Consignor
receives 40% of the selling price
for the item

Store Specials: Dollar rack always
available, Select color tag sales
every week!

Present this coupon at
Second Hand Rose
303 Depot Street
Bennington, Vermont & save
10% off your total purchase

Expiration Date: 12/31/99

Burlington

The Garment Gallery
266 Pine Street
Burlington, Vermont 05401

Store Hours:
Monday-Saturday 10am-6pm

Sunday 12pm-5pm

Contact: Leigh Brisson
Phone: 802-860-2388

Vintage, casual clothing for men,
women & children, jewelry, hats
& shoes
Accepts cash & checks

Store Policy: Items purchased
outright

Store Specials: On going sales

Present this coupon at
The Garment Gallery
266 Pine Street
Burlington, Vermont &
save 20% off one item

Expiration Date: 12/31/99

Ludlow

The Black River Good
Neighbor Food Shelf/
Thrift Shop
105 Main Street
Ludlow, Vermont 05149

Store Hours:
Monday-Saturday 10am-3pm

Contact: Pati Trapeni-LaPlante
Phone: 802-228-3663

Clothing for the entire family,
household items and much more
Accepts cash or checks

Store Policy: Donations welcome
All clothing must be clean and in
good condition

Store Specials: End of the season sales

All proceeds from the shop are used to support the Food Shelf which helps those in need in the community.

Middlebury

Neat Repeats
Bakery Lane
Middlebury, Vermont 05753

Store Hours:
Monday-Saturday 9:30am-4:30pm

Contact: Kathy Caswell & Linda Waterman
Phone: 802-388-4488

Clothing for the entire family, jewelry, household items & collectibles
Accepts cash & checks

Consignment Policy:
50/50 split for items up to $15.00
65/45 split for items over $15.00

Store Specials: Twice a year big seasonal sales

Neat Repeats helps the community by presenting grants to various organizations.

Vergennes

Your Turn Consignment
Shop/Sports Exchange
151 Main Street
Vergennes, Vermont 05491

Store Hours:
Monday-Friday 10am-5pm

Contact: Marion Sullivan
Phone: 802-877-3915

Clothing for the entire family, household items and sporting goods
Accepts cash & checks

Consignment Policy:
50/50 split up to $30.00
65/45 over $30.00
Items consigned for 6 weeks

White River Junction

Listen, Inc.
Route 5
Near Hartford Highschool
White River Junction,
Vermont 05001

Store Hours:
Monday-Saturday 10am-5pm
Sunday 12pm-5pm

Phone: 802-295-9259

Clothing for the entire family, housewares, furniture & bric-a-brac
Accepts cash, checks & credit cards

Store Policy: Donations welcome

Vermont

Woodstock

Who Is Sylvia?
26 Central Street
Woodstock, Vermont 05091
Located in one of the most
picturesque New England towns.

Store Hours:
Monday-Sunday 10am-5pm

Contact: Elizabeth McCrae
Phone: 802-457-1110
Fax: 802-457-4489

Who Is Sylvia carries vintage
clothing & accessories circa
Victorian era through the 1950's
for men, women & children,
linens & lace
Accepts cash, checks & credit
cards

Store Policy: Items purchased
outright

*A wide variety of fine antique
linens is available at Who Is
Sylvia? in Woodstock, Vermont*

Alexandria

Alexandria Consignments
110 S. West Street
Alexandria, Virginia 22314

Located in historic Olde Town Alexandria surrounded by quaint antique shops.

Store Hours:
Monday, Tuesday, Wednesday, Friday & Saturday 11am-6pm
Call for seasonal store hours

Phone: 703-684-9140
e-mail: AlxConsign@aol.com

Designer clothing for women sizes 2-22, vintage clothing & accessories for women & men circa 1930's to 1960's. Full line of tuxedos for men. Lots of costume jewelry including some great vintage pieces.

Consignment Policy:
50/50 split
$10.00 annual fee to consign items
Items consigned for 60 days

Store Specials: Seasonal sales are held & special discounts may apply to mailing list members

> Present this coupon at
> *Alexandria Consignments*
> *110 S. West Street*
> *Alexandria, Virginia*
> & save 20% off a total sale
>
> (Coupon may not be combined with other sales or offers)
> Expiration Date: 12/31/99

Blacksburg

Second Seasons, Inc.
208 N. Main Street
Blacksburg, Virginia 24060

Store Hours:
Monday-Friday 10am-6pm
Saturday 10am-5pm
Sunday 1pm-5pm

Contact: Dorothy Lemme Egger
Phone: 540-552-7412

Women's clothing & accessories, shoes, jewelry, new clothing items & maternity wear
Accepts cash, checks, Visa & Mastercard

Consignment Policy: Consignments accepted by appointment
Consignor receives 40% of the selling price for the item
Items are consigned for 90 days

Store Specials: Select tickets reduced monthly

> Present this coupon at
> *Second Seasons*
> *208 N. Main Street,*
> *Blacksburg, Virginia* &
> save 10% off any purchase on regular priced items
>
> (Can not be used for discounted items)
> Expiration Date: 12/31/99

Virginia

Centreville

Designer Consignor, Ltd.
Village Center
Shopping Plaza
5651 Stone Road
Centreville, Virginia 20120

Store Hours:
Tuesday-Friday 11am-7pm
Saturday 10am-7pm
(Check in the Summer for
extended hours)
Sunday 12pm-6pm

Phone: 703-266-7667
Fax: 703-266-7804
e-mail: ADixon1@aol.com or
ConsignBiz@aol.com

Specializing in designer & brand
name better clothing for the
entire family, accessories, shoes,
decorative household items,
antiques, prints, gift items,
jewelry, sunglasses & more!

Consignment Policy:
Consignments accepted by
appointment only
$10.00 semi-annual consignment
fee & consignors receive 10%
discount on items
50/50 split

Store Specials: 50% off red dot
items
After 30 days items reduced 25%

■ Present this coupon at ■
■ *Designer Consignor, Ltd.* ■
■ *5651 Stone Road* ■
■ *Centreville, Virginia* & ■
■ save 25% off any single full ■
■ priced item ■
■ (Coupon is not valid for previously ■
■ discounted or red dot/clearance items) ■
■ Expiration Date: 12/31/99 ■

258

Charlottesville

Kids Kaboodle
1756 Rio Hill Center
Charlottesville, Virginia
22901

Store Hours:
Monday-Thursday 10am-6pm
Friday 10am-7pm & Saturday
10am-4pm

Phone: 804-974-7063

High end childrens' clothing &
baby equipment

Chesapeake

Uniquely Yours
1457 Mt. Pleasant Road
Chesapeake, Virginia 23322

Store Hours:
Monday 10am-3pm
Tuesday & Friday 10am-5pm
Wednesday 10am-7pm
Saturday 10am-4pm

Upscale clothing for women &
children, jewelry, toys & furniture

Over three hundred new items
arrive daily!

Danville

Kid's Stuff
Consignment Boutique
1083 Piney Forest Road
Danville, Virginia 24540

Store Hours:
Monday-Thursday 9am-5pm
Friday & Saturday 9am-6pm

Phone: 804-836-1450

Quality brand name clothing for children to size 14, maternity wear, shoes including tap & ballet, scout uniforms, Halloween costumes, toys, games, books & baby furnishings

Consignment Policy:
Consignments accepted Monday-Friday 9am-5pm
Consignor receives 40%

Kid's Stuff has a great play area for kids!

Herndon

Once Cherished Consignments, Inc.
141-A Spring Street
Herndon, Virginia 20170

Store Hours:
Tuesday, Wednesday, Thursday 11am-6pm
Friday & Saturday 11am-5pm

Contact: Alice Stellabotte
Phone: 703-435-5141

Designer & better label women's wear, jewelry, furniture, antiques, collectibles & home accessories
Accepts cash, checks, Visa & Mastercard

Consignment Policy:
50/50 split
Items consigned for 60 days
No annual fee

Store Specials:
After 30 days items reduced 25%
After 60 days items reduced 50%
Lay-a-way available

Newport News

Disabled American Veterans Thrift Store
15265 Warwick Blvd.
Newport News, Virginia 23608

Store Hours:
Monday-Friday 9:30am-8:30pm

Phone: 757-877-0999

Clothing for the entire family, bric-a-brac, books, furniture & more!

Richmond

Private Collections Consignments
Oxbridge Square Shopping Center
9957 Hull Street Road
Richmond, Virginia 23236

Store Hours:
Monday-Friday 10am-7pm
Saturday 10am-5pm

Phone: 804-674-1993

Clothing & accessories for women & children, maternity wear & bridal gowns

Consignment Policy: 50/50 split

Virginia

Second Impressions
Tuckernuck Square
9058 West Broad Street
Richmond, Virginia 23294

Store Hours:
Monday-Friday 10:30am-6:30pm
Saturday 10:30am-4:30pm

Contact: Linday Weinstein
Phone: 804-346-4968

Contemporary apparel for
women, specializing in maternity
& bridal wear.
One of the largest selection of
bridal gowns in the Richmond
area. Over 250 current gowns &
over 100 headpieces, some never
worn!
Accepts cash & checks
Consignment Policy:
First time consignors need an
appointment

Store Specials: Lay-a-way
available

Present this coupon at
Second Impressions
9058 West Broad Street
Richmond, Virginia & save
10% off any one item
during one visit
(Offer not valid with bridal or
any other offers)
Limit one per customer
Expiration Date: 12/31/99

Virginia Beach

Second Time Around
3772 Virginia Beach Blvd.
Virginia Beach, Virginia
23452

Store Hours:
Monday-Saturday 10am-6pm

Phone: 757-498-3927
Fax: 757-498-1145

Excellent quality clothing &
accessories for women & children

Consignment Policy: 50/50 split

Bellevue

Dark Horse Boutique
11810 N.E. 8th
Bellevue, Washington 98005

Store Hours:
Monday, Tuesday, Wednesday
& Friday 10:30am-6pm
Thursday 10:30am-8pm
Saturday 10:30am-5pm

Phone: 425-454-0990

Apparel & accessories for
men & women & books
Accepts cash, checks & credit
cards

Store Specials: Items reduced
after 30 days

Bremerton

Almost New Furniture
1640 Navy Yard Highway
Bremerton, Washington
98312

Store Hours:
Monday-Saturday 10am-6pm
Sunday 12pm-5pm

Phone: 360-405-1812

Featuring over 7700 square feet of
almost new furniture & household
accessories

Kennewick

Mother's World, Inc.
127 W. Kennewick Avenue
Kennewick, Washington
99336

Store Hours:
Monday, Tuesday, Wednesday &
Friday 10am-5:30pm
Thursday 10am-7pm
Saturday 9am-5pm

Contact: Della Farance
Phone: 509-586-0272

Clothing for women including
maternity wear, juniors, children,
infants, toys, handcrafts & baby
equipment

Consignment Policy: Items are
consigned for 90 days

Store Specials: Quarterly bag sales

Over 6000 square feet of
merchandise!

Mount Vernon

The Encore Shoppe
1501 Parker Way #102
Mount Vernon, Washington
98273

Store Hours:
Tuesday-Friday 9:30am-5:30pm
Saturday 9:30am-5pm

Contact: Sandy Youngren
Phone: 360-424-8099

Quality new & "nearly new"
apparel for women, men &
children
Accepts cash, checks, Visa,
Mastercard & Discover

Washington

Consignment Policy: Items are consigned for 90 days
Consignor receives 40%

Seattle

Ah Nuts
601 N. 35th
Seattle, Washington 98103

Store Hours:
Monday-Sunday 11am-5pm

Contact: Josh Logan
Phone: 206-633-0664

The most unique collection of "junque" in the Northwest. Vast array of antiques & collectibles. Accepts cash & credit cards

Store Policy: Barter

Store Specials: Dealer discounts available

Alexandra's
412 Olive Way
Seattle, Washington 98101

Store Hours:
Monday-Saturday 10am-6pm
Friday until 7pm
Sunday 12pm-4pm

Phone: 206-623-1214

Designer labels for women & men including Armani, Escada, Donna Karan & accessories

Consignment Policy: Consignor receives 40% of the selling price

American Cancer Society
Discovery Shop
4535 California Ave. SW
Seattle, Washington 98116

Phone: 206-937-7169

Store Hours:
Monday-Saturday 9:30am-4:30pm

New & gently used clothing, kitchenware, books & collectibles

Store Policy: Donations welcome

Cecil's Consignment
2224 Queen Anne Avenue N.
Seattle, Washington 98109

Store Hours:
Monday-Friday 10am-7pm
Saturday 10-am-5pm
Sunday 12pm-5pm

Phone: 206-283-3676

Women's designer clothing & accessories

Children's Hospital
Thrift Stores
2026 3rd Ave.
Seattle, Washington 98121-2494

Store hours:
Monday-Saturday 9:30am-5pm

Phone: 206-448-7609

Furniture, household items, office & kitchenware, designer boutique & clearance center

Store Policy: Donations welcome

Proceeds from the Children's

Washington

Hospital Thrift Stores benefit Chldren's Hospital & Regional Medical Center which provides quality care to all children in need.

Other Locations:

4800 Sandpoint Way NE
Seattle, Washingon 98105

Store Hours:
Monday-Friday 9am-5pm
Saturday-Sunday
11am-3pm

Phone: 206-526-2238

Fine gift items, vast array of stuffed animals, toys, dolls, beanie babies, jewelry, candy & cards

Store Specials: Gift orders may be taken over the phone for patients

8310 Greenwood Ave.
N. Seattle, Washington 98103

Store Hours:
Monday-Friday 10am-6pm
Saturday 10am-2pm

Phone: 206-782-7287

Seasonal & hand-made items for children, the home & Christmas cards

572 Winslow Way
Bainbridge Island,
Washington 98110
Located near the ferry

Store Hours:
Monday-Saturday 10am-5pm

Phone: 206-842-5567

15137 NE 24th
(Overlake Square)
Redmond, Washington 98052

Store Hours:
Monday-Saturday 9:30am-5:30pm

Phone: 425-746-3092

Clothing for the entire family, household items & collectibles

303 West Meeker
Kent, Washington 98032

Store Hours:
Monday-Saturday 9am-5pm

Phone: 253-850-8216

Clothing, household items & collectibles

Attractive selection of clothing for the entire family including a large selection of party dresses, household items, vintage & collectibles

1024 Lawrence Street
Pt. Townsend, Washington
98268

Store Hours:
Monday-Saturday 9am-5pm

Phone: 360-385-6639

Clothing for the entire family & household items

Washington

<u>Vancouver</u>

Country Second Hand
10918 NE 152nd Street
Vancouver, Washington 98682

Store Hours:
Monday-Sunday 11am-4:30pm

Phone: 360-892-3618

Clothing for the entire family &
collectibles

**Christ Child
Opportunity Shop
1427 Wisconsin Ave. NW
Washington, DC 20007**

Store Hours:
Tuesday-Saturday 10am-3:45pm

Phone: 202-333-6635

Gently used clothing for the
entire family, household items &
collectibles

Consignment Policy:
Consignments accepted on
Wednesday & Thursday 10am-
2pm

**Clothes Encounter
(...of a second kind)
202 7th Street SE
Washington, DC 20003**

Store Hours:
Monday-Friday 11am-6pm
Thursday until 7pm
Saturday 10am-6pm
Sunday 12pm-4pm

Phone: 202-546-4004

Gently used women' clothing

Consignment Policy:
50/50 split
Accepts cash, checks & credit
cards

> Present this coupon at
> *Clothes Encounter*
> *202 7th Street SE*
> *Washington, DC* & save
> 10% off a purchase
>
> Expiration 12/31/99

**Meeps & Aunt Neensie's
U Street NW
Washington, DC 20009**

Store Hours:
Thursday 3pm-7pm
Friday 3pm-7pm
Saturday 12pm-7pm
Sunday 2pm-6pm

Phone: 202-265-6546

Vintage clothing & accessories
for women & men
Accepts cash, Visa & Mastercard

**Once Is Not Enough
4830 MacArthur Boulevard
N.W.
Washington, D.C. 20007**

Located near the French &
German embassies

Store Hours:
Monday-Saturday 10am-5pm

Contact: Inge Guen
Phone: 202-337-3072

Haute couture women's designer
clothing from Washington's elite
featuring labels designed by
Armani, Chanel, St. John, Ungaro,
YSL, Escada Sensational
accessories, including designer
handbags, shoes, scarves &
jewelry.

Consignment Policy: Items are
consigned for two months

Store Specials: Personal shopping
is available at no extra cost

Secondi
1702 Connecticut Avenue
Washington, DC 20009

Store Hours:
Monday, Tuesday & Saturday
11am-6pm
Wednesday, Thursday & Friday
11am-7pm
Saturday 11am-6pm
Sunday 1pm-5pm

Phone: 202-667-1122

Upscale clothing for women &
men & accessories

Consignment Policy: 50/50 split

The Pinnacle
4932 Wisconsin Avenue N.W.
Washington, D.C. 20016

Store Hours:
Monday-Saturday 11am-6pm

Phone: 202-244-6300

High fashion women's apparel &
accessories

Consignment Policy: 50/50 split
Items are consigned for 90 days

Fairmont

Re-Runs For Wee-Ones
201 Morgantown Avenue
Fairmont, West Virginia
26554

Store Hours:
Monday-Friday 10am-5:30pm
Saturday 10am-5pm

Phone: 304-366-5437

Children's clothing from sizes
newborn to 16, maternity wear &
toys

Consignment Policy: 50/50 split

Kingwood

Connie's Closet
115 S. Price Street
Kingwood, West Virginia
26537

Store Hours:
Tuesday-Friday 10am-5pm
Saturday 10am-2pm

Contact: Connie Finamore
Phone: 304-329-1679

Clothing for women & children,
handmade decorations, cards &
gifts

Huntington

GallaherVillage
Consignment Shop
403 Norway Avenue
Huntington, West Virginia
25705
Store Hours:
Monday-Saturday 10am-5pm

Contact: Judy Aycock
Phone: 304-529-4827

Quality clothing for the entire
family
Accepts cash, store credit,
Mastercard, Visa & Discover

Consignment Policy: 50/50 split
Items marked down 50% after 60
days

Store Specials: Private parties
after hours with refreshments &
drawing

Princeton

Repeat Performance
829 Mercer Street
Princeton, West Virginia
24740

Store Hours:
Monday-Friday 10am-6pm
Saturday 10am-5pm

Contact: Carol French
Phone: 304-425-4860

Clothing for the entire family &
housewares

Wheeling

Abbrakidabbra
75 Edgington Lane
Wheeling, West Virginia
26003

Store Hours:
Monday-Saturday 10am-5pm

Contact: Jane Dorisio
Phone: 304-242-4692

West Virginia

New & gently used children's & maternity clothing, accessories, books, toys & more

Accepts cash, checks, Visa, Master card, Novus

Consignment Policy: Consignor receives 40% of the selling price

Store Specials: On-going discounts on select merchandise

Present this coupon at
Abbrakidabbra
75 Edgington Lane
Wheeling, West Virginia & save

10% off all merchandise

(Excluding Olsen)
Expiration Date: 12/31/99

Brookfield

Playroom Closet
13470 W. Greenfield
Brookfield, Wisconsin 53005

Store Hours:
Tuesday & Wednesday 10am-5pm
Thursday & Friday 12pm-7pm
Saturday 12pm-4pm

Contact: Laure Benetti
Phone: 414-785-9091

Clothing for children, toys &
furniture
Accepts cash, checks & credit
cards

Fond du Lac

Act II
14 E. Second Street
Fond du Lac, Wisconsin 54935

Store Hours:
Monday-Friday 10am-5pm
Saturday 9am-1pm
Phone: 920-923-3180

Designer clothing, household
items, furniture, collectibles &
more!
Accepts cash & checks

Store Policy: Donations welcome

Store Specials: Two dollar bag sale
the first day of each month

Janesville

Carousel Consignments
31 South Main
Janesville, Wisconsin 53545

Store Hours:
Monday-Saturday
10am-5:30pm
Contact: Joni Bozart
Phone: 608-758-0553

Antiques, collectibles & household
items
Accept cash, checks, Mastercard
& Visa

Madison

Women & Kidstore Resale
6798 Watts Road
Madison, Wisconsin 53719

Store Hours:
Monday-Thursday 10am-8pm
Friday & Saturday 10am-5pm

Contact: Marilyn Wedberg
Phone: 608-274-4477

Clothing for women & children,
maternity wear & toys
Accepts cash, checks, Visa,
Mastercard & Discover

Menomonie

Affordable Adorables
1403 9th Street
Menomonie, Wisconsin 54751

Store Hours:
Monday-Friday 10am-5:30pm
Saturday 10am-5pm

Contact: Patty Engler &
Katherine Grubb
Phone: 715-235-8044

Gently used childen's clothing &
accessories

Wisconsin

Ms.ellaneous
320 on the Main
Menomonie, Wisconsin 54751

Store Hours:
Monday-Friday 10am-5pm
Saturday 10am-3pm or by
appointment

Contact: Sandy Ott
Phone: 715-235-3599

Women's elite fashions "worth
repeating"
Accepts cash, checks, Visa,
Mastercard & Discovery

Consignment Policy: 50/50 split
Items are consigned for 90 days

Store Specials: Sale room featuring
merchandise discounted 20% to
50%

Milwaukee

American Council of the
Blind Thrift Store
109 West Wilbur Ave.
Milwaukee, Wisconsin 53207

Store Hours:
Monday-Friday 9am-9pm
Saturday 9am-8pm

Phone: 414-483-5955

Clothing for the entire family,
furniture, antiques & more

Store Policy: Donations welcome

Store Specials: Senior discount on
Monday

Cheyenne

The Salvation Army
Thrift Store
1401 East Lincolnway
Cheyenne, Wyoming 82003

Store Hours:
Monday-Saturday 9am-5pm

Phone: 307-637-8073

Clothing for the entire family,
bric-a-brac, appliances, furniture
& more

Store Policy: Donations welcome
& a receipt may be provided for
tax purposes

Store Specials: Senior discount

Cody

Bargain Box
1644 Alger Avenue
Cody, Wyoming 82414

Store Hours:
Tuesday-Friday 11am-6pm
Saturday 10am-5pm
Phone: 307-587-6666

Clothing for the entire family &
household items

Store Policy: Donations welcome

Laramie

Jean's Closet
223 Garfield
Laramie, Wyoming 82070

Store Hours:
Tuesday-Friday 10am-6pm
Saturday 10am-5pm

Contact: Diane Kopulos
Phone: 307-742-7309

Clothing for women from casual
to dressy
Accepts cash, checks, Visa &
Mastercard

Consignment Policy: 50/50 split
Items are consigned for 60 days

Riverton

Unique Boutique &
Flea Market
119 N. Broadway
Riverton, Wyoming 82501

Store Hours:
Monday-Friday 9am-5pm
Saturday 10am-4pm

Phone: 307-856-0431

Clothing, antiques, collectibles &
more!

WearAgains
103 North 5th East
P.O. Box 1548
Riverton, Wyoming 82501

Store Hours:
Monday-Friday 12pm-6pm
Saturday 12pm-5pm

Contact: Sue Peters & Ed Peters
Phone: 307-856-7977

Clothing for the entire family,
accessories, jewelry, bridal & gifts
Accepts cash, checks, Visa &
Mastercard

Wyoming

Consignment Policy: Items are
consigned for 60 days

Store Specials: Periodic markdowns

Second Location:
**411 Lincoln
Lander, Wyoming 82520
Phone: 307-332-2665**

Worland

**St. Alban's Born
Again Clothing
824 Big Horn Avenue
Worland, Wyoming 82401**

Store Hours:
Monday-Saturday 10am-4pm

Phone: 307-347-2047

Clothing for the entire family,
household items & vintage
clothing
Accepts cash

Store Policy: Donations welcome

Store Specials: Seasonal sales

American Cancer Society Discover Shops

Established in 1965 by a volunteer in California, The Discovery shops have expanded to many locations throughout the United States.

The Discovery shops carry upscale clothing for the entire family, jewelry, small furniture, household items, books, antiques & collectibles. The shops accept cash, checks, Visa & Mastercard. Several sales & promotions are offered each month.

Proceeds benefit programs & research by the American Cancer Society to help fight cancer. The shops are run by dedicated volunteers & donations are welcome.

Bremerton

714 Lebo Blvd.
Bremerton, Washington 98310
Phone: 360-373-1025
Winter Hours:
Monday-Saturday 10am-4:30pm
Summer Hours: Monday-Saturday 10am-6pm

Everett

1001 N. Broadway A-3
Everett, Washington 98201
Phone: 425-339-4141
Store Hours:
Monday-Saturday 10am-5pm

Kent

225 First Avenue S.
Kent, Washington 98032

Phone: 253-852-9696
Store Hours:
Monday-Saturday 10am-4:30pm

Redmond

14840 NE 24th Street
Redmond, Washington 98052
Phone: 425-869-7523
Store Hours:
Monday-Friday 10am-5pm

Seattle

4535 California Ave SW
W. Seattle, Washington 98116
Phone: 206-937-7169
Store Hours:
Monday-Saturday 9:30am-4:30pm

2005 NW Market
Seattle, Washington 98107
Phone: 206-782-7763
Store Hours:
Monday-Saturday 10am-5pm

6814 Roosevelt NE
Seattle, Washington 98115
Phone: 206-524-3399
Store Hours:
Monday-Thursday & Saturday 9:30am-4pm
Friday 9:30am-7pm

Spokane

805 W. Garland
Spokane, Washington 99205
Phone: 509-328-9373
Store Hours:
Winter Monday-Saturday 9:30am-4pm
Summer: 9:30am-4:30pm

Tacoma

2512 N. Proctor
Tacoma, Washington 98406

Store Hours:
Monday-Saturday 10am-5pm
Phone: 253-759-2823

Vancouver

2011 Main Street
Vancouver, Washington 98660
Phone: 360-695-8215
Store Hours:
Monday-Friday 9:30am-4:30pm
Saturday 9:30am-4:30pm

Yakima

513 W. Yakima Avenue
Yakima, Washington 98902
Phone: 509-575-1236
Store Hours:
Monday-Saturday 9:30am-4:30pm

Baubles & Beads

Baubles & Beads locations offer a very large selection of upscale apparel & accessories for women featuring designers such as Ralph Lauren, DKNY, Escada, Armani, Bob Mackie & more. Visit A Man's Resale for excellent quality clothing for men.
Consignors receive 50% of the selling price and items are consigned for 90 days.
Web site: www.flash.net/~activate/

Store Locations

3603 W. Park Row
Arlington, Texas 76013
Phone: 817-460-5825

4107 S. Capital of Texas
Highway
Austin, Texas 78704
Phone: 512-912-0204

4254A S. Alameda
Corpus Christi, Texas 78412
Phone: 512-991-6181

6387 G Camp Bowie
Fort Worth, Texas 76116
Phone: 817-732-5451

66 Woodlake Square
Houston, Texas 77063
Phone: 713-785-2646

1945 West Gray
Houston, Texas 77019
Phone: 713-524-4100

9715 Katy Freeway
Houston, Texas 77024
Phone: 713-468-3544

9710 Hillcroft

Houston, Texas 77096
Phone: 713-729-0200

603 East Main
League City, Texas 77573
Phone: 281-554-2588

2000 W. Parker Road #170
Plano, Texas 75075
Phone: 972-612-6260

2885 Promenade
Richardson, Texas 75080
Phone: 972-690-4692

999 East Basse Road #184
San Antonio, Texas 78209
Phone: 210-828-8032

2267 N.W. Military #117
San Antonio, Texas 78213
Phone: 210-341-8491

3613 State Highway 6
Sugarland, Texas 77478
Phone: 713-980-7600

5311 W. Navarro
Victoria, Texas 77904
Phone: 512-572-3555

110 F.M. 1960
West Houston, Texas 77090
Phone: 281-537-2223

5464 F.M. 1960
West Houston, Texas 77069
Phone: 281-893-1962

A Man's Resale

14020 Memorial
Houston, Texas 77079
Phone: 281-531-0008

2437 Bissonnet
Houston, Texas 77005
Phone: 713-522-5645

**Bethesda Lutheran Homes &
Services Inc.
700 Hoffman Drive
Watertown, Wisconsin 53094**

Executive Director:
David Geske, Ph.D.
Contact: Ronald C. Furno
Phone: 1-800-369-4636

Established in 1958, Bethesda's
thrift stores have provided the
Bethesda community with a wide
selection of great clothing &
household items at affordable
prices.
With over twenty thrift stores run
by dedicated volunteers, the stores
rely heavily on the hundreds of
good quality donations received by
wonderful local supporters. The
volunteers enjoy working in the
stores and feel it is "a nice way to
enjoy Christian fellowship while
giving something back to the
community".
Over twenty stores have provided
more that $1.4 million in
resources which benefit resident
care. With fifty-two facilities and
services in eleven states, Bethesda
provides quality Chrisitan care for
more than seven hundred
mentally retarded children
and adults.
Bethesda offers free resources and
referral services which are
supported through donations and
the thrift stores. Contact
Bethesda for more information
at 1-800-369-4636.
All Bethesda stores carry
excellent quality clothing for the
entire family, household goods,
appliances, antiques & collectibles
at affordable prices. Some store
locations also carry furniture.

The stores accepts cash. Special
sales held on an ongoing basis.

Illinois

**Bethesda Thrift Shop
Route 14 & Keith Avenue
Crystal Lake Plaza, #26
Crystal Lake, Illinois**
Phone: 815-455-2325

Kansas

**Faith Village Thrift & Gift
520 County Line Road
Kansas City, Kansas**
Phone: 913-262-9447

Michigan

**Bethesda Thrift Shop
208 S. Michigan
Saginaw, Michigan**
Phone: 517-792-0391

Minnesota

**Bethesda Thrift Shop
913 Main Street
Hopkins, Minnesota**
Phone: 612-939-0988

**Bethesda Thrift Store
Economy
Center
934 N. Rice Street
St. Paul, Minnesota**
Phone: 612-488-9326

Texas
**Good Samaritan Thrift
Center
5111 Burnet**
Austin, Texas
Phone: 512-451-2652

Good Samaritan Thrift Mart
817 W. Pioneer Parkway
Grand Prairie, Texas
Phone: 972-660-4802

Good Samaritan Resale Shop
241 W. 19th Street
Houston, Texas
Phone: 713-861-9453

Good Samaritan Thrift Shop
5131 Ella Blvd.
Houston, Texas
Phone: 713-686-3931

Good Samaritan Thrift Mart
28575 Tomball Parkway
Tomball, Texas
Phone: 281-255-9441

Wisconsin

Bethesda Thrift Shop
2812 London Road
Queens Plaza
Eau Claire, Wisconsin
Phone: 715-834-7875

Bethesda Thrift Shop
336 N. Military Avenue
Green Bay, Wisconsin
Phone: 920-494-2921

Bethesda Country Fair Store
104 Clinton Street
Horicon, Wisconsin
Phone: 920-485-4113

Bethesda House of Thrift
474 N. Sherman Avenue
Madison, Wisconsin
Phone: 608-246-0889

Dress for Less
Economy Center
7814 W. Burleigh
Milwaukee, Wisconsin
Phone: 414-442-2272

Bethesda Thrift Mart
998 Winneconne Avenue
Neenah, Wisconsin
Phone: 920-725-7467

Bethesda Thrift Store
1019 N. 8th Street
Sheboygan, Wisconsin
Phone: 920-452-5212

Bethesda Thrift Shop
800 Montgomery Street
Watertown, Wisconsin
Phone: 920-261-7030

Bethesda Thrift Store
329 N. First Avenue
Wausau, Wisconsin
Phone: 715-845-1878

Bethesda Upscale Resale
Thrift Store
7210 W. Greenfield Avenue
West Allis, Wisconsin
Phone: 414-453-3254

Present this coupon at
*Bethesda Thrift Shop*s
& save $10.00 off
purchase of $20.00 or more
Expiration Date: 12/31/99
The Ultimate Consignment & Thrift Store
Guide

Buffalo Exchange

Buffalo Exchange stores offer the latest styles in designer wear, vintage clothing, leather, accessories & unique items entice customers to return.
A customer may buy, sell or trade stylish merchandise through the Buffalo Exchange stores.
Buffalo Exchange has been rated the best used clothing store by the readers of the *Berkeley East Bay Express, The Berkeley East Bay Guardian, The Phoenix Times, The Tucson Weekly & The San Francisco Bay Guardian.*
Buffalo Exchange supports protection of the enviornment through recycling.
Web site:
www.buffaloexchange.com

Arizona

1113 South Plaza Way
Flagstaff, Arizona 86001
*Franchise location
Store Hours:
Mondy-Saturday 11am-7pm
Sunday 11am-5pm
Phone: 520-556-0472

724 E. Glendale
Phoenix, Arizona
Store Hours:
Monday-Friday 10am-8pm
Saturday 10am-7pm
11am-6pm
Phone: 602-870-8507

227 W. University
Tempe, Arizona
Store Hours:
Monday-Friday 10am-9pm
Saturday 10am-8pm
Sunday 11am-6pm
Phone: 602-968-2557

2001 E. Speedway
Tucson, Arizona
Store Hours:
Monday-Friday 10am-8pm
Saturday 10am-7pm
Sunday 11am-6pm
Phone: 520-795-0508

7045 E. Tanque Verde
Tucson, Arizona
Store Hours:
Monday-Saturday 10am-6pm
Sunday 12pm-5pm
Phone: 520-885-8392

California

2512 Telegraph Avenue
Berkeley, California
Store Hours:
Monday-Saturday 11am-7pm
Sunday 12pm-5pm
Phone: 510-644-9202

3333 Lakeshore Avenue
Oakland, California
Store Hours:
Monday-Saturday 11am-7pm
Sunday 12pm-6pm
Phone: 510-452-4464

1555 Haight Street
San Francisco, California
Store Hours:
Monday-Saturday 11am-7pm
Sunday 12pm-6pm
Phone: 415-413-7733

1800 Polk Street
San Francisco, California
Store Hours:
Monday-Saturday 11am-7pm
Sunday 12pm-6pm
Phone: 415-346-5726

**1007 Garnet Avenue
(Pacific Beach)
San Diego, California**
Store Hours:
Monday-Friday 11am-8pm
Saturday 11am-7pm
Sunday 11am-6pm
Phone: 619-273-6227

**3862 Fifth Avenue
San Diego, California**
Store Hours:
Monday-Friday 11am-8pm
Saturday 11am-7pm
Sunday 11am-6pm
Phone: 619-298-4411

Colorado

**1717 Walnut
Boulder, Colorado**
*Franchise location
Store Hours:
Monday-Saturday 11am-7pm
Sunday 11am-5pm
Phone: 303-938-1924

New Mexico

**3005 Central Ave NE
Albuquerque, New Mexico**
Store Hours:
Monday-Saturday 10am-7pm
Sunday 12pm-6pm
Phone: 505-262-0098

Nevada

**4110 S. Maryland Parkway
Las Vegas, Nevada**
Store Hours:
Monday-Saturday 11am-7pm
Sunday 12pm-6pm
Phone: 702-791-3960

Oregon

**1420 SE 37th
Portland, Oregon**
Store Hours:
Monday-Saturday 11am-7pm
Sunday 12pm-6pm
Phone: 503-234-1302

Texas

**2904 Guadalupe Street
Austin, Texas**
Store Hours:
Monday-Friday 11am-7pm
Saturday 11am-8pm
Sunday 12pm-6pm
Phone: 512-480-9922

Washington

**216 Broadway Avenue East
Seattle, Washington**
Store Hours:
Monday-Saturday 11am-7pm
Sunday 12pm-5pm
Phone: 206-860-4133

**4546 University N.E.
Seattle, Washington**
Store Hours:
Monday-Saturday 11am-7pm
Sunday 12pm-5pm
Phone: 206-545-0175

Children's Orchard

Children's Orchard
Corporate Headquarters
315 E. Eisenhower Parkwy
Suite 316
Ann Arbor, Michigan 48108

Contact: Cathy Marks
Phone: 313-994-9199
Fax: 313-994-9323
e-mail: ChildOrch@aol.com
Web site: www.ChildOrch.com

Founded in 1980, Children's
Orchard offers a vast array of
name brand gently used clothing
for children's clothing, sizes
newborn to 8, toys, books, baby
equipment, furniture & accessories.
Cash is paid on the spot for
merchandise and all season items
are accepted year round.
Most locations are open seven
days a week & some evenings.
Most store locations offer 20%
off select merchandise, cash
bonuses for top brand name
clothing, coupons, raffles &
grandparent discounts.

California

5647 Canan Road
Agoura Hills, California
91301
Phone: 818-889-2776

5769D E Santa Ana
Canyon Road
Anaheim Hills, California
92807
Phone: 714-998-5648

13291 S. Street
Cerritos, California 90703
Phone: 310-865-9422

369 East 17th Street
Costa Mesa, California 92627
Phone: 714-650-2243

10135 Valleyview
Cypress, California 90630
Phone: 714-827-2550

998 W. El Norte Parkway
Escondido, California 92026
Phone: 619-738-7296

18645 Brookhurst
Fountain Valley, California
92708
Phone: 714-964-3488

7171 Warner Ave. Suite C
Huntington Beach, California
92647
Phone: 714-842-5209

5323 University Drive
Irvine, California 92612
Phone: 714-857-KIDS

28985 St of Golden Lantern
Laguna Niguel, California
92677
Phone: 714-249-3736

22953 Ridge Route Drive
Lake Forest, California 92630
Phone: 741-951-0444

28771 Los Alisos Blvd
Suite D-2
Mission Viejo, California
92692
Phone: 714-551-2007

3841 Plaza Drive #901
Oceanside, California 92056
Phone: 760-941-1083

132 E. Yorba Linda Blvd.
Placentia, California 92870

Phone: 714-792-0760

9430-5B Mira Mesa Blvd
San Diego, California 92126
Phone: 619-586-7313

867 West Arrow Highway
San Dimas, California 91773
Phone: 909-394-7338

26576 Bouquet Canyon Road
Santa Clarita, California
91350
Phone: 805-262-1484

26431 Ynez Road #14C
Temecula, California 92591
Phone: 909-676-1643

2801 Pacific Coast Highway
Torrance, California 90505
Phone: 310-517-0422

17941 Martha Anne Drive
Tustin, California 92780
Phone: 714-832-7373

Colorado

205B. W Rockrimmon Blvd.
Colorado Springs, Colorado
80919
Phone: 719-620-0557

Conneticut

1131-P Tolland Turnipike
Manchester, Conneticut
06040
Phone: 203-643-0525

3089 Berlin Turnpike
Newington, Conneticut 06111
Phone: 203-666-KIDS

Florida

6000 Lake Gray Blvd #B-1
Jacksonville, Florida 32244
Phone: 904-573-0300

14444 Beach Blvd. #57
Jacksonville, Florida 32250
Phone: 904-223-0012

Kentucky

171 Lowry Lane Suite I
Lexington, Kentucky 40503
Phone: 606-260-1400

Illinois

668 East Rand Road
Arlington Heights, Illinois
60004
Phone: 847-259-KIDS

331 Rand Road
Lake Zurich, Illinois 60074
Phone: 847-438-3415

Maine

US Route I
Falmouth, Maine 04105
Phone: 207-781-7777

Maryland

9150-7 Baltimore National
Pike
Ellicott City, Maryland 21042
Phone: 410-750-8600

Children's Orchard

Massachusetts

2088 Commonwealth Ave
Auburndale, Massachusetts
02166
Phone: 617-244-0300

446 Boston Street
Billerica, Massachusetts
01821
Phone: 978-671-0008

807 Boylston Street
Chestnut Hill, Massachusetts
02167
Phone: 617-277-3006

139 Endicott Street
Danvers, Massachusetts 01923
Phone: 978-777-3355

861 Edgell Road
Framingham, Massachusetts
01701
Phone: 508-788-0072

65 Independence Way
Hyannis, Massachusetts
02601
Phone: 508-775-4121

132 East Central Street
Natick, Massachusetts 01760
Phone: 508-651-9386

45 Storey Ave.
Newburyport, Massachusetts
01950
Phone: 978-462-KIDS

90 Main Street (Rt. 28)
No. Reading, Massachusetts
01864
Phone: 508-664-0009

1001 Providence Highway
Norwood, Massachusetts 02062
Phone: 781-769-4388

225 Newburyport Turnpike
Rowley, Massachusetts 01969
Phone: 978-948-6600

20 Commerce Way
Seekonk, Massachusetts 02771
Phone: 508-336-7757

Shaw's Plaza Rte 138
Stoughton, Massachusetts
02072
Phone: 781-297-0004

15 Scammel Street
Quincy, Massachusetts 02169
Phone: 617-770-4979

18 Lyman Street
Westboro, Massachusetts
01581
Phone: 508-366-KIDS

Michigan

1727 Plymouth Road #25
Ann Arbor, Michigan 48105
Phone: 734-761-7103

2216 S Main Street
Ann Arbor, Michigan 48102
Phone: 734-995-8889

43319 Joy Road
Canton, Michigan 48187
Phone: 313-453-4811

3050 Union Lake Suite 3-D
Commerce Turnpike,
Michigan
48382
Phone: 248-366-9393

561 Lawndale Court
Holland, Michigan 49423
Phone: 616-494-0778

2309 Portage Street
Kalamazoo, Michigan 49001
Phone: 616-373-4269

5246 Easter S.E.
Kentwood, Michigan 49508
Phone: 616-261-1526

6749 South Westnedge Ave
Portage, Michigan 49002
Phone: 616-329-4397

2020 S Airport Road W
Traverse City, Michigan 49684
Phone: 616-929-1700

6629 Orchard Lake Road
W. Bloomfield, Michigan
48322
Phone: 248-626-0690

Missouri

722 South 7 Highway
Blue Springs, Missouri 64014
Phone: 816-224-0887

3906 Peachtree Drive Suite E
Columbia, Missouri 65203
Phone: 573-443-5700

4514 S. Noland Road
Independence, Missouri
64055
Phone: 816-373-4585

1173 NE Rice Road
Lee's Summit, Missouri
64063
Phone: 816-524-7303

12714 Olive Street
St. Louis, Missouri 63141
Phone: 314-453-0609

Nevada

881 S Rainbow Blvd
Las Vegas, Nevada 89128
Phone: 702-877-2223

New Hampshire

4 Orchard View Drive #8
Londonberry, New Hampshire
03053
Phone: 603-434-3284

1525 S Willow St #1
Manchester, New Hampshire
03103
Phone: 603-644-3700

112 Daniel Webster Highway
Nashua, New Hampshire
03060
Phone: 603-888-0803

427 Ameherst Street
Nashua, New Hampshire
03063
Phone: 603-880-6760

5 Plaistow Road Route 125
Plaistow, New Hampshire
03865
Phone: 603-382-1332

1981 Woodbury Ave
Portsmouth, New Hampshire
03801
Phone: 603-436-8704

224 North Broadway
Salem, New Hampshire 03079
Phone: 603-894-5549

Children's Orchard

Route 9
Somersworth,
New Hampshire 03878
Phone: 603-749-1515

7820 East 101st Suite D
Tulsa, Oklahoma 74133
Phone: 918-369-4642

New Jersey

240 Route 10
East Hanover, New Jersey
07936
Phone: 973-515-1151

New York

5507 Nesconset Highway
Mt. Sinai, New York 11766
Phone: 516-474-9174

North Carolina

5865 Holly Springs Road
Raleigh, North Carolina
27606
Phone: 919-852-0550

Ohio

8440 E Washington Street
Chagrin Falls, Ohio 44023
Phone: 216-543-4443

Oklahoma

13801 N Penn Suite K
Oklahoma City, Oklahoma
73134
Phone: 405-748-6294

7002 NW Expressway Suite A
Oklahoma City, Oklahoma
73123
Phone: 405-720-2302

Texas

3000 Custer St. #130
Plano, Texas 75075
Phone: 972-612-7177

18502 Kuykendahl Road
Spring, Texas 77379
Phone: 281-528-9543

Established in 1988, Computer Renaissance ® has proven to be the leader in buying and selling gently used & new computers. Choose from a wide selection of quality new & gently used computers, monitors, modems and software, all at affordable prices. Buy, trade or sell your computer through Computer Renaissance. Whatever your computer needs are, Computer Renaissance is the place to find it. For more information on Computer Renaissance store franchises call 1-800-868-8974 or visit their Web site at www.crl.com. Computer Renaissance, Disc Go Round, Once Upon A Child, Music Go Round & Play It Again Sports are concept franchises that have been developed by Grow Biz International ® Inc. In 1996, Inc. Magazine ranked Grow Biz 23rd among the 100 fastest growing companies.

Alaska

211B E. Dimond Blvd.
Anchorage, Alaska 99515
Phone: 907-3244-6565

Alabama

143 S Cox Creek Parkway
Florence, Alabama 35630
Phone: 205-765-0000

5000 Whitesburg Drive
Suite 125
Huntsville, Alabama 35802
Phone: 205-880-3707

6385 Atlanta Highway
Montgomery, Alabama 36117
Phone: 334-395-7879

Arizona

1235 S. Plaza Way
Flagstaff, Arizona 86001-631
Phone: 520-679-2424

13637 N. Tatum Blvd. Ste.#18
Phoenix, Arizona 85032
Phone: 602-765-1020

2814 W Bell Road Suite 1485
Phoenix, Arizona 85023
Phone: 602-504-6771

8940 E Indian Bend Road
Suite B1
Scottsdale, Arizona 85250
Phone: 602-443-1067

6151 E. Broadway
Tucson, Arizona 85711
Phone: 520-790-5720

4132 N Oracle Road
Tucson, Arizona 85705
Phone: 520-888-8100

California

5610 Stockdale Highway
Bakersfield, California 93309
Phone: 805-395-5860

2260 Otay Lakes
Road Suite 106
Chula Vista, California
91915
Phone: 619-656-6606

7947 Greenback Lane
Citrus Heights, California
95620
Phone: 916-721-0249

393 West Shaw Ave. #A20
Clovis, California 93612
Phone: 209-324-0250

280 Metro Center 41
Colma Blvd.

Colma, California 94014
Phone: 415-758-1181

8396 Parkway Drive
La Mesa, California 91942
Phone: 619-464-3711

8953 Tampa Ave.
Northridge, California 91324
Phone: 818-727-9150

8440 Rio San Diego
Drive #B-103
San Diego, California 92108
Phone: 619-298-7125

7305B Clairemont Mesa Blvd.
San Diego, California 92111
Phone: 619-576-2001

5263 Prospect Road
San Jose, California 95129
Phone: 408-873-8070

Colorado

7691 W 88th Avenue
Arvada, Colorado 80005
Phone: 303-422-3334

1260 South Abilene Street
Aurora, Colorado 80012
Phone: 303-752-1948

2525 Arapahoe E10
Boulder, Colorado 80302
Phone: 303-938-4034

1065 N Academy Blvd.
Colorado Springs, Colorado
80909
Phone: 719-574-8998

2721 S. College Ave.
Ft. Collins, Colorado 80525
Phone: 970-223-8398

8086 W. Bolwes Unit F
Littleton, Colorado 80123
Phone: 303-904-9441

Connecticut

376 W Middle Turnpike
Manchester, Connecticut
06040
Phone: 860-646-6667

116 Post Road
Orange, Connecticut 06477
Phone: 203-795-1805

Delaware

3617 Silverside Road
Taylleville Shp
Wilmington, Delaware 19810
Phone: 302-529-5760

Florida

8903 Glades Road
Boca Raton, Florida 33434
Phone: 561-477-4880

1925 W. Brandon Street
Brandon, Florida 33511
Phone: 813-662-0469

16008 US 19
Clearwater, Florida 33764
Phone: 813-781-2005

3600 SW Archer Road
Suite C
Gainesville, Florida 32608
Phone: 352-381-0030

10131-15 San Jose Blvd.
Jacksonville, Florida 33257
Phone: 904-880-1177

PO Box 54271
698 N Wickham
Merritt Island, Florida 32954
Phone: 407-259-1735

8809 SW 107th Ave.
Miami, Florida 33176
Phone: 305-271-1775

1129 Apalachee Parkway
Tallahassee, Florida 32302
Phone: 904-878-3088

14405 N Dale Mabry
Tampa, Florida 33618
Phone: 813-968-2005

525 S. Semoran Blvd.
Winter Park, Florida 32792
Phone: 407-671-8800

Georgia

5975 Roswell Road Suite 309
Atlanta, Georgia 30328
Phone: 404-256-2626

2235 W. Broad Street
Athens, Georgia 30606
Phone: 706-546-9199

800 W Barrett Parkway
Suite 31B
Kennesaw, Georgia 30144
Phone: 770-218-2500

3555 Mercer University Drive
Suite 102-1
Macon, Georgia 31204
Phone: 912-757-9299

1100 Johnson Ferry Road
Suite 400
Marietta, Georgia 30068
Phone: 770-579-8887

592 Bobby Jones Expressway
Martinez, Georgia 30907
Phone: 706-854-9474

Idaho

8073 Fairview Ave.
Boise, Idaho 83704
Phone: 208-321-0088

Illinois

91 W Rand Road
Arlington Heights, Illinois
60004
Phone: 847-259-2300

330 N. Randall Road
Batavia, Illinois 60510
Phone: 630-761-1010

316 West Army Trail
Road #120
Bloomingdale, Illinois 60106
Phone: 630-307-9787

2103 N. Veterans
Parkway #304
Bloomington, Illinois 61701
Phone: 309-662-2667

7776 South Cierco Ave.
Burbank, Illinois 60459
Phone: 708-422-0220

907 W. Marketview Drive #2
Champaign, Illinois 61821
Phone: 217-351-1111

2954 Finley Road
Downers Grove, Illinois 60515
Phone: 630-495-6570

103 Frey Lane
Fairview Heights, Illinois
62280
Phone: 618-628-3990

618 S Rte 59 Suite 120
Naperville, Illinois 60540
Phone: 630-961-0444

8618 West Golf Road
Niles, Illinois 60714
Phone: 847-827-8800

Computer Renaissance

15868 S LaGrange Road
Orland Park, Illinois 60462
Phone: 708-873-0300

3125 N. University
Peoria, Illinois 61614
Phone: 309-688-1888

1663 N. Alpine Road
Rockford, Illinois 81107
Phone: 815-395-9001

2515 Schaumberg Dr
Schaumberg, Illinois 60194
Phone: 847-584-4788

Indiana

271 Merchants Square
Drive #C6B
Carmel, Indiana 46032
Phone: 317-844-3978

833 N Green River Road
Evansville, Indiana 47715
Phone: 812-485-0200

515 E Coliseum Blvd
Ft. Wayne, Indiana 46805
Phone: 219-471-0023

8636 Purdue Road
Indianapolis, Indiana 46268
Phone: 317-228-0222

5880 E 82 St
Indianapolis, Indiana 46250
Phone: 317-842-2000

Iowa

1146 Blairs Ferry Road NE
Cedar Rapids, Iowa 52402
Phone: 319-378-4274

2824 E 53rd Street
Davenport, Iowa 52807
Phone: 319-344-9685

1821 22nd Street
Des Moines, Iowa 50266
Phone: 515-223-9676

1755 Boyrum
Iowa City, Iowa 52240
Phone: 319-337-4142

Kansas

1525 W. 6th St. Suite C
Lawrence, Kansas 66044
Phone: 785-843-9922

12042 W 95th St
Lenexa, Kansas 66215
Phone: 913-438-8902

315 Fort Riley Blvd
Manhattan, Kansas 66502
Phone: 913-537-4413

Kentucky

291 N. Hubbards Lane
Louisville, Kentucky 40207
Phone: 502-896-4828

3160 Parisa Drive
Paducah, Kentucky 42003
Phone: 502-443-5800

Louisiana

4031 Veterans Blvd
Metairie, Louisiana 70002
Phone: 504-779-7999

Massachusetts

Porter Square Galleria/One
Porter
Cambridge, Massachusetts
02140
Phone: 617-354-0007

Maryland

167W Jennifer Road
Annapolis, Maryland 21401
Phone: 410-573-6806

5244 Randolph Road
Rockville, Maryland 20852
Phone: 301-881-7111

Maine

11 Bangor Mall Blvd. Suite A
Bangor, Maine 04401
Phone: 207-942-9505

Michigan

877 West Eisenhower
Parkway
Ann Arbor, Michigan 48103
Phone: 313-994-1030

2843 E Grand River Suite 170
E. Lansing, Michigan 48823
Phone: 517-332-6480

29316 Orchard Lake Road
Farmington Hills, Michigan
48334
Phone: 810-851-6611

G-4270 Miller Road
Flint, Michigan 48507
Phone: 810-720-0540

2923 Breton SE
Grand Rapids, Michigan
49512
Phone: 616-243-7078

3095 Bay Plaza Drive
Saginaw, Michigan 48604
Phone: 517-249-4250

3674 Rochester Road
Century Plaza
Troy, Michigan 48083

Phone: 810-740-9940

Minnesota

14023 Grand Ave S
Burnsville, Minnesota 55337
Phone: 612-898-4438

5115 Burning Tree Road
Suite 306
Duluth, Minnesota 55811
Phone: 218-727-0040

574 Eden Prairie
Center Drive
Eden Prairie, Minnesota
55344
Phone: 612-942-5062

1305 W Lake Street
Minneapolis, Minnesota
55408
Phone: 612-825-3007

12981 Ridgedale Drive
Minnetonka, Minnesota
55305
Phone: 612-545-2302

720 W. 78th Street
Richfield, Minnesota 55423
Phone: 612-866-1986

822 S. Broadway
Rochester, Minnesota 55902
Phone: 507-281-9892

2335 Fairview Ave N
Roseville, Minnesota 55113
Phone: 612-638-9808

2958 1/2 W Division St
St. Cloud, Minnesota 56301
Phone: 320-654-9703

1580-2 Woodlane Drive
Woodbury, Minnesota 55125
Phone: 612-730-5262

Computer Renaissance

Missouri

15289 Machester Road
Ballwin, Missouri 63011
Phone: 314-207-9640

19130C E 39th Street
Independence, Missouri 64057
Phone: 816-795-9550

2401 E. 32nd Street Suite 13
Joplin, Missouri 64804
Phone: 417-626-9100

89381 Hillcrest Road
Kansas City, Missouri 64138
Phone: 816-761-5522

6102 NW Barry Road
Kansas City, Missouri 64154
Phone: 816-746-5030

9811 Watson Road
St. Louis, Missouri 63126
Phone: 314-821-3237

3899 S Service Road Suite D
St. Peters, Missouri 63376
Phone: 314-936-0404

1145 E. Republic Road
Springfield, Missouri 65807
Phone: 417-889-4818

Mississippi

1189 E County Line Road
Suite 1020
Jackson, Mississippi 39211
Phone: 601-956-0999

Montana

2695 King Ave West
Billings, Montana 59102
Phone: 406-652-9442

North Carolina

450 Crossroads Blvd
Cary, North Carolina 27511
Phone: 919-851-1995

8128 Providence Road
Suite 300
Charlotte, North Carolina
28277
Phone: 704-341-4252

349 E Copperfield Blvd
Concord, North Carolina
28025
Phone: 704-786-1102

4421-119B Six Forks Road
Raleigh, North Carolina
27609
Phone: 919-786-0608

North Dakota

4340 13th Ave SW
Fargo, North Dakota 58103
Phone: 701-281-0566

Nebraska

8054 S. 84th Street
La Vista, Nebraksa 68128
Phone: 402-537-0800

330 N 48th Street Suite B
Lincoln, Nebraska 68504
Phone: 402-465-4040

723 N 114th
Omaha, Nebraska 68154
Phone: 402-445-2200

New Jersey

325 Route 10
East Hanover, NJ 07936
Phone: 201-428-1898

556 Route 17
Paramus, New Jersey 07652
Phone: 201-670-8283

New Mexico

11130 Lomas Blvd NE Suite F4
Albuquerque, New Mexico
87112
Phone: 505-332-1000

Nevada

4624 West Sahara Avenue
Suite 1
Las Vegas, Nevada 89102
Phone: 702-870-1962

New York

421 Central Ave
Hartsdale, New York 10530
Phone: 914-328-2955

297 N. Broadway
Jericho, New York 11753
Phone: 516-939-0190

376 Jefferson Road
Rochester, New York 14623
Phone: 716-424-2050

Ohio

3464 New Germany Trebein
Road
Beavercreek, Ohio 45431
Phone: 513-897-0115

9281 Governor's Way
Cincinnati, Ohio 45249
Phone: 513-697-0266

1761 Tiffin Ave.
Findlay, Ohio 45840
Phone: 419-427-3323

1148 N Memorial Drive
Lancaster, Ohio 43130
Phone: 614-654-4555

2361 Elida Road
Lima, Ohio 45805
Phone: 419-331-8706

4856 Northfield Road
N. Randall, Ohio 44128
Phone: 216-518-9989

Oklahoma

6813 N. May Ave.
Oklahoma City, Oklahoma
73116
Phone: 405-848-6767

Oregon

Beavertown Town Square SW
Beavertown, Oregon 97005
Phone: 503-644-1989

956 NW Circle Blvd
Corvallis, Oregon 97330
Phone: 541-752-2958

2265 Lancaster Drive
Salem, Oregon 97305
Phone: 503-585-0936

Pennsylvania

5206 Simpson Ferry Road
Mechanicsburg, Pennsylvania
17055
Phone: 717-261-0533

Paoli Shopping Center
Paoli, Pennsylvania 19301
Phone: 610-296-4020

1158 Baltimore Pike
Springfield, Pennsylvania
19064
Phone: 610-543-1443

Computer Renaissance

South Carolina

599 Haywood Road
Greenville, South Carolina
29607
Phone: 864-234-6888

South Dakota

907 Jackson Blvd
Rapid City, South Dakota
57701
Phone: 605-341-0101

Tennessee

714 Germantown Parkway
Suite 1
Cordova, Tennessee 38018
Phone: 901-752-4400

5564 Nolensville Road
Nashville, Tennessee 37211
Phone: 615-837-4554

Texas

201 Westgate Parkway Suite E
Amarillo, Texas 79121
Phone: 806-359-6820

10740 Research Blvd
Suite 120
Austin, Texas 78759
Phone: 512-342-2667

5425 S Padre Island Drive
Suite 163
Corpus Christi, Texas 78411
Phone: 800-280-1004

13396 Preston Road
Dallas, Texas 75240
Phone: 972-503-1111

9501 Gateway W
El Paso, Texas 79925
Phone: 915-594-4005

745 Mesa Hills Suite D
El Paso, Texas 79925
Phone: 915-584-8855

2501 S. WS Young Dr. Suite
107
Killeen, Texas 76542
Phone: 254-554-8800

4551 FM 1960 W
Houston, Texas 77069
Phone: 713-444-2627

6602 Slide Road #6
Lubbock, Texas 79424
Phone: 806-794-9988

Utah

2120 South 700 East Suite C
Salt Lake City, Utah 84106
Phone: 801-486-5586

5602 S. Redwood Road
Taylorsville, Utah 84123
Phone: 801-966-6556

Virginia

265 South Van Dorn Street
Alexandria, Virginia 22304
Phone: 703-823-5455

837 Eden Way N.
Suite 144
Chesapeake, Virginia 23320
Phone: 757-523-5714

4501 H Warwick Blvd.
Newport News, Virginia 23608
Phone: 757-872-0123

9704 Midlothian Turnpike
Richmond, Virginia 23235
Phone: 804-330-2600

Computer Renaissance

2219 Colonial Ave.
Roanoke, Virginia 24015
Phone: 540-342-6070

8428 Old Keene Mill Road
Springfield, Virginia 22152
Phone: 703-913-6023

2728 N. Mall Drive Suite 113
Virginia Beach, Virginia
23452
Phone: 757-631-8898

Washington

2120 S 320th Street Suite C7
Federal Way, Washington
98003
Phone: 253-941-0900

1218 N Columbia
Center Blvd.
Suite 16
Kennewick, Washington
99336
Phone: 509-783-2499

11310 NE 124th Street
Kirkland, Washington 98034
Phone: 425-814-7000

3333 184th St. SW #T
Lynnwood, Washington 98037
Phone: 206-771-2911

15230 NE 24th Street
Redmond, Washington 98052
Phone: 206-562-1190

2827 2nd Ave.
Seattle, Washington 98121
Phone: 206-448-9566

3299 Randall Way NW
Suite 103
Silverdale, Washington 98383
Phone: 360-613-9760

1901 S. 72nd Street
Suite A-06
Tacoma, Washington 98408
Phone: 253-474-2188

17304 Southcenter Parkway
Tukwila, Washington 98188
Phone: 206-575-2225

8101 NE Parkway Drive
Suite D-2
Vancouver, Washington 98662
Phone:360-944-1234

615 N. Sullivan Road Suite B
Veradale, Washington 99037
Phone: 509-926-2003

21 E Yakima Ave Suite A
Yakima, Washington 98901
Phone: 509-453-1404

Wisconsin

1005 Mutual Way
Appleton, Wisconsin 54915
Phone: 920-993-9950

17000-F Blue Mound Road
Brookfield, Wisconsin 53005
Phone: 414-860-8777

7475 Mineral Point Road
Madison, Wisconsin 53717
Phone: 608-833-7050

4625 75th Street
Pleasant Prairie, Wisconsin
53142
Phone: 414-697-4850

3337 South Business Drive
Sheboygan, Wisconsin 53081
Phone: 920-457-1000

4412 Rib Mountain Drive
Wausau, Wisconsin 54401
Phone: 715-359-9970

Computer Renaissance

3168 Dunmore Road S.E.
Medicine Hat, AB T1B 2X2
Phone: 403-526-5053

Unit 14 1415 Hillside Drive
Kamloops. BC V2E 1A9
Phone: 604-314-0461

102-1980 Cooper Road
Kelowna, BC V1Y 8K5
Phone: 250-763-2492

27 Elizabeth Ave.
St. John's, NF A1A 1W6
Phone: 709-726-2410

201 Chain Link Drive
Suite 15
Bayer Lake
Halifax, NS B3S 1C8
Phone: 902-450-5466

Kmart Plaza
465 University Ave.
Charlottetown, PE C1A 4N9
Phone: 902-566-2667

#24 2077 Pembina Highway
Winnipeg, Canada R3T 519
Phone: 204-261-8900

Disc Go Round ® offers new & pre-owned compact discs for music afficiendos at great prices. You can preview your selections at the listening station in the shop and even peruse the look-up station in order to preview their inventory. Sell your pre-owned CDs to make room for new ones. Disc Go Round offers great savings when it comes to compact discs. For more information on Disc Go Round franchises call 1-800-842-4356 or visit their Web site at http://www.dgr1.com/home.html

Alabama

6125 University Drive Suite D13
Huntsville, Alabama 35806
Phone: 205-922-0905

Arizona

1225 W. Main St. Plaza Suite B113
Mesa, Arizona 85201
Phone: 602-827-2020

8969 E. Indian Bend Road Suite C5
Scottsdale, Arizona 85250
Phone: 602-368-5430

777 S Mill Ave
Tempe, Arizona 85281
Phone: 602-829-4990

California

200 Main Street #113
Huntington Beach, California 92648
Phone: 714-536-7544

72-270-Highway 111 Suite B3
Palm Desert, California 92260
Phone: 760-568-6557

Colorado

8745 North Wadsworth Boulevard
Arvada, Colorado 80005
Phone: 303-422-1837

8280 B S Quebec
Englewood, Colorado 87523
Phone: 303-730-2403

5066 S Wadsworth Unit 105
Littleton, Colorado 80123
Phone: 303-973-4147

Delaware

45 Main Street
Newark, Delaware 19711
Phone: 302-369-3334

4563 Kirkwood Highway
Wilmington, Delaware 19808
Phone: 302-995-6611

Talleyville Shopping Center 3615 Silversi
Wilmington, Delaware 19810

Florida

10991-29A San Jose Blvd.
Jacksonville, Florida 32223
Phone: 904-288-9171

2742 E Colonial Drive
Orlando, Florida 32803
Phone: 407-896-1535

2732 E Fowler Ave
Tampa, Florida 33612
Phone: 813-632-8835

Disc Go Round

Georgia

2280B Peachtree Road
Atlanta, Georgia 30309
Phone: 404-351-7005

2997 Cumberland Circle
Atlanta, Georgia 30339
Phone: 770-803-9947

6690 Roswell Road Suite C4
Atlanta, Georgia 30328
Phone: 404-256-0057

596 Bobby Jones Expressway
Augusta, Georgia 30907
Phone: 706-651-0101

2180 Pleasant Hill Road
Suite B14
Duluth, Georgia 30136
Phone: 770-623-1552

50 Barrett Parkway
Suite 1240
Marietta, Georgia 30066
Phone: 770-425-3472

1100 Morrow Ind Blvd
Suite 2A
Morrow, Georgia 30260
Phone: 770-960-8099

Iowa

526 Main Street
Ames, Iowa 60010
Phone: 515-233-8860

124 Collins Road NE
Cedar Rapids, Iowa 52402
Phone: 319-373-9604

1800 NW 86th Street Suite 13
Clive, Iowa 50325
Phone: 515-270-8847

2188 W Kimberly Road
Davenport, Iowa 52806
Phone: 319-386-8632

6055 SE 14th Street
Des Moines, Iowa 50320
Phone: 515-256-0436

1519 E. San Marnan
Waterloo, Iowa 50702
Phone: 319-236-7242

Illinois

1701 E Empire
Bloomington, Illinois 61701
Phone: 309-662-8595

8050 S Cierco Ave
Burbank, Illinois 60459
Phone: 708-499-0777

3182 N Clark Street
Chicago, Illinois 60657
Phone: 773-404-4955

2412 North Lincoln Ave.
Chicago, Illinois 60614
Phone: 773-529-1133

4634 N Harlem
Harwood Heights, Illinois
60656
Phone: 773-867-9144

4601 16th Street
Moline, Illinois 61265
Phone: 309-762-8655

7313 W 25th St B17
North Riverside, Illinois
60546
Phone: 708-442-6112

5301 E State Street Suite 110
Rockford, Illinois 61108
Phone: 815-399-0093

Indiana

883 College Mall Road
Bloomington, Indiana 47401
Phone: 812-337-1990

1960 E Stop 13 Road
Indianapolis, Indiana 46227
Phone: 317-888-3472

10030 E Washington Street
Room 168
Indianapolis, Indiana 46229
Phone: 317-898-4148

6245 N. College Ave.
Indianapolis, Indiana 46220
Phone: 317-251-1964

4219 Grape Road
Mishawaka, Indiana 46545
Phone: 219-277-9222

Kentucky

387 Rose Street
Lexington, Kentucky 40508
Phone: 606-254-9196

1931 S Hurstbourne Parkway
Louisville, Kentucky 40220
Phone: 502-499-9999

620 Eastern Bypass
Richmond, Kentucky 40475
Phone: 606-625-0101

Louisiana

8939 Jewella Ave Suite 112
Shreveport, Louisiana 71118
Phone: 318-688-4286

Maryland

1306 West Patrick Street
Suite 14
Frederick, Maryland 21703
Phone: 301-695-6009

Michigan

1203 S. University Ave.
Ann Arbor, Michigan 48104
Phone: 313-996-9010

28 Abbott Road
East Lansing, Michigan 48823
Phone: 517-333-6616

3728 Alpine
Grand Rapids, Michigan
49321
Phone: 616-785-0566

12465 James Street
Holland, Michigan 49424
Phone: 616-394-4800

Westwedge Ave.
Portage, Michigan 49002
Phone: 616-329-4642

Minnesota

119 23rd Street NE
Bemidj, Minnesota 56601
Phone: 218-751-6636

748 Highway 10 NE
Blaine, Minnesota 55434
Phone: 612-783-9960

6070 Shingle Creek Parkway
Brooklyn Cntr., Minnesota
55430
Phone: 612-560-5111

1254 City Road 42
Burnsville, Minnesota 55337
Phone: 612-898-4955

5115 Burning Tree Road
Suite 312
Duluth, Minnesota 55811
Phone: 218-727-0193

7101 France Ave S
Edina, Minnesota 55435
Phone: 612-926-1951

582 Prairie Center Drive
Eden Prairie, Minnesota
55344
Phone: 612-947-9318

7967 Wedgewood Lane North
Maple Grove, Minnesota
55369
Phone: 612-420-6377

1440 W Lake Street
Minneapolis, Minnesota
55408
Phone: 612-827-2155

410 14th Ave SE
Minneapolis, Minnesota
55414
Phone: 612-623-3799

2981 Ridgedale Drive
Minnetonka, Minnesota
55305
Phone: 612-545-1595

2480 Fairview Ave N
Roseville, Minnesota 55113
Phone: 612-633-7557

2958 Division St W Suite 2B
St. Cloud, Minnesota 56302
Phone: 320-203-9509

North Carolina

1283 NW Maynard Road
Cary, North Carolina 27613
Phone: 919-461-0805

601 S Kings Drive Suite O
Charlotte, North Carolina
28204
Phone: 704-333-3472

4600 Chapel Hill Blvd
Durham, North Carolina
27707
Phone: 919-490-1499

433 WestWood Shop Ctr
Fayetteville, North Carolina
28314
Phone: 910-868-9611

6300 Creedmoor Road
Suite 116
Raleigh, North Carolina
27612
Phone: 919-848-3472

341-12 S College Road
Wilmington, North Carolina
28403
Phone: 910-792-0082

North Dakota

4325 13th Ave SW
Fargo, North Dakota 58103
Phone: 701-281-0950

Nebraska

5001 O Street
Lincoln, Nebraska 68510
Phone: 402-486-0047

New Jersey

28A Diamond Spring Road
Denville, New Jersey 07834
Phone: 201-983-0035

3585 US Highway 9 Unit 9
Freehold, New Jersey 07728
Phone: 908-845-9607

700 Haddonfield-Berlin Road
Suite 1
Voorhees, New Jersey 08043
Phone: 609-309-9445

Nevada

3967 South Maryland
Parkway
Las Vegas, Nevada 89119
Phone: 702-731-1445

2570 South Decatur
Las Vegas, Nevada 89102
Phone: 702-222-1759

New York

1004 North Street
Endicott, New York 13760
Phone: 607-785-5157

2080 Western Ave. Suite 126
Guilderland, New York 12084
Phone: 518-452-0338

Ohio

3464 New German-Trebein
Road
Beavercreek, Ohio 45431
Phone: 937-320-1974

4746 Ridge Road
Brooklyn, Ohio 44144
Phone: 216-398-0506

101 E Alex Bell Road
Suite 152
Centerville, Ohio 45459
Phone: 937-435-5333

4394 Eastgate Drive
Suite 1800
Cincinatti, Ohio 45245
Phone: 513-753-8877

9982 Kings Auto Mall Drive
Cincinnati, Ohio 45249
Phone: 513-583-1900

9982 Kings Auto Mall Drive
Cincinnati, Ohio 45249
Phone: 513-583-1900

1 University Plaza/Kilcawley
Cent
Youngstown, Ohio 44555
Phone: 330-742-4005

Oregon

18021 NW Evergreen Parkway
Beaverton, Oregon 97006
Phone: 503-531-0264

Pennsylvania

3100 Tilghman Street/Village
West
Allentown, Pennsylvania
18104
Phone: 610-439-4914

201 West Ridge Pike
Conshohocken,Pennsylvania
19428
Phone: 610-828-8434

3095 William Penn Highway
Easton, Pennsylvania 18045
Phone: 610-253-1666

Disc Go Round

6825 Peach Street Suite A9
Erie, Pennsylvania 16509
Phone: 814-864-1844

1000 W Pittsburgh Street
Suite3
Greensburg,Pennsylvania
15601
Phone: 412-836-6888

3832 Union Deposit Road
Harrisburg, Pennsylvania
17109

3832 Union Deposit Road
Harrisburg, Pennsylvania
17109
Phone: 717-657-5336

4900 Carlisle Pike
Mechanicsburg, Pennsylvania
17055
Phone: 717-731-1120

219 South Street Abbott
Square
Philadelphia,Pennsylvania
19147
Phone: 215-574-9072

4885 McKnight Road
Pittsburgh, Pennsylvania
15237
Phone: 412-366-6210

228 W College Ave
State College, Pennsylvania
Phone: 814-234-9044

South Carolina

593 Haywood Road Suite 593
Greenville, South Carolina
29607
Phone: 864-627-0606

South Dakota

1001 W 41st Street
Sioux Falls, South Dakota
57105
Phone: 605-373-9969

Tennessee

5335 Mt. View Road
Antioch, Tennessee 37013
Phone: 615-731-0063

2855 Bartlett Blvd
Bartlett, Tennessee 38135
Phone: 901-384-9434

2143 Gallatin Pike North
Madison, Tennessee 37115
Phone: 615-851-1535

Texas

10710 Research Blvd
Suite 328
Austin, Texas 78759
Phone: 512-349-7590

2025 Guadalupe Suite 266
Austin, Texas 78705
Phone: 512-479-7779

113 College Main
College Station, Texas 77841
Phone: 409-846-6620

1233 Airline Suite B
Corpus Christi, Texas 78412
Phone: 512-980-0440

80 FM1960 West
Houston, Texas 77090
Phone: 281-586-0700

Utah

79 S State Street
Orem, Utah 85048
Phone: 801-235-9850

2250 N University Parkway
Suite C54
Provo, Utah 84604
Phone: 801-371-8686

2120 S 700 E Ste E
Salt Lake City, Utah 84106
Phone: 801-483-2966

Vermont

198 College Street
Burlington, Vermont 05401
Phone: 802-660-8150

Washington

Fred Meyer Plaza
5050 State Highway
Bremerton, Washington
98311
Phone: 360-405-0878

1514 3rd Place
Kirkland, Washington 98033
Phone: 206-828-4481

4527 University Way NE
Seattle, Washington 98105
Phone: 206-632-7713

532 Queen Anne Ave N
Seattle, Washington 98109
Phone: 206-285-4605

111 Broadway East
Seattle, Washington 98102
Phone: 206-323-7374

6009 N Division Street
Spokane, Washington 99216
Phone: 509-483-1038

4027 Tacoma Mall Blvd
Tacoma, Washington 98409
Phone: 206-474-0521

Wisconsin

117D N Badger Ave
Appleton, Wisconsin 54914
Phone: 920-733-1094

19555 West Bluemound Road
Brookfield, Wisconsin 53005
Phone: 414-780-0700

1428 East Brady Street
E. Milwaukee, Wisconsin
53202
Phone: 414-273-0736

2773 South Oneida Street
Green Bay, Wisconsin 54304
Phone: 920-497-8665

1695 Main Street
Green Bay, Wisconsin 54302
Phone: 414-468-7230

4975 S 76th Street
Greenfield, Wisconsin 53220
Phone: 414-281-0700

Disc Go Round

2025 Old Hunes Road
Janesville, Wisconsin 53547
Phone: 608-758-7288

6708 Odana Road
Madison, Wisconsin 53719
Phone: 608-829-3472

640 State Street
Madison, Wisconsin 53707
Phone: 608-255-3472

8360 W Brown Deer Road
Milwaukee, Wisconsin 53223
Phone: 414-365-2774

2310 S Green Bay Road
Unit H
Racine, Wisconsin 53406
Phone: 414-554-1319

Wyoming

4250 S Polar Street
Casper, Wyoming 82601
Phone: 307-266-1314

Canada

28 2077 Pembina Highway
Winnipeg, MB R3T 5J9
Phone: 204-275-1414

1609 Regent Ave Unit 5
Winnipeg, MB R2C 3B5
Phone: 204-661-2300

1090 Memorial Ave
Thunder Bay, ON P7B 4A3
Phone: 807-625-9700

Music Go Round ® carries a wide selection of new & gently used musical instruments including guitars, amps, keyboards, drums, studio equipment, P.A. equipment, home audio & video supplies, accessories & much more, at prices everyone can afford! Musical instruments & equipment may be bought, sold or traded. For more information about Music Go Round franchise stores call 1-800-645-7298 or visit their Web site at www.musicgoround.com

Arizona

1312 W Southern Ave Suite 4
Mesa, Arizona 85202
Phone: 602-610-1717

9620 N Metro Parkway W
Suite B3
Phoenix, Arizona 85051
Phone: 602- 943-5511

Georgia

6120 N Point Parkway Suite 100
Alpharetta, Georgia 30202
Phone: 770-410-9555

4153 Lawrenceville Highway
US 29
Lilburn, Georgia 30047
Phone: 770-931-9190

Illinois

862 W Main
West Dundee, Illinois 60118
Phone: 847-426-1223

Indiana

709 Northcrest Shopping

Ft. Wayne, Indiana 46805
Phone: 219-471-2999

2727 E 86th Street Suite 208
Indianapolis, Indiana 46204
Phone: 317-254-8100

1212 E McGalliard Road
Muncie, Indiana 47303
Phone: 765-287-1421

Iowa

3200 16th Avenue SW
Cedar Rapids, Iowa 52404
Phone: 319-362-2062

Kansas

7397 Quivira Road
Shawnee, Kansas 66216
Phone: 913-268-5900

Kentucky

2052 Hurstbourne Parkway
Louisville, Kentucky 40220
Phone: 502-495-2199

Maryland

8450 Baltimore National Pike
Ellicott City, Maryland 21043
Phone: 410-203-0752

56 Mountain Road.
Glen Burnie, Maryland 21061
Phone: 410-760-5102

Michigan

2791 Oak Valley Drive
Ann Arbor, Michigan 48103
Phone: 313-662-1080

26116 Ingersol Drive
Novi, Michigan 48375
Phone: 248-348-7773

Music Go Round

Minnesota

14025 Grand Ave S
Burnsville, Minnesota 55337
Phone: 612-898-3393

223 Willow Bend
Crystal, Minnesota 55429
Phone: 612-535-5311

1301 W Lake Street
Minneapolis, Minnesota
55408
Phone: 612-822-7602

3434 55th St NW, #100
Rochester, Minnesota 55901
Phone: 507-287-8784

1722 Lexington Ave N
Roseville, Minnesota 55113
Phone: 612-487-7937

4170 Division #100
St. Cloud, Minnesota 56301
Phone: 320-252-4288

2032 Ford Parkway
St. Paul, Minnesota 55116
Phone: 612-695-9630

7060 Valley Creek Drive
Suite 10
Woodbury, Minnesota 55125
Phone: 612-714-1460

North Carolina

3719 Highpoint Road
Greensboro, North Carolina
27407
Phone: 910-854-4460

North Dakota

3207 Main Ave
Fargo, North Dakota 58103
Phone: 701-237-5516
304

Ohio

3464 New Germany Trebein
Road
Beavercreek, Ohio 45431
Phone: 937-427-4382

833 E Bethel Road
Columbus, Ohio 43214
Phone: 614-457-9328

Oklahoma

2320 N Meridian
Oklahoma City, Oklahoma
73107
Phone: 405-943-1177

Pennsylvania

3747 William Penn Highway
Monroeville, Pennsylvania
15146
Phone: 412-856-8742

2810 DeKalb Pike
Norristown, Pennsylvania
19401
Phone: 610-279-2400

South Dakota

1216 W. 41st Street
Sioux Falls, South Dakota
57105
Phone: 605-339-4393

Texas

12344 H Gulf Freeway
Houston, Texas 77034
Phone: 713-910-8863

3521 N Beltline Road
Irving, Texas 75062
Phone: 972-258-4830

Washington

14150 NE 20th
Bellevue, Washington 98007
Phone: 206-747-8794

3333 184th St SW Unit H
Lynnwood, Washington 98037
Phone: 425-774-7111

Wisconsin

5012 S 74th Street
Greenfield, Wisconsin 53220
Phone: 414-281-2777

688 S. Whitney Way
Madison, Wisconsin 53711
Phone: 608-271-3939

6901 W Brown Deer Road
Milwaukee, Wisconsin 53223
Phone: 414-355-7244

Once Upon A Child

Once Upon A Child ® offers quality brand name new & gently used children's clothing, accessories, furniture and toys, all for a fraction of their original cost. Great way to outfit your children in the latest fashions and still have money left over! The shops purchase merchandise outright from customers. For more information about Once Upon A Child franchise stores call 1-800-445-1006 or visit their Web site at http://www.ouac.com.

Alaska

1006 West Northern Lights Blvd.
Anchorage, Alaska 99503
Phone: 907-562-8777

Alabama

1000 Beltline Rd SW Suite V1
Decatur, Alabama 35603
Phone: 205-355-5555

Arizona

1994 North Alma School Road
Chandler, Arizona 85224
Phone: 602-963-9092

9201 N 29th Ave Suite 41 & 42
Phoenix, Arizona 85051
Phone: 602-906-8944

3860 W Ina Road Suite 122
Tucson, Arizona 85741
Phone: 520-744-3868

Arkansas

2810 E Highland Dr Suite E
Jonesboro, Arkansas 72401
Phone: 870-930-3700

California

2728 Ming Ave
Bakersfield, California 93304
Phone: 805-834-9961

5489 Sunrise Blvd.
Citrus Heights, California 95610
Phone: 916-966-1144

121 N El Camino Real Suite B
Encinitas, California 92024
Phone: 760-943-0111

703-3 E Bidwell
Folsom, California 95630
Phone: 916-983-6185

2607 Foothill Blvd
La Crescenta, California 91214
Phone: 818-248-9996

3440 McHenry Ave
Modesto, California 95350
Phone: 209-575-3554

1929 W El Camino Real
Mountain View, California 94040
Phone: 415-960-6822

5462 New Park Mall Road
Newark, California 94560
Phone: 510-494-8822

8945 Tampa Ave
Northridge, California 91324
Phone: 818-882-7777

2455 K Vista Way
Oceanside, California 92054
Phone: 760-722-7896

384 Roseville Square
Roseville, California 95678
Phone: 916-774-0852

3186 Arden Way
Sacramento, California 95825
Phone: 916-488-8861

916 N Main Sts
Salinas, California 93906
Phone: 408-443-4648

1609 Meridian Ave
San Jose, California 95125
Phone: 408-265-6800

5756 Pacific Ave
Stockton, California 95207
Phone: 209-478-8539

450 N Moorpark Road
Thousand Oaks, California
91360
Phone: 805-379-1663

504 E First Street
Tustin, California 92780
Phone: 714-505-2119

4711-4 Telephone Road
Ventura, California 93003
Phone: 805-654-0123

Colorado

8025 Sheridan Blvd Suite M
Arvada, Colorado 80003
Phone: 303-427-5437

3110 D Blake Ave
Glenwood Springs, Colorado
81601
Phone: 970-945-1513

Connecticut

99 Farmington Ave
Bristol, Connecticut 06010

Phone: 860-584-8131

Brookside Plaza
24 Hazard Ave
Enfield, Connecticut 06082
Phone: 860-745-9599

410C West Middle Turnpike
Manchester, Conneticut
06040
Phone: 860-649-1577

1055A Silas Deane Highway
Weathersfield, Conneticut
06109
Phone: 860-571-8773

Florida

109 Brandon Town Center
Brandon, Florida 33511
Phone: 813-661-0331

1249 Semoran Blvd
Casselberry, Florida 32707
Phone: 407-673-9449

11380-8 Beach Blvd
Jacksonville, Florida 32246
Phone: 904-998-7722

11112-14 San Jose Blvd
Jacksonville, Florida 32223
Phone: 904-886-7071

10500 Ulmreton Road
Suite 292
Largo, Florida 33771
Phone: 813-586-4606

14839 N Dale Mabry
Tampa, Florida 33618
Phone: 813-264-6119

Georgia

4880 Lower Roswel Road
Suite 610
Marietta, Georgia 30067
Phone: 770-509-7966

140 Peach Tree E
Peach Tree City, Georgia
30269
Phone: 770-487-2441

7201-C Hodgson Memorial
Drive
Savannah, Georgia 31406
Phone: 912-351-0555

Idaho

435 N Milwaukee
Boise, Idaho 83704
Phone: 208-376-1077

2291 East 17th Street
Idaho Falls, Idaho 83404
Phone: 208-528-6124

1000 Pocatello Creek Road
Suite E 10
Pocatello, Idaho 83201
Phone: 208-235-1428

Illinois

2103 Veterans Parkway
Suite 312
Bloomington, Illinois 61704
Phone: 309-662-3414

318-110 West Army Trail Road
Bloomingdale, Illinois 60108
Phone: 630-295-9622

333 North Naperville Road
Bolingbrook, Illinois 60440
Phone: 630-759-3545

5316 No Milwaukee
Chicago, Illinois 60630
Phone: 773-594-1705

251 Commons Drive
Chicago Ridge, Illinois 60415
Phone: 708-857-7005

737 W Golf Road
Des Plaines, Illinois 60016
Phone: 847-427-9651

1220 W 75th St
Downers Grove, Illinois 60516
Phone: 630-663-9211

1406 Butterfield Road
Downers Grove, Illinois 60515
Phone: 630-932-0883

1275 S Naper Blvd
Naperville, Illinois 60540
Phone: 630-357-8390

572 S Rte 59
Naperville, Illinois 60540
Phone: 630-416-9344

801 W Lake Ave
Peoria, Illinois 61614
Phone: 309-686-7603

868 West Main Street
West Dundee, Illinois 60118
Phone: 847-836-8945

6215 E State Street
Rockford, Illinois 61108
Phone: 815-399-1177

835 E Rollins Road
Round Lake Beach, Illinois
60073
Phone: 847-548-9994

1117 S Roselle Road
Schaumberg, Illinois 60193
Phone: 847-301-9250

15935 S Harlem
Tinley Park, Illinois 60477
Phone: 708-633-8364

Indiana

706 E Highway 131
Clarksville, Indiana 47129
Phone: 812-218-8888

865 N Green River Road
Evansville, Indiana 47715
Phone: 812-477-5165

1204 West 86th Street
Indianapolis, Indiana 46260
Phone: 317-846-7011

5990 East 71st Street
Indianapolis, Indiana 46220
Phone: 317-842-0533

7007 S US 31
Indianapolis, Indiana 46227
Phone: 317-888-7013

9477 E Washington
Indianapolis, Indiana 46229
Phone: 317-897-9009

124C Farabee Drive N
Lafayette, Indiana 47905
Phone: 765-449-1299

5685 Crawfordsville Road
Speedway, Indiana 46224
Phone: 317-486-8010

Iowa

1945 51st Street NE
Cedar Rapids, Iowa 52402
Phone: 319-378-9844

10201 University Ave
Clive, Iowa 50325
Phone: 515-222-0774

1754 Hamilton Blvd
Sioux City, Iowa 51103
Phone: 712-255-7112

1239 Anborough Ave
Waterloo, Iowa 50701
Phone: 319-234-5228

Kansas

320 N Rock Road
Suite 2
Derby, Kansas 67037
Phone: 316-789-0007

8912 W 95th Street
Overland Park, Kansas 66212
Phone: 913-381-9685

1311 W Crawford
Salina, Kansas 67401
Phone: 913-825-6500

12204 Shawnee
Mission Parkway
Shawnee, Kansas 66216
Phone: 913-631-3700

3101 North Rock Road
Suite 185
Wichita, Kansas 67226
Phone: 316-634-6996

Kentucky

1805 Campbell Lane
Bowling Green, Kentucky 42104
Phone: 502-796-5085

3138 Richmond Road
Lexington, Kentucky 40509
Phone: 606-269-5359

8087 Connector Drive
Florence, Kentucky 41042
Phone: 606-282-8922

3944 Taylorsville Road
Louisville, Kentucky 40220
Phone: 502-451-2345

Massachusetts

100-A Boston Turnpike Rte 9
Shrewsbury, Massachusetts
01545
Phone: 508-755-2323

Maryland

8450 Baltimore National Pike
Ellicott City, Maryland 21043
Phone: 410-418-4707

Michigan

3426 Washtenaw Ave
Ann Arbor, Michigan 48104
Phone: 313-973-3111

5804 N Sheldon Drive
Canton, Michigan 48187
Phone: 313-459-6669

13060 Riverdale Drive #700
Coon Rapids, Michigan 55448
Phone: 612-421-3879

13587 Eureka Road
Southgate, Michigan 48195
Phone: 313-246-5400

6029 Rochester Road
Troy, Michigan 48098
Phone: 248-828-7474

1260 28th Street West
Wyoming, Michigan 49509
Phone: 616-531-5715

Minnesota

107 23rd Street
Bemidji, Minnesota 56601
Phone: 218-751-9100

772 Highway 10 NE
Blaine, Minnesota 55434
Phone: 612-784-9545

7971 South Town Center
Bloomington, Minnesota
55431
Phone: 612-881-2220

13965 Grand Ave So
Burnsville, Minnesota 55337
Phone: 612-892-1540

8471 Easst Point
Douglas Road
Cottage Grove, Minnesota
55106
Phone: 612-768-7511

574 Eden Prairie
Center Drive
Eden Prairie, Minnesota
55344
Phone: 612-941-3515

13596 80th Circle N
Maple Grove, Minnesota
55369
Phone: 612-494-8687

2525 White Bear Ave
Suite A4
Maplewood, Minnesota 55109
Phone: 612-773-5122/3

14200 Wayzata Blvd
Minnetonka, Minnesota
55305
Phone: 612-540-0477

1665 W Co Road C
Roseville, Minnesota 55113

Phone: 612-628-0120

1300 Salem Road SW
Rochester, Minnesota 55902
Phone: 507-252-5090

3419 W Division Street
St. Cloud, Minnesota 56301
Phone: 320-253-7193

5021 Excelsior Blvd
St. Louis Park, Minnesota
55416
Phone: 612-922-6535

Missouri

15425 Manchester Road
Ballwin, Missouri 63011
Phone: 314-230-2922

11445 Olive Street Road
Creve Coeur, Missouri 63141
Phone: 314-993-5437

1225 S Kirkwood Road
Kirkwood, Missouri 63122
Phone: 314-966-1844

4418 Lemay Ferry Road
St. Louis, Missouri 63129
Phone: 314-845-0806

266 Mid Rivers Center
St. Peters, Missouri 63376
Phone: 314-970-6270

Montana

918 Grand Avenue
Billings, Montana 59012
Phone: 406-259-0990

North Carolina

2326 D South Church Street
Burlington, North Carolina
27215
Phone: 910-222-9212

435G Dolly Madison Road
Greensboro, North Carolina
27410
Phone: 910-855-9914

341-16 S College Road
Wilmington, North Carolina
28403
Phone: 910-452-9976

608 Hanes Mall Blvd
Winston-Salem,
North Carolina 27103
Phone: 910-768-9100

North Dakota

4340 13th Ave SW
Suite R
Fargo, North Dakota 58103
Phone: 701-282-5222

Nebraska

E View Shopping Center
233 N 48th Street
Lincoln, Nebraska 68504
Phone: 402-464-4443

New Jersey

135 W Main Street
Somerville, New Jersey 08876
Phone: 908-218-0600

Nevada

7161 South Eastern Ave
Las Vegas, Nevada 89119
Phone: 702-269-9590

4040 Kietzke Lane
Reno, Nevada 89502
Phone: 702-825-4448

New York

7206-3rd Ave
Brooklyn, New York 11209
Phone: 718-491-0300

808 Hicksville Road
N. Massapequa, New York
11758
Phone: 516-541-5300

2305 Richmond Ave
Staten Island, New York
10314
Phone: 718-370-3006

Ohio

4369 Whipple Ave NW
Canton, Ohio 44718
Phone: 330-493-8668

8315 Beechmont Ave
Cincinnati, Ohio 45255
Phone: 513-474-5105

9976 Kings Auto Mall Dr
Cincinnati, Ohio 45249
Phone: 513-677-5700

5138 Glen Crossing Way
Cincinnati, Ohio 45238
Phone: 513-451-7600

2733 Madison Road
Cincinnati, Ohio 45209
Phone: 513-871-8700

9727 Montgomery Road
Cincinnati, Ohio 45242
Phone: 513-791-1199

9904 Colerain Ave
Cincinnati, Ohio 45251
Phone: 513-385-3034

7420 Sawmill Road

Columbus, Ohio 43235
Phone: 614-791-3900

6026-28 E Main Street
Columbus, Ohio 43213
Phone: 614-863-9777

1901 Northwest Blvd.
Columbus, Ohio 43212
Phone: 614-488-8806

2964 E Broad Street
Columbus, Ohio 43209
Phone: 614-236-5550

5760 Frantz Road
Dublin, Ohio 43017
Phone: 614-761-8488

4150 Tuller Road Suite 206
Dublin, Ohio 43107
Phone: 614-791-0000

7255 Dixie Highway K/L
Fairfield, Ohio 45014
Phone: 513-860-0770

3900 Medina Street Suite T
Fairlawn, Ohio 44333
Phone: 330-670-0019

385 StoneRidge Lane
Gahanna, Ohio 43230
Phone: 614-337-0200

2199 Stringtown Road
Grove City, Ohio 43213
Phone: 614-875-9000

1536 Spring Meadows Drive
Holland, Ohio 43528
Phone: 419-865-1166

1532 River Valley Circle S.
Lancaster, Ohio 43130
Phone: 614-653-8335

5135 Mayfield Road
Lyndhurst, Ohio 44124
Phone: 216-446-9595

8210 Macedonia
Commons #24
Macedonia, Ohio 44056
Phone: 216-467-0881

7537 Mentor Ave
Mentor, Ohio 44060
Phone: 216-951-7222

218 W. 4th Street
Ontario, Ohio 44906
Phone: 419-747-7006

1943 East South Boundary
Perrysburgh, Ohio 43551
Phone: 419-874-3606

15135 Pearl Road
Stongsville, Ohio 44136
Phone: 216-846-0000

4272 Kent Road #10
Stow, Ohio 44224
Phone: 330-688-7176

6600 Sylvania Ave
Sylvania, Ohio 43560
Phone: 419-882-0004

399 S State Street
Westerville, Ohio 43081
Phone: 614-899-6654

25028 Center Ridge Road
Westlake, Ohio 44145
Phone: 216-899-1100

644 High Street
Worthington, Ohio 43085
Phone: 614-885-0885

Oklahoma

615 N May Ave
Oklahoma City, Oklahoma
73116
Phone: 405-842-8795

Oregon

3698 S 6th
Klamath Falls, Oregon 97603
Phone: 541-883-2321

1114 Lancaster Drive NE
Salem, Oregon 97301
Phone: 503-362-2229

Pennsylvania

10 Millcreek
Erie, Pennsylvania 16565
Phone: 814-866-3803

6019 Allentown Blvd
Harrisburg, Pennsylvania
17112
Phone: 717-540-7840

2994 E State Street
Hermitage, Pennsylvania
16146
Phone: 412-342-6353

2644 Mosside Blvd
Monoreville, Pennsylvania
15146
Phone: 412-374-9932

2040 W State Street
New Castle, Pennsylvania
16101
Phone: 412-656-9309

645 Clariton Blvd
Pleasant Hills,
Pennsylvania 15236
Phone: 412-653-9922

Wexford Plaza
10648 Perry Highway
Wexford, Pennsylvania 15090
Phone: 412-933-1660

South Carolina

30 Orchard Park Drive
Suite 12
Greenville, South Carolina
29615
Phone: 864-297-5558

South Dakota

3804 S Western
Sioux Falls, South Dakota
57105
Phone: 605-334-0922

Tennessee

2200 Hamilton Place Blvd
Chattanooga, Tennessee
37421
Phone: 423-894-1700

2880 Wilma Rudolph Place
Blvd
Clarksville, Tennessee 37040
Phone: 615-645-9346

112 Watson Glen Highway 96
Franklin, Tennessee 37604
Phone: 615-790-8081

Texas

2816 Soncy Road
Amarillo, Texas 79121
Phone: 806-354-0071

2220 Texas Ave South
College Station, Texas 77840
Phone: 409-696-7161

5425 S Padre Island Drive
Suite 167
Corpus Christi, Texas 78411
Phone: 512-993-8581

5102 B 60th St
Lubbock, Texas 79414
Phone: 806-788-1555

2734 N. Grandview Ave
Odessa, Texas 79762
Phone: 915-550-3883

7200 Independence Parkway
Suite 240
Plano, Texas 75025
Phone: 972-618-5800

3916 Kemp Blvd
Suite J2
Witchita Falls, Texas 76308
Phone: 940-691-8687

Vermont

299-2 Williston Road
Williston, Vermont 05495
Phone: 802-878-5434

Virginia

360A Arbor Drive
Christianburg, Virginia
24073
Phone: 540-382-5045

192 S Gate Squre
Colonial Heights, Virginia
23834
Phone: 804-526-1333

17860 Forest Road Suite 6
Forest, Virginia 24551
Phone: 804-385-4387

9111 Midlothian Turnpike
Richmond, Virginia 23236
Phone: 804-272-2229

3536 Electric Road
Roanoke, Virginia 24018
Phone: 540-774-3639

1371 Town Square Blvd
Roanoke, Virginia 24012
Phone: 540-563-9891

Washington

4217 Wheaton Way Ste N
Bremerton, Washington
98310
Phone: 360-377-4850

1218 N Columbia Center Blvd
Suite 14
Kennewick, Washington
99336
Phone: 509-783-6913

26121 104th Ave SE
Kent, Washington 98031
Phone: 253-850-7585

3225 Alderwood Mall Blvd
Suite E
Lynnwood, Washington 98036
Phone: 425-774-8393

E 88 Francis
Spokane, Washington 99207
Phone: 509-482-4696

7901 S Hosmer Street
Suite C7
Tacoma, Washington 98408
Phone: 253-473-4555

11505 NE 4th Plain Road F-4
Vancouver, Washington 98662
Phone: 360-253-7742

Wisconsin

710 North Casaloma Drive
Appleton, Wisconsin 54915
Phone: 414-738-9600

1142 S Military Ave
Green Bay, Wisconsin 54304
Phone: 920-498-9591

5020 S 74th Street
Greenfield, Wisconsin 55220
Phone: 414-325-7511

1625 Thierer Road
Madison, Wisconsin 53704
Phone: 608-243-1284

706 S Gammon Road
Madison, Wisconsin 53519
Phone: 608-276-8076

867 N Mayfair Road
Wauwatosa, Wisconsin 53226
Phone: 414-477-4957

West Virginia

2715 Murdoch Ave
Parkersburg, West Virginia
26101
Phone: 304-422-2005

Canada

Coakers Meadow
286 Torbay Road
St. Johns, NF A1A 4E1
Phone: 709-754-6200

75 Bayly Street West Suite 17
Ajax, Ontario L1S 7K7
Phone: 905-427-4194

347 Bayfield Street North
Barrie, Ontario L4M 2C3
Phone: 705-726-7577

1505 Guelph Line
Burlington, Ontario LP7 3B6
Phone: 905-335-3352

4625 Varsity Drive NW
Calgary, AB T3A 0Z9
Phone: 403-543-1068

180 94th Ave SE Unit 30E
Calgary, AB T2J 3GB
Phone: 403-543-1066

1024 Upper Wentworth Street
Hamilton, Ontario L9A 4V9
Phone: 905-318-8685

1295 Highbury Ave. #A10
London, Ontario NSV 5L3
Phone: 519-659-2231

2555 Dixie Road Suite 4
Mississauga, Ontario L4C
4Y4
Phone: 905-276-7799

16655 Yonge Street
New Market, Ontario L3V
1V6
Phone: 905-715-7939

1881 Steeles Ave W Suite 3
North York, Ontario M5H 5Y4
Phone: 416-661-0678

2423 Trafalgar Road #1
Oakville, Ontario L6H 6K7
Phone: 905-257-5775

1386 Bayview Ave
Toronto, Ontario M4G 3A1
Phone: 416-485-2776

4261 Highway 7
Unionville, Ontario L3R 9W6
Phone: 905-477-8983

1645 Dundas Street East
Whitby, Ontario L1N 2K9
Phone: 905-579-7679

22 C Allen Street
Charlottetown, PE C1A 2V3
Phone: 902-892-2505

Bring In The Old.

Catch Something New.

Trade In. Trade Up.

Whether it's practically new - or has seen the glory of 14 seasons - your quality used gear is wanted at Play It Again Sports. So trade in to trade up on some new gear and save big. Or get cash instead. Catch something new. Trade up and play it again.

PLAY IT AGAIN SPORTS®

Why Not Play it Again

Look For Us In The Guide

Play It Again Sports ®
Grow Biz Corporation
Corporate Office
4200 Dahlberg Drive
Minneapolis, MN 55422
Phone: 1-800-592-8046
Website:
www.playitagainsports.com

Established in 1983 by Martha
Morris with a great idea and a
gently used backpack, Play It
Again Sports ® has successfully
grown to hundreds of locations
conveniently located throughout
the US and Canada.
Play It Again Sports offers the
best value and selection on new
and gently used sporting goods
for the novice to the avid sports
enthusiast, they have it all. Most
stores are open seven days a week
and accept major credit cards. You
may choose to buy, sell or trade
your gently used sporting goods.
Extraordinary selections, fantastic
prices and great customer service
makes Play It Again Sports a must
for all shoppers. For more
information on Play It Again
Sports store franchises call 1-800-
592-8046 or visit their Web site
at www.playitagainsports.com.

758 E. Glen
Auburn, Alabama 36830
Phone: 334-887-2424

1728 2nd Avenue SW
King Ed. Pl
Cullman, Alabama 35055
Phone: 205-734-9414

1000 South Beltline Road,
Plumtre
Decatur, Alabama 35601
Phone: 205-350-8500

3121 Ross Clark Circle
Dothan, Alabama 36303
Phone: 334-677-8154

127 Cox Creek Parkway
Florence, Alabama 35630
Phone: 205-767-4800

2806C Memorial
Parkway Swm
Huntsville, Alabama 35801
Phone: 205-533-7373

7950 Highway 72W Suite K
Madison, Alabama 35758
Phone: 205-721-9993

3980 Airport Blvd.
Mobile, Alabama 36608
Phone: 334-304-0400

149 Eastern Bypass
Montgomery, Alabama 36117
Phone: 334-213-0042

12 Merchants Walk
Suite 5-A
Tuscaloosa, Alabama 35406
Phone: 205-752-0400

Play It Again Sports

Alaska

2636 Spenard Road
Anchorage, Alaska 99503
Phone: 907-278-7529

29 College Road
Unit 8B
Fairbanks, Alaska 99503
Phone: 907-457-7427

Arkansas

3029 N College
Fayetteville, Arkansas 72703
Phone: 501-442-7529

4300 Rodgers Avenue Suite 55
Fort Smith, Arkansas 72903
Phone: 501-783-3342

400 McCaine Blvd.
North Little Rock, Arkansas
72116
Phone: 501-791-7333

Arizona

1411 Milton Road
Flagstaff, Arizona 86001
Phone: 520-556-0304

5846 N 43rd Avenue
Glendale, Arizona 85301
Phone: 602-939-7799

1954 W Broadway Road
Suite 103
Mesa, Arizona 85202
Phone: 602-834-0005

3405 W. Thunderbird Road
Suite 1
Phoenix, Arizona 85203
Phone: 602-942-9224

3414 E Thomas Road
Phoenix, Arizona 85018
Phone: 602-468-9929

3143 E. Greenway Road
Phoenix, Arizona 85032
Phone: 602-971-8604

370 E Fry Blvd
Sierra Vista, Arizona 85635
Phone: 520-459-4009

2825 North Scottsdale Road
Scottsdale, Arizona 85251
Phone: 602-994-4958

8880 East Via Linda #110
Scottsdale, Arizona 85254
Phone: 602-661-1858

161 E Deuce of Clubs
Showlow, Arizona 85901
Phone: 520-537-0451

1840 E Warner Road
Suite 126
Tempe, Arizona 85284
Phone: 602-345-6109

7280 E. Broadway Blvd
Tucson, Arizona 85710
Phone: 520-296-6888

4128 N. Oracle Road
Tucson, Arizona 85705
Phone: 520-293-2010

4648 E Speedway
Tuscon, Arizona 85712
Phone: 520-795-0363

280 W 32nd Street
Yuma, Arizona 85364
Phone: 520-782-1401

California

30317 Canwood Street
Suite 37
Agoura Hills, California
91301
Phone: 818-879-5083

2228B Southshore Center
Alameda, California 94501
Phone: 510-521-3833

6300 White Lane Suite M
Bakersfield, California 93309
Phone: 805-832-7767

2065 Whitman Avenue
Suite 4C
Chico, California 95928
Phone: 530-345-7427

475A Philadelphia Street
Chino, California 91710
Phone: 909-590-4700

7348 Greenback Lane
Citrus Heights, California
95621
Phone: 916-721-7660

10155 Valley View Avenue
Cypress, California 90630
Phone: 714-828-9994

1351 B W Covell Blvd
Davis, California 95616
Phone: 530-756-4691

2801 Diamond Bar Blvd
Diamond Bar, California
91765
Phone: 909-468-9193

258A N El Camino Real
Encinitas, California 92024
Phone: 760-633-3966

1348 West Valley Parkway
Escondido, California 92029
Phone: 760-489-1644

1016-1 Riley Road
Folsom, California 95630
Phone: 916-983-6376

4035 Mowry Avenue
Fremont, California 94538
Phone:510-505-9696

5193 N. Blackstone
Fresno, California 93710
Phone: 209-221-8832

720 N Harbor Blvd
Fullerton, California 92632
Phone: 714-449-0113

220 E 10th Street Suite K
Gilroy, California 95020
Phone: 408-847-7678

105 N Central Avnue
Glendale, California 91203
Phone: 818-553-0940

18352 Beach Blvd
Huntington Beach,
California 92648
Phone: 714-848-6788

3800 Barranca Parkway #3
Irvine, California 92604
Phone: 714-654-1235

140 French Bar Road
Jackson, California 95642
Phone: 209-223-1223

319

3157 Foothill Blvd.
La Crescenta, California
91214
Phone: 818-249-4222

27241A S LaPaz Road
Laguna Nigel, California
92656
Phone: 714-831-3030

5538 Woodruff Avenue
Lakewood, California 90713
Phone: 562-920-9994

8366 Parkway Drive
LaMesa, California 91942
Phone: 619-667-9499

2228 Bellflower Blvd
Long Beach, California 90815
Phone: 562-598-9888

4916 El Camino Real
Los Altos, California 94022
Phone: 415-988-6800

1836 N Sepulveda Blvd
Manhattan Beach, California
90266
Phone: 310-796-5595

McCarthy Ranch Market
Place 238R
Milpitas, California 95035
Phone: 408-945-1808

25565 Jeronimo Road
Mission Viejo, California
92691
Phone: 714-586-6091

2720 McHenry Avenue
Suite N
Modesto, California 95350
Phone: 209-521-4664

522 W Huntington Drive
Monrovia, California 91016
Phone: 626-305-5770

8947 Tampa Avenue
Northridge, California 91324
Phone: 818-701-7056

3809 Plaza Drive
Oceanside, California 92056
Phone: 760-630-6156

1215-C Olive Drive
Oildale, California 93308
Phone: 805-399-4300

2348 N. Orange Mall
Orange, California 92865
Phone: 714-921-8242

279 N McDowell Avenue
Petaluma, California 94954
Phone: 707-765-1564

4571 Century Blvd
Pittsburgh, California 94565
Phone: 510-778-8805

3302 E Yorba Linda Blvd
Placentia, California 92831
Phone: 714-993-6383

1601 Contra Costa Blvd
Pleasant Hill, California
94523
Phone: 510-825-3396

5548 Springdale Avenue
Suite A
Pleasanton, California 94588
Phone: 510-734-6750

1619 Hilltop Drive Suite I
Redding, California 96002
Phone: 916-223-2646

3640 N Rosemead Blvd
Rosemead, California 91770
Phone: 818-312-3550

3176 Arden Way
Sacramento, California 95825
Phone: 916-971-1269

848 Playa Avenue
Sand City, California 93955
Phone: 408-899-7766

9969 Mira Mesa Blvd
Suite 6-7
San Diego, California 92131
Phone: 619-695-3030

1401 Garnet Avenue
San Diego, California 92109
Phone: 619-490-0222

45 W Portal Avenue
San Francisco, California
94127
Phone: 415-753-3049

2081 Camden Avenue
San Jose, California 95124
Phone: 408-371-4531

31882 Del Obispo Street
Suite 156
San Juan Capistrano,
California 92675
Phone: 714-661-4313

55 Bellam Blvd
San Rafael, California 94901
Phone: 415-453-7260

4850 BB Hollister Avenue
Santa Barbara, California
93111
Phone: 805-967-9889

26837 Bouquet Canyon Road
Santa Clarita, California
91350
Phone: 805-297-3579

1231 Wilshire Blvd
Santa Monica, California
90403
Phone: 310-395-8229

2735 Santa Rosa Avenue
Santa Rosa, California 95407
Phone: 707-527-7678

2691 Cochran Street
Simi Valley, California 93065
Phone: 805-520-6053

4770 Soquel Drive
Soquel, California 95073
Phone: 408-475-1988

828 W Benjamin Holt Drive
Stockton, California 95207
Phone: 209-474-1944

12038 Ventura Blvd
Studio City, California 91064
Phone: 818-752-9123

1046 East El Camino
Sunnyvale, California 94087
Phone: 408-247-1234

25365C Crenshaw Blvd.
Torrance, California 90505
Phone: 310-534-5760

2751 Geer Riad
Turlock, California 95380
Phone: 209-669-8541

Play It Again Sports

12872 Newport Avenue
Tustin, California 92680
Phone: 714-669-3734

830 E. Foothill Blvd.
Upland, CA 91786
Phone: 909-466-7611

4705 Telephone Road Suite 4
Ventura, California 93003
Phone: 805-644-4948

1101 South Mooney Blvd
Visalia, California 93277
Phone: 209-734-5616

973 S. Glendora Avenue
W. Covina, California 91790
Phone: 818-337-3364

15025 E Whittier Blvd
Whittier, California 90605
Phone: 310-698-5353

Colorado

7651 W 88th Avenue
Arvada, Colorado 80005
Phone: 303-431-6585

1090 South Sable Blvd
Aurora, Colorado 80012
Phone: 303-337-2737

653 S. Broadway
Boulder, Colorado 80303
Phone:303-499-2011

653 S. Broadway
Boulder, Colorado 80303
Phone:303-499-2011

12 East Kiowa
Colorado Springs, Colorado
80903

Phone: 719-635-5550

2223 S Monaco Parkway D-12
Denver, Colorado 80222
Phone: 303-756-6223

4619 South Mason
Ft. Collins, Colorado 80525
Phone: 970-223-9820

3820 W 10th Street
Greeley, Colorado 80634
Phone: 970-356-8808

8601 W Cross Drive Unit A6
Littleton, Colorado 80123
Phone: 303-979-3379

151 W Mineral Avenue
Littleton, Colorado 80120
Phone: 303-798-8824

3977 East 120th Avenue
Thornton, Colorado 80233
Phone: 303-280-9520

Connecticut

92 Bridgeport Avenue
Milford, Connecticut 06460
Phone: 203-877-8403

278 Boston Post Road
Orange, Connecticut 06477
Phone: 203-799-3700

738 Wolcott Street
Waterbury, Connecticut
06705
Phone: 203-756-2773

15 S Main Street
W. Hartford, Connecticut
06107
Phone: 860-523-4692

Delaware

1237 Dupont Highway N
Dover, Delaware 19901
Phone: 302-672-9366

Florida

3611 First Street East #710
Bradenton, Florida 34208
Phone: 941-745-2959

744 West Lumsden Road
Brandon, Florida 33511
Phone: 813-661-4141

1500 Beville Road Suite 702
Daytona Beach, Florida 32114
Phone: 904-238-6949

1091 Federal Highway South
Deerfield Beach, Florida
33441
Phone: 954-427-9774

5226 Bank Street
Ft. Myers, Florida 33907
Phone: 941-277-9889

3425 W University Avenue
Gainesville, Florida 32607
Phone: 352-377-7666

4919 A Sheridan Street
Hollywood, Florida 33021
Phone: 954-983-4171

11701 San Jose Blvd Suite 23
Jacksonville, Florida 32258
Phone: 904-880-5090

10769 Unit 8 Beach Blvd
Jacksonville, Florida 32216
Phone: 904-565-9003

2211 S Florida Ave-
Southgate S
Lakeland, Florida 33803
Phone: 941-688-7757

3649 Lake Emma Road
Lake Mary, Florida 32779
Phone: 407-333-0340

10601 US Highway 441
Suite E3-5
Leesburg, Florida 34788
Phone: 352-365-9996

4760 North Congress
Lantana, Florida 33462
Phone: 561-963-7427

10500 Ulmerton Road
Largo, Florida 33771
Phone: 813-530-9730

9019 SW 107th Avenue
Miami, Florida 33176
Phone: 305-596-6380

2208 N Tamiami Trail
Naples, Florida 33940
Phone: 941-263-6679

11859 US Highway 1
N. Palm Beach, Florida 33408
Phone: 561-775-1703

1827 E Silver Springs Blvd
Ocala, Florida 32670
Phone: 352-622-1122

195 3 Blanding Blvd
Orange Park, Florida 32073
Phone: 904-272-1242

2425 Hiawassee Road
Orlando, Florida 32835
Phone: 407-578-6200

33649 US Highway 19N
Palm Harbor, Florida 34684
Phone: 813-781-7700

658 W 23rd Street
Panama City, Florida 32045
Phone: 904-769-7611

6601 N Davis Highway
Pensacola, Florida 32504
Phone: 904-477-7407

1900 Tamiami Trail Suite 139
Port Charlotte, Florida 33948
Phone: 941-255-1378

5407 Fruitville Road
Sarasota, Florida 34232
Phone: 941-378-1477

3942 Tyrone Blvd
St. Petersburg, Florida 33709
Phone: 813-344-0601

3400 Fourth Street N
St. Petersburg, Florida 33704
Phone: 813-528-1115

3351 SE Federal Highway
Stuart, Florida 34997
Phone: 407-286-9552

4139 N Pine Island Road
Sunrise, Florida 33351
Phone: 954-746-0055

1201 Apalachee Parkway
Tallahasse, Florida 32301
Phone: 904-878-2163

13238 N Dale Mabry Highway
Tampa, Florida 33618
Phone: 813-969-0855

921 15th Place Lurias Plaza
Vero Beach, Florida 32960
Phone: 561-563-0026

5622 Cypress Garden Blvd
Winter Haven, Florida 33884
Phone: 941-318-0001

7628 University Blvd
Winter Park, Florida 32792.
Phone: 407-677-5007

Georgia

711 Westover Suite B
Park Place
Albany, Georgia 31706
Phone: 912-883-9983

4279 Roswell Road NE
Atlanta, Georgia 30342
Phone: 404-257-0229

596 Bobby Jones
Expressway Suite 14
Augusta, Georgia 30907
Phone: 706-650-8767

3814 Atlanta Highway
Bogart, Georgia 30622
Phone: 706-369-3477

5715B Altama Avenue
Brunswick, Georgia 31525
Phone: 912-267-0520

410 Cherokee Place
Cartersville, Georgia 30121
Phone: 770-386-8866

1543 Highway 38 Suite N
Conyers, Georgia 30013
Phone: 770-918-1001

1931 Auburn Avenue
Columbus, Georgia 31906
Phone: 706-561-1777

3151 Highway 5
Douglasville, Georgia 30135
Phone: 770-947-5895

174B Banks Crossing
Shopping Center
Fayetteville, Georgia 30214
Phone: 770-460-7511

1080 A Dawsonville Highway
Gainsville, Georgia 30501
Phone: 770-503-0470

1687 Expressway
Griffin, Georgia 30223
Phone: 770-227-6789

800 W Barrett Parkway
Suite 30
Kennesaw, Georgia 30144
Phone: 770-429-8636

2100 Riverside Parkway
Suite 104A
Lawrenceville, Georgia 30043
Phone: 770-338-9444

5015 Floyd Road
Mabelton, Georgia 30059
Phone: 770-739-5514

3715 Bloomfield Road
Summit Center
Macon, Georgia 31204
Phone: 912-471-8211

440 Roswell Road Suite 140
Marietta, Georgia 30062
Phone: 770-565-5200

1250 Tech Drive Northwest
Norcross, Georgia 30093
Phone: 770-806-9166

7050 Jimmy Carter Blvd
Suite 106F
Norcross, Georgia 30092
Phone: 770-242-9788

7175 Georgia Highway 85
Riverdale, Georgia 30274
Phone: 770-907-1338

2204 Shorter Avenue
Rome, Georgia 30165
Phone: 706-232-2002

10800 Alpharetta Highway
Suite 144
Roswell, Georgia 30076
Phone: 770-642-4880

7929 Abercorn St. Suite 640
Savannah, Georgia 31406
Phone: 912-927-1886

1825 Rock Bridge Road SW
Suite 16A
Stone Mountain, Georgia
30087
Phone: 770-413-7333

1200 D North Street
Augustine Road
Valdosta, Georgia 31601
Phone: 912-245-8077

Hawaii

4400 Kalanianaole Highway
Honolulu, Hawaii 96821
Phone: 808-737-5537

74-5615 Luhia Street
Kailua-Kona, Hawaii 96740
Phone: 808-334-0051

Idaho

1467 North Milwaukee
Boise, Idaho 83704
Phone: 208-378-0053

380 S Woodruff
Idaho Falls, Idaho 83401
Phone: 203-523-7797

Play It Again Sports

401 N. Veterans Parkway
Bloomington, Illinois 61704
Phone: 309-662-7744

109 C Village Square
Shopping Center
Route 50
Bradley, Illinois 60915
Phone: 815-933-7978

1227 Dundee Road
Plaza Verde
Buffalo Grove, Illinois 60089
Phone: 847-797-1442

503 S. Mattis Avenue
Champaign, Illinois 61821
Phone: 217-355-0027

2101 W Irving Park Road
Chicago, Illinois 60618
Phone: 773-463-9900

28 W Crystal Lake Plaza
Crystal Lake, Illinois 60014
Phone: 815-459-1717

4240 N Prospect Drive
Decatur, Illinois 62526
Phone: 217-872-2434

Oakland Plaza
2587 Sycamore Road
DeKalb, Illinois 60115
Phone: 815-758-1180

1540 Ogden
Downers Grove, Illinois 60515
Phone: 630-810-9811

649 42nd Avw
East Moline, Illinois 61244
Phone: 309-755-9297

35 E North Avenue
Glendale Heights, Illinois
60139
Phone: 630-510-8733

9270 Joliet Road
Suite 800
Hodgkins, Illinois 60525
Phone: 708-485-4851

2736 Plainfield Road
Joliet, Illinois 60435
Phone: 815-254-9100

721 W Main Street
Lake Zurich, Illinois 60047
Phone: 847-726-9044

1014 S Elmhurst Raod
Mt. Prospect, Illinois 60056
Phone: 847-228-9859

24 W Gartner Road Suite 104
Naperville, Illinois 60540
Phone: 630-355-1121

475 Waukegan
Brookside Plaza
Northbrook, Illinois 60062
Phone: 847-564-9180

1544 W Highway 50
O' Fallon, Illinois 62269
Phone: 618-628-2345

5600 W 95th Street
Oak Lawn, Illinois 60453
Phone: 630-636-6311

9200 159th Street
Orland Park, Illinois 60462
Phone: 708-460-7760

2601 W Lake Avenue A3
Peoria, Illinois 61615
Phone: 309-685-8911

839 E Rollins Road
Round Lake Beach, Illinois
60073
Phone: 847-223-6446

1127 S Roselle Road
Schaumburg, Illinois 60193
Phone: 630-894-8914

5373 W Touhy Avenue
Skokie, Illinois 60077
Phone: 847-674-6900

2761 S 6th Street
Springfield, Illinois 62703
Phone: 217-522-7427

1501 W Main
St. Charles, Illinois 60174
Phone: 630-584-7334

874 West Main Street
West Dundee, Illinois 60118
Phone: 847-428-7529

Indiana

1211 S College Mall Road
Bloomington, Indiana 47401
Phone: 812-336-0600

271 Merchants Square
Drive C-6A
Carmel, Indiana 46032
Phone: 317-848-1815

1160 E. Highway 131
Clarksville, Indiana 47129
Phone: 812-288-8656

3527 S Main
Elkhart, Indiana 46517
Phone: 219-293-2462

101B Green River Road
Evansville, Indiana 47715
Phone: 812-474-1992

8923 S. Meridian
Indianapolis, Indiana 46217
Phone: 317-889-9978

2110 E 62nd Street
Indianapolis, Indiana 46220
Phone: 317-257-0036

9455 E Washington Street
Indianapolis, Indiana 46229
Phone: 317-897-4020

2324 Miracle Lane
Mishawaka, Indiana 46545
Phone: 219-255-5631

6129A Crawfordsville Road
Speedway, Indiana 46224
Phone: 317-481-9750

3450 Riverside Plaza
Terre Haute, Indiana 47802
Phone: 812-234-5434

Iowa

526 Main Street Suite F
Ames, Iowa 50010
Phone: 515-233-8606

3657 1st Ave SE
Cedar Rapids, Iowa 52403
Phone: 319-366-8664

2124 E Kimberly Road
Davenport, Iowa 52807
Phone: 319-359-4982

5126 SE 14th Street
Des Moines, Iowa 50230
Phone: 515-287-1767

2714 Beaver Avenue
Des Moines, Iowa 50310
Phone: 515-274-6475

1690 JFK Road
Dubuque, Iowa 52001

Play It Again Sports

Phone: 319-557-9694
1705 1st Avenue
Iowa City, Iowa 52240
Phone: 319-354-4777

1631 4th Street SW Suite 109
Mason City, Iowa 50401
Phone: 515-424-5256

4277 Sergeant Road
Sioux City, Iowa 51106
Phone: 712-276-5509

3740 University Avenue
Waterloo, Iowa 50701
Phone: 319-233-0078

Kansas

1029 Massachusetts Street
Lawrence, Kansas 66044
Phone: 913-841-7529

12980 W 87th Street
Lenexa, Kansas 66215
Phone: 913-599-1818

5305 Johnson Drive
Mission, Kansas 66205
Phone: 913-722-3600

13511 Mur-Len Road
Suite 133
Olathe, Kansas 66062
Phone: 913-782-2999

1311 Crawford
Salina, Kansas 67401
Phone: 913-826-4900

2130 SW Wanamker Road
Topeka, Kansas 66614
Phone: 913-272-5665

8815 W 13th Street
Wichita, Kansas 67212
Phone: 316-729-0300

7300 E Kellogg Suite 180

Wichita, Kansas 67207
Phone: 316-681-2670

Kentucky

6827 Alexandria Pike
Alexandria, Kentucky 41001
Phone: 606-635-6388

1805 Campbell Lane
Bowling Green, Kentucky
42104
Phone: 502-796-4199

8119 Connector Drive
Florence, Kentucky 40142
Phone: 606-282-6565

305 Leonardwood Drive
Suite 4
Frankfort, Kentucky 40601
Phone: 502-875-7609

4138 Outer Loop
Louisville, Kentucky 40219
Phone: 502-968-5354

291 North Hubbard Lane
Suite B-4
Louisville, Kentucky 40207
Phone: 502-897-3494

636 Southtown Boulevard
Suit 5
Owensboro, Kentucky 42301
Phone: 502-686-8060

3401 Park Avenue Suite 3
Paducah, Kentucky 42001
Phone: 502-575-3655

Louisiana

9626 Airline Highway Suite
C2B
Baton Rouge, Louisiana
70808

Phone: 504-924-4907

1000 W Esplanade Suite 207
Kenner, Louisiana 70065
Phone: 504-469-1303

2981 Highway 190
Mandeville, Louisiana 70471
Phone: 504-727-1997

Maine

250 Center Street
Auburn, Maine 04210
Phone: 207-777-7427

114 Western Avenue
Capital Shopping
Center
Augusta, Maine 04330
207-621-9968

270 State Street
Brewer, Maine 04412
Phone: 207-989-8350

147 Bath Road Unit B8
Brunswick, Maine 04011
Phone: 207-725-6800

315 Marginal Way
Portland, Maine 04101
Phone: 207-773-6063

16 Saco Valley
Shopping Center
Saco, Maine 04072
Phone: 207-286-1444

Maryland

167 G Jennifer Road
Annapolis, Maryland 21401
Phone: 410-224-6180

519 Baltimore Pike
Bel Air, Maryland 21014
Phone: 410-838-0404

10037 York Road
Cockeysville, Maryland 21030
Phone: 410-683-7427

9150 3 Baltimore
National Pike
Ellicott City, Maryland 21043
Phone: 410-418-9371

1039 W Patrick Street
Frederick, Maryland 21702
Phone: 301-698-2407

1334 B Defense Highway
Gambrills, Maryland 21054
Phone: 301-261-3021

30 Mountain Road
Glen Burnie, Maryland 21060
Phone:410-761-5003

13102A Penn Avenue
Hagerstown, Maryland 21742
Phone: 301-790-1365

14130 Baltimore Avenue
Laurel, Maryland 20707
Phone: 301-317-3943

18145 Village Mart Drive
Olney, Maryland 20832
Phone: 301-570-9745

745 Solomons Island
Road-Fox Run
Prince Frederick, Maryland
20678
Phone: 410-535-6912

250 Englar Road
Unit 20
Westminster, Maryland 21157
Phone: 410-876-0600

Play It Again Sports

11981-83 Reisterstown Road
Reisterstown, Maryland
21136
Phone: 410-833-8812

Massachusetts

750 Belmont Street
Brockton, Massachusetts
02401
Phone: 508-559-5100

626 Washington Street
Dedham Plaza
Dedham, Massachusetts 02026
Phone: 617-320-8108

280 Worcester Road
Framingham, Massachusetts
01701
Phone: 508-626-2828

25 Iyanough Road
Hyannis, Massachusetts
02601
Phone: 508-771-6979

187 Sumner Court
Cranberry Crossing
Kingston, Massachusetts
02364
Phone: 617-585-5955

814 N Main Street
Leominster, Massachusetts
01452
Phone: 508-537-2063

42 Boston Post Road
Marlborough, Massachusetts
01752
Phone: 508-485-7042

265 Main Street
North Reading,
Massachusetts 01864
Phone: 508-664-9363

8 Bourbon Street
Peabody, Massachusetts 01960
Phone: 508-535-5506

660 Merrill Road
Pittsfield, Massachusetts
01201
Phone: 413-442-9003

339 Squire
North Gate Plaza
Unit 124
Revere, Massachusetts 02151
Phone: 617-289-4997

20 Commerce Way
Seekonk, Massachusetts
02771
Phone: 508-336-0565

62 E Montvale Ave
Stoneham, Massachusetts
02180
Phone: 617-438-2399

550 Adams Street Plaza
Quincy, Massachusetts 4128
Phone: 617-479-0065

367 Memorial Avenue
West Springfield,
Massachusetts 01089
Phone: 413-734-7529

Michigan

1422 S Main Street Suite B
Adrian, Michigan 49221
Phone: 517-264-6969

2461A W Stadium Blvd
Ann Arbor, Michigan 48103
Phone: 313-747-6277

2535 M 139 South
Benton Harbor, Michigan
49022
Phone: 616-926-0021

620 West Grand River
Brighton, Michigan 48816
Phone: 810-227-6877

50607 Gratiot Road
Chesterfield Township,
Michigan 48051
Phone: 810-598-7700

1032 N Crooks Suite L
Clawson, Michigan 48017
Phone: 810-435-7240

28942 Orchard Lake Road
Farmington Hills, Michigan
48334
Phone: 248-737-0970

G4205 Miller Road
Flint, Michigan 48507
Phone: 810-732-3675

4130 24th Avenue
Ft. Gratiot Township,
Michigan 48059
Phone: 810-385-5800

16054 15 Mile Road
Fraser, Michigan 48026
Phone: 810-294-8665

2915 Breton Road SE
Grand Rapids, Michigan
49512

Phone: 616-241-2550

3575 Alpine Avenue NW
Grand Rapids, Michigan
49504
Phone: 616-785-3000

12465 James Street Suite B
Holland, Michigan 49424
Phone: 616-399-9906

316 N. Wisner
Jackson, Michigan 49202
Phone: 517-789-9967

5017 W Main Street
Kalamazoo, Michigan 49009
Phone: 616-344-5571

5441 W Saginaw
Lansing, Michigan 48917
Phone: 517-321-6162

2168 US Highway 41 W
Marquette, Michigan 49885
Phone: 906-225-0099

301 S Saginaw
Midland, Michigan 48640
Phone: 517-832-4125

503 N Telegraph Road
Monroe, Michigan 48162
Phone: 313-457-3366

4128 E Bluegrass
Mt. Pleasant, Michigan 48858
Phone: 517-775-8888

2977 Henry Street
Muskegon, Michigan 49441
Phone: 616-733-6490

5730 S Westnedge
Portage, Michigan 49002
Phone: 616-345-9119

Play It Again Sports

3236 Orchard Lake Road
Orchard Lake, Michigan
48324
Phone: 248-682-4335

1397 Walton Blvd.
Rochester Hills, Michigan
48309
Phone: 248-650-5300

21323 Harper
St. Clair Shore, Michigan
48080
Phone: 810-772-0600

14854 Dix Toledo
Southgate, Michigan 48195
Phone: 313-284-7488

3951 West Road
Trenton, Michigan 48185
Phone: 313-692-6470

45410 Van Dyke Ave
Utica, Michigan 48317
Phone: 248-731-5530

4288 Dixie Highway
Waterford, Michigan 48329
Phone: 248-674-8220

1049 28th Street SW
Wyoming, Michigan 49509
Phone: 616-530-9779

2345 Ellsworth Road
Ypsilanti, Michigan 48197
Phone: 313-572-0943

Minnesota

609 Broadway
Alexandria, Minnesota 56308
Phone: 320-762-1323

1401 1st Avenue SW
Austin, Minnesota 55912
Phone: 507-433-2881

750 Paul Bunyan Drive
Bemidji, Minnesota 56601
Phone: 218-759-9225

7811 Southtown Center
Bloomington, Minnesota
55431
Phone: 612-888-4620

6248 Lakeland Avenue N
Brooklyn Park, Minnesota
55428
Phone: 612-533-1004

1313 Highway 25 Suite F
Buffalo, Minnesota 55313
Phone: 612-682-9334

13957 Grand Ave S
Burnsville, Minnesota 55337
Phone: 612-898-1878

2613 Coon Rapids Blvd
Coon Rapids, Minnesota
55433
Phone: 612-754-1230

1300 Arrowhead Drive
Duluth, Minnesota 55811
Phone: 218-724-1700

1256 Tower Center
Eagen, Minnesota 55123
Phone: 612-452-8151

8025 Glen Land
Eden Prairie, Minnesota
55344
Phone: 612-944-8265

19268 Evans Street NW
Elk River, Minnesota 55330
Phone: 612-241-9876

616 N Lake Street
Highway 61
Forest Lake, Minnesota 55025
Phone: 612-464-8445

2645 White Bear Avenue
Maplewood, Minnesota 55109
Phone: 612-777-6899

1829 Adams Street
Mankato, Minnesota 56001
Phone: 507-625-2000

3505 Hennepin Ave S
Minneapolis, Minnesota
55408
Phone: 612-824-1231

11317 Highway 7
Minnetonka, Minnesota
55343
Phone: 612-935-4999

202 W Bridge Street
Owatonna, Minnesota 55060
Phone: 507-455-1198

102 Elton Hills Drive NW
Suite 200
Rochester, Minnesota 55901
Phone: 507-281-1943

2575 W Fairview
Roseville, Minnesota 55113
Phone: 612-639-9500

524 25th Ave N
St. Cloud, Minnesota 56303
Phone: 612-259-7980

53 S Cleveland
St Paul, Minnesota 55105
Phone: 612-698-3773

14375 N 60th Street Suite B
Stillwater, Minnesota 55082
Phone: 612-351-7588

15620 Wayzata Blvd
Wayzata, Minnesota 55391
Phone: 612-449-0919

2020 South Robert
W. St. Paul, Minnesota 55118
Phone: 612-451-1225

1305 S 1st Street
Willmar, Minnesota 56201
Phone: 320-235-9508

1705 Weir Drive Suite 5
Woodbury, Minnesota 55125
Phone: 612-730-9093

Missouri

1412 AB South Highway 7
Blue Springs, Missouri 64014
Phone: 816-228-8220

2136 Williams
Town Plaza Shopping Center
Cape Girardeau, Missouri
63701
Phone: 573-339-5888

122 Four Seasons
Shopping Center
Chesterfield, Missouri 63017
Phone: 314-576-7900

1500 170 Drive SW
Columbia, Missouri 65203
Phone: 573-442-9291

8 Paddock Hills Plaza
Florissant, Missouri 63033
Phone: 314-830-3900

13811A East 40 Highway
Independence, Missouri
64055
Phone: 816-373-8885

1704 Missouri Boulevard
Jefferson City, Missouri
65101
Phone: 573-635-9391

Play It Again Sports

2401 E 32nd St Suite 18
Joplin, Missouri 64801
Phone: 417-626-7529

2107 Zumbell Road
St Charles, Missouri 63303
Phone: 314-949-5600

2207 N Belt Highway
Suite B
St Joseph, Missouri 64506
Phone: 816-364-1688

12460 Tesson Ferry Road
St. Louis, Missouri 63128
Phone: 314-849-7300

3303 South Campbell
Springfield, Missouri 65807
Phone: 417-883-7444

Mississippi

2650 Beach Blvd Suite 16
Biloxi, Mississippi 39531
Phone: 601-388-7638

2523 Highway 9
Clara Point Plaza
Gautier, Mississippi 39553
Phone: 601-497-6888

6380 E Ridgewood Court
Jackson, Mississippi 39211
Phone: 601-956-5500

2606 W Main Street
Tupelo, Mississippi 38801
Phone: 601-840-9300

Montana

1005 24th Street Suite 3
Billings, Montana 59102
Phone: 406-652-3662

4305 10th Avenue S
Great Falls, Montana 59405
Phone: 406-453-8199

2230 Reserve Street Suite 305
Missoula, Montana 59802
Phone: 406-549-1580

Nebraska

2418 N Webb Road Suite T
Grand Island, Nebraska 68803
Phone: 308-381-0123

3540 Village Drive
Lincoln, Nebraska 68156
Phone: 402-421-8423

5141 O Street Suite A
Lincoln, Nebraska 68510
Phone: 402-483-7447

906 Omaha Avenue
Norfolk, Nebraska 68701
Phone: 402-371-6757

7928 Dodge Street
Omaha, Nebraska 68114
Phone: 402-393-3003

2809 South 125th Avenue
Omaha, Nebraska 68144
Phone: 402-333-0911

810 Tara Plaza
Papillion, Nebraska 68128
Phone: 402-339-3999

New Hampshire

PO Box 3159
Rte 16 Conwark Market
Conway, New Hampshire
03818
Phone: 603-447-3052

441 Amherst Street
Nashua, New Hampshire
03063
Phone: 603-594-0800

37 Plaistow Road Suite 5
Plaistow, New Hampshire
03865
Phone: 603-382-3580

775 Lafayette Road
Portsmouth, New Hampshire
03801
Phone: 603-431-7627

New Jersey

149 Route 31
Flemington, New Jersey
08822
Phone: 908-284-9227

Todays Man-Marshalls Mall
240
East Hanover, New Jersey
07936
Phone: 201-581-1404

4 Village Center Drive
Freehold, New Jersey 07728
Phone: 732-863-1770

731 Rte 33
Mercerville, NJ 08169
Phone: 609-586-8989

Middletown Shopping Center
1165 Route 35
Middletown, New Jersey
07748

Phone: 908-957-0355

4201 Church Road
Mt. Laurel, New Jersey 08054
Phone: 609-235-2573

566 Milltown Road
Brunswick Shopping Center
North Brunswick, New Jersey
08902
Phone: 908-846-3242

801 Tilton Road
Northfield, New Jersey 08225
Phone: 609-569-0099

308 Orlando Drive
Route 206 South
Raritan, New Jersey 08869
Phone: 908-725-2232

275 State Highway Route 10E
Succasunna, New Jersey
07876
Phone: 201-252-1147

1334 Lakewood Rod
Toms River, New Jersey 08753
Phone: 732-341-0200

501 State Highway 42
Turnersville, New Jersey
08012
Phone: 609-232-1100

1597 Rte 22W
Watchung, New Jersey 07060
Phone: 908-322-1001

1172 Hamburg Turnpike
Wayne, New Jersey 07470
Phone: 201-633-7633

New Mexico

7401 Menaul NE
Albuquerque, New Mexico

Play It Again Sports

87110
Phone: 505-881-0551

10131 Coors Road NW
Suite E2
Albuquerque, New Mexico
87114
Phone: 505-890-6117

3030 E Main Street Suite L
Farmington, New Mexico
87402
Phone: 505-327-5403

2010 Cerrillos Road
Suite 21-22
Santa Fe, New Mexico 89510
Phone: 505-438-6006

Nevada

3331 Highway 50 East Suite 5
Carson City, Nevada 89701
Phone: 702-882-1224

8380 W. Cheyenne
Suite 102-103
Las Vegas, Nevada 89128
Phone: 702-645-5548

2001 S Rainbow Blvd Suite A
Las Vegas, Nevada 89102
Phone: 702-228-1713

651 E Moana Lane
Reno, Nevada 89502
Phone: 702-825-6311

New York

4144 Union Road
Buffalo, New York 14225
Phone: 716-626-6600

223 Glen Cove Road
Carle Place, New York 11514
Phone: 516-873-8874

3232 Erie Blvd E
Dewitt, New York 13214
Phone: 315-446-7670

1912 Jericho Turnpike
E. Northport, New York 11731
Phone: 516-462-1024

3840 S McKinley Parkway
Hamburg, New York 14219
Phone: 716-826-3867

106 Alexander Ave
Lake Grove, New York 11755
Phone: 516-724-7427

952 Troy Schenectady Road
Latham, New York 12110
Phone: 518-785-6587

802 Hicksville Road
Massapequa, New York 11758
Phone: 516-541-3290

1109 Commercial Drive
New Hartford, New York
13413
Phone: 315-736-5336

3910 Brewerton Road
North Syracuse, New York
13212
Phone: 315-457-7101

46 Atlantic Avenue
Oceanside, New York 11572
Phone: 516-678-7900

499 Sunrise Highway
Patchogue, New York 11772
Phone: 516-289-1791

30 Plattsburgh Plaza
Plattsburgh, New York 12901
Phone: 518-566-6026

2199 E Henrietta Road
Rochester, New York 14623
Phone: 716-359-0740

3564 A Ridge Road W
Rochester, New York 14626
Phone: 716-723-8210

2855 Sheridan Drive
Tonawanda, New York 14150
Phone: 716-832-3800

3701 Vestal Parkway East
Suite 40
Vestal, New York 13850
Phone: 607-770-6059

1900 Empire Blvd
Webster, New York 14580
Phone: 716-671-8816

757 Montauk Highway
W. Babylon, New York 11704
Phone: 516-422-8591

North Carolina

611 Tunnel Road
Asheville, North Carolina
28805
Phone: 704-299-1221

2142 S Church Street
Burlington, North Carolina
27215
Phone: 910-570-3020

421 Crossroads Blvd
Cary, North Carolina 27511
Phone: 919-851-1851

1800-12E Franklin Street
Chapel Hill, North Carolina
27514
Phone: 919-967-8010

741-29 E Independence Blvd.
Charlotte, North Carolina
28227
Phone: 704-531-1337

245 Westwood
Shopping Center
Fayetteville, North Carolina
28314
Phone: 919-967-8010

2711 Battleground Avenue
Greensboro, North Carolina
27408
Phone: 910-288-5088

146 SW Greenville Blvd
Greenville, North Carolina
27834
Phone: 919-353-4344

114 Henderson Crossing
Hendersonville,
North Carolina 28792
Phone: 704-698-1988

2156 Highway 70 SE
Hickory, North Carolina
28602
Phone: 704-261-0044

274 E Chester Drive
High Point, North Carolina
27262
Phone: 910-869-8539

6282 102 Glenwood Ave
Raleigh, North Carolina
27612
Phone: 919-787-9060

530 S College Road
Wilmington, North Carolina
28412
Phone: 910-791-1572

127 Jonestown Road
Winston-Salem, North
Carolina 27104
Phone: 910-760-1470

North Dakota

204 W. Front
Bismarck, North Dakota
58504
Phone: 701-255-6068

3405 W Main Ave
Fargo, ND 58103
Phone: 781-293-1721

Ohio

2202 Romig Road
Akron, Ohio 44320
Phone: 330-848-1811

1300 N Fairfield
Beaver Creek Plaza
Beavercreek, Ohio 45432
Phone: 937-427-1961

813 Boardman Poland Road
Boardman, Ohio 44512
Phone: 330-629-2828

4778 Ridge Road
Brooklyn, Ohio 44144
Phone: 216-459-8586

8223 Colerain Ave
Cincinnati, Ohio 45239
Phone: 513-245-2006

4394 Eastgate Square Drive
Cincinnati, Ohio 45245
Phone: 513-752-9808

6149 Glenway Ave
Cincinnati, Ohio 45211
Phone: 513-661-8833

9990 Kings Auto Mall Drive
Cincinnati, Ohio 45249
Phone: 513-583-0040

3880P Paxton Ave
Cincinnati, Ohio 45209
Phone: 513-321-1711

573 Emporium Sq Drive
Columbus, Ohio 43231
Phone: 614-890-2110

6011 E Main Street
Columbus, Ohio 43123
Phone: 614-868-0018

7412 Sawmill Road
Columbus, Ohio 43235
Phone: 614-791-9344

597 Howe Ave
Cuyahoga Falls, Ohio 44221
Phone: 330-922-0606

6625 Dixie Highway
Fairfield, Ohio 45014
Phone: 513-870-0010

2179 Springtown Road
Grove City, Ohio 43123
Phone: 614-539-8881

959 Hebron Road
Heath, Ohio 43056
Phone: 614-522-5376

4714 Cemetary Road
Hilliard, Ohio 43206
Phone: 614-529-9100

1532 Spring Meadow Drive
Holland, Ohio 43528
Phone: 419-868-8533

7763 Old Troy Pike
Huber Heights, Ohio 45424
Phone: 937-236-9969

1144 Memorial Drive
Lancaster, Ohio 43130
Phone: 614-654-9555

8210 Macedonia
Commons Blvd
Macedonia, Ohio 44056
Phone: 216-467-0788

321 N Lexington
Spring Mill Road
Mansfield, Ohio 44906
Phone: 419-529-9977

875 N Court
Medina, Ohio 44256
Phone: 330-723-3337

9156 Mentor Ave
Mentor, Ohio 44060
Phone: 216-974-3225

535 S Breiel Blvd
Middletown, Ohio 45044
Phone: 513-424-9800

4733 Great Northern Blvd
N. Olmsted, Ohio 44070
Phone: 216-777-5569
1608 Upper Valley Pike
Springfield, Ohio 45504
Phone: 937-324-1144

16895 Chagrin Blvd
Shaker Heights, Ohio
44120
Phone: 216-751-2400

5333 Monroe Street Suite 16
Toledo, Ohio 43623
Phone: 419-843-4230

Oklahoma

580 SE Washington Blvd
Bartlesville, Oklahoma 74006
Phone: 918-331-9888

100 E 15th Street
Edmond, Oklahoma 73013
Phone: 405-348-6171

2316 W Owen K Garriot Road
Enid, Oklahoma 73703
Phone: 405-242-2228

101 N Douglas Blvd
Suite 101A
Midwest City, Oklahoma
73130
Phone: 405-732-4700

2203 W Main Street Suite 2
Norman, Oklahoma 73069
405-364-0080

8531 N Rockwell
Oklahoma City, Oklahoma
73132
Phone: 405-722-2723

2209 SW 74th St. Suite 303
Oklahoma City, Oklahoma
73159
Phone: 405-682-5551

211 N Perkins Suite 36
Stillwater, Oklahoma 74075
Phone: 405-372-7200

7127 S Mingo Road
Tulsa, Oklahoma 74133
Phone: 918-250-4515

Play It Again Sports

Oregon

1255 NE 3rd St
Bend, Oregon 97701
Phone: 503-382-0506

9248 SW Beaverton-Hillsdale
Highway
Beaverton, Oregon 97005
Phone: 503-292-4552

1422 NW 9th
Corvallis, Oregon 97330
Phone: 541-754-7529

2598 Williamette Street
Eugene, Oregon 97405
Phone: 541-342-4041

10355 NE Halsey
Portland, Oregon 97220
Phone: 503-254-4993

11350 SE 82nd Ave Suite 305
Portland, Oregon 97266
Phone: 503-786-0484

1911 Lancaster Drive NE
Salem, Oregon 97305
Phone: 503-378-7283

Pennsylvania

415 N Orchard Plaza
Altoona, Pennsylvania 16602
Phone: 814-946-3223

Great South Shopping Center
Route 50
Bridgeville, Pennsylvania
15017
Phone: 412-257-2455

3401 Hartzdale Drive
Camp Hill, Pennsylvania
17011
Phone: 717-731-9899

20808 Rte 19
Cranberry Township,
Pennsylvania 16066
Phone: 412-776-1820

1617 S. Braddock Ave
Edgewood, Pennsylvania
15218
Phone: 412-243-9510

847 Pittsburgh Ave
Erie, Pennsylvania 16505
Phone: 814-453-3332

434 W Lincoln Highway
Exton, Pennsylvania 19341
Phone: 610-429-9764

447 Oxford Valley Road
Suite 475
Fairless Hills, Pennsylvania
19030
Phone: 215-945-4800

Hemphield Plaza Route 30
Suite 26
Greensburgh, Pennsylvania
15601
Phone: 412-834-1211

4415A Buffalo Road
Harbor Creek, Pennsylvania
16510
Phone: 814-898-2965

2984 E State
Hermitage Hills Plaza
Hermitage, Pennsylvania
16148
Phone: 412-347-6330

105 Town Center
King of Prussia, Pensylvania
19006
Phone: 610-265-4300

850 Plaza Road
Lancaster, Pennsylvania
17601
Phone: 717-291-9997

Ralphs Corner Shopping
Center
Route 463
Lansdale, Pennsylvania 19446
Phone: 215-361-8100

3847 Washington Road
McMurray, Pennsylvania
15317
Phone: 412-942-4777

Walmart Plaza Route 18 &
Route 51
Monaca, Pennsylvania 15061
Phone: 412-774-6244

880 Narrows Run Road
Moon Township, Pennsylvania
15108
Phone: 412-264-7577

Holiday Center
3747 William Penn Highway
Monroeville, Pennsylvania
15146
Phone: 412-372-3380

1828 Union Ave
Natrona Heights,
Pennsylvania 15065
Phone: 412-224-7240

9181 Roosevelt Blvd
Philadelphia, Pennsylvania
19114
Phone: 215-969-5521

4885 McKnight Road
Pittsburgh, Pennsylvania
15237
Phone: 412-366-8480

Southland Shopping Center
525 Clariton B
Pittsburgh, Pennsylvania
15236
Phone: 412-653-3328

223 Shoemaker Road
Pottstown, Pennsylvania
19456
Phone: 610-323-7100

3951 Perkiomen Avenue
Reading, Pennsylvania 19606
Phone: 610-779-8360

1149 Lancaster Avenue
Rosemont, Pennsylvania
19010
Phone: 610-519-9530

735 Scranton Carb Highway
Scranton, Pennsylvania
18508
Phone: 717-347-4148

500 Baltimore Pike
Springfield, Pennsylvania
19064
Phone: 610-543-2008

225 S Allen Street
State College, Pennsylvania
16801
Phone: 814-237-7066

Route 611 S.
Tannersville Plaza
Tannersville, Pennsylvania
18372
Phone: 717-620-9777

Play It Again Sports

864 West Street Road
Warminster, Pennsylvania
18974
Phone: 215-443-5661

Shop Rite Shopping Center
1115 Westchester
West Chester, Pennsylvania
19380
Phone: 610-429-9764

500 N York Road
Willow Grove, Pennsylvania
19090
Phone: 215-657-7001

2556 MacArthur Road
White Hall, Pennsylvania
18052
Phone: 610-770-7850

Rhode Island

52 Frenchtown Road
N Kingston, Rhode Island
02852
Phone: 401-885-6760

South Carolina

3501 Clemson Blvd
Anderson, South Carolina
29621
Phone: 864-231-9268

7372A Two Notch Road
Columbia, South Carolina
29223
Phone: 803-419-8303

1234B Pleasantburg Drive
Greenville, South Carolina
29607

Phone: 864-268-2407

7800 Rivers Avenue
Suite 1250
North Charleston,
South Carolina 29406
Phone: 803-572-8255

445 S Blackstock Road
Spartanburg, South Carolina
29301
Phone: 864-595-9911

South Dakota

224 S. Main Street
Aberdeen, South Dakota
57401
Phone: 605-225-8281

660 N LaCrosse
Rapid City, South Dakota
57701
Phone: 605-341-7529

3109 W 41st Street Suite 3
Sioux Falls, South Dakota
57105
Phone: 605-339-2444

Tennessee

5354B Mt. View Road
Antioch, Tennessee 37103
Phone: 615-731-9077

6227 Lee Highway Suite C
Chattanooga, Tennessee
37421
Phone: 423-855-4672

2880 Wilma Rudolph Blvd
Clarksville, Tennessee 37040
Phone: 615-645-8033

1791 Germantown Parkway
Cordova, Tennessee 38018
Phone: 901-753-7337

1745 Galleria Blvd Suite 2010
Franklin, Tennessee 37604
Phone: 615-771-8811

8422 Kingston Pike
Knoxville, Tennessee 37919
Phone: 423-694-8129

3650 Ridgeway Road
Memphis, Tennessee 38115
Phone: 901-797-9819

2107 Gallatin Road North
Madison, Tennessee 37115
Phone: 615-851-6190

Texas

4657 South 14th Street
Abilene, Texas 79605
Phone: 915-692-7427

7306 W 34th Street Suite C7
Amarillo, Texas 79121
Phone: 806-353-5201

2223 W Park Row Drive
Arlington, Texas 76013
Phone: 817-277-2313

2620 S Lamar
Austin, Texas 78704
Phone: 512-444-2270

2923 W Anderson Lane
Austin, Texas 78757
Phone: 512-451-8976

13450 Research Blvd Suite
102
Austin, Texas 78750
Phone: 512-331-9739

2661 Midway Road Suite 219
Carrollton, Texas 75006
Phone: 972-380-5550

2218 S Texas Ave
College Station, Texas 77840
Phone: 409-764-8285

14902 Preston Road Suite 506
Dallas, Texas 75240
Phone: 972-720-9666

366 Hillside Village
Dallas, Texas 75214
Phone: 214-821-7737

901 N Polk Street Suite 365
Desoto, Texas 75115
Phone: 972-224-1700

5232 S Hulen Suite 280
Ft. Worth, Texas 76123
Phone: 817-263-0003

13837 Breck
Houston, Texas 77066
Phone: 281-587-0707

19645 Highway 59
Houston, Texas 77338
Phone: 281-446-7529

3557 North Beltline
Irving, Texas 75062
Phone: 972-258-6440

1773 Fry Road
Katy, Texas 77449
Phone: 281-578-6633

405 W Loop 281 Suite J
Longview, Texas 75605
Phone: 903-663-6800

3801 50th Street Suite 13A
Lubbock, Texas 79413
Phone: 806-788-0144

1100 N Towncast Blvd
Suite 102
Mesquite, Texas 75150

Phone: 972-681-1777
3211 West Wadley Suite 22
Midland, Texas 79705
Phone: 915-699-4332

3952A E. 42nd Street
Odessa, Texas 79762
Phone: 915-550-6236

3115 W Parker Road
Suite 335
Plano, Texas 75023
Phone: 972-612-1101

3254 Sherwood Way
San Angelo, Texas 76901
Phone: 915-944-9662

2120 E. South Lake Blvd
Suite C
South Lake, Texas 76092
Phone: 817-329-9090

3374 Highway 6 South
Sugarlands, Texas 77478
Phone: 281-265-9883
473 Sawdust Road
The Woodlands, Texas 77380
Phone: 281-364-9883

1936 ESE Loop 323
Tyler, Texas 75701
Phone: 903-526-7427

6245 Rufe Snow Drive Suite
804
Watauga, Texas 76148
Phone: 817-577-3729

3916 Kemp Blvd Suite N
Wichita Falls, Texas 76308
Phone: 940-691-5200

Utah

1490 N Main
North Logan, Utah 84341
Phone: 801-753-6595

4048 S Riverdale Road
Ogden, Utah 84405
Phone: 801-393-5566

894 N State Street
Orem, Utah 84057
Phone: 801-226-0909

946 W Sunset Blvd Suite J
St George, Utah 84770
Phone: 801-652-8086

2120 S 700 E
Salt Lake City, Utah 84106
Phone: 801-466-4499

6910 S Highland Drive
Salt Lake City, Utah 84121
Phone: 801-944-0094

45 West 10600 S
Sandy, Utah 84070
Phone: 801-576-9000

Virginia

1808 Rio Hill Center
Charlottesville, Virginia
22901
Phone: 804-973-2638

4300 Portsmouth Blvd
Unit 142
Chesapeake, Virginia 23321
Phone: 757-465-4049

1220 Greenbrier Parkway
Suite 130
Chesapeake, Virginia 23320
Phone: 757-382-9592

3195 N Franklin Street
Christianburg, Virginia
24073
Phone: 540-381-1261

5750 Union Mill Road
Clifton, Virginia 22024
Phone: 703-266-8677

305 Mount Cross Road
Danville, Virginia 24540
Phone: 804-752-1620

1116 West Broad Street
Falls Church, Virginia 22046
Phone: 703-241-8304

17860 Forest Road
Forest, Virginia 24551
Phone: 804-385-5811

1249 Jefferson Davis Highway
Fredericksburg, Virginia
22401
Phone: 540-374-9284

1790-100 E Market St
Harrisonburg, Virginia 22801
Phone: 540-568-1816

7356 Bell Creek Road Unite
#15
Mechanicsville, Virginia
23111
Phone: 804-559-1474

4150 Meadowdale Blvd
Richmond, Virginia 23234
Phone: 804-275-9264

8003 W Broad Street
Richmond, Virginia 23294
Phone: 804-527-1988

11523 A Midlothian Turnpike
Richmond, Virginia 23235
Phone: 804-897-3500

4208 K Franklin Road
Roanoke, Virginia 24014
Phone: 540-774-6809

1469 W Main Street
Salem, Virginia 24153
Phone: 540-387-1560

2720 N Mall Drive Suite 112
Virginia Beach, Virginia
23452
Phone: 757-463-1008

Vermont

150 Dorset Street
So. Burlington, Vermont
05043
Phone: 802-865-3021

Washington

14339 NE 20th St
Bellevue, Washington 98007
Phone: 425-643-2599

185 Cascade Mall Drive
Burlington, Washington
98233
Phone: 360-757-7529

309 E. Casino Road Suite B
Everett, Washington 98204
Phone: 425-356-2776

1400 S. 312th St, Suite 1
Federal Way, Washington
98003
Phone: 253-946-2029

755 NW Gilman Blvd Suite R
Issaquah, Washington 98027
Phone: 425-837-9515

371 Triangle Mall
Longview, Washington 98632
Phone: 360-423-3405

731 N Columbia Center
Suite 120
Kennewick, Washington
99336
Phone: 509-736-0890

19513 Highway 99
Lynnwood, Washington 98036
Phone: 425-670-1184

1246 A State Street
Marysville, Washington
98270
Phone: 360-651-7529

17622 108th SE
Renton, Washington 98055
Phone: 425-227-8777

901 East Pike Street
Seattle, Washington 98122
Phone: 206-329-8605

E 14208 Sprague
Spokane, Washington 99216
Phone: 509-924-4031

86 E Francis
Spokane, Washington 99207
Phone: 509-484-1551

8101 NE Parkway Drive
Vancouver, Washington 98662
Phone: 360-260-9440

147 Easy Street
K Mart Plaza Suite 106
Wenatchee, Washington
98807
Phone: 509-663-4103

13210 NE 175th Street
Woodinville, Washington
98072
Phone: 425-481-8676

West Virginia

1804 Grand Central
Vienna, West Virginia 26105
Phone: 304-295-0770

115 Bridge Street Plaza
Wheeling, West Virginia
26003
Phone: 304-243-1477

Wisconsin

611 W Northland Ave
Appleton, Wisconsin 54911
Phone: 920-735-0432

Kings Plaza 3006
London Road
Eau Claire, Wisconsin 54701
Phone: 715-834-0602

3765 S 108th Street
Greenfield, Wisconsin 53228
Phone: 414-541-8848

1924 Ridge Road
Green Bay, Wisconsin 54304
Phone: 414-497-1420

1801 Ward Ave
Hudson, Wisconsin 54016
Phone: 715-386-3993

3000 Milton Ave
Janesville, Wisconsin 53545
Phone: 608-754-3131

5600 75th St
Kenosha, Wisconsin 53142
Phone: 414-694-6640

4100 E Washington Ave
Madison, Wisconsin 53704
Phone: 608-249-5201

720 S Gammon Road
Madison, Wisconsin 53719
Phone: 608-277-1988

North 96 West 18743 City
Line Road
Menomonie Falls, Wisconsin
53051
Phone: 414-250-1506

6905 W Brown Deer Road
Milwaukee, Wisconsin 53223
Phone: 414-355-8776

561 Highway 51 S
Minocqua, Wisconsin 54548
Phone: 715-356-3302

6508 E 27th Street
Oak Creek, Wisconsin 53154
Phone: 414-761-2446

9380 Highway 16
Onalaska, Wisconsin 54650
Phone: 608-783-4932

1924 South Koeller
Oshkosh, Wisconsin 54901
Phone: 920-231-5200

1620 S Main Stret
Rice Lake, Wisconsin 54868
Phone: 715-234-9141

1699 Schofield Ave Suite 200
Scholfield, Wisconsin 54476
Phone: 715-359-9240

559 South Taylor Drive
Sheboygan, Wisconsin 53081
Phone: 920-458-3844

3272 Church St
Stevens Point, Wisconsin
54481
Phone: 715-341-1762

8020 Durand Ave
Sturtevant, Wisconsin 53177
Phone: 414-886-4949

114 Belknat
Superior, Wisconsin 54880
Phone: 715-392-3700

608 S. Church Street
Watertown, Wisconsin 53094
Phone: 920-261-8588

W229 N 1416 Westwood Drive
Waukesha, Wisconsin 53228
Phone: 414-542-7962

10111 W Capital Drive
Wauwatosa, Wisconsin 53222
Phone: 414-461-5600

Wyoming

303 Cole Shopping Center
Cheyenne, Wyoming 82001
Phone: 307-637-4030

Canada

24 Stewart Green SW
Calgary, AB T3H 3C8
Phone: 403-686-4228

H2-55 Castle Ridge Blvd. NE
Calgary, AB T3J 3J8
Phone: 403-280-0425

9726 170 Street
Edmonton, AB T5T 5L5
Phone: 403-448-5858

220 Manning Crossing
Edmonton, AB T5A 1A5
Phone: 403-448-1251

Play It Again Sports

222 Baseline Road #378
Sherwood Park, AB T8H 1S8
Phone: 403-417-0488

244 Highway 97 N
Kelowna, BC V1Z 4J2
Phone: 250-868-2115

2748 Laughead Highway
Suite 106
Port Coquitlam, BC V3B 6P2
Phone: 604-464-7529

420 500 Notre Dame Drive
Kamloops, BC V2C 6T6
Phone: 250-851-9799

1601 Victoria Street
Prince George, BC V2L 2L4
Phone: 250-562-1951

1180 Marine Drive
Vancouver, BC V7P 1S8
Phone: 604-988-5557

1717 Bedford Highway
Bedford, NS B4A 3X1
Phone: 902-835-8187

Woodlawn Shopping Center
Woodland R
Dartmouth, NS B2W 2S7
Phone: 902-434-7979

3627 Joseph Howe Drive
Halifax, NS B30 4H8
Phone: 902-454-4400

212 McAllister Drive
Saint John, NB E2H 2L1
Phone: 506-652-2030

516 Topsail Road
St. Johns, NF A1E 2C5
Phone: 709-745-7533

152 Prince Street
Sydney, NS B1P 3K5
Phone: 902-562-7200

184 Arthur Street
Truro, NS B2N 5B2
Phone: 902-895-7778

75 Bayley Street W
Ajax, Ontario L1S 7K8
Phone: 905-428-2272

4 Elgin Street
Amprior, Ontario K7S 1N3
Phone: 613-623-1599

165 Wellington Street W.
Barrie, Ontario L4N 1L7
Phone: 905-270-3731

366 N Front Street
Belleville, Ontario K8P 5E6
Phone: 613-966-4401

258 A. Queen Street E
Brampton, Ontario L6V 1B9
Phone: 905-456-1331

245 King George Road
Brantford, Ontario N3R 7N7
Phone: 519-751-7378

3315 Fairview Street
Burlington, Ontario L7N 3N9
Phone: 905-639-8872

37 9th Street East
Cornwall, Ontario K6H 6R3
Phone: 613-936-2020

138 Hurontario Street
Collingwood, Ontario L9Y
2L8
Phone: 705-446-0633

773C The Queens Way
Etobicoke, Ontario M8Z 1NZ
Phone: 416-503-2288

218 Silver Creek Parkway
Guelph, Ontario N1H 7P8
Phone: 519-822-0900

1025 Upper Wentworth
Hamilton, Ontario L9A 5B3
Phone: 905-387-9900

640 Bath Road
Kingston, Ontario K7M 4X6
Phone: 613-389-8647

500 Fairway Road South
Suite 2-3
Kitchner, Ontario N2C 1X3
Phone: 519-748-5809

9275 Markham Road
Markham, Ontario L6E1 A11
Phone: 905-471-9652

3825 Richmond Road
Nepean, Ontario K2H 1A5
Phone: 613-820-3600

1495 Seymour Street
North Bay, Ontario P1B 8G4
Phone: 705-840-2513

2701 St Joseph Blvd
Orleans, Ontario K1C 1G4
Phone: 613-837-7529

1679 Carling Ave.
Ottawa, Ontario K2A 1C4
Phone: 613-798-5000

1721 Bank Street
Ottowa, Ontario K1V 7Z4
Phone: 613-731-6006

1135 Lansdown St NE Suite 23
Peterborough, Ontario K9J
7M2
Phone: 705-741-6110

318 Ontario Street
St Catharines, Ontario L2R

5L8
Phone: 905-688-6226

165 Indian Road South
Sarnia, Ontario N7T 3W3
Phone: 519-344-7400

126 Great Northern Road
Sault St Marie, Ontario
P6B 4Z1
Phone: 705-949-7009

2488 Gerrard Street E
Scarborough, Ontario
M1N1 W8
Phone: 416-690-0666

2055 Lawrence Ave. East
Scarborough, Ontario
M1R 2Z4
Phone: 416-285-7529

900 LaSalle Blvd. #R
Sudbury, Ontario P3A 5W8
Phone: 705-566-1236

414 Algonquin Blvd East
Timmins, Ontario P4N 1B6
Phone: 705-267-7427

1082 Memorial Avenue
Thunder Bay, Ontario
P7B 4A3
Phone: 807-622-8282

3456 Yonge Street
Toronto, Canada M4N 2N4
Phone: 416-488-6471

2625 C Weston Road Unit 38
Weston, Ontario M9N 3V9
Phone: 416-244-9640

5980 Tecumseh Road E
Windsor, Ontario N8T 1E3
Phone: 519-945-2202

1801 Dundas Street E Suite 24
Whitby, Ontario L1N 2L3
Phone: 905-728-8881

Play It Again Sports

655 University Ave
Charlottetown, PE C1E 1E5
Phone: 902-628-1223

2973 St Charles Road
Kirkland, PQ H9J IN5
Phone: 514-697-1079

2100 Decarie Blvd
Montreal, PQ H4A 3J3
Phone: 514-484-5150

550 Rue Marais Unit 19
Quebec City, PQ G1M 3R1
Phone: 418-688-3311

Photos courtesy of Play It Again Sports

3838 Tacherau Blvd
Greenfield Park, PQ J4V 2H9
Phone: 514-923-1023

365 Blvd Harwood
Dorion, PQ J7V 7W1
Phone: 514-455-6464

3260 St. Martim Blvd West
Laval, PQ H7T 1A1
Phone: 514-681-8008

816 Albert Street
Regina, SK S4R 2P5
Phone: 306-757-7529

318 Main Street N.
Moose Jaw, SK S6H 319
Phone: 306-693-0768

TVI Inc - Corporate Office
11400 SE 6th Street
Suite 220
Bellevue, Washington 98004
Phone: 425-462-1515
Web site: http://
www.valuevillage.com

Established in Renton,
Washington in 1966, Value
Village, Savers and Village des
Valeurs stores have grown into
over 150 highly successful
locations throughout the United
States, Canada & Australia.

The stores purchase their
merchandise from over sixty
various charities such as Big
Brothers, Big Sisters, United
Cerebral Palsy & the Canadian
Diabetes Association.

Known for their professional and
friendly service, the stores
average 20,000 spacious square
feet of wonderful merchandise.
They carry men's, women's &
children's apparel, plus sizes,
maternity wear, vintage clothing,
household items & much more at
prices that are hard to beat.

Some of the store locations offer
a 20% senior discount once a
week (inquire at store location).

Visa, Mastercard, Discover &
personal checks are accepted in
most locations. In Canadian
locations bank debit cards are
accepted. Within seven days
tagged merchandise can be
exchanged for a store credit.

Other promotions throughout the
year include 50% off everything
sale which is held on June 13 &
December 5, 1998.

The stores have been featured on
TV, newspapers and on the radio
including *The Today Show, The
The Wall Street Journal and
Forbes Magazine.*

By the year 2000 there will be
two hundred fantastic store
locations.

Photos courtesy of TVI, Inc.

Alaska

Value Village
5437 E. Northern Lts. Blvd.
Anchorage, Alaska 99504
Phone: 907-337-2184

Value Village
501 E Dimond Blvd.
Anchorage, Alaska 99515
Phone: 907-522-9090

Value Village
3027 Airport Way
Fairbanks, Alaska 99701
Phone: 907-474-4828

Arkansas

Savers
2516 Cantrell Road
Little Rock, Arkansas 72202
Phone: 501-603-9831

Arizona

Savers
1106 N. Arizona Avenue
Chandler, Arizona 85224
Phone: 602-899-7776

Savers
5060 N. Highway 89
Flagstaff, Arizona 86004
Phone: 520-526-1066

Savers
2049 West Broadway Road
Mesa, Arizona 85202
Phone: 602-962-1552

Savers
13621 N. 32nd Street
Phoenix, Arizona 85032
Phone: 602-971-7704

Savers
2929 N. 75th Ave. #18A
Phoenix, Arizona 85033
Phone: 602-849-8580

Savers
3517 West Bell Road
Phoenix, Arizona 85023
Phone: 602-938-1616

Savers
5542 E. Thomas Road
Phoenix, Arizona 85018
Phone: 602-840-3181

Savers
2625 W. Bethany Home Road
Phoenix, Arizona 85017
Phone: 602-242-4288

Savers
290 West Fort Lowell Road
Tucson, Arizona 85705
Phone: 520-292-6330

Savers
5845 E. Broadway Blvd.
Tucson, Arizona 85711
Phone: 520-571-2001

California

Savers
2840 Geneva Avenue
Daly City, California 94014
Phone: 415-468-0646

Savers
19131 Magnolia Street
Huntington Beach,
California 92646
Phone: 714-962-6881

Savers
60 S. Dempsey Road
Milpitas, California 95035
Phone: 408-263-8338

Savers
875 Main Street
Redwood City, California
94063
Phone: 415-364-5545

Savers
2222 Business Circle
San Jose, California 95128
Phone: 408-287-0591

Colorado

Savers
12303 E Mississippi Avenue
Aurora, Colorado 80012
Phone: 303-365-2450

Savers
695 S. Broadway
Boulder, Colorado 80303
Phone: 303-499-6979

Savers
1977 Sheridan Blvd.
Edgewater, Colorado 80214
Phone: 303-274-8452

Savers
4106 S. College Ave #100
Ft. Collins, Colorado 80525
Phone: 970-282-9446

Savers
1400 W. Littleton Blvd.
Littleton, Colorado 80120
Phone: 303-794-6640

Hawaii

Savers
1505 Dillingham Blvd
Honolulu, Hawaii 96817
Phone: 808-842-0061

Savers
25 Kaneohe Bay Drive
Kailua, Oahu Hawaii 96734
Phone: 808-254-1118

Savers
326 Hanamau Street
Kahului, Hawaii 96732
Phone: 808-871-7244

Idaho

Savers
10475 Fairview Avenue
Boise, Idaho 83704
Phone: 208-377-2001

Massachusetts

Savers
109 S. Mariano Bishop Blvd.
Fall River, Massachusetts
02720
Phone: 508-675-6592

Savers
1277 Liberty Street
Springfield, Massachusetts
01104
Phone: 413-746-2242

Savers
1024 Kings Highway
New Bedford, Massachusetts
02745
Phone: 508-998-3899

Savers
126 Parkingway
Quincy, Massachusetts 02169
Phone: 617-479-7033

Savers
1600 VFW Parkway
West Roxbury, Massachusetts
02132
Phone: 617-323-8231

Minnesota

Savers
8049 Morgan Circle
Bloomington, Minnesota
55431
Phone: 612-881-7300

Savers
4849 Central Ave NE
Columbia Heights,
Minnesota 55421
Phone: 612-571-1319

Savers
2124 E Lake Street
Minneapolis, Minnesota
55407
Phone: 612-729-9271

Savers
3326 W. Division Street
St. Cloud, Minnesota 56301
Phone: 320-203-0558

Savers
235 E Maryland Avenue
St. Paul, Minnesota 55117
Phone: 612-488-6293

Nebraska

Savers
4690 Leighton Avenue
Lincoln, Nebraska 68504
Phone: 402-467-1991

Nevada

Savers
5130 Spring Mountain Road
Las Vegas, Nevada 89102
Phone: 702-220-7350

1100 E. Charleston Blvd.
Las Vegas, Nevada 89104
Phone: 702-474-4773

Savers
3145 E. Tropicana Ave.
Las Vegas, Nevada 89121
Phone: 702-433-1402

Savers
2350 Oddie Blvd.
Sparks, Nevada 89431
Phone: 702-359-4244

New Mexico

Savers
3300 San Mateo Blvd. NE
Albuquerque, New Mexico
87110
Phone: 505-888-0116

Ohio

Savers
6272 Pearl Road
Parma Heights, Ohio 44130

Phone: 216-887-0870

Oregon

Value Village
850 Biddle Road
Medford, Oregon 97504
Phone: 541-770-6829

Value Village
18625 SE McLoughlin Blvd
Milwaukie, Oregon 97222
Phone: 503-653-7333

Value Village
5050 SE 82nd Street
Portland, Oregon 97266
Phone: 503-771-5472

Value Village
2460 Mission SE
Salem, Oregon 97302
Phone: 503-362-8858

Value Village
555 W. Centennial Blvd.
Springfield, Oregon 97477
Phone: 541-747-8339

Value Viallge
12060 SW Main
Tigard, Oregon 97223
Phone: 503-684-1982

Rhode Island

Savers
1925 Pawtucket Avenue
East Providence, Rhode Island
02914
Phone: 401-438-1955

Savers
1525 Smith Street
N. Providence, Rhode Island
02908

Savers, Value Village & Village des Valeurs

Texas

Savers
10780 Pebble Hills Blvd.
El Paso, Texas 79935
Phone: 915-590-9070

Savers
7645 Dashwood Drive
Houston, Texas 77036
Phone: 713-772-8003

Savers
2015-50th Street
Lubbock, Texas 79412
Phone: 806-747-7500

Utah

Savers
39 West 7200 South
Midvale, Utah 84047
Phone: 801-561-4199

Savers
3833 Washington Blvd.
Ogden, Utah 84403
Phone: 801-399-3919

Savers
81 North State Street
Orem, Utah 84057
Phone: 801-225-9445

Savers
4145 S. Redwood Road
Taylorsville, Utah 84123
Phone: 801-262-2150

Washington

Value Village
3390 Meridian Street
Bellingham, Washington
98226
Phone: 360-733-2333

Value Village
3449 Wheaton Way
Bremerton, Washington
98310
Phone: 360-479-7998

Value Village
131 SW 157th
Burien, Washington 98166
Phone: 206-246-6237

Value Village
6220 Evergreen Way
Everett, Washington 98203
Phone: 206-355-8320

Value Village
32945 Pacific Highway S.
Federal Way, Washington
98003
Phone: 253-874-3966

Value Village
27241 132nd Ave. SE
Kent, Washington 98042
Phone: 253-630-9885

Value Village
17216 Highway 99
Lynnwood, Washington 98036
Phone: 425-745-6603

Value Village
525 E. College Way
Mt. Vernon, Washington
98273
Phone: 360-416-0104

Value Village
2100 West Harrison
Olympia, Washington 98501
Phone: 360-786-5630

Value Village
1124 River Road
Puyallup, Washington 98371
Phone: 253-848-1582

Value Village
16771 Redmond Way
Redmond, Washington 98052
Phone: 425-883-2049

Value Village
1222 Bronson Way N.
Renton, Washington 98055
Phone: 425-255-5637

Value Village
12548 Lake City Way NE
Seattle, Washington 98125
Phone: 206-365-8232

Value Village
2929 27th Ave. S
Seattle, Washington 98144
Phone: 206-723-5000

Value Village
8700 15th Ave. NW
Seattle, Washington 98117
Phone: 206-783-4648

Value Village
1525 11th Avenue
Seattle, Washington 98122
Phone: 206-322-7789

Value Village
West 708 Boone
Spokane, Washington 99201
Phone: 509-325-2569

Value Village
13112 East Sprague
Spokane, Washington 99216
Phone: 509-921-7889

Value Village
8025 South Hosmer Street
Tacoma, Washington 98408
Phone: 253-539-0886

Value Village
2503 Main Street
Union Gap, Washington
98903
Phone: 509-454-4060

Value Village
7110 NE Fourth Plain Road
Vancouver, Washington 98661
Phone: 360-944-5225

Wisconsin

Savers
3015 E. Hamilton Avenue
Eau Claire, Wisconin 54701
Phone: 715-835-8500

Savers
1880 E. Washington Avenue
Madison, Wisconsin 53704
Phone: 608-240-0768

Canada

Value Village
104-58th Ave. SE
Calgary, AB T2H ON7
Phone: 403-255-5501

Value Village
104-58th Ave. SE
Calgary, AB T2H ON7
Phone: 403-255-5501

Value Village
3405-34th Street NE
Calgary, AB T1Y 6J6
Phone: 403-291-3323

Value Village
8930-82nd Avenue
Edmonton, AB T6C 0Z3
Phone: 403-468-1259

Value Village
11850-103rd Street
Edmonton, AB T5G 2J2
Phone: 403-477-0025

Value Village
9450-163rd Street
Edmonton, AB T5P 3M7
Phone: 403-484-4177

Thrift Village
1616 Mayor Magrath Drive
Lethbridge, AB T1K 5X7
Phone: 403-320-5358

Value Village
2235 50th Avenue
Reed Deer, AB T4R 1L2
Phone: 403-343-3000

Value Village
7350 Edmonds Street
Burnaby, BC V3N 1A8
Phone: 604-540-4066

Value Village
31970 S. Fraser Way
Clearbrook, BC V2T 1W6
Phone: 604-850-3712

Value Village
540 Clarke Road
Coquitlam, BC V3J 3X5
Phone: 604-937-7087

Value Village
444 Seymour Street
Kamloops, BC V2C 2G6
Phone: 250-374-6609

Value Village
190 Aurora Crescent
Kelowna, BC V1X 7M3
Phone: 250-491-1356

Value Village
5666 Glover Road
Langley, BC V3A 4H8

Phone: 604-533-1663

Value Village
110-22255 Dewdney
Trunk Road
Maple Ridge, BC V2X 3J1
Phone: 604-467-5585

Value Village
530-5th Street Suite 101
Nanaimo, BC V9R 1P2
Phone: 250-741-0803

Value Village
1666 Spruce Street
Prince George, BC V2L 2R3
Phone: 250-561-0311

Value Village
10642 King George Highway
Surrey, BC V3T 2X3
Phone: 604-588-5225

Value Village
1820 E. Hastings Street
Vancouver, BC V5L 1T2
Phone: 604-254-4282

Value Village
6415 Victoria Drive
Vancouver, BC V5P 3X5
Phone: 604-327-4434

Value Village
1810 Store Street
Victoria, BC V8T 4R4
Phone: 250-380-9422

Village des Valeurs
3860 Blvd. Taschereau
Greenfield Park, PQ J4V 2H9
Phone: 514-923-4767

Village des Valeurs
7401 Newman Blvd.
LaSalle, PQ H8N 1X3
Phone: 514-595-8101

Village des Valeurs
875 Cure Labelle

Laval, PQ H7V 2V2
Phone: 514-978-4191

Village des Valeurs
4906 W. Jean Talon Street
Montreal, PQ H4P 1W9
Phone: 514-739-1962

Village des Valeurs
6779 Jean Talon East
Montreal, PQ H1S 1N2
Phone: 514-254-0433

Village des Valeurs
2033 Pie IX
Montreal, PQ H1V 9Z7
Phone: 514-528-8604

Village des Valeurs
2555 Boul Montmorency
Quebec City, PQ G1J 5J3
Phone: 418-660-5840

Village des Valeurs
3355 de la Perade
Ste. Foy, PQ G1X 3V3
Phone: 418-651-2772

Village des Valeurs
6055 Boul. Jean XXIII
Trois Rivieres, PQ G8Z 4NB
Phone: 819-694-9929

Village des Valeurs
1730 Boulevard Talbot
Ville de Chicoutimi G7H 587
Phone: 418-690-2030

Value Village
1695 Ellice Ave.
Winnipeg, MB R3H 0A9
Phone: 204-774-1315

Value Village
942 Jefferson Avenue
Winnipeg, MB R2P 1W1
Phone: 204-694-6844

Value Village
1729 Pembina Highway
Winnipeg, MB R3T 2G6
Phone: 204-261-8719

Value Village
1560 Regent Avenue
Winnipeg, MB R2C 3D4
Phone: 204-661-9045

Value Village
42 Canal Street
Dartmouth, NS B2Y 2W3
Phone: 902-463-4054

Value Village
Unit A
209 Chain Lake Drive
Halifax, NS B3S 1C9
Phone: 902-450-5134

Value Village
212 McAlister Drive
St. John, NB E2L 3S2
Phone: 506-696-5301

Value Village
161 Kenmount Road
St. Johns, NF A1B 3P9
Phone: 709-726-5200

Value Village
298 Wayne Gretzky Parkway
Barntford, ON N3S 7P2
Phone: 519-751-4424

Value Village
150 West Drive
Brampton, ON L6T 4P9
Phone: 905-451-7975

Value Village
480 Hespeler Road
Cambridge, ON N1R 7R9
Phone: 519-624-1812

Value Village
2340 Fairview Street
Burlington, ON L7R 2E3
Phone: 905-631-6990

Value Village
1520 Steeles Avenue West
Concord, ON L4K 3B9
Phone: 905-761-7990

Value Village
45 Woodbine Downs Blvd.
Etobicoke, ON M9W 6N5
Phone: 416-675-7450

Value Village
214 Silvercreek Parkway N.
Guelph, ON N1H 7PS
Phone: 519-821-9994

Value Village
530 Fennell Ave.
Hamilton, ON L8V 1S9
Phone: 905-318-0409

Value Village
412 Bath Road
Kingston, ON K7M 4X6
Phone: 613-544-4849

Value Village
120 Ottawa Street N.
Kitchener, ON N2H 3K5
Phone: 519-576-4403

Value Village
4464 Wellington Road
London, ON N6E 2Z8
Phone: 519-680-3711

Value Village
3130 Dixie Road
Mississauga, Ontario L4Y 1Z9
Phone: 905-949-4440

Value Village
2345 Keele Street
North York, ON M6M 4A3
Phone: 416-247-7372

Value Village
1824 Bank Street
Ottawa, ON K1Z 7Y6
Phone: 613-526-5551

Value Village
1162 Cyrville Road
Ottawa, ON K1J 7S9
Phone: 613-749-4977

Value Village
1230 Broad Street
Regina, SK S4R 1Y3
Phone: 306-522-1228

Value Village
10620 Yonge Street
Richmond Hill, ON L4C 3C8
Phone: 905-737-7444

Value Village
1379 London Road
Sarnia, ON N7S 1P6
Phone: 519-541-0153

Value Village
2115 Faithfull Avenue
Saskatoon, S7K 1T8
Phone: 306-668-6161

Value Village
360 Ontario Street E.
St. Catharines, ON L2R 5L8
Phone: 905-688-7764

Value Village
248 Northern Ave. E
Sault Ste. Marie, ON P6B
4H1
Phone: 705-256-1801

Value Village
3701 Lawrence Ave. E. #1
Scarborough, ON M1G 1P7
Phone: 416-439-4464

Value Village
840 Queenston Road
Stoney Creek, ON L8G 4A8
Phone: 905-664-8884

Value Village
799 Notre Dame Avenue
Sudbury, ON P3A 2T2
Phone: 705-525-2339

Value Village
45 Keltic Drive
Sydney River, ON B1S 1P4
Phone: 902-562-6205

Value Village
1319 Bloor Street W.
Toronto, ON M6H 1P3
Phone: 416-539-0585

Value Village
2119 Danforth Avenue
Toronto, ON M4C 1J9
Phone: 416-698-0621

Value Village
924 Queen Street E.
Toronto, ON M4M 1J5
Phone: 416-778-4818

Value Village
2411 Dougall Avenue
Windsor, ON N8X 1T3
Phone: 519-250-8818

Australia

Savers
330 Sydney Road
Brunswick, Victoria 3056
Phone: 139-281-2800

Women's American ORT

Women's American ORT
National Office
315 Park Avenue South
New York, New York 10010
Phone: 212-505-7700

Founded in Brooklyn, New York back in 1927, Women's American ORT is a membership-based Jewish organization whose fund-raising activities support the worldwide ORT network of vocational & technological training in Israel, the United States, South America, France, India, cities in the former Soviet Union & Eastern Europe. As part of their fund-raising effort, Women's American ORT runs numerous thrift shops throughout the United States that carry a vast assortment of clothing, accessories, housewares & more.

California

Clothesport
3702 Grand Avenue
Oakland, California 94610

Store Hours
Monday-Saturday 11am-4pm
Phone: 510-547-2656

Clothing for women, jewelry, handbags, hats & shoes
Accepts cash, checks,
Visa & Mastercard

Store Policy: Donations accepted anytime
Store Specials: Occasional sales throughout the year

Florida

ORT Thrift Shop
5400 N. Dixie Highway
Boca Raton, Florida 33487

Store Hours:
Monday-Friday 10am-4pm
Saturday 10am-3pm
Phone: 561-997-6160

Clothing for women & men, shoes, toys, furniture, jewelry & bric- a-brac all at great prices!
Accepts cash & checks

Store Policy: Donations accepted during store hours

Store Specials: Occasional sales throughout the year

ORT'S Nearly New Shop
3188 S. University Drive
Miramar, Florida 33025

Store Hours:
Monday-Saturday 10am-5pm
Phone: 954-436-3184

Clothing for men & women, furniture, jewelry, bric-a-brac & books
Accepts cash & checks

Store Policy: Donations welcome during store hours & pick-up is available for furniture

Illinois

ORT Resale Shop
915 Chicago Avenue
Evanston, Illinois 60202

362

Store Hours:
Monday-Saturday 9am-5pm
Phone: 847-864-6099

Clothing for the entire family,
furniture, jewelry, bric-a-brac &
books
Accepts cash, checks, Visa &
Mastercard

Store Policy: Donations accepted
anytime during store hours

Store Specials: Monthly sales on
select merchandise

Mention this listing in
*The Ultimate Consignment &
Thrift Store Guide* at
ORT Resale Shop
915 Chicago Avenue
Evanston, Illinois & save 25%
off one clothing purchase

ORT Resale & Book Shop
800 Central Avenue
Highland Park, Illinois 60035

Store Hours:
Monday-Friday 9am-4:30pm
Phone: 847-433-1697

Clothing for the entire family,
furniture, jewelry, bric-a-brac,
books, toys, housewares & linens
Accepts cash & checks

Store Policy: Donations welcome
Store Specials: Daily specials!

Iowa

Ortique
329 5th Street
West Des Moines, Iowa 50265

Store Hours:
Monday-Saturday 10am-5pm
Phone: 515-279-0288

Designer clothing for women &
men, jewelry & handbags
Accepts cash, checks, Visa,
Mastercard & Discover

Store Policy: Donations accepted
by appointment

Store Specials: Occasional sales
throughout the year

Michigan

Clothesport
3026 W. Twelve Mile Road
Berkeley, Michigan 48072

Store Hours:
Monday-Saturday 10am-5pm
Phone: 248-395-5019

Clothing for the entire family,
jewelry, bric-a-brac, books, small
household items & linens
Accepts cash, checks, Visa &
Mastercard

Store Policy: Donations welcome
Store Specials: Weekly sales on
select merchandise

New Jersey

Once Again Shop
1350 Queen Anne Road
Teaneck, New Jersey 07666

Store Hours:
Monday, Tuesday, Wednesday &
& Friday 10am-5pm
Thursday 10am-7pm
Phone: 201-833-0027

Clothing for the entire family, small furniture, jewelry, bric-a-brac, housewares, paintings & toys
Accepts cash & checks

Store Policy: Donations accepted anytime during store hours

Store Specials: Occasional sales throughout the year

Ohio

S'ORT of New
4469 Mayfield Road
South Euclid, Ohio 44121

Store Hours:
Monday-Saturday 10am-5:45pm
Phone: 216-382-3530

Clothing for the entire family, furniture, jewelry, bric-a-brac, books & sports equipment
Accepts cash, Visa & Mastercard

Store Policy: Donations accepted anytime during store hours
Store Specials: On Mondays, select items are half price

Second Act
5201 Monroe Street
Toledo, Ohio 43623

Store Hours:
Monday-Saturday 10am-5pm
Phone: 419-885-2224

Clothing for women & men, furniture, jewelry, bric-a-brac & books
Accepts cash, checks, Visa & Mastercard

Store Policy: Donations accepted anytime during store hours

Pennyslvania

S'ORT of New Shop
7592 Haverford Avenue
Philadelphia, Pennsylvania
19157

Store Hours:
Monday, Tuesday 9am-5:30pm,
Wednesday & Thursday 9:30am-7pm
Friday 9:30am-5pm
Saturday 10am-4pm
Sunday 11:30am-3:30pm
Phone: 215-473-5590

Clothing for women & men, furniture, jewelry & bric-a-brac
Accepts cash, Visa, Mastercard & Discover

Store Policy: Donations welcome Tuesday-Friday 11am-4pm

Store Specials: On-going store sales throughout the year

ORT Value Center
29 South 19th Street
Philadelphia, Pennsylvania
19103

Store Hours:
Monday, Tuesday, Thursday & Friday 10am-4:45pm
Wednesday 9:30am-5:15pm
Phone: 215-563-2377

Clothing for the entire family, jewelry, bric-a-brac & books
Accepts cash, Visa & Mastercard

Store Policy: Donations accepted anytime during store hours

Store Specials: Seniors receive a 10% discount

Act II
5503 Centre Avenue
Pittsburgh, Pennsylvania
15232

Store Hours:
Monday-Friday 10am-5:30pm
Wednesday 10am-7pm
Saturday 10am-4pm
Phone: 412-682-3932

New & gently used designer
clothing for women at discounted
prices, jewelry, handbags, shoes &
hats
Accepts cash, checks, Visa &
Mastercard

Store Policy: Donations accepted

Store Specials: Seniors receive a
10% discount on Tuesday
$1.00 clearance room

Virginia

Act II
10353 Warwick Blvd.
Newport News, Virginia 23601

Store Hours:
Monday-Saturday 9:30am-4:30pm
Phone: 757-595-0507

Clothing for women & jewelry
Accepts cash, checks, Visa,
Mastercard & Discover

Store Policy: Donations accepted
during store hours

Store Specials: Seniors receive a
10% discount on Mondays
Discount sales rack

Act II
816-A West 21st Street
Norfolk, Virginia 23517

Store Hours:
Monday-Saturday 10am-5pm
Phone: 757-622-1533

Clothing for women, new jewelry
& bric-a-brac

Australia

A Bride To Be
Treatts Road
Sydney, Australia

Store Hours:
Monday-Saturday by appointment

Contact: Pam Kirwan
Phone & Fax: 02 94165418

New & pre-loved designer bridal
gowns all at 1/2 to 1/3 off original
cost
Accepts cash, bank cheque or
cheque

Consignment Policy: Gowns must
be in immaculate condition & no
older than eighteen months

Blue Spinach
Recycled & New Designer
Clothing For Men & Women
348 Liverpool Street
Darlinghurst NSW 2010
Sydney, Australia

Store Hours:
Monday-Saturday 10am-6pm &
late trading on Thursday until
8pm

Contact: Mark Thompson &
Jane Wigzell
Phone: 612 9331 3904
Fax: 612 9360 3036

Designer secondhand labels such as
Versace, Armani, Calvin Klein,
Moschino, Dolce & Gabbana &
more for men & women, shoes &
accessories all in excellent
condition. Items sold at a fraction
of original cost.

Consignment Policy: 50/50 split

Items consigned for two months
& must be in pristine condition

Encore La Chance
No 7 Enoggera Terrace
Red Hill
Brisbane, Queensland 4059
Australia

Store Hours:
Monday-Friday 10am-5pm
Saturday 10am-4pm

Contact: Megan Glore
Phone: 07 33683252

Designer label clothing for women
with labels such as Lisa Ho, Adele
Palmer, Country Road, Robert
Burton & more!

Consignment Policy: 50/50 split
Items reduced 20% after three
months

Brotherhood of St Laurence
Head Office
67 Brunswick Street Fitzroy,
3056
Victoria, Australia

Phone: 61 3 9419 7055
Fax: 61 3 9417 2691
e-mail: bhstl@vicnet.net.au
Web site: www.bsl.org.au

The Brotherhood of St. Laurence
provides a wide range of services
for those in need of improving
their economic, social and
personal circumstances in
Australia. The Brotherhood
organization works towards
positive change through
community education, research,
social action and advocacy.

In order to raise funds for the
organization, the Brotherhood

operates more than twenty opportunity shops (thrift shops) throughout Melbourne.
The stores carry a wide variety of clothing for the entire family, books, bric-a-brac and lots of other treasures waiting to be discovered.

Most stores are open from Monday-Friday 9am/9:30am-5pm Saturday from 9am-1pm-some stores are open until 4pm

**Bentleigh:
518 Centre Road**
Phone: 03 9557 6130

Box Hill 948 Whitehorse Road
Phone: 03 9898 6504

Brunswick Clothing: 109 Brunswick Road
Phone: 03 9387 3359

Brunswick Furniture: 132 Barkly Street
Phone: 03 9387 3359

Campbellfield: 1799 Hume Highway
Phone: 03 9303 4128

City: Royal Arcade basement Bourke Street, Melbourne
Phone: 03 9650 3011

City: Shop 51, Ground Floor, Royal Arcade, Bourke Street, Melbourne
Phone: 03 9650 1843

150-152 Smith Street-A Retro Fashion Shop
Phone: 03 9486 0027

Dandenong: 235 Thomas Street
Phone: 03 9792 4414

Eltham Mall, 10 Arthur Street
Phone: 03 9439 3483

Frankston: 19 Rosmith Avenue-New super store!
Phone: 03 9783 5821

Glen Huntly: 1143 Glen Huntly Road
Phone: 03 9571 3879

Greensborough: Rear shop, 106 Main Street
Phone: 03 9434 4221

Ivanhoe: 200 Upper Heidel-berg Road
Phone: 03 9499 1111

Malvern: 215 Glenferrie Road
Phone: 03 9509 2443

Mt. Waverley: 11 Hamilton Walk
Phone: 03 9807 6449

Australia

Niddrie: 2/302-308 Keilor Road
Phone: 03-9374 2655

Northcote: 358 High Street
Phone: 03 9489 6183

Ormond: 5 Katandra Road
Phone: 03 9578 1912

Pakenham: 166 Main Street
Phone: 03 5941 4343

**Rosebud: Shop 2
2/13 Rosebud Parade**
Phone: 03 5986 5488

**Seaford: Shop 1
3 Station Street**
Phone: 03 9786 7015

**Watsonia: Diamond Village
78 Nepean Street**
Phone: 03 9435 1444

**Recycle
433 Bourke Street,
Melbourne
Victoria 3000 Australia**

Store Hours:
Monday-Thursday 10am-6pm
Friday 10am-8pm &
Saturday 10am-3pm

Contact: Peter Harris &
Anita Harris
Phone: 03 9 670 9997
Fax: 03 9 614 0043

High quality pre-loved clothing
for women & men. Featuring
labels like Armani, Zegna, Prada
and leading Australia designers

Consignment Policy: Items must
be in style & no more than 18
months old

Store Specials: January & July
select merchandise is reduced 10%
to 20%

**Re-Cycology
Shop M9/10, Menzies Arcade
Wynard, Sydney 2000
Australia**

Store Hours:
Monday-Friday 8:30am-5:30pm

Contact: Linda Connell
Phone: 02 9290 2630

Upscale designer clothing &
accessories for women. Ventillo,
Trent Nathan, Country Road &
Chanel, just to name a few.

Consignment Policy: 50/50 split

A favorite shop among overseas
airline employees!

The Look Shops provide high
quality clothing at very reasonable
prices. The shops are sponsored
by the Wesley Mission which is
the largest Christian organization
of its type in Australia. The
Wesley Mission Centers provide
services such as counseling,
pastoral services, child and family
care and services to the homeless
and many other wonderful
programs in Australia for those in
need.
Donation bins are located
throughout the Sydney metropolitan area, or items may be donated
at store locations. Pickup is
available for large donations.

Blacktown: 1/107 Main Street
Phone: 9676 2001

Botany: 1375 Botany Road
Phone: 9666 4137

**Campbelltown: 135-141
Queen Street**
Phone: 4628 9366

**City: Level 6, Gowings
Building
Cnr George & Market Street**
Phone: 9267 8637

Fairfield: 1/43 Ware S
Phone: 9755-0619

**Glebe: Shop 10, Glebe Place
131-145 Gelbe Point Road**
Phone: 9566 1525

**Lakemba: Shop 4,
Lakemba Arcade
132 Haldon Street**
Phone: 9759 2836

Leichardt: 93 Norton Street
Phone: 9560 4451

**Liverpool: 4/196 Macquarie
Mall**
Phone: 9822 7051

Newton: 230 King Street
Phone: 9550 2455

Penrith: 470 High Street
Phone: 4732 1422

Randwick: 2 Belmore Road
Phone: 9399 7092

**Rockdale: 478 Princes
Highway**
Phone: 9567 9315

Brussels

**Timeless
Avenue Louise 142A
1050 Brussels
Belgium**

Store Hours:
Tuesday-Friday 1:30pm-7pm
Other days by appointment only

Contact: Rita De Kerpel
Phone: 32.2.64.84.552
e-mail: timeless@skynet.be
Web site: http://www.timeless-antiques.com

Established in 1987, Timeless is Belgium's finest vintage boutique. The store carries a vast selection of high end European vintage clothing including cocktail, evening dresses, jackets & coats circa 1920 to 1960's.
French haute couture clothing from Chanel & Hermes.
A vast selection of in vogue accessories, hats, handbags, scarves, high quality European vintage silver & costume jewelry.
Art deco & nouveau objects.
Accepts cash, Eurocheque, Travelers checks, Amex, Diner's Club, Visa, Mastercard & Eurocard

Store Policy: Items purchased outright

Store Specials: Quantity & dealer discounts available

Bermuda

Bears Repeating
"A Baby & Children's
Consignment Store"
The Marshall Building
#8 South Road
Smith's Parish, Bermuda

Located in the Phase 1 building on
South Shore Road between A-1
Grocery & Mailboxes at
Collectors Hill

Store Hours:
Monday-Saturday 9am-5pm

Contact: Lorene Gibson
Phone: 441-232-2474

High quality name brand children's
clothing, equipment, accessories
& toys including cute teddy bears,
all at great prices!

Consignment Policy
50/50 split on most items except
larger items which consignor
receives 40% of the selling price

Store Specials: Consignments
accepted Monday to Saturday
from 9am-5pm
Twenty item limit per day
excluding maternity

The Barn
44 Devon Springs Road
Devonshire
Bermuda

Mailing address:
The Barn
Box DV273
Devonshire, DVBX
Bermuda

Store Hours:
Thursday & Saturday 9am-12pm

Contact: Lorraine Bills &
Mary Morris
Phone: 441-236-3155
e-mail: lbills@ibl.bm

Clothing for the entire family,
toys, books, CDs, tapes, linens,
jewelry, magazines, bric-a-brac
& much more!
Accepts US & Bermuda dollars,
local, foreign & travelers checks

Store Policy: Donations accepted
Monday-Saturday 9am-12pm

The Barn is operated by the
Hospital Auxiliary of Bermuda
and proceeds are donated to the
hospital. Bargain hunters usually
arrive around 8:30am waiting for
the shop to open. If you want to
avoid the frenzy, arrive after
10am. Lots of hidden treasures
waiting to be discoverd here!

Edmonton

Lasting Impressions
14903-111 Ave
Edmonton, Ab
Canada T5M-2P6

Store Hours: Call for store hours

Phone: 1-800-993-3464
Fax: 403-483-1707
e-mail: lasting@compusmart.ab.ca
Web site: www.comusmart.ab.ca/
lasting

All inclusive shop for brides
including pre-owned & new gowns,
veils, crinolines & shoes,
bridesmaid dresses, mother-of-the
bride dresses & evening wear for
the bridal party
Accepts cash, cheques, Visa &
Mastercard

Store Specials: In house seam-
stress & lay-a-way available

Miramichi

Shared Treasures
484 King George Highway
Miramichi, NB
E1V 1M4
Canada

Store Hours:
Wednesday-Saturday 10am-5pm

Phone: 506-622-2822

Apparel for women including
bridal gowns, evening wear, prom
dresses & fur coats

Consignment Policy: Consignments accepted on Monday &
Tuesday 10am-5pm by appointment

> Present this coupon at
> *Shared Treasures*
> *484 King George*
> *Highway, Miramichi, NB &*
> save 20% off a purchase
>
> Expiration Date: 12/31/99

Pickering

Mulberry Bush
376 Kingston Road
Pickering, Ontario

Store Hours:
Monday, Tuesday, Wednesday &
Saturday 10am-5pm
Thursday & Friday 10am-8pm
Sunday 10am-3pm

Phone: 905-509-6750
e-mail: mulbush@idirect.com
Web site:
www.themulberrybush.com

New & nearly new clothing for
children, boys, books, baby
equipment, nursery furniture &
much more!

Scarborough

Better Beginnings
2849 Kingston Road
Scarborough, Ontario M1M
1N2

Store Hours:
Tuesday & Wednesday 10am-5pm
Thursday & Friday 10am-7pm
Saturday 11am-5pm

Contact: Shirley Sophie
Phone: 416-261-1866

Clothing for the entire family, maternity wear, baby items & more!
Accepts cash, Visa & Interact

Goodwill Toronto-Corporate Office
234 Adelaide Street
Toronto, Ontario M5A 1M9

Phone: 416-362-4711

Goodwill carries clothing for the entire family, furniture, books, small appliances, electronics and housewares. Most shops are open Monday to Friday 9am-9pm, Saturday 9am-6pm & Sunday 10am-5pm. Accepts cash, Interac, Visa & Mastercard.
Goodwill Canada is a non-profit organization whose proceeds provide funds for work training & employment programs to help people become more independent though employment.

250 Bayly St. W.
Ajax, ON L1S 3V4
Phone: 905-428-9130

Barrie
534 Bayfield Street
Barrie, ON L4M 5A3
Phone: 705-737-1286

14 Cedar Pointe Drive
Units 10, 11, 12
Barrie, ON L4N 5R7
Phone: 705-721-5630

382 Queen St. E.
Brampton, ON L6V 1C3
Phone: 905-453-5252

2400 Parkedale Avenue
Brockville, ON K6V 3G8
Phone: 613-498-1103

720 Burnhamthorpe Rd. W.
Unite 3, Credit View Centre
Mississauga, ON L5C 3G1
Phone: 905-949-8660

234 Adelaide Street E.
Toronto, ON M5A 1M9
Phone: 416-362-4710

1224 Dundas St. E., Unit 4
Mississauga, ON L4Y 4A2
Phone: 905-276-5177

548 College Street
Toronto, ON L4Y 4A2
Phone: 416-967-0364

293-299 Coxwell Ave.
Toronto, ON M4L 3B5
Phone: 416-465-8569

1224 Dundas St. E., Unit 2
Mississauga, ON L4Y 4A2
Phone: 905-276-6879

2800 Eglinton Ave. E.
Scarborough, ON M1J 2C9
Phone: 261-7610

4975 Dundas St. W.
Etobicoke, ON M9A 1B6
Phone: 207-9691

3905 Keele St.
Downsview, ON M3J 1N6
Phone: 398-6416

4568 Kingston Road
Scarborough, ON M1E 2P2
Phone: 284-0146

1316 Princess Street
Kingston, ON K7M 3E2
Phone: 613-545-3643

2985 Lakeshore Blvd. W.
Etobicoke, ON M8V 1J8
Phone: 255-3211

9275 Highway #48
Markham, ON L6E 1A1
Phone: 905-201-9311

1111 Davis Drive Unit 1
Newmarket, ON L3Y 7V1
Phone: 905-898-5911

1300 King Street E.
Oshawa, ON L1H 8J4
Phone: 905-434-8202

50 Northside Rod
Nepean, ON K2H 5Z6
Phone: 613-820-8253

60 Overlea Blvd., Unit 4
Toronto, ON M4H 1B6
Phone: 422-0998

306 Gerrard Street East
Toronto, ON M5A 205
Phone: 416-921-3396

9625 Yonge Street
Richmond Hill
ON L4C 572
Phone: 905-737-6460

28 Roncesvalles Road
Toronto, ON M6R 2M6
Phone: 416-534-1686

585 St. Clair Avenue W.
Toronto, ON M6C 1A3
Phone: 416-656-5550

2625A Weston Road
North York, ON M9N 3V8
Phone: 241-2020

2075 Lawrence Ave. E.
Scarborough, ON M1R 2Z4
Phone: 755-1248

1121 Dundas St. E.
Whitby, ON L1N 2K4
Phone: 905-430-6093

Kany's International
773 Annette Street
Toronto, Ontario M6S 2E4

Store Hours:
Tuesday-Friday & Saturday
11am-6pm

Phone: 416-766-6257

Home accessories & gift items
including figurines, curtains,
mirrors, rugs, lamps, artwork, wall
frames, pottery, tableware, dishes
& lots more!

Consignment Policy: 50/50 split
Items consigned for 90 days

Store Specials: After 30 days
items reduced 15%

KidSmart Consignment and
Boutique
419 Jane Street
Toronto, Ontario

Store Hours: Call for store hours

Phone: 416-760-9624

Specializing in gently used
clothing for children & equipment

Off The Cuff
5 Broadway Ave.
Toronto, Canada M4P 177
Located two blocks north of
Eglinton, East of Yonge

Store Hours:
Tuesday & Wednesday 10am-6pm
Thursday 12pm-8pm
Friday 10am-5pm & Saturday
10am-4pm

Canada

Contact: Shelley Romberg
Phone: 416-489-4248

Upscale designer clothing new &
nearly new exclusively for men
Accepts, cash, bankcards,
Mastercard & Visa

**STARticles Film & Music
Artifacts
58 Stewart Street #301
Toronto, Ontario
Canada M5V 1H6**

Store Hours: 11am-7pm

Phone: 416-504-8286
e-mail: info@starticles.com
Web site: www.starticles.com

STARTicles specializes in film &
music artifacts, props & wardrobes. Featuring items such as
Robert DeNiro's custom made
shirt worn in "New York, New
York", Sylvester Stallone's sci-fi
prop gun from "Judge Dredd",
guitar signed by the band "Oasis"
and collections of private letters
including those from Henry Miller
& vintage autographs from
Katherine Hepburn, Bogart &
Gable.
Accepts cash, cheques, Visa,
American Express & International money orders

Other fantastic items received
over the years through STARticles
include a Beatles gold record,
Kirk's tunic from the original Star
Trek, Elvis Presley's stage worn
wardrobe, Dorothy's dress from
The Wizard of Oz, Clint
Eastwood's saddle from
"Unforgiven", just to name
a few. Shopping here will be a

great experience. You are sure to
find that unique, one-of-a-kind
valuable gift at STARticles.

**The Repeat Rider
1777 Avenue Road
Toronto, Ontario
Canada M5M 3Y8**

Store Hours:
Monday, Tuesday, Wednesday &
Friday 10am-6pm
Thursday 10am-7pm
Call for store hours during the
month of December

Contact: Evelyn Teversham
Phone: 416-256-5899
Fax: 416-256-0584
e-mail: et@repeatrider.com

Established over five years ago,
The Repeat Rider offers resale
riding apparel for equestrians &
horse back riding, tack & saddles,
some seconds too!
Accepts cash, cheques, Visa,
Mastercard, American Express &
Debit cards

Consignment Policy: Items
consigned for one year
50/50 split on most items except
saddles
Consignors receive 75%

American Classics
404 Kings Road
Chelsea, SW10
London, England
Store Hours:
Monday-Saturday
10am-6:30pm
Sunday 1pm-5pm

Contact: Peter Rogers
Phone: 0171-351-5229
Fax: 0171-352-9525

Vintage American clothing circa
1940 to 1980
Accepts cash & all major credit
cards

Store Specials: 10% discount
with a cash purchase over 50
pounds

Any Amount Of Books
62 Charing Cross Road
London WC2 HOBB
England

Store Hours:
Monday-Sunday 10:30am-9:30pm

Phone: 0171 836 3697
Fax: 0171 240 1769
Web site:
www.anyamountofbooks.com

Second Location:

Charing Cross Road
Bookshop at 56
London, England

Any Amount Of Books offers a
wide variety of rare books, first
editions, antiquarian,
leatherbound, art & literature.
Many collections are obtained
from mansions, country houses,

villas & chateaus. If you are
looking to create your own
instant library Any Amount of
Books can help you customize
your library according to your
specifications. The shop also
buys books "anywhere in the
known world".

Accepts cash, checks, Visa,
Mastercard & Access

Cenci
31 Monmouth Street
London, England WC2

Store Hours:
Monday-Friday 10:30am-7pm
Saturday 10:30am-6:30pm

Phone: 0171 836 1400
Fax: 0181 766 8564

Vintage clothing & accessories
Accepts cash, checks, American
Express, DC, Visa, Mastercard,
JCB & Switch

Store Specials: Bargain basement-
select items half price

Designs On Her
60 Rosslyn Hill
Hampstead, London NW3
1ND

Store Hours:
Monday-Saturday 10am-5:45pm

Contact: Dominique Cussen
Phone: 0171 435 0100
Fax: 0171 431 3151

Designer clothing & accessories
including belts, handbags, shoes &
jewelry for women, girl's clothing
sizes 0 to 8 & men's ties
Accepts cash, credit cards, Euro

cheques & travellers checks

Consignment Policy:
Items accepted for consignment
Monday, Tuesday & Friday
between 10am-1pm & Thursday
4:30pm to 6:30pm or by special
arrangement
Minimum of three items, must
be fashionable, dry cleaned & in
excellent condition & no more
than two years old
Items consigned for six weeks

Store Specials: Receive a privilege
card when you spend 250 pounds

Designers For Less
203 Uxbridge Road
London W13 9AA

Store Hours:
Monday-Saturday 9am-6pm

Phone: 0181 5795954
Fax: 0181 579 4463

Clothing for women & men
including new & gently used items
& factory seconds

Store Specials: Two clearance sales
per year

Dynasty
Almost New Designer Wear
12A Turnham Green Terrace
Chiswick, London
W4 1QP

Store Hours: Daily 10:30am-5pm

Phone: 0181 995 3846

Top designer clothing for women
Accepts all forms of payment

Store Specials: End of the season
reductions

L'Homme Designer Exchange
50 Blanford Street
London W1
Located off Baker Street

Store Hours:
Monday-Friday 11am-6pm
Thursday 11am-7pm
Saturday 11am-5pm

Phone: 0171 224 3266

Exclusive shop catering to
the "fashion conscious man".
Ties, shirts, sweaters, trousers,
suits & jackets for that perfect
wardrobe. Designers such as Prada,
Versace, Claude Montana, Thierry
Mugler, Gucci & more. Many
items are received from famous
film, TV and music stars.
Inventory is constantly changing!

Pandora
16122 Cheval Place
Knightsbridge
London, England

Store Hours:
Monday-Saturday 9am-6pm

Phone: 0171 589 5289
Fax: 0171 581 9256

Featuring over 5000 items of
clothing & accessories for women

Consignment Policy: Items
consigned for approximately
six months

Store Specials: Seasonal merchandise reduced 30% in July, August
December & January. Select
merchandise reduced 20% in
September & February

Rokit
225 Camden High Street
Camden
London, England

Store Hours:
Monday-Friday 10:30am-6:30pm
Saturday & Sunday 10am-7pm

Phone: 0171 267 3046

Second Location:

23 Kensington Gardens
Brighton
London, England

Store Hours:
Monday-Friday 10:30am-6pm
Saturday 10:30am-6:30pm

Phone: 1273 672 053

Clothing for ladies & gents
featuring labels such as Lee,
Levi's, Wrangler jeans, cords,
cotton shirts, shirts, dresses, furs,
leathers, suedes & leathers,
vintage stock, capital "E" jeans,
jackets & gabardine shirts
Accepts cash, cheques, travellers
cheques (with proper ID) & major
credit cards

Store Specials: 10% discount to
students with valid student ID

Steinberg & Tolkien
193 King's Road
Chelsea
London SW3 5ED

Store Hours:
Monday-Saturday 10:30am-7pm
Sunday 12pm-6pm

Phone: 0171 376 3660

Fax: 0171 360 3630

Vintage couture specializing in
period costume jewelry circa
1900 through 1960. Over 40,000
items on display for the discerning
shopper. World famous shop is
popular among models & fashion
designers.
Accepts cash, checks & all credit
cards

The shop has been featured in
British Vogue.

The Loft
35 Momouth Street
Covent Garden, London WC2
9DD
Nearest tube stop is Covent
Garden

Store Hours:
Monday-Saturday 11am-6pm

Phone: 0171 240 3807

Excellent quality secondhand
designer items for women & men.
Helmut Lang, Comme De
Garcons, Paul Smith, Armani &
more. The boutique type
atmosphere adds to the ambience
of this shop.

The Penguin Society
144 West End Lane
West Hamstead
London NW6 1SD

Store Hours:
Monday-Friday 11am-7pm
Saturday 11am-5:30pm

England

Phone: 0171 625 7778
Fax: 0171 794 6383

Located in "magical privileged village" of West Hampstead in Northwest London, The Penguin Society stocks and trades a vast array of international designer fashions for men & women by top British designers such as Vivienne Westwood, Jasper Conran, Alexander McQueen, English Eccentrics & more.
Decorative jewelry, accessories & bric-a-brac are among other items found at this shop.

Consignment Policy: Clothing may be consigned appointment in the shop or viewed at your home Items consigned for eight weeks

The Penguin Society helps to raise funds for many charities which include health projects, AIDS & children in need.

**The Wedding Shop
171 Fulham Road
Chelsea, London SW3 6JW**

Store Hours:
By appoinment Monday-Saturday

Phone: 0171 838 0171
Fax: 0171 838 1177

Exquisite designer couture wedding dresses at fabulous prices. Choose among gowns designed by Jasper Conran, Neil Cunningham, Anouska Hempel, Phillipa Lepley Catherine Walker and several more.

**Sense
The National Deafblind and Rubella Association**

**Unit 6, Murray Business Centre
Murray Road
Oprington
Kent BR5 3RE**
Phone: 01689 827030
Fax: 01689 821577
Web site: www.Sense.Org.UK

Sense currently operates forty-six charity shops throughout the U.K. & Scotland. All funds from the shops benefit 23,000 deafblind people in the UK and worldwide. Over a million garments are displayed in the shops each year. The shops carry high quality designer label clothing for the entire family, accessories, household items, charity Christmas cards & craft goods produced by deafblind students at the Manor House Craft Centre. The shops accept cash & cheques and are generally open from 9am-4:30pm or 9:30am-5pm.
Due to their great merchandise, twelve new shops per year are are planned to open. Donations are welcome.

Midlands

**182, High Street
Blackheath
Birmingham B65 ODU**
Phone: 0121 561 5684

1, Hampton Walk
Queens Square

165, Castle Square
Weoley Castle
Birmingham B29 2DP
Phone: 0121 427 8935

Wolverhampton WV1 1TQ
Phone: 01902 710192

413, Birmingham Road
Wylde Green
Birmingham B72 1AU
Phone: 0121 384 7514

120, High Street
Cradley Heath
Birmingham B64 5HE
Phone: 01384 637686

2274, Coventry Road
Sheldon
Birmingham B26 3JR
Phone: 0121 722 2515

4, Blackwell Street
Swan Centre
Kidderminster
Worcester DY10 2DP
Phone: 01562 862788

179-181 Church Road
Yardley
Birminghan B25 8UN
Phone: 0121 789 8677

21, Market Street
Kingswinford
West Midlands DY6 9JS
Phone: 01384 402564

17/18 Kingstanding Shopping
Centre
Kingstanding
Birmingham B44 9HH
Phone: 0121 355 1552

15 Royal Sqaure
Kingsfisher Shopping Center
Redditch B97 4HU
Phone: 01527 591993

Southern

60A Station Road
Birchington
Kent CT7 9RA
Phone: 01843 847143

43, Station Approach
Hayes
Kent BR2 7EB
Phone: 0181 462 2160

126, High Street
Margate
Kent CT9 1JW
Phone: 01843 297666

117, Queensway
Petts Wood
Kent BR5 1DG
Phone: 01689 875002

54, Queen Street
Ramsgate
Kent CT11 9EE
Phone: 01843 850998

41, Central Parade
New Addington
Croydon CR0 0JD
Phone: 01689 848008

189, Broadway
Bexleyheath
Kent DA6 7ER
Phone: 0181 301 4426

40, High Street
Dover
Kent CT16 1EA
Phone: 01304 213827

England

Unit 23
Rainham District Shopping
Centre
Rainham
Kent ME8 7HW
Phone: 01634 262638

Unit 4, Winslade Way
Catford Shopping Centre
London SE6 4JU
Phone: 0181 314 0568

6, St. Marys Walk
Hailsham
East Sussex BN27 1AF
Phone: 01323 441915

Eastern

7 Ironmonger Street
Stamford
Lincs PE9 IPL
Phone: 01789 755850

323 Lincoln Road
Peterborough
Cambs PE1 2PF
Phone: 01733 311271

34, High Street
Hunstanton
Norfolk PE36 5AF
Phone: 01485 535008

75, Gold Stret
Kettering
Northants NN16 8JB
Phone: 01536 483327

3A Southgate
Sleaford
Lincolnshire NG34 7SY
Phone: 01529 307606

9, Lumley Road
Skegness
Lincolnshire PE25 3LL
Phone: 01754 760428

54c High Street
Hucknall
Notss NG15 7AX
Phone: 01159 632202

6-8 Silver Street
Gainsborough
Lincs DN21 2DP
Phone: 01427 811577

26 Market Gates
Shopping Centre
Great Yarmouth
Norfolk NR30 2AX
Phone: 01493 745889

2 Sovereign Way
Anglia Square
Norwich NR3 1ER
Phone: 01603 612373

E. London/Essex

585, Leabridge Road
Leyton
London E10 6AJ
Phone: 0181 521 5077

95, The Broadway
Leigh On Sea
Essex SS9 1PG
Phone: 01702 470017

159, High Street
Hornchurch
Essex RM11 3YP
Phone: 01708 620432

52, Furtherwick Road
Canvey Island
Essex SS8 7AE
Phone: 01268 511526

6, St. Johns Way
Corringham
Essex SS17 7LJ
Phone: 01375 671556

9-11 North Mall
Edmonton Green Shopping
Centre
Edmonton
London N9 0EQ
Phone: 0181 803 1141

46 Farnham Road
Harold Hill
Romford
Essex RM3 8DX
Phone: 01708 342547

307 Mare Street
Hackney
London E8 1EJ
Phone: 0181 968 0494

57 Seven Sisters Road
Holloway
London N7 6BH
Phone: 0171 561 9199

43 Rye Lane
Peckham
London SE15 5ER
Phone: 0171 639 1077

Scotland

168 Dumbarton Road
Glasgow G11 6XE
Phone: 0141 334 9675

1109 Cathcart Road
Mount Florida
Glasgow G42 9HF
Phone: 0141 649 0888

30 Westmuir Street
Parkhead
Glasgow G31 5BH
Phone: 0141 551 9705

Unit 29 Castlemilk Arcade
The Braes Shopping Center
Glasgow G45 9AA
Phone: 0141 631 4977

Link Romania, Link House
59/61 Lyndhurst Road
Worthing, West Sussex BN11
2DB
UK

Contact: Mark Shipperlee
Phone: 0044 1903 529333
Fax: 0044 1903 529007
e-mail:
mark_shipperlee@linkrom.org
admin@linkrom.org
Web site: www.linkrom.org

Link Romania is a Christian
charity based in the UK. Through
their charity shops in the UK and
Romania they help provide much
needed financial support for
charitable & educational projects
in Romania. The shops carry
clothing & bric-a-brac. This
organization is constantly in need
of clothing. For more information
in helping Link Romania contact
Mark Shipperlee.

England

26 South Street
Tarring, Worthing
West Sussex, UK

Store Hours:
Monday-Friday 10am-5pm
Saturday 10am-1pm

A boutique style charity shop
featuring a vast array of clothing

35 South Street
Tarring, Worthing
West Sussex, UK

Store Hours:
Monday-Friday 10am-4pm

England

Located up the road from the clothing shop, this spacious shop carrys furniture for the home and office

45 Broadwater Street West Worthing, West Sussex UK

Store Hours:
Monday-Friday 10am-4pm
Saturday 10am-1pm

Clothing & bric-a-brac

4 Wick Parade Littlehampton, West Sussex UK

Store Hours:
Monday-Friday 10am-4pm
Saturday 10am-1pm

Phone: 44-1903-733408

Clothing & bric-a-brac

Locations in Romania

Deva

Nexus, Boulevard Decebal, Bloc 5
Ground Floor

Manageress Adela Bujorean

Iasi

Contact Arpi Foszto at Fundatia Link Romania-Moldavia at 032-139915 to guide you to the shops.

Crinii de Camp (Lilies of the Field)Str Canta nr 58
Manageress Liliana Apostu

Filomarket, Str Vasile Lupu nr 29
Manageress Silvia Chipei

Gloria, Boulevard N. Iorga nr 905a
Manageress Ada Chitescu

Petrila

Omnis, Str Republicii Bloc 70 Parter (Ground Floor)

Contact Cristi & Coco Bulica at 094-555400 to guide you to the shops in Timisoara.

Timisoara

Betamarket, Str Iosif Preyer Nr 30
Manageress Viorica Tamas

Betamarket Cl, Str. Calea Lipovei
Nr 28
Manageress Lidia Dancea

Paris

Anna Lowe
104, Rue Du FG Saint Honore
75008 Paris
France
Metro: Miromesuil

Store Hours
Monday-Saturday 10am-7pm

Contact: Suzy Goei
Phone: 01 42 66 11 32
Fax: 01 40 06 00 53

Located on the famous Rue Du
FG Saint-Honore where haute
couture reigns, Anna Lowe is a
well known premiere boutique for
designer label fashions at discount
prices.

Several garments at Anna Lowes
have been worn on the runway by
many fashion models.
Other items are last season or
current collections that have
never been worn.
Many items are 1/2 off their
original retail price. Designer
clothing from Chanel, Valentino,
Armani & more are 1/4 off
original price.
Accepts cash & all major credit
cards

Store Specials: Alternations are
available for a small fee

Annexe Des Createurs
Designer Sale Shop
19 Rue Godot de Mauroy
75099 Paris
France
Metro: Madeleine or
Havre-Caumartin

Store Hours:
Monday-Saturday 11am-7pm

Phone: 01 42 65 46 40

Designer clothing for women &
men from former haute couture
collections, accessories & more.
Versace, Moschino, Dolce &
Gabbana, Westwood, Thierry
Mugler, Helmut Lang, Galliano &
more available at 40% to 70% off
original price.
Accepts cash, Mastercard & Visa

Store Specials: Alterations
available for a small fee

Diableries
67 Place dt Felix O' Bligeois
75017 Paris
France

France

Store Hours:
Tuesday-Saturday
11am-7:30pm
Monday 1:30pm-6pm

Contact: Jo Maurin
Phone 42.29.99.70

Diableries is named after a famous perfume that rose to popularity during the 1930's in France. Situated near a church, Diableries carries a vast array of garments circa 1930 to 1950, a wonderful selection of capes, hats, retro bags, earrings by Jo, jewelry, embroidered hankies and many other unique pieces, all with a timeless quality.

GD Expansion
19 Rue du Sentier
75022 Paris

Store Hours:
Monday-Saturday 10am-7pm

Contact: M. Roubine
Phone: 01 42 33 38 39
Fax: 01 42 33 37 82

Designer apparel for men & women including designs by Mas Mara, Week End, Marella, Olivier Strelli, Dimension, Pabls, Caractere, Helena Sorel, Zapa & more.

Les Mauvais Garcons
(The Bad Boys)
20 Rue Voltaire
93100 Montreuil
Paris

Store Hours:
Monday-Saturday 9:30am-6:30pm

Contact: Rozenkopf Laurent
Phone: 01.49.88.17.17
Fax: 01.49.88.15.07

Choose from over 15,000 garments for men, women & children circa 1890 to 1998 available for rental. The shop is frequented by famous designers who rent clothing for their collections. The shop carries the best selection merchandise all in excellent condition.

L'Occaserie
30, Rue de la Pompe
75116 Paris
France

Store Hours:
Monday-Saturday 11am-7pm

Phone: 01 45 03 16 56

Designer clothing for men & women. Over five store locations on the famous "16ieme arrondissement".

Mamie
73 Rue De Rochechouart
Paris
Metro Anvers

Store Hours:
Tuesday-Friday 11am-1:30pm & 4pm-8pm
Saturday 4pm-8pm

Contact: Yannick Lettione & Brigitte Chiron
Phone: 01 42 82 09 98

Authentic boutique featuring retro vintage clothing from the 30's, 40's, 50's & 60's for men & women, accessories, shoes & furniture from Europe & the United States

Opportune
114 Avenue du General
Michel
Bizot
75012 Paris
France

Store Hours:
Tuesday-Friday 3pm-7pm
Saturday 10:30am-1pm & 3pm-6pm

Phone: 01 43 44 54 50

Opportune shop carries excellent quality secondhand clothing for women, jewelry, antiques & bibelots (little objects).

Consignment Policy: 50/50 split

Passe' Devant
62 Rue d'Orsel
75018 Paris
France

Store Hours: Tuesday-Saturday
11am-12:30pm & 1:30pm-7pm
Sunday & Monday 2pm-7pm

Contact: M.E. Thebault
Phone: 01 42 54 75 15

Excellent quality designer clothing for women & accessories

Rag
83 Rue St. Martin
75004 Paris
France

Store Hours:
Monday-Sunday 10am-8pm

Vertiges
85 Rue St. Martin
75004 Paris
France

Store Hours:
Monday-Sunday 10am-8pm

Phone: 01.48.87.39.69

Vintage clothing from the 40's to the 70's & bell bottoms galore!

Reciproque
88, 89, 92, 93, 95, 123, 101, 97
Rue de la Pompe
75116 Paris
Metro: Pompe

Store Hours:
Tuesday-Friday 11am-7:30pm
Saturday 10:30am-7:30pm

Contact: Madame Nicole Morel
Phone: 01.47.04.30.28

Located in one of the most elegant neighborhoods in Paris, Reciproque spans the Rue de la Pompe with several locations. You will find racks of couture clothing & accessories for men & women featuring designs by Chanel, Christian Dior, Versace, Hermes, Lacroix, Herve Leger, Vuitton, Gucci, Moschino, Prada & Vivienne Westwood, jewelry, handbags, evening & party dresses, furs, shoes, coats, hats, crystal & beautiful gift items. A shopper's dream! Upscale items for the distinguished shopper at great prices.

France

Hundreds of new arrivals daily!
Accepts cash, Visa & American
Express
Bilingual staff available.

Stocklux
8 Place Vendome
75007 Paris
France
Store Hours:
Monday-Saturday 10am-7:30pm

Contact: Michele Cohen
Phone: 01.49.27.09.31

Couture apparel & accessories for
men & women. Casual wear by
Christian Lacroix, Claude
Montana, Thierry Mugler
& other designers discounted
60%-70%.

Store Specials: Alterations
& delivery available

Terran Vogue
13 R Keller
75011 Paris
France

Store Hours:
Monday-Saturday 11am-8pm

Phone: 33.43.14.03.23

Secondhand trendy clothing for
women & men from some of
France's best designers

Troc Parnass
Depot Vente
58, Rue du Montparnasse
75014 Paris

Store Hours:
Tuesday-Saturday
11:30am-7:30pm
Phone: 01.43.22.72.53

Designer clothing, career to casual
wear from Georges Rech, Sonia
Rykiel, Lolita Lempicka & Gerard
Darel

Dublin

Cheeverstown
Kilvare
Templeogue
Dublin 6W
Ireland

Phone: 01 490 4681
Fax: 01 490 5753
e-mail: Cheeverstownpr@itw.ie
Web site: http://www.itw.ie/
cheeverstown/

Cheeverstown is a centre for
mentally handicapped children
and adults which provides
residential care and workshops.
Two charity shops sell & accept
clothing, furniture & bric-a-brac.
Donations are welcome. As part
of an ongoing fund-raiser,
Cheeverstown sells Shamrock pins
via their web site.

Stock Xchange
8 Upper Baggot Street
Dublin 4
Ireland

Located on the 2nd & 3rd floors
over the shop called "Number"
and next to Burger King. The
shop is about a ten minute walk
from Grafton Street, Ireland's
premier shopping street.

"Where you can indulge your
passion for fashion without
seriously damaging your wealth!"

Store Hours:
Monday-Friday 10am-6pm for
sales

Monday-Friday 11am-5pm for
consignments

Contact: Kathryn Fitzgibbon
Phone: 01 668 8010
Fax: 01 280 2959

Upscale designer clothing for
women with labels such as Versace,
Moschino, Armani, Ralph Lauren
& more! A special room is
available for plus sizes 12-20.
Lots of beautiful designer samples
too!

Consignment Policy: Items must
be less than two years old and in
new condition
Items consigned for five weeks

Established over twenty-one years
ago, Stock Xchange is Dublin's
largest and most popular designer
consignments (swap) shop. Many
customers travel from all areas of
Ireland & abroad to shop and
consign clothing to the Stock
Xchange.
The shop is a favorite among
women seeking excellent quality
clothing at amazing prices.

● ● ● ● ● ● ● ● ● ● ● ● ● ●
●   Present this coupon at   ●
●   *Stock Xchange*   ●
●   *8 Upper Baggot Street*   ●
● *Dublin 4, Ireland* & save 10% ●
●   off a regular priced item   ●
●   ●
●   Expiration Date: 12/31/99   ●
● ● ● ● ● ● ● ● ● ● ● ● ● ●

Cerebral Palsy Ireland
Shops Division
Headquarters
25 Capel Street
Dublin 1
Phone: 01 872 7155
Fax: 01 872 7181

Ireland

Since 1987, Cerebral Palsy Ireland has been operating several shops throughout Ireland. The shops carry good quality, gently used clothing for women, gents & children, accessories, footwear, bric-a-brac, toys, books & household items. Most shops are open from 9am-5pm in Dublin & 9am-5:30pm in the rest of the country. The shops accept cash, cheques & cheque cards Donations are welcome & the organization operates a weekly van collection service for items to donate. Proceeds benefit the Capital Development Fund which was developed to improve existing facilities and services for the disabled throughout Ireland.

25 Capel Street
Dublin 1
Phone: 873 3867

8 South Great Georges
Dublin 8
Phone: 478 2763

28 Lr. Camden Street
Dublin 8
Phone: 468 0647

69 Thomas Street
Dublin 8
Phone: 454 2681

43 Main Street
Finglas, Dublin 11
Phone: 834 7304

32 Shop Street
Drogheda

041 39650

Unit 2, Kennedy Road
Navan, Co Meath
Phone: 046 73466

Unit 2, Wine Street
Car Park, Sligo
Phone: 071 50259

4 Upper William Street
Limerick
Phone: 061 314334

24/24 High Street
Galway
091 564857

32 North Main Street
Cork City
021 278280

39 Princes Street
Cork City
Phone: 021 278280

9 Mary Street
Clonmel
Phone: 052 26202

14 Broad Street
Waterford
Phone: 051 841696

Kfar Saba

The Second Hand Store
78 Rothschild
Kfar Saba
Israel 44201

Store Hours:
Sunday, Monday, Wednesday &
Thursday 10am-1pm &
4:30pm-7pm
Tuesday & Friday 10am-1pm

Contact: Rina Moran
Phone: 972 9 7672963

Consignment clothing, shoes,
jewelry, hangings, curtains,
antiques, art work & a vast array
of beautiful ornaments

Consignment Policy: Items are
consigned for 90 days
Items are reduced after two
months
Consignor receives 1/3 of the
selling price

Jerusalem

Kol-Bo "Ofer" Second Hand
Paran st. 7
Ramat Eshkol Shopping
Center
Jerusalem, Israel

Store Hours:
Sunday-Friday 9am-1pm
Sunday-Tuesday 4pm-7pm

Considered a very special
consignment shop, customers are
greeted warmly by Chan & Yossi,
the store owners.
The shop offers clothing for the
entire family, housewares,
electrical appliances, lighting
fixtures, jewelry, toys, books &
much, much more! Consignments
are welcome & all unsold items
are donated to hospitals,
orphanages & geriatric centers.
Specializing in serving & pleasing
their customers and great prices!
"A special shopping experience
indeed".

Israel

Tel-Aviv

**Second Hand on the
Second Floor
84 Ben Yehuda Street
Tel-Aviv, Israel**

Store Hours:
Sunday, Monday & Tuesday
12pm-7pm
Wednesday & Thursday 11am-
7pm & Friday 9:30am-2:30pm

Contact: Meira Erez
Phone: 972 35276614

Beautiful clothing, jewelry,
decorative small items including
glass, porcelain, silver & artwork
Accepts cash & checks

Consignment Policy: 50/50 split

A.N.G.E.L.O.
Vintage Palace
Via Garibaldi, 59
48022 Lugo (RA)

Store Hours:
Monday 3pm-7pm
Tuesday-Saturday 10:30am-7pm
Closed on Sunday

Contact: Angelo Caroli
Phone: 0545 35200
Fax: 0545 34440
e-mail: angelo@angelo.it
Web site: www.angelo.it

A.N.G.E.L.O. offers over 50,000
carefully pre-selected garments
and accessories. Hundreds of
pairs of jeans & vintage time
period pieces from around the
world.
The shop has been featured in *The
New York Times, Fashion,
Glamour & L'Uomo.*
The attic section is available to
rent for television events, fashion
shows, theatre, cinema & fashion
shoots.
Also featuring a great archive of
civil and military items from the
1920's to the 1980's.
Accepts cash & all major credit
cards

A.N.G.E.L.O. Vintage Jeans
Ravenna Via Baccarini, 18
Phone: 39-55-218313

A.N.G.E.L.O. Block 60
Riccione Via Milano, 60
Phone: 39-541-607828

Upstairs/ c/o Fiorucci Warehouse
Milano Galleria Passerella, 2
Phone: 39-2-76006051

Muffa
Forli' Via C. Cignani, 23
Phone: 0543/36171

Gassosa
Cesena Via Montalti, 17
Phone: 39-0547-611187

Tribu Used Store
Reggio Emilia Viale Isonzo,
14
Phone: 39-055-300039

Gerard Loft
Firenze Viadei Pecori, 34/36
rosso
Phone: 39-055-282491

Fashion Market
Civitanova Marche Corso
Umberto, 123
Phone: 39-733-812563

Suprefly
Giulianova Via Galilei
Phone: 39-85-8025025

M.A.R.I.O.
Senigallia Piazza Saffi, 9
Phone: 39-71-7928512

Double Five
Boy's & Girl's
Brescia Corso Garibaldi, 19

Italy

Verona Via Adua, 16
Phone: 045 8031014

Messi Una Volta
Abbigliamento per bambini
Via Salaria 93
00198 Roma Italy

Store Hours:
Monday-Saturday 10am-8pm

Contact: Daniela Andreoli
Phone: 0039-6-8411374
Fax: 0039-6-3294906

Clothing for infants & children
featuring labels such as Levi's, Osh
Kosh & much more!

The shop was the first of its kind
in Rome and is frequented by
many movie stars.

Auckland

Collections Clothing
14/254 Lincoln Road
Auckland, New Zealand

Store Hours:
Monday, Tuesday, Wednesday
9am-5pm,
Thursday 9am-7pm
Friday 9am-6pm
Saturday 9am-4pm

Contact: Dell or Pam
Phone: 09-837-2613

Pre-loved quality designer clothing
for women & some new items
too!
Accepts cash, Mastercard, Visa &
American Express

Consignment Policy: 50/50 split
Items consigned for 60 days

Emporio 'U'
9 High Street-Basement
Auckland, New Zealand

Store Hours:
Monday-Thursday 10am-5pm
Friday 10am-6pm
Saturday 11am-2pm

Contact: Ute Bohnert
Phone: 09-356-6985

Designer secondhand clothing for
women
Accepts cash & cheques

Consignment Policy: Consignor
receives 60%

The Recycle Boutique
14 Darby Street
(Off Queen Street)
Auckland City, New Zealand

Store Hours:
Monday-Thursday 9am-5:30pm
Friday 9am-8:30pm
Saturday 10am-4pm
Sunday 12pm-4pm

Phone: 09-379-8891

Second Location:

8 Anzac St
Takapuna
Located near Shore City

Store Hours:
Monday, Tuesday, Wednesday &
Friday 9am-5:30pm
Thursday 9am-8pm
Saturday 10am-4pm
Sunday 9am-2pm

Phone: 09-486-5413

The Recycle Boutique is
Auckland's largest consignment
shop. Featuring a vast array of
upscale clothing for the entire
family, jewelry & accessories.
Over 1200 new garments arrive
weekly!
Accepts cash, personal &
travellers cheques, credit & debit
cards

Consignment Policy:
50/50 split
Items marked half price after
four weeks

Norway

Scotland

Tonica Second-Hand Boutique
Sorgenfrigaten 1
0365 Oslo
Norway

Store Hours:
Monday, Tuesday, Wednesday &
Friday 11am-5pm
Thursday 11am-6pm
Every first Saturday of each
month 11am-5pm

Phone: 0047-22-60-22-06
Fax: 0047-22-49-44-22
Accepts cash & cheques

Established in 1976, Tonica
Boutique carries designer clothing
for women

Consignment Policy: Items are
consigned for one month

The Address Designer
Exchange
3 Royal Exchange Court
Glasgow, Scotland G1 3DB

Store Hours:
Tuesday-Saturday 10am-5pm

Contact: Lorri & Celia
Phone: 0141 221 6898

New & "as new" designer clothing
for women. Choose from day &
evening wear, casual, wedding
dresses & accessories. Featuring
designers such as Escada, Cerruiti,
Chanel, Dolce & Gabbana, Mondi,
Alberta Ferretti & more.
Accepts cash, Visa, Mastercard &
Delta

Consignment Policy:
Items must be in pristine
condition, on hangers & less than
two years old
50/50 split
Items consigned for two months

Store Specials: Sample sales &
stock clearance lines

South Africa | Sweden

Second Time Around
196 Long Street
Cape Town
South Africa

Store Hours:
Monday-Friday 9am-5pm
Saturday 9am-2pm

Phone: 021 23-1674

Vintage original clothing &
accessories for men & women.
Tuxedos, tails, hats, wigs, gloves,
scarves, ties, furs & jewelry.
Contemporary clothing & leather
wear too.
Hire (rental) of clothing available
for dances, wedding, parties,
theatre, television & film

Old Touch
Upplandsgatan 43
11328 Stockholm
Sweden

Store Hours:
Monday-Friday 11am-6pm
Saturday 11am-3pm

Contact: Birgitta Gardner
Phone: 01046-8-349005

Vintage clothing circa 1890-1950,
lace & beautiful embroidery
Accepts cash & Swedish bank
checks

Store Policy: Bartering is
acceptable here

Present this coupon at
Old Touch
Upplandsgatan 43
11328 Stockholm, Sweden
& save 10% off one item of
clothing

Expiration Date: 12/31/99

395

Switzerland   Taiwan

Switzerland

Taipei

**Phylli's Top Second Hand
in the old railroad station
Hofwieaenstrasse 369
8050 Zurich
Switzerland**

Store Hours:
Tuesday-Friday 10am-1:30pm &
3pm-6:30pm
Saturday 10am-4pm

Contact: Phyllis Castelli
Phone: 01-312.66.55
Fax: 01-312.66.60

Featuring first class second hand
clothing from the world's most
famous designers, Versace, Annex,
Armani, Jil Sander, Anne Klein &
more. A special section with new
dresses, jeans. leisure clothing &
shoes. All at great prices!

Store Specials: End of the season
sale 20% to 50% off select
merchandise

Present this coupon at
*Phylli's Top Second Hand
in the old railroad station
Hofwieaenstrasse 369 Zurich,
Switzerland* & save
10% off an item

Expiration Date: 12/31/99

**Curious Goods
Room 703., No. 155
Section 4
Chung Shiao East Road
Taipei, Taiwan**

Store Hours:
Monday-Saturday
12:30pm-8:30pm

Contact: Amanda Chen
Phone: 886-2-2781-2104
e-mail:
curious@mail.intellect.com.tw

Upscale designer secondhand
clothing & jewelry. Chanel
Armani, Donna Karan & more.
Accepts cash

Consignment Policy: Consignor
receives 70% of the selling price
for the item

Present this coupon at
*Curious Goods
Room 703, No. 155, Chung
Shiao East Road,
Taipei,Taiwan*
& save 20% ~ 25% off
your first visit

Expiration Date: 12/31/99

Great Resources

Rummaging Through
Northern California
Harris Publications
P.O. Box 297
Sonoma, California 95476-
0297
Phone: 707-939-9124
Fax: 707-939-9579
e-mail: rtnc@sonic.net
Website: www.secondhand.com

Newspaper & guide to consignment & thrift shops, rummage
sales, sample sales, flea markets,
resale shows, surplus salvage,
antiques & "cheap thrills"
covering Northern California.

Set Your Table
13419 Van Buren Street NE
Ham Lake, Minnesota 55304

Phone & Fax: 612-754-6483
Phone & Fax: 800-600-2127
Website:http://
www.setyourtable.com
e-mail: sranta@setyourtable.com

Annual discontinued tableware
dealers directory. All inclusive
information on locating dinnerware, glassware & flatware.

The "No Nonsense" Antique
FDS Antiques, Inc.
101 Brown Street
P.O. Box 188
Higginsport, Ohio 45131
Phone: 937-375-4395
Fax: 937-375-4394
e-mail: FDSINC@BRIGHT.NET

The dedicated antiquer's guide to
more than 5,000 Antique malls,
centers & multi-dealer shops.

To The Trade

Complete Computer Solutions Of Ohio, Inc.
780 Nilles Road Suite D2
Fairfield, Ohio 45014

Contact: Whittney Sink
Phone: 800-433-0812
Fax: 513-829-6572
e-mail: sales@ccsofoh.com
Web site: www.ccsofoh.com

Specializing in software and hardware designed for the the consignment industry.

Display Innovations U.S.A., Inc.
81 Hanse Avenue
PO Box 548
Freeport, New York 11520

Contact: Frank Timlin
Phone: 516-623-3100/1-800-949-6330
Fax: 516-623-3310
e-mail: DisplayInnovations@usa.net
Web site: www.displayinnovations.com

Clothing racks, hangers, price tags, showcases, gondolas & gridwalls for stores. Custom metal & acrylic work available. Call for a catalog.

Fashion Design Studio
Via S. Giorgio, 27
50047 Prato (PO)
Florence, Italy

Phone & Fax: 39 574 21859
Contact: Serena Fumanti
Web site: www.fashionart.it/fashion
e-mail: fashion@fashionart.it

Fashion Design Studio offers seasonal garments and shoes, jewelry, leather clothes, handbags & sample collections.

Jay Jewelry, Inc.
119 Citation Court
Birmingham, Alabama 35209

Contact; Robert S. Pathman
Phone: 205-870-0908/1-800-633-4774
Fax: 205-870-9569

Established over fifty years ago, Jay Jewelry offers fashion & sterling jewelry wholesale.

Katydid Press
2592 York Road
Columbus, Ohio 43221

Contact: Kate Holmes
Phone & Fax: 614-487-0709
e-mail: Katetgtbt@aol.com
Web site: www.tgtbt.com

Bimonthly industry newsletter "Too Good To Be Threw" & other publications for the consignment industry.

To The Trade

Liberty Systems Inc.
906 N. Pine Hills Road
Orlando, Florida 32808

Contact: Ed Davies
Phone: 800-858-1758
Fax: 407-297-0640
e-mail: sales@libery-systems.com
Web site: www.liberty-
systems.com

Sophisticated, powerful software
that is easy to learn & use
for resale shops.

National Association of
Resale & Thrift Shops
P.O. Box 80707
St. Clair Shores, MI 48080-
0707

Phone: 800-544-0751
Fax: 810-294-6776
e-mail: Webmaster@narts.org
Web site: www.narts.org

National organization dedicated
to the professionalism of the
resale industry.

Sean James Enterprises
425 Tribble Gap Road
Cumming, Georgia 30040

Contact: John Harrington
Phone: 888-866-9826
Fax: 888-808-9046
e-mail: seanjames@msn.com

Superb quality rolling garment
racks & baskets, garment bags &
covers & accessories. The best
the industry has to offer at
reasonable prices.

The Consignment Workbook
Scandia International
133 Olney Road
Petersburgh, New York 12138

Contact: Sue Harris
Phone: 518-658-3724

Publishes "The Consignment
Workbook" step by step guide
for new consignment store
owners.

The Ultimate Consignment & Thrift Store Guide

Published by Consignment & Thrift Store Publishing, Inc.
442 Route 202-206 North Suite 274
Bedminster, New Jersey 07921
Phone: 908-781-2589
Fax: 908-781-8598
e-mail: carolyn@net-lynx.com
Web site: www.consignmentguide.com

Order Form

Date: _____

Name: _____

Street: _____

City/State/Zip _____

Country _____

Phone: _____

Quantity	Description	Amount	Total
_____	The Ultimate Consignment & Thrift Store Guide	$16.95 per copy	_____
	New Jersey buyers add 6.0% sales tax		_____
	Shipping & Handling within the US add $3.00 for the first copy & $1.00 for each additional copy		_____
	Outside the United States add $6.95 for the first copy & $2.00 for each additional copy (US funds only, please)		

Subtotal _____

Total _____

___ Check/Money Order ___ Mastercard ___ Visa

Account Number _____ *Exp. Date* _____

Name on card _____

Signature _____

Thank you for ordering The Ultimate Consignment & Thrift Store Guide. Satisfaction Guaranteed!

About the Author

Carolyn Schneider began secondhand shopping over eleven years ago. Her career in the corporate world required that "designer look" but her pocketbook required affordable prices. After years of discovering fabulous buys in secondhand stores, Carolyn decided to write The Ultimate Consignment & Thrift Store Guide. The first of its kind, the all inclusive guide is designed specifically to save the smart shopper time and money. When she is not secondhand shopping, Carolyn loves to spend time with family and friends and travel. Carolyn has been interviewed on TV, numerous radio shows and newspapers throughout the United States sharing her secrets about secondhand shopping.

On the front cover, Carolyn is wearing a gently used elegant ruby Chanel suit & Chanel black suede pumps from Nicole's Revival in Westland, Michigan.
Gently used designer clothing & accessories courtesy of Nicole's Revival
Black hat & necklace from Apparel Revisited in North Plainfield, New Jersey.
Elegant glass pin from Reciproque in Paris, France.
All gently used sporting goods courtesy of Play It Again Sports in Raritan, New Jersey.
Gently used men's blue sweater from Savers Thrift Store in Quincy, Massachusetts

Notes

Notes

Notes

Notes

Notes

Notes

Notes